HEAT

HEAT

Extreme Adventures at the Highest
Temperatures on Earth

RANULPH FIENNES

**SIMON &
SCHUSTER**

London · New York · Sydney · Toronto · New Delhi

A CBS COMPANY

First published in Great Britain by Simon & Schuster UK Ltd, 2015
A CBS COMPANY

1 3 5 7 9 10 8 6 4 2

Simon & Schuster UK Ltd
1st Floor
222 Gray's Inn Road
London WC1X 8HB

www.simonandschuster.co.uk

Simon & Schuster Australia, Sydney
Simon & Schuster India, New Delhi

The author and publishers have made all reasonable efforts
to contact copyright-holders for permission, and apologise
for any omissions or errors in the form of credits given.
Corrections may be made to future printings.

A CIP catalogue record for this book
is available from the British Library

Hardback ISBN: 978-1-4711-3795-2
Trade paperback ISBN: 978-1-4711-3796-9
eBook ISBN: 978-1-4711-3798-3

Typeset in Sabon by M Rules
Printed and bound by CPI Group (UK) Ltd, Croydon, CR0 4YY

Simon & Schuster UK Ltd are committed to sourcing paper
that is made from wood grown in sustainable forests and supports the Forest
Stewardship Council, the leading international forest certification organisation.
Our books displaying the FSC logo are printed on FSC certified paper.

For Mark, the bravest man Louise and I have ever known
Mark Reeves RIP

Contents

Preface

All my life I have read tales of desert exploration. Over forty years I have travelled in many hot places, whether fighting in an Arab army, searching for a lost desert city, or merely seeing for myself those lands where the Sun God rules and where man must be tough to survive.

My experiences have often depended on those of my predecessors, so I have mingled their observations with mine. The common denominator is the all-powerful effect of great *heat*. So, fetch a cool drink, switch up the air-conditioning and read on.

Exmoor,
May 2015

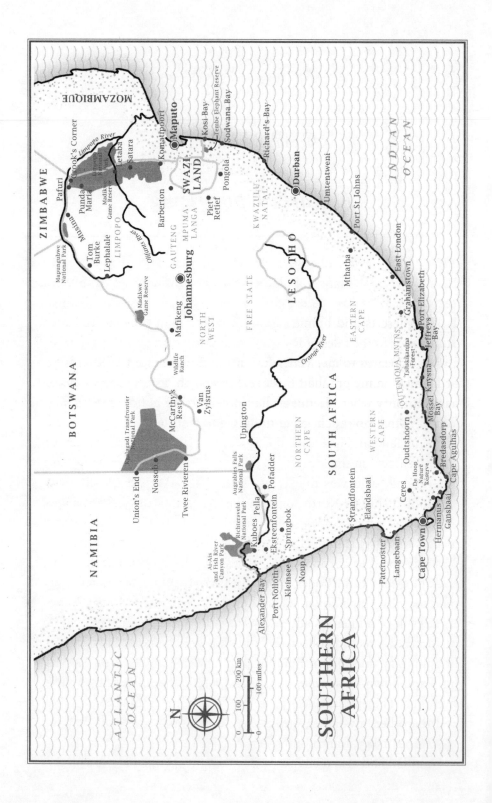

SOUTHERN AFRICA

CHAPTER 1

A Warm Upbringing

Hot deserts and humid jungles, the exotic but menacing backdrops to the tales of Rudyard Kipling and *Arabian Nights*, have always appealed to me. Maybe this attraction is in my DNA and can be blamed on my grandad Eustace. He was born in the family castle near Banbury where Fienneses have lived for six hundred years. The firstborn male of each generation spent his life looking after the castle, its land and its locals, but any other children were expected to choose careers in the army, the church or the colonies.

Grandad, who was the second son, heard about the Gold Rush and took a ship to North America. He failed to strike gold and was a failure as a fur trapper, so he joined the Mounties and was given medals for his part in quelling the Louis Riel rebellion in Alberta. He was promoted to corporal but, restless and hearing about the maverick pioneer Cecil Rhodes in South Africa, spent his Mountie wages on a berth to Cape Town, where he joined the South African Police. As a result of numerous adventures fighting Zulus, Boers and others, he received a record collection of medals which is currently housed in a military museum in Edinburgh Castle. He retired with Florrie, his Cape Town-born wife, to England where they brought up their two sons. The eldest, Uncle John, was killed on the Somme in 1917 and the other, my father, died commanding his regiment in Italy in November 1943, four months before I was born.

Grandad had also died in 1943, so Granny, by then in her eighties, decided to end her days back in her Cape Town home among her blood relatives. Strong willed, she persuaded my widowed mother to accompany her, along with my three older sisters and me.

So, from cool Windsor aged two, I was shunted to warm Constantia, a paradise of vineyards beneath the majestic ramparts of Table Mountain.

Florrie was welcomed back into the bosom of her Rathfelder family, who owned much of Constantia and its vineyards, and she set about building a house there which she named Broughton after the family castle back in England. The house cost £17,000 to build.

A stream trickled through our valley which had a marshy stretch known as the Vlei, and this separated us from the Cape Coloured folk who lived in a cluster of shacks under the shade of a pine tree grove. The strict apartheid rules of that time did not apply to children, at least not in Constantia, and, as a child, I joined the local gang which, in school holidays, roamed the forested Tokai foothills of Table Mountain and threw *donnerball* firecombs at each other, at baboons and at packs of skulking wild dogs.

My three sisters aged ten, eight and five years older than me, did well at school and Gill, the youngest of the three, won rosettes at local gymkhanas. I was encouraged to ride a Zulu pony named Zimba, but I preferred to run barefoot with the gang.

My mother hated the apartheid regime and joined the Black Sash movement in Cape Town, helping to collect 90,000 signatures on behalf of coloured people's rights. She also gave her personal wealth, all of it, to help build Cafda Village to house the poor and the homeless.

One morning, when waking up my mother by drawing the curtains in her bedroom, a sizeable black spider dropped down the neck of my pyjama top. I screamed and squashed it as it bit my shoulder. For years afterwards I was terrified of spiders, even little English ones.

Many children at the four Cape Town schools that I went to suffered from verrucas, and I well remember the sharp pain of the red-hot needle used in those days by doctors to burn out the roots of the offending warts. Equally vicious were the antiquated drills of our Cape Town dentist.

Summers were hot when the infamous *berg* winds roasted Constantia. The grapes loved it, but I wilted and the Vlei gang patrolled our forest fiefdom without me. At night I would keep my curtains drawn so that I couldn't see the great fires that roared through the foothills and the tinder-dry undergrowth below the moonlit outlines of Devil's Peak and Lion's Head. Air-conditioning did not exist, even in the homes of the super-rich. When the fires eventually died down, thousands of acres of brush were left black and seemingly dead until the following spring, and our vines were left scattered with ash.

I found my father's service pistol loaded under my mother's pillow one day when she was away, and I threatened Christine, the cook, with it in order to obtain chocolate cake from the locked larder. She screamed and later told my mother who, quite rightly, beat my backside with a cane.

There was crime in the Cape and we were lucky, since we had no adult male in the family, not to experience any bad incidents, other than the sudden appearance one afternoon of a copiously bleeding Zulu who was dragged to our garden gate by two very large locals from the Vlei who said that he was a thief and could we call the police. When he tried to speak to my mother, they hit his head against the gate.

During holidays, my mother drove us to other parts of South Africa, and in 1954 she took my sisters to the Kruger National Park. On that occasion my mother and sisters went without me, but I did get to the park on a later trip. It is a huge tract of wild land, the eastern boundary of which marks the frontier with Mozambique, and its demarcation fence helps reduce the killing of park animals by cross-border poaching gangs.

Many diseases thrive in the Kruger heat, including sleeping sickness caused by the tsetse fly, malaria and water-borne bilharzia. In the 1890s a Portuguese settler tried to found a colony there, but the area was formally designated as a national park in 1898 by the South African government.

During the Second World War the unmarked border was rife with rumours of Nazi spies and armed units up to no good in the park.

Later still, during the Mozambique civil war, anti-government forces and units of the South African Defence Force would rendez-vous along the border fence. The fence was eventually electrified in key parts of the border in order to prevent large numbers of unem-ployed refugees entering South Africa. This has proved only partially successful, since hundreds cross in the non-electrified zones by climb-ing over the fence after dark and avoiding the night patrols. They often do this for any job which offers a mere pittance of pay. Some local farmers take them on as tomato crop pickers at rock-bottom wages, and they have been known to call the border police to arrest and deport them just before pay day.

On both sides of the Limpopo River, which splits the park, there are prides of lions who have learnt that many immigrants follow the line of the electricity pylons which runs from Mozambique into South Africa. So they lie in wait once they have developed a taste for human flesh and then eat their fill of would-be refugees just short of the border.

Sometimes the Limpopo dries up, except for the deeper pools where crocodiles congregate. Grandfather Eustace had a close encounter with crocodiles in this area. In 1879 some 5,000 British troops crossed into Zululand intent on forcing the Zulu king to accept the status of a British protectorate. While the troops were camped at Isandlwana they were attacked by 10,000 Zulus with spears. The British fixed bayonets but were soon massacred. The Zulus swept on to the isolated garrison of Rorke's Drift, held by 120 mostly Welsh soldiers who somehow repulsed the attacking horde.

My great uncle Geoffrey Fiennes was part of Disraeli's response to the massacre, a second army of 23,000 men sent out to avenge the dead of Isandlwana. Grandad Eustace was his younger brother and he, no doubt inspired by Geoffrey, joined the British South Africa Police to do his bit 'in the colonies'.

When my mother and sisters went to the Kruger without me because I was considered too young, I was sent to stay with Aunt 'Utcha', the daughter of Granny Florrie's first marriage. Utcha lived with her thirty-year-old son Michael on their chicken farm near Kommetjie Sands. The woods there were wild and tangled and alive with all manner of insects, snakes and lizards. The puff adder and *boomslang* or tree snake were to be avoided, my cousin warned me, but he had lived there all his life and had never been bitten.

Resting during searingly hot afternoons in the shade of the farm-stead's 'stoep' veranda, I could hear the non-stop boom of the Cape breakers on the other side of the nearby dunes. Not far away two great oceans – the Atlantic and the Indian – came together at Cape Agulhas. The Agulhas Bank, the richest fishing zone in the Southern Hemisphere, stretched away for 180 miles.

The Portuguese named the Cape 'the Cape of the Needles' because their compass needles showed nil magnetic variation once there. Now a fine lighthouse warns sailors of the lethal conditions offshore, but prior to its installation a great many ships had foundered there and thousands of bodies washed up on the fine white sandy beaches, where they provided food for vultures and crabs after locals had removed their clothes and valuables.

Aunt Utcha's farm was colourful with proteas, the national flower, ericas and wild rosemary. Ticks and biting flies were in constant attendance. Along the coast road a touch towards Sea Point was a notice: 'STOPPING AND FEEDING OF BABOONS PROHIBITED'.

At school I learnt Afrikaans and Latin (both of little value later in life) and about the country's history, which was summarized as: 'Two thousand years ago Bantu tribes moved south and their descendants include Zulus, Tswana, Xhosa and Sotho. Jan van Riebeeck claimed the land for the Dutch in 1652, but the British formed a Cape Colony early in the nineteenth century. There are 40 million South Africans, of whom 70 per cent are Christian and one per cent Muslim. The North West of the country is arid and includes the Namib Desert and the few surviving Bushmen of the Kalahari.'

We were taught our history starting in 1601 when British ships first entered Table Bay and twenty years later claimed the Cape for King James I. The Dutch, arriving thirty years on, ignored this British claim and set up a commercial base. At that time the land all the way south to Cape Agulhas was rich in game, which Dutch nomadic 'trekkers' began to decimate. They also killed off great numbers of the desert-dwelling Kalahari San or Bushmen. One group of Dutch 'Boers' proclaimed their own free state in which 'Every Bushman shall for life be the lawful property of such burghers as may possess them and serve in bondage from generation to generation.'

This happy Dutch settlement was upset when in 1806 the British, at war with Napoleonic France as well as Holland, sent six thousand troops and sixty ships to occupy the Cape.

Thereafter Britain ruled the same area of South Africa as had the Dutch, determinedly forbidding any extension of the Cape Colony to the north of the Orange River, beyond which fierce African tribes held sway. Likewise, they left Mozambique to their long-time allies, the Portuguese.

But, unlike today, communications between individuals in far-flung colonies and Westminster were not instantaneous. As a result, the strictly limited size of the South African colony, as desired and ordered by the Colonial Office, was often expanded by rogue Britons without their government's immediate knowledge or consent.

My grandad was one of those guilty parties in this private empire-grabbing activity, despite having been a teenage best friend, neighbour and fellow Territorial Army officer of Winston Churchill, and later his personal assistant during the Gallipoli Campaign.

Another eastern part of South Africa, which I visited later in life and with my wife, was Swaziland. I gave lectures alongside Dr Richard Leakey, the famous Zimbabwean conservationist, in the Swazi capital of Mbabane. In 1968 Swaziland became an independent kingdom, and in neighbouring Zululand my sister Celia became a doctor at the Missionary Hospital in Nqutu. A Swazi friend, Sibusiso Vilane, with whom I later climbed, became the first black man to reach the summit of Everest.

The hottest area of South Africa, halfway between the two oceans and spreading west into the Namib Desert to the Skeleton Coast, is the Kalahari Desert, the second biggest continuous stretch of sand in the world which reaches as far north as the rain forests of the Congo. As a general rule, the western half of South Africa becomes drier and less populated the further you travel towards the Atlantic.

In the Nama tongue, Namib means 'a place where there is nothing', and the Namib desert itself reaches south 1,000 kilometres from the Namib border to the Oliphants River in the Cape Province. The sands of the Namib date back some 55 million years, making it the oldest desert in the world, and some of its dunes reach to over 900 feet in height. There are few drier deserts anywhere and its shoreline is spattered with the skeletons of many hundreds of ships and, some several miles inland, the skeletons of crew members who survived shipwreck only to die of thirst.

The only place, apart from Omani and Yemeni deserts, where I have seen oryx is the Kalahari where they are known as *gemsbok*. In their Arabian home they have only human hunters to fear. In South West Africa they are prey also to the big cats that lie in wait by pools in largely dry riverbeds.

In the most northern tip of South Africa, in the Kgalagadi Transfrontier, there appears to be no possible reason for humans to fight each other, since nothingness is all that exists there. Yet I was told by a ranger that, when the region was a German colony, local Khoikhoi Namibians rebelled and attacked a German outpost at dawn. Victorious, they stripped the Germans naked and shot them all in the back.

Where South Africa meets Namibia and Botswana, an electrified fence delineates the 20th degree of longitude through hundreds of miles of sand in a dead straight line.

Because my wife and I travelled the Kalahari in the month of July, night temperatures were near freezing, which made it difficult to accept that the Kalahari is one of the hottest of all deserts and is hostile to human settlement. Sadly, the earliest known tribe who did manage to survive and even to thrive there has now been all but killed off by fellow humans, rather than by the rigours of the desert. They were of the San tribe, referred to by early European explorers as Bushmen.

Today the Kalahari extends from South Africa into Botswana and Namibia, all now separate and independent nations.

The first Europeans to rule what is now Namibia were the Germans who, in 1915, were defeated by South African troops. The new rulers called the region South West Africa and, after years of civil war between them and the locals, gave the country independence in 1990 as Namibia.

The Namib Desert has vast zones of high sand dunes, with many weird plants finding water only by means of very deep roots. One such, the *Welwitschia*, is known to live for over a thousand years, but has only two leaves issuing out of a single woody stem.

One major difference and advantage which the Namib has over

most other deserts is its proximity to the Atlantic coastline from which banks of fog creep over the sands leaving them briefly damp. Various species of sand dwelling insects emerge at night and, lined up facing the sea (like so many meerkats), they stand on their heads hour after hour letting the fog's moisture condense on their bodies and drip down into their mouths. Bushmen used equally clever ways to benefit from their surroundings. But for a handful, they are all now tragically gone but at least their hot weather survival tricks were noted by early European explorers' records, and they make fascinating reading.

Bushmen's bodies adapted themselves over the centuries, rather like camels, to desert living. We can all store food by way of fat to serve as a larder for lean times, but, as I have learnt to my cost during desert ultra-marathons, such fat deposits are a huge disadvantage to strenuous hot-weather exercise because bodily exertion generates heat in muscle and surplus fat blocks the urgent need to lose heat through the skin to stay cool. So heart and lungs have to work extra hard.

Bushmen's, and especially Bushwomen's, bodies avoided this problem by concentrating their reserves of fat in their voluminous buttocks, which looked quite out of keeping with the rest of their lean, stringy bodies.

The well-known South African traveller and academic, Laurens van der Post, described the buttocks of Bushmen as sponges. Despite their resulting unsexy silhouettes, Bushwomen were much coveted as slaves or wives by their Bantu neighbours due to their delicate limbs and honey-coloured skin.

Bushmen learnt how to suck moisture from seemingly desiccated desert weeds. They would use a stick to dig away the sand around the weed's thin stems until they unearthed the 'water tanks' where the stems swelled to football-sized, jelly-filled balls which, when squeezed, produced liquid. This the Bushmen would drink and wipe on their bodies to moisten their skin.

William Burchell, a botanist from Kew Gardens, spent many years in South Africa during the early nineteenth century, and he greatly admired the Bushmen. He commented on the graceful ways of the women, and noted how the boys stood 'still as herons' for hours on end in the pools of dried riverbeds waiting to spear fish. He noted too that Bantu bands would soon wipe out all Bushmen in their zeal to take over their hunting grounds. He added that the poor Bushmen might first be killed off by neighbouring Hottentot tribes who feared the lethal desert poisons of Bushmen arrows, or by Boer farmers whose cattle the Bushmen were prone to rustle.

One of the Bushmen's favourite foods, found on their desert boundaries along the Orange and Limpopo rivers, was the hippopotamus. They called the meat of these 3,500-pound beasts 'sea-cow pork', and since animal fat was their ultimate delicacy, they went out of their way to trap them.

Hippos are the most lethal of Africa's riverine denizens, with more deaths per year to their credit than even crocodiles. Highly territorial when cut off from their pools, their aggressive and surprisingly agile attacks on land or in water make them particularly dangerous to hunt. So Bushmen dug deep hippo pits with camouflaged covering along known hippo tracks. Once killed, the beasts' thick pelts would be peeled back like banana skins.

A fully grown hippo carries more dense fat than any other animal kilo for kilo, and they are so heavy that they can walk about under water, grazing on water weeds for five minutes with a lungful of air.

Burchell himself loved hippo steak which he would consume, while his Bushmen friends carved off great chunks of fat to dry on thorn bushes, drank bowls of melted fat, munched on entrails and offal, and 'all around me was carving, broiling, gnawing and chewing'.

An eccentric Scot, named Gordon Cumming, who left Eton at nineteen, joined the army in India and later in the Cape. After resigning in 1843 he went on a five-year safari, which took him all over South Africa, often alone.

Resented early on by his man servant (a Cockney ex-cab driver), he hunted at times with a Hottentot tracker he called Hendrick. But a lion ate Hendrick one day, leaving only one leg (knee down) with a shoe on it. Cumming then tracked and killed the lion.

He disliked the Boers and their treatment of Bushmen. He noted that hunting licences in the Boer Republic included 'two Bushmen in each seasonal game permit'.

He was highly impressed by the Bushmen, whose women carried hollowed-out ostrich eggs full of water over great distances of arid desert, hiding some in secret places along ancient Bushmen 'escape routes'.

He noted in his meticulous diaries how Bushmen, when hunting the hyper-shy ostrich, would wear ostrich skins and strut about in imitation of that bird's standard gait until close enough to use a poisoned arrow.

Cumming was a canny Scot and he appreciated the cunning ways of the Bushmen, who would garner whatever meat might be available within reach of their desert hideouts, whether that meat was wild or owned by farmers. He admired their meticulous withdrawal plans following a rustling raid, and how they would, on reaching their desert hideouts, drive the stolen cattle barefoot into the most arid zones where their mounted pursuers dared not follow.

A contemporary of Cumming, William Oswell, was another British hunter who admired the Bushmen. Oswell was himself of a fearless nature, and whereas Cumming was wont to shoot at a charging lion from seventy metres, Oswell favoured a mere thirty. This sometimes backfired, and on one occasion, hunting with a companion of David Livingstone, he and his horse were thrown to the ground and gored by a white rhinoceros. Oswell's scalp was literally torn from his head, but somehow he survived. Much of his bush and survival craft was learnt from dwelling with the families of Bushmen, who, to an outsider, appeared to live for weeks without water amid their dunes and endless plains of salt pans, thorny acacias and confusing mirages.

His diary notes that, elephant-like, they chew the bitter flesh of the Kalahari *tsamma* melon. I have tasted one and instantly spat it out, but the evil flavour lingered in my mouth for hours.

Bushmen, Oswell wrote, copy the habits of the desert *gemsbok*, sucking dry hidden tubers by somehow knowing where to dig for them. In places with no apparent water source at all, they hand-dig a shaft into which they plunge a long pole and then revolve this, drill-like, down to hollows in the substratum to form a *mamina* hole from which they suck water through a long hollow reed.

Cumming returned to Scotland in 1850 and, twenty years later, his books attracted Frederick Selous, then a boy at Rugby School, to give up his plans to be a doctor and instead go to Africa to hunt big game. Selous was to become acknowledged as the greatest of all the white hunters of the nineteenth century and he noted the Bushmen as the most proficient trackers in Africa. He admired their boxes of acacia bark lined with gum in which, despite great heat, they stored live poisonous caterpillars to keep their *n'gwa* toxin fresh for arrow tips. How, too, they left the skins of their prey hanging from bushes along their secret paths for a rainy day, when the leather might keep them alive.

Selous envied their ability to successfully digest decomposing meat and slimy offal. And, he noted, when hunting man-eating lions with a taste for Bushmen, how fastidious the lions often were with their kills. First their abrasive tongues would lick the skin off their victims, then suck the blood from the flayed bodies before eating them, feet first.

Dr Livingstone himself, although not long in the Kalahari, also spoke highly of the patience of Bushmen hunters who would wait motionless for hours watching a lion gorge on a kill. Then, when the lion eventually slept satiated from its feast, they would creep up and fire poisoned arrows into the big cat's belly.

The records of hunters and explorers towards the end of the nineteenth century mention Bushmen less frequently. By the 1870s safari hunters like Cornwallis Harris described the few Bushmen that he met as desperate survivors, hunted to near extinction by both Boer and Bantu; no longer daring to rustle cattle or stray from the inner sanctums of their deserts, they lived off ant larvae, locusts and roots. Knowing that their hunters ambushed water holes, the Bushmen filled their ostrich egg water bottles only when in the direst of need. Harris described them as walking skeletons.

Harris himself subsequently met the chief of one of the Zulu tribes who massacred many Bushmen, the Matabele chief Mzilikazi. In the 1830s Mzilikazi's tribe was thrown out of Bechuanaland by the Boers and driven 700 miles to land north of the Limpopo, having slaughtered many of the Mashona who they displaced in what is now Zimbabwe. (Robert Mugabe is himself a Mashona, and he has in his time as leader murdered over 30,000 Matabele.) Harris was warned by the Bushmen of Mzilikazi's bad habits, including decapitation, genital amputation and impalement, but he eventually charmed and gifted his way into the Zulu chief's favour and hunted all over his land.

Although the Bushmen clans survived Mzilikazi's atrocities, their end nearly came in the 1890s when one of the last desperate clans of San Bushmen raided veldt-grazing cattle and were pursued by vigilante Boer farmers. The raiders usually managed to escape into a mountainous outcrop, their last refuge, but unfortunately for them this hideout, located by chance in its secret valley, was attacked by Boer commandos. Many of the San, whose ancestors sired all indigenous South Africans, were wiped out that day. Half breeds still survive, but few pure DNA members of the First People, the greatest known true desert dwellers in African history. DNA researchers at the Nanyang Technological University in Singapore in 2013 traced existing Bushmen in Namibia and compared their DNA with 420,000 variants across 1,462 genomes from forty-eight ethnic groups worldwide

Professor Stephan Schuster, the project leader, says of the Khoisan people, including the Kalahari Bushmen, 'Our study proves that they belong to one of mankind's most ancient lineages and that they did not interbreed with any other ethnic groups for 150,000 years.'

Sadly, the Bushmen of today are under great pressure to leave their historic homeland which, in 1961, was known as Bechuanaland. That year the British rulers designated an area twice the size of Wales as the Central Kalahari Game Reserve (CKGR) which was designed to protect the last refuge of a people who had lived across southern Africa for tens of thousands of years until they were gradually exterminated by all the races that came after them. This guarantee that Bushmen could live in this reserve unmolested was enshrined in the new country's constitution when Botswana won independence in 1966.

But diamonds were discovered inside the reserve in the 1980s and the Botswana government told the Bushmen to move out. Despite global censure, the authorities pressed ahead with the evictions, forcing the Bushmen to an arid settlement where, like Australian Aboriginals and Canadian Inuit in similar plight decades before, they lost the will to live and turned to alcohol and despair in the ghetto which they named the place of death.

A friend of mine, Robin Hanbury-Tenison who, to help remote jungle tribes in Brazil, had set up the now global concern called Survival International for indigenous peoples under threat, had taken legal steps on behalf of the Bushmen.

Despite this and Survival's successes in the Botswana High Court in 2006 and 2011, the government ignored the court rulings, denied the Bushmen access to the only available water supplies and to the hunting rights that they had always lived off in the reserve. If caught hunting, government agents now arrest, torture or shoot them.

Botswana's President, Ian Khama, is personally determined to drive every last Bushman out of the reserve so that the diamond operations there can be expanded.

When I was twelve, my South African granny having died, my mother decided to take all four of us children back to England. She bought a cottage in Sussex, toned down our South African accents and registered us in English schools. I fell in love with a nine-year-old next-door neighbour named Ginny, but she failed, for at least four years, to notice. Her father disliked me, but after teenage years of clandestine meetings, we knew that we were, as the saying goes, made for each other.

Long after we were married I returned with her many times to Africa to show her my old Constantia haunts and to explore elsewhere.

One of our journeys took us in search of my grandfather's Mozambique adventures a century before. We drove a rickety rental car up the coast road, the so-called Garden Route, passing by Ceres where, on a hillside, an imposing white chapel with pillars overlooks the coastline far below. This is the memorial shrine of Cecil Rhodes, land-grabber extraordinary and Grandad's one-time boss.

Our route was the same as that taken by most of the white settlers who arrived in Cape Town and headed east to find their own patch of the promised land. We stopped to walk on a wild beach beyond Gansbaai and tipped a one-legged self-styled beach attendant. The other, he said, had been removed by a white shark 'in the surf out there'. He reeled off coastal history to earn his tip and told us of shipwrecks all along the Agulhas Coast. 'Right there,' he pointed, 'the *Birkenhead* went down in the 1850s full of Brit troops come to fight the Zulus. Four hundred and fifty drowned. She was one of many.' Turning round and waving one crutch inland, he assured us that in his grandmother's day this coastal plain had shaken to the gallop of buck and sable, the air rent with the scream of elephants and the roar of lions, while hippos and crocs splashed in the freshwater lagoons. Then he sighed, 'We Boers and you Brits turned paradise to hell. Now only dogs, baboons and ostrich survive – if they don't get run over.'

Like the settlers, we followed the corridor of red aloe trees and low veldt, with the Outeniqua Mountains always to our left and the sea to our right. The British Army had fought a dozen Frontier Wars to force the Xhosa tribes back north and so hand good farming land to the settlers. Beyond Cape Agulhas we camped at Mossel Bay, as did Bartholomew Dias from Portugal in 1488.

Dias was then, and still is, a hero of mine. I have had two great dreams in my life. First, to emulate my father by becoming colonel of, to me, the most famous regiment in the world. In my Constantia nursery there was a photo (now in my office) of Dad, somewhere in Scotland, riding at the head of 300 grey horses mounted by soldiers of the Royal Scots Greys. My second sacred ambition, less specific but no less present, was to see for myself the steaming jungles, great deserts and remote rumbling volcanoes described by famous explorers whose books I had devoured from an early age.

I marvelled at the daring of the great navigators and conquistadors of Portugal and Spain who risked horrific deaths to sail into the unknown. Dias had, on his Mossel Bay landing, discovered that the coast of Africa ran east and not south, as had been thought. He had, without at the time realizing the enormity of his discovery, found the way to the East, to the fabulous wealth of the Indies.

It was clear to me that all worthwhile exploration must be to dangerous places where sandstorms, thirst, scorpions, huge spiders, alligator swamps, fierce bedu on camels and terrible disease were to be found.

My earliest heroes' journeys were always described in books with lively drawings of curling waves higher than their ships or, on land, spear-throwing natives.

Marco Polo's book *Travels* concerns his journeys overland during a period of twenty-three years, which took him across the Gobi Desert to little-known China, and eventually, by way of India and Persia, back to Venice. His stories inspired the subsequent voyage of the Italian Christopher Columbus under the patronage of the King of Spain.

Some thirty years after Marco Polo, a Berber scholar from Tangier named Ibn Battuta set out in 1325 on a pilgrimage to Mecca. This turned into a remarkable twenty-four-year journey of 75,000 miles, taking in the Sahara down to Timbuktu, much of Arabia, India, Indonesia, and a side voyage to Peking. His well-observed account of his travels were and remain a unique record of the society and culture of the fourteenth-century world of Islam.

A century after Battuta's journey, Columbus set sail from Spain heading due west from the Canary Islands because, unlike other great navigators of the time, he believed that he could reach the Indies that way. He is famous today for having 'discovered America', whereas he actually landed in the Bahamas and Cuba. He also recorded the first ever horizontal journey around Earth. (In the late twentieth century I led the first vertical journey around Earth.) Out of personal pride, he maintained all his life that he had found a new route to Asia. He was later subjected to disbelief and derision and he died embittered aged fifty-five.

Ten years after the 1487 Mossel Bay landing of Bartholomew Dias, the Portuguese King, Dom Manuel, sent a little-known Lisbon aristocrat named Vasco da Gama south with four well-stocked vessels to follow the Dias route. Like Dias, they made a landfall on the Cape coast but, unlike him, they carried on east to the busy ports of Mozambique and Mombasa where they encountered traders doing regular business across the Indian Ocean. They took on local pilots who guided them in a little over three weeks to the spices entrepôt of Calicut in India.

Da Gama had found the long sought sea route to the Indies from which subsequent European 'empires' would be built which in turn would lead to a truly global economy.

From Mossel Bay Ginny and I passed to Oudtshoorn, where burly
Boer honey farmers vied with each other to lift great tins of delicious
smelling 'protea honey', and where we bought tickets to ride gallop-
ing ostriches around a ring. In the Tsitsikamma Forest we passed
families of baboons foraging along the verges, and then at Port
Elizabeth the road became a four-lane highway.

We were now in the Eastern Cape, in a region much contested
between Xhosa, Boer and Brit over a century. After the Napoleonic
Wars Britain suffered a depression and, just as criminals were deposited in Australia, so a flotilla of twenty ships in 1820 dropped off
some four thousand would-be 'settlers' with their basic belongings
on to the Port Elizabeth beaches. Few survived.

Driving through KwaZulu-Natal, we came at last to the Swazi
border at Kosi Bay. Now we were in the region where Grandad went
maverick.

In the late nineteenth century the South African President, Paul
Kruger, wanted Kosi Bay as a key trading port, but Queen Victoria's
government had other concerns and made a pact with the Zulus
which brought the region under imperial jurisdiction. Since the
Portuguese in Mozambique were also keen to claim Kosi Bay for
themselves, patient diplomacy was needed.

But patience and diplomacy were not the preserves of Cecil
Rhodes, nor of my grandfather Eustace. I mentioned the latter's
colonial wanderings earlier, but the Kosi Bay Limpopo region
was nearly his undoing. He had left the Canadian Police in 1888
and made his way to Africa, initially to Egypt with the job of
news reporter for the *Morning Post*. He then joined the staff of
General Kitchener, who was busy retaking Sudan after the rebellious Dervishes of the Mahdi had earlier killed General Gordon
at Khartoum. Eustace fought with Kitchener's army at the Battle
of Gemaizah, but it would be ten years before the final defeat of
the Mahdi's successor, the Khalifa, at Omdurman and the annexation of all Sudan by Britain. Eustace left Kitchener's forces in
March 1890 and joined the British South Africa Company's
police as a sub-lieutenant in Kimberley. This force had been
formed by Cecil Rhodes the previous year to help protect pioneers travelling north into Mashonaland (now part of

Zimbabwe). Eustace did well and was soon promoted to full lieutenant with his own police troop.

Just as the East India Company in India and the Hudson Bay Company in Canada preceded British territorial gains in those countries, so Cecil Rhodes' British South Africa Company expanded British territory in southern Africa. Hence Rhodesia. Eustace did his bit. The *History of the British South Africa Police* described Eustace (spelling his surname 'ffiennes') as: 'Not a regular soldier, he was the son of a lord and a member of the London Stock Exchange although he had served, by some unexplained circumstances, in the Canadian militia.'

Pennyfeather's Column of Pioneers to Southern Rhodesia, which began in late June 1890, made inevitable a confrontation with Portugal, Britain's oldest ally, because Portugal had laid claim to the whole area through which the Rhodes pioneers had to travel to reach Rhodesia, and many of his men, including Pennyfeather and, later, Grandfather Eustace, were dead keen to grab territory for the motherland wherever they could. Shortly before Eustace joined the BSAP, an energetic Portuguese soldier, Major Paiva d'Andrada, formed a Rhodes-type commercial company and established a fortress at Massi Kessi, twenty miles from where Eustace's police were based at Umtali.

In November 1890 a small armed force under Eustace attacked three hundred Portuguese levies on the ridge above Massi Kessi. Andrada was captured and his fort seized. Andrada was sent back to Portugal where he caused a great stir against British aggression on Portuguese territory. Later, when four separate Portuguese forces arrived to retaliate, including a thousand volunteers with artillery, they found overland travel a much harder foe than the British. It was easy to get lost in the dense tropical vegetation. Rations were meagre. Malaria and dysentery struck men daily. Horses died or contracted tsetse fly-induced sickness. Rivers had to be crossed, swollen and full of crocodiles. Tracks were deep in mud. The heat and humidity were exhausting.

In March 1891, according to the book *Men Who Made Rhodesia*, Eustace was stationed at Umtali when he received a messenger. Two of his men were down with fever at an outpost.

Fiennes at once called for volunteers who were good swimmers, and selected two. The three men then set out on a 23 mile journey over slippery mountain paths at the height of the rainy season when all rivers were in flood. Rain had fallen incessantly for months, and 52 inches had been recorded for the season against a normal 30 inches. When they got to the Revué River they found it to be 'raging like a miniature sea, mountainous waves roaring like thunder'. In spite of this, Fiennes attempted the crossing alone; he was carried down the stream for half a mile and was once entangled in reeds. Nevertheless he managed to gain the far bank after half an hour in the water.

At the outpost he found that one man had been dead for a week and Glover, the other, was in a dreadful condition. He began to dig a grave with his own hands. Building a small raft, Fiennes and another man got Glover back over the crocodile river and, in a rough litter, over the mountains to their base. Glover lived until 1950. The account continued: 'Fiennes' part in the rescue was one of calculated courage of the highest order; the odds in favour of his crossing the Revué were very slender.'

Eustace then took part in the Battle of Chua Hill when a Portuguese attack was repulsed. Next day the Massi Kessi Fort's garrison was found to have fled and Fiennes was sent forward with his mounted men along the paths towards Beira to follow up the enemy and keep going east to the sea. At Chimoio, 130 miles from Umtali, he located a manned Portuguese fort, observed it and decided to attack the next day. While preparing the attack he was surprised by a white man whom he nearly shot, believing him to be Portuguese. But this was the British Bishop of Mashonaland who told him not to attack the Portuguese as the arrival of Major Sapte, the military secretary to the British High Commissioner, was imminent. This man duly arrived and ordered Eustace not to attack because peace had been made by the two governments the previous day.

According to the official *History of the British South Africa Police*: 'When Rhodes heard what had happened, and that the swashbuckling attempt to add Portuguese East Africa to his territories had again been abandoned, he said, "Why didn't Fiennes say Sapte was drunk and put him in irons?"' On 30 May 1891 Lord Salisbury and the Portuguese government finally signed an agreement, which has lasted until the present day. At the time, Queen Victoria was greatly relieved, being closely related to the Portuguese king. Eustace, unaware of the narrow scrape he had experienced in sparking off a potentially major international embarrassment, was sent back to Umtali.

That July, Rose Blennerhassett, in charge of a group of nursing sisters posted to the Umtali region, wrote in her book, *Adventures in Mashonaland*: 'Foremost amongst our friends was Lieutenant Eustace Fiennes whom we came to regard as a special providence. He saved us as far as possible from difficulties, was kind, courteous and helpful, to say nothing of being a very jolly young fellow and excellent company.' In December, however, Eustace's health broke down and he resigned his commission.

His subsequent attempts to buy stakes in the Kimberley gold mines and to start a farm in Matabeleland came to nothing.

In 1899 Eustace, back home with his little family, various medals and tales of derring-do, contested North Oxfordshire as the Liberal candidate. He was defeated by 700 votes.

Since his political aspirations had not initially worked out, Eustace kept his ears attuned to the South African scene. In October that year the Dutch, or Boer, leader in South Africa formally declared war on Britain unless British troops were withdrawn from the twin Boer republics of Transvaal and the Orange Free State. Since one of Britain's main geopolitical goals was to bring both these gold-rich Boer provinces under direct British rule, war was exactly what Prime Minister Salisbury wanted, especially (PR-wise) if the Boers were seen to make the first aggressive move. Militarily Britain was confident of quickly defeating them. Eustace, along with many other Liberals, did not approve in principle of the idea of fighting the Boers to gain their gold. So he said so in public and was promptly labelled 'pro-Boer' by prominent Tories.

Originally the Cape, already settled by the Dutch, had been occupied by the British to safeguard the route to India. Various plans to incorporate the Boers into a federation were discussed and then, in 1877, imposed on them. But four years later the Boers had rebelled and their two states were given a loose independence. This had worked until both gold and diamonds were discovered on Boer land, and Cecil Rhodes goaded the Boers' leader, Paul Kruger, into his 1899 declaration of war.

Eustace discussed joining up for the Boer War with his old friend Winston Churchill, who had a similar background of fighting in various foreign wars, including in the Sudan, and he had also reported on them for the *Morning Post*.

Churchill's family, the Spencers, owned the Blenheim estate close to Broughton, had intermarried with the Fienneses years before and, although Winston was at this stage a Tory, before switching to Liberal and then back again, he thought along similar political lines to Eustace on most things. They would later work well together but, back in 1900, Eustace was attracted by Winston's war stories, not his politics. The previous year Winston had achieved brief fame through his own *Morning Post* reports of rescuing an armoured train from the Boers and then, after being captured, effecting a daring escape. So Eustace, like Winston, signed up with the local regiment, the Oxfordshire Imperial Yeomanry, said goodbye to Granny Florrie and was shipped back to sunny South Africa to kill Boers instead of Portuguese.

Unfortunately things did not go as planned for the British Army. The superior mobility, field skills and firepower of the Boers led to many embarrassing British defeats and the siege of various garrisons, including Mafeking. Britain's enemies all over the world sniggered and gloated, though Eustace did well and was twice mentioned in dispatches, adding to his colourful collection of medals. Such had been the humiliating effect on the British public of the previous long history of defeats by the Boers that the May 1900 relief of Mafeking was greeted with nationwide rejoicing. The garrison commander, Colonel Robert Baden-Powell, who years later founded the Boy Scout and Girl Guide movements, had saved many lives during the siege by boiling whole horse corpses in vats to provide 'the Colonel's Soup'.

At the close of 1900, Kitchener of Khartoum took over in the Cape with a Commonwealth army of half a million troops in order to clean up the remnants of a Boer force that never exceeded 50,000 soldiers. The latter resorted to the guerrilla tactics at which they were adept and to which the terrain was ideally suited. To retaliate, the British invented concentration camps and long lines of blockhouses, 8,000 of them, connected by tangled hedges of barbed wire. Boer farms were burnt and civilians were shut up in the camps where 25,000 died of disease. Finally, in May 1902 Kitchener signed a peace treaty with the Boers, whose two states became British colonies but with internal self-government.

By the time Ginny and I visited Kosi Bay and the Mozambique border in the 1970s, Britain and Portugal were still the best of friends and were celebrating the five hundredth anniversary of their 'unbroken Alliance'.

Having spent my formative years, thanks to the South African adventures of Grandad Eustace, in a land proud of its explorers and white hunters and where I had long daydreamed of King Solomon's Mines, there lurked in the back of my mind the thought of how nice it would be to find my own lost city somewhere in a Congolese or Brazilian jungle or, better yet, in the great dunes of some far-flung oven-like desert.

CHAPTER 2

A Talent for Trouble

After the four schools I had attended in South Africa, Eton was definitely a cultural shock, but five years as a boarder there left me plenty of time in which to daydream and to further my reading about exotic adventures.

I excelled at none of the school's 'mainline' sports, such as cricket and football, but I did well, in my own unorthodox manner, at boxing. One *Eton Chronicle* match report stated:

The School versus Charterhouse
Fiennes beat Goodman. He was not quite so wild as usual but persists in using his head. If he can overcome these two faults he will do well as he is very strong and courageous.

and

The School versus Bloxham College
Fiennes beat Fowler. This was a wild brawl and Fiennes must remember to use neither his head nor the inside of his glove for disabling his opponent. This will not only enable him to see, but also to score the odd point or two. This was a close win for Eton.

I was beaten with a cane five times for breaking rules at Eton and became adept at avoiding many other deserved beatings through a mixture of low cunning and careful planning. This would later hold me in good stead in facing the odds when travelling the great deserts of the world.

One cardinal crime I committed at Eton was in response to an addiction I picked up during my last two years there, that of stegophily, the official name for the sport of climbing up the outside of buildings, particularly by night, and leaving items on their topmost spire, dome or lightning conductor. My climbing partner, a senior prefect in his House, was caught one night when we were heard affixing a flag to the 'summit' of School Hall's dome. I managed to escape in the ensuing chase, but he was sadly asked to leave at the end of that term.

Due to over-training for the boxing team when I was sixteen, I began to suffer from shooting cramp-like chest pains and I was diagnosed as suffering from rheumatic fever. My heart, the doctor said, would be in danger of permanent damage unless I took a complete rest for six months. No boxing, no night-climbing and (good news) no school.

That summer, at home in the record heatwave of 1960, introduced me to the wonderful new world of explosives. I had not done well in school chemistry lessons with Bunsen burners, but my best friend in our Sussex village (later to become a senior officer in the Fire Service) helped me experiment in our garden shed with various easily purloined 'chemicals', such as sugar and weedkiller. To ignite the resulting cocktails we used our pocket money to purchase Jetex fuse wire so that we could sprint to cover behind the garden wall after lighting the fuse ends.

After satisfying weeks of explosives around the house, a thirty-foot-high mushroom-shaped cloud which followed the shattering of the 'bomb's' container, my mother's best brass flower vase, finally decided her. She banned all future bomb-making. If only I had obeyed her ban, my life would have taken a very different course.

After the six months' 'rest', I shed the chest pains, grew six inches and moved into the light heavyweight boxing grouping. I went to hospital for three days with double vision, my two front teeth were chipped, my nose was broken and both thumbs swelled up due to oft-repeated hooks with the forbidden insides of my gloves.

During my final Eton year, and in order to increase my pocket money, I joined forces with Jeremy Deedes, whose father edited the *Daily Telegraph*, and with Chris Cazenove, who was later to become a Hollywood-based film star. We organized a method of avoiding detection by patrolling school masters whose duties included apprehending any Etonian caught in forbidden parts of Windsor. By changing in a back street from our easily spotted Eton tailcoats into working men's boiler suits and cloth caps, we would buy Black Russian and Abdulla cigarettes plus mini-bottles of cherry brandy, which we then sold at a profit to senior boys back at school.

Aged seventeen I won my school Boxing Cap and was told by our boxing coach that I would be School Boxing Captain if I stayed on for another year. But my mother, on the advice of my House Master, sent me to a language crammer in Brighton for specialist training in order to ensure that I passed the vital A-Level exams needed to enter Sandhurst and obtain a Regular Commission in the army. I chose languages because there was no chance at all of my obtaining A-Levels at any other subject. I had been taught French by David Cornwell (who later wrote spy novels under the name of John le Carré).

My chief ambition, out of several, was still to emulate my father and become commanding officer of the Royal Scots Greys cavalry regiment, the position that he had held when he was killed in Italy in the war.

Aged eighteen, my long-time calf-love for Ginny was thwarted by her father's belief that I was too wild for his daughter, and he issued me with a court 'banning order'. This served only to encourage a growing love affair over our teenage years.

Meanwhile, my time at the Brighton language school coincided with the height (literally) of the miniskirt fashion era, so that I found concentration in the mixed-sex language classes to be impossible and I failed my A-Levels twice.

Additionally, my previous fascination with explosives was rekindled by a nocturnal raid by fellow students on a local girls' boarding school, after which I was prosecuted in court for 'malicious damage caused by a smoke bomb'. This was reported in the national newspapers and further set Ginny's father against me. By then I was the proud possessor of a Vespa scooter on which I would scoot from Brighton by night to visit Ginny in the fourth floor attic room of her boarding school in nearby Eastbourne.

Once it had become clear that I would never gain an A-Level, it was decided that I should try for a Short Service Commission at Mons Cadet School, a poor alternative to Sandhurst, but better than nothing.

At Mons I met a fellow building-climber and, under his guidance one night scaled the west wing wall of Heathfield Girls' School, where we were unfortunately caught by the police. My friend, who had hit out when apprehended, was removed from Mons, whereas I, who had avoided physical contact with our captors, was merely awarded a 'Restriction of Privileges' for fifty-six days, which involved two hours in uniform and standing to attention every evening outside the Guard Room when all other cadets had local leave.

My platoon sergeant-major informed me, in what I thought was a tone of slight respect, that I had chalked up the record number of RPs since Mons was first formed.

In the spring of 1962 I was passed out by Her Majesty as a second lieutenant in the Royal Scots Greys. With a friend who passed into the regiment from Mons at the same time, I planned to spend the month's leave, before joining the Scots Greys in Germany, crossing the Anatolian Desert in Turkey by camel.

Unfortunately, the Ministry of Defence heard of our intentions and, due to the 'political climate in Anatolia', forbade us to go.

We quickly switched from Anatolia to the Pyrenees and from camels to a mule and cart – a first taste of expeditioning. This was followed by courses in tank maintenance and gunnery, learning how to destroy Soviet tanks a mile away. That Christmas there was a spectacular blizzard and more snow was recorded throughout England than in any year since 1881. In the New Year, my tank training complete, I said goodbye to my family and to Ginny and joined the regiment in Germany to help defend Western Europe against the fairly likely event of invasion by the massed armoured regiments of the Warsaw Pact.

Each of our tank squadrons had four troops of three tanks. Three of these troops had 50-ton Centurion tanks and the fourth crewed

70-ton Conquerors, which could only fire their great 120mm shells when halted. I was given a Conqueror troop and we referred to the Centurions as 'bubble cars'.

I grew to love my tanks, my crew members (the vast majority of whom were from Scotland) and the regiment as a whole.

Since many of my fellow officers were avid polo players or drag-hunt fanatics, there were luckily few contenders for those army sports involving your feet rather than your horse, or, in the case of boxing, your hands (not head).

I won the regimental heavyweight boxing class which, according to Tarry Shaw, the long-term Boxing Officer, had once been won by my father.

I signed up for the Cross-Country Running Team, the Langlauf (cross-country) Skiing Team, and founded a Canoe Club by persuading wannabe canoeists to buy a quarter share in one of sixteen two-seater craft.

For the next three years, every summer I spent two months teaching soldiers how to canoe. We travelled down various European rivers, including the Elbe, the Oste, the Weser, the Rhône, the Loire, the Rhine and the Danube, up to the border of neutral Austria. The hottest of those journeys, which averaged two weeks per river, was the descent of the Danube, especially when, in a heatwave, we reached the village of Donauesverschwunden (which translates as 'Disappearance of the Danube'). At this point the river really did disappear, leaving a steaming hot, dry riverbed for some nine miles. Each two-man crew had to carry all their kit, their paddles and their heavy fibreglass touring canoes on their sunburnt shoulders. Horseflies descended on bare shoulders in their swarms and, with no spare hands to wave them off, there was a great deal of swearing (and glaring at me) as though I was personally responsible for the discomfort.

On the banks of the Kiel Canal one night, I was in charge of some eighty Greys men, half of whom were my canoeists and the other half were two-man teams of trekkers. I had not actually received training permits from the Canal Authority for the simple reason that I knew all training activities on the canal were forbidden to British troops, so there was no point in applying for any permits. So we and our four 3-ton army lorries were over 100 miles from the Schlei River where I *did* have permission to train.

Unfortunately one of my corporals, acting as 'enemy' on the canal's southern bank, saw a canoe riding the wash of a huge Russian tanker gliding down the canal. So he fired off a Schermuly parachute illuminating flare which landed by mistake on the tanker's deck. We later discovered that all the tanker's crew had to wear special rubber-soled boots, due to the highly flammable nature of their cargo, in order to avoid creating any spark.

Our flare hissed and burned away fiercely on the boat deck and in a short while the klaxon and red light system, which is installed along the Kiel Canal banks right across Europe, began to honk and flash as though World War Three was about to erupt. Loudspeakers crackled and a disembodied male voice spoke to us with British Rail-like lack of intelligibility. I understood only two words with crystal clarity: '*Engländer Soldaten*.' A British-style beret or cap comforter must have been spotted on a canoeist.

I radioed the lorry drivers and all the 'enemy' posts along the canal and ordered the immediate end of the exercise. Somehow, within two hours all but four of the men were assembled in one place. All grey berets were removed and mud was smeared on the vehicle number plates. Those soldiers who were temporarily with us from other regiments were told to keep their black berets on and to sit prominently beside the drivers.

We sped north on our way back to our own training area, but the driver of my open jeep (or *champ* as they were known) grew sleepy, so I told him that we must change places. Officers were forbidden to drive MoD vehicles, but I felt sure that I was doing the right thing in order to avoid a possible crash. A short while later I woke from a drowsy trance to find myself driving straight towards a German pine tree. I jerked the steering wheel around, but it was too late. I sheered the off-front wheel clean from its axle, flung both my passengers into the dark undergrowth and generally redesigned the shape of the jeep. I seemed to be unhurt but for a bruised ribcage and forehead. The Jocks were bloody but healthily voluble.

Back in Fallingbostel, I was ordered to report to the divisional commander, General Miles Fitzalan-Howard, shortly to become

Duke of Norfolk. For my misdemeanour (the crash), I was fined £25 and given a stern warning. Luckily, there seemed to be no MoD central filing system which cross-checked the growing number of disciplinary incidents I had accrued, and, more fortunately, the Russian tanker mishap had not been blamed on the Greys.

Telegrams had flown to all regimental commanders. My own had quite rightly protested innocence. It appeared that because of the flare, all canal traffic across Europe had stopped for five hours, which was an expensive delay. Six months later some busybody forester found a Grey's beret by the canal and handed it to the *polizei*, who gave it to the local British Army liaison officer. Within twenty-four hours my CO had summoned me, and this time I saw a different general, received a heavier fine and a dozen extra orderly officer duties. Did I realize the possible consequences had the Soviet tanker exploded? I assured the general that I did, but that I had acted in innocence and with only the interests of training in mind. I persuaded myself that the matter would be forgotten and that I had as yet done nothing which might slow down my progress towards command of the regiment.

That winter my short-service commission with the Greys was to end. I took and passed a lieutenant-to-captain promotion exam but was still, due to my Mons background, a second lieutenant, and my many months of adventure training rather than concentration on tank training had not improved my qualifications.

I was about to apply for a one-year extension, the longest then allowed for someone in my position, when I spotted a three-line advertisement in regimental orders. 'Officers wishing to apply for secondment to the 22nd Special Air Service should obtain the relevant form from the Orderly Office.' Only a week before I had listened spellbound to a Mess story of SAS patrols in Borneo, the only war zone where the British Army was still in action. Here was an open invitation to a three-year secondment with this little-known but élite regiment, after which I could apply to extend my commission with the Greys.

In November 1965 I was told to report to SAS headquarters the following January for a selection course in the Welsh mountains. This turned out to be extremely rigorous, and 90 per cent of the 136 entrants were eliminated over the next four weeks.

One test involved a theoretical bank raid and, after completing a careful reconnaissance of the target bank in Hereford, I stupidly left in a restaurant my outline notes on how I would complete the raid.

Two days later the national newspapers screamed 'BIG BANK RAID MYSTERY' and 'MINISTRY ENQUIRY INTO BANK RAID SCARE'. These headlines were then followed by 'ARMY INITIATION UPSETS POLICE' in the *Daily Mail*.

It turned out that a weekend-long security operation had stopped all police leave because every bank in Hereford had been surrounded, owing to the lack of a specific identification of the target in my plans.

Future SAS selection courses no longer involved theoretical bank raids.

In the winter of 1966 I was officially accepted into the hallowed ranks of the 22nd SAS Regiment as a captain, at that time being the youngest captain in the British Army.

Continuation training then followed to teach us 'students' the gentle arts of demolition, CQB (close-quarter battle), resistance to interrogation, fast response shoot-to-kill, parachuting, field medicine, and field survival. Failure to pass subsequent tests on these topics was not permitted.

I disliked the eye, stomach and artery operations we had to watch in surgeries as much as I enjoyed the demolition classes which were tutored by a diminutive Welsh sergeant with a squint and rock-steady hands. Under the gentle lilt of his quaint accent we learnt to demolish steel girders and pear trees with maximum economy of explosives. With self-deprecating humour Taff-Bang (his nickname) labelled his work bags as Explosives. I became adept at 'minimal usage' and ended up with a good supply of detonators, plastic explosives and ancillaries. These should have been returned to the Stores, but I took them home at weekends.

In June 1967 I was due to fly to Malaysia for intensive SAS jungle training, but an Old Etonian friend, by then a wine salesman, had inveigled me into helping him destroy the filmset of Twentieth Century Fox's *Doctor Dolittle*, starring Rex Harrison, on the night before the film crew began production. My friend's aim was to prevent lasting damage by the film-makers to the village of Castle

Combe, recently voted by the British Travel Association as 'the prettiest village in England'.

Unfortunately, our operation was betrayed upfront by a journalist, the police pounced, and I spent a night in the local prison.

A week later I was expelled from the SAS and demoted to second lieutenant. Back home, Ginny's father telephoned my mother to say that he would call the police if I ever tried to see his daughter again.

Subsequent Assizes found that my use of army explosives to destroy civilian property was 'indefensible', and I was heavily fined.

The Army Council, satisfied that there was no criminal involvement with the Castle Combe incident, allowed me to rejoin the Royal Scots Greys in Germany. I spent another year there back in tanks, a year in which I learnt for sure that my long-term dream of commanding the regiment would never happen, since my own goal at Castle Combe might be forgiven but never, on my file, forgotten.

Suspicious that Ginny had purloined the explosives that I had used from his chalk quarry works in Sussex, her father sent her away to stay with an American cousin who lived in Spain because that country had no extradition rights with the UK and he was convinced, despite Ginny's protestations of innocence, that her arrest by the police was imminent.

So, on my next home leave from Germany, I found myself Ginny-less and without the long-term army goal I had lived for all my life. My future was therefore a void, and determined to do something meaningful, I applied to MI6. The ensuing interview (carried out by a woman with no name somewhere in Earls Court) was quick, negative and mentioned Castle Combe.

At that time a friendly major in the regiment sent me a letter postmarked the Sultanate of Oman, where he was serving on a two-year posting. He knew that I was looking for a change from tank exercises in Germany and suggested that I volunteer to join the Sultan's Forces, just as he had.

I learnt at that time from the barrister who had defended me at the Assizes that, due to IRA terrorists blowing up targets on mainland Britain, I would now have received a minimum sentence of seven years in prison for my Castle Combe offence. I had been extremely lucky.

My application to join the Sultan's Armed Forces was accepted and I said goodbye to my Scots Greys friends. For three months I learnt basic Arabic in a north London language school, together with seven other officers from various regiments. They all passed the course. I failed, but was still eligible for the two-year posting.

Apart from learning Arabic, I would also need to know the basic facts of dealing with military activity in conditions of extreme heat. A manual, translated from French, summarized Foreign Legion advice thus:

— To maintain mental alertness, avoid dehydration. Just before sunrise, wipe rocks with an absorbent cloth to collect dew.
— On the move, avoid talking. Never shout. Breathe only through your nose. Keep your head and neck covered.
— Observe animals and birds. They circle water and recent corpses. Doves and bats can lead you to well shafts.
— Dig where animals have scratched or where flies crawl, as such places may recently have been damp. Signs of much camel dung may indicate a nearby water source. So too old campfire sites.
— Cactus pulp can often be sucked.
— Mix urine with sand and rub it on your skin to help keep cool.
— Above all, remember in hot deserts the air can be so dry that your sweat evaporates at once so that a litre of water can be lost in a single hour. In such conditions you can die in a single day with no water.

Despite ongoing opposition from her father, I had loved Ginny for twelve years and when I asked her to marry me, she nodded and I told her that I was as happy as a sandboy. 'That,' she said, 'is exactly what you are about to be ... an Arab sandboy.'

I left for Arabia in June 1968.

CHAPTER 3

'Never come here by yourself without a gun'

An RAF VC10 aircraft flew me and the seven other seconded officers via Rome to Bahrain. I had never been anywhere hotter than South Africa, and our arrival in mid-summer Arabia was a memorable experience. The wet heat was immediately exhausting, even during short outings from the air-conditioned cool of our hotel.

Our onward flight connection to Muscat, the capital of Oman, was by British Overseas Airways Corporation and they decided to go on strike that week. So we were stranded for the next eight days, which proved an excellent way to start acclimatizing to these new and debilitating hothouse conditions.

I met an air stewardess whose boyfriend, a medic in the local forces hospital, had told her of a British officer just arrived, badly wounded, from Muscat. This I soon discovered was the same officer, Major Richard John, whose initial letter a year before had given me the idea of joining the Sultan's Army.

I failed to make contact with Richard before his onward evacuation to hospital treatment back in Britain, but was told that a Marxist terrorist had shot him.

Richard's tales of sun and sand had enthused me to apply for my posting to Oman but now he was gone. He had promised to give me a thorough briefing on the Oman situation on my arrival. As it was and in his absence I studied the notes he had sent me some months before which summarized the short history of the Sultan's Forces.

The Sultan, my new boss, was hereditary leader of Muscat and Oman. In reality there had always been an Imam who was voted for by the populace and who ruled the interior of Oman, while the Muscat-based Sultan ruled the coastal fringe and handled Oman's foreign relations and sea trade.

For a while my boss had ousted the current Imam, one Ghalib bin Ali, and by 1957 was contentedly ruling from a beachfront palace in Dhofar, the southernmost province of Oman, well away from both the great heat of Muscat and the troublesome, fractious tribes of the Omani interior. Keeping a semblance of order up north was left to three small independent forces of the Muscat Infantry, the Batinah Force and the Oman Field Force. In March that year they were each turned into fully fledged regiments, respectively the Muscat Regiment, the Northern Frontier Regiment and the Oman Regiment. I would be joining the Muscat Regiment.

In June 1957 with support from the Saudis, the Sultan's chief enemy, the brother of Ghalib, the ex-Imam of Oman, Talib bin Ali, invaded with several hundred trained soldiers of his Oman Liberation Army (OLA) and reinstated Ghalib as Imam.

In July the Sultan sent the Oman Regiment to fight against the Imamate force, but they were badly defeated and were later disbanded. The rebels had seized the Omani inland capital of Nizwa, so the Sultan had requested immediate assistance from his old Treaty friends, the British. There is an old saying, 'He had them over a barrel' (in this case an oil barrel) and Whitehall responded by sending basic military assistance quickly (but quietly in order to avoid international criticism, bearing in mind the Suez Crisis the previous year). That August a mixed force of soldiers from the Sultan's Army, the Trucial Oman Scouts from the Gulf States and the Cameronians from the UK recaptured Nizwa and attempted unsuccessfully to dislodge the main rebel force from their stronghold on the 10,000-foot-high Jebel Akhdar (Green Mountain), considered by the Sultan's British advisers to be impregnable by the forces available to the Sultan.

That autumn rebel groups made constant sorties from the Jebel in order to lay mines and to attack Sultanate outposts. The British then sent further assistance, and in November a concerted attack was made on two sides of the Jebel. RAF Venom fighters, and later Shackleton bombers, bombed and rocketed known rebel hideouts on the upper slopes, but the rebels were adept at camouflage and easily defended the few vertiginous ascent routes to the upper plateaux.

The attack was a failure and only served to increase rebel sorties. So many vehicles were blown up on the main access road to the Fahud oil sites that the oil company drivers refused to use it.

Through the spring and summer of 1958 over a hundred powerful anti-tank mines were laid and over 80 per cent destroyed Sultanate or British armoured cars, Land Rovers and trucks. Sultanate camps were mortared and some of the rebel mines and hand grenades were found to be from American sources.

That November the British sent detachments of Ferret armoured cars from regiments including the Life Guards and a squadron of the Special Air Service.

One night in December the SAS spearheaded an attack on the Jebel using ropes to climb a difficult cliff in order to achieve surprise. They killed nine rebels and although they could not retain their hold on the cliff top, they had gained valuable knowhow for a future assault with more support.

During the full-moon nights of late January 1959 a number of diversionary attacks and RAF strikes were made prior to the SAS scaling a cliff face or spur between two valleys on the south side of the Jebel. They reached the cliff top by dawn and consolidated there before the rebels realized that they had been duped. Victory for the Sultan's forces soon followed and all rebel strongholds on the Jebel were taken.

The hardcore rebel leaders escaped to Saudi Arabia, but from then on permanent Sultanate garrisons were established on the Jebel. For the rest of the year, although the SAS were withdrawn, some British and Trucial Oman Scout units remained to mop up rebel guerrilla bands and block ongoing weapons and mines reaching them from Saudi Arabia.

By the time, nine years later, that I arrived in Bahrain, all British forces had withdrawn, leaving only the agreement that a limited number of serving army and air force officers could volunteer to join the Sultan's Army. When in the early 1960s Saudi troublemaking against the Sultanate switched to Dhofar, virtually all rebel activity up north had ceased.

While delayed in Bahrain, I met an old friend, Nick Holder, who had been at Mons Cadet School with me before he joined the Parachute Regiment. After his three years with them he had left the army and joined Gillette. In Bahrain, he told me, selling razor blades was proving extremely tough because nearly all the males wore long beards and bushy moustaches. But he was happy, for he loved a challenge and didn't seem to mind the oppressive climate.

Like everyone else in Britain at the time, Nick was unaware of the nature of British involvement in Oman because a D-Notice was firmly in place which effectively prevented the media from reporting from the war zone. I had myself signed a form agreeing not to disclose details of military activities that I observed or was involved in. As far as I know this was the last conflict in which British forces were to be involved where D-Notices were tolerated by the public. It was some nine years between the mid 1960s and 1970s that British seconded officers fought and died for the Sultan in bitter but unsung fighting in Dhofar, about which the taxpayer, who paid their salaries, knew little or nothing.

Looking back, this was strange, although I never questioned the policy at the time, since on the outcome of the fight between our Marxist-supported enemy and our Sultanate forces would hang the energy lifeblood of the West, enmeshed as it then was in a critical energy crisis.

More than two-thirds of the crude oil needs of the free world during those dangerous Cold War years derived from the countries of the Persian Gulf. All of the giant tankers heading south from the shallow waters of the Gulf had to pass through the narrow bottleneck of the Straits of Hormuz, at an average rate of one every ten minutes every day of the year.

These stormbound straits are twenty-five miles wide, only nine miles of which are navigable by tankers. They are guarded to the east by the Iranian navy. To the west the coast is commanded by the United Arab Emirates and the Sultanate of Oman, and it was here that the USSR was conducting a carefully planned war on two fronts.

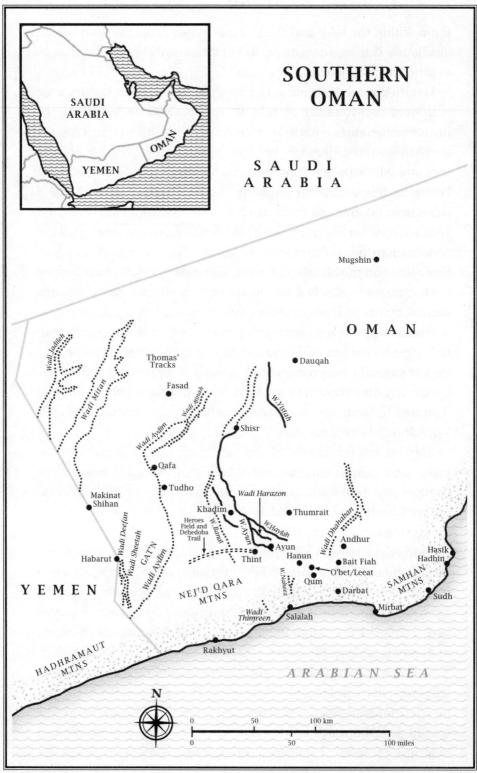

* Locations are approximate

From within the UAE and the Sultanate creeping subversion spread insidiously side by side with persistent terrorist plots, and from without the attack was overt, for Oman's southern province of Dhofar, a mountain-girt wonderland no bigger than Wales, abuts onto Aden.

In June 1967, under Harold Wilson's expedient guidance, the British imperialists withdrew from Aden, and within three months the Russian and Chinese imperialists moved into the resulting power vacuum; Marxism had now achieved a firm basis in the Arabian Peninsula from which to spread its wings. The land so long called Aden now became the People's Democratic Republic of Yemen, or South Yemen for short, an official Marxist state that soon attracted revolutionaries from the far corners of Arabia, ablaze with desire to spread abroad the blessings of revolution. Dhofar was naturally their nearest target and only Dhofar and Oman blocked the way to the narrow Straits of Hormuz and the oil of the Persian Gulf.

Dhofar was ruled by the ageing Sultan of Oman whose reactionary rule and longstanding friendship with Britain were tailor-made for propaganda purposes. The people were oppressed and poverty-stricken, the army was poorly armed and consisted of under a thousand fighting men, half of whom were Baluchi mercenaries with a handful of British volunteers in command. Since the Sultan had no friends but the British, the Marxists feared no outside intervention and rightly gauged that the British, still smarting from memories of Suez, would not wish any significant involvement in Dhofar. If pushed, they would withdraw smartly, abandoning the Sultan rather than risk a furore in the British Parliament and press.

Readily available to help the Marxists with their initial moves was Musallim bin Nuffl, leader of the local rebels inside Dhofar, who had become fed up with the Sultan's repressive measures as far back as 1964. When foreign oil prospectors had arrived in Dhofar, bin Nuffl had been lucky enough to obtain one of the few new jobs available, as a lorry mechanic. He soon learnt of the prosperity in other oil-rich Arab lands and noted that the Sultan used Indian and African labourers, not Dhofaris, to help the American oilmen in Dhofar. No bicycles, no transistor radios, and not even dark glasses might be bought by Dhofari townspeople, none of whom were allowed to hold any position of influence. Frustrated and enraged, bin Nuffl stirred up others of his tribe and after killing a few oil workers and destroying some lorries, he had taken his fledgling force off to Saudi Arabia and Iraq to train, calling them the Dhofar Liberation Front.

Once trained, they returned to harass the Sultan's forces in the mountains and to stir up trouble among the tribes. Bin Nuffl and his faction were not initially Marxists but non-revolutionary Muslims who wanted Dhofar for the Dhofaris. Nothing more. They were simple-minded nationalists who would ultimately have to be purged from the rebel leadership once Russian- and Chinese-trained Dhofaris were ready to take the helm.

The Sultan himself had long since left his traditional palace in Oman's capital city of Muscat, where his ancestors had faced civil war and inter-family or fraternal rivalry, and had settled in Salalah, the capital of Dhofar, leaving the troublesome north to be governed by a handful of trusted and well-paid Britons who were mostly ex-colonial administrators from the Indian Empire where he, the Sultan, had spent his youth. He had taken over the Sultanate on his father Taimur's abdication in 1932.

The ever-increasing dangers posed by the Marxist threat seemed to pass unnoticed by the Sultan in his coastal palace alongside an idyllic stretch of the white sands and palm trees of the Indian Ocean.

Under pressure from his ageing British retainers he did stir himself sufficiently to slightly increase the strength of his army, but found it difficult to recruit local, loyal and professional officers. He relied largely on professional mercenaries recruited from Pakistan, India, Britain and South Africa, but the ones he could afford were scarce on the ground so he had pushed the Harold Wilson regime to honour a long-standing Anglo-Omani Agreement to allow any British officer who volunteered for a two-year posting to his Sultan's Armed Forces (SAF) to do so without hindrance.

In return for this officer loan system, the Sultan agreed to allow two key RAF stations to be based in Oman, one close to his Salalah Palace and the other on Masirah Island just off the Dhofar coast.

When Richard John first told me of the chance to escape from the routine of boring tank exercises in Germany, he had described desert patrols in unexplored dune country and the search for terrorist arms caches buried in the sand. When he had additionally mentioned the presence of mountain lions, snakes, wolves and hyenas, I was truly hooked but blissfully unaware of the growing list of dead and wounded British officers, due to the D-Notice rulings.

This was corrected when I met a friendly officer, Peter Southward-Heyton of the Muscat Regiment, who had had plenty of experience of the Dhofar war zone. I will précis some of the information that he passed to me over several glasses of 'dark rum and coke'.

On leaving their bases in the East Aden Protectorate the previous year, the British forces handed over large quantities of weapons and ammunition to their successors, the Federal Regular Army. Unfortunately Aden's new government quickly turned Marxist-Leninist and switched the Dhofar rebellion from being merely troublesome at the time that Richard John's letter had attracted me to sign up, to a seriously escalating conflict soon after my arrival in Oman.

A few months before, in December 1967, major arms supplies and military leaders, well trained in the Soviet Union, arrived over the 'Aden' (Yemen) border, and within weeks of their arrival an *adoo* ambush killed five SAF soldiers and wounded seven. SAF vehicles were increasingly blown up by mines and their bases targeted by heavy mortar fire.

China, Peter added, was now vying with the Soviets to pour in arms and advisers, as well as providing guerrilla training at the Anti-Imperialist School in Beijing.

Helicopters were far too expensive for the Sultan, whose budget was dependent mainly upon dates and a £1 million annual gift from the British government. So when men were wounded and needed evacuation, donkeys were the only answer, and then only when the often precipitous terrain permitted.

Richard John from my regiment, badly wounded in the chest and shoulder during a patrol far from his mountain base, was laid across the back of a donkey and jolted over rocky ground for twelve hours in order to reach the nearest level clearing where the Sultan's only light Beaver aircraft could land. He was in great pain but there was only enough morphine for three hours. He finally reached hospital treatment and surgery some thirty-six hours after being wounded.

*

DHOFAR/OMAN

BAHRAIN

Manama

IRAN

P E R S I A N
G U L F

Mussundam
Hormuz
Ras al Khaimah
Khasab

Doha

Dubai

QATAR

Fujairah

GULF OF
OMAN

Abu Dhabi

HAFEET MTNS

BATINA

Khaburah

Muscat

UNITED ARAB
EMIRATES

Dhank
Rostaq
Bidbid
Wadi Tayin

HAJAR MTNS

Qalhat
Sur

Ibri
Wadi Samail
Naqsi
Hindarut

Ras al Hadd

Sayq
Sharaijah
Wadi Mayan
SHARQIYAH

Nizwa
Izki

Balad Bani
Bu Ali

SAUDI ARABIA

Adam
Zayan

WAHIBA SANDS

OMAN

Masirah
Island

JIDDAT
AL HARASIS

HARASIS

Mugshin

Fasad
Dauqah

Khor Ruri

Shisr

ARABIAN
SEA

Khadim

Andhur
Muria
Kuria

YEMEN

SAMHAN MTNS

Salalah
Sudh
Mirbat

N

HADHRAMAUT
MTNS

| 0 | 50 | 100 | 150 km |
| 0 | 50 | 100 | 150 miles |

* Locations are approximate

Leaving my brother officers playing interminable games of poker in our Bahrain hotel, I wandered the nearby streets, and in a minor hotel's restaurant decided to test my Arabic on a local. I noticed, sitting at a table by himself, an Arab gentleman wearing spectacles and whose dress and hairstyle looked different to any other Arab that I had observed in Bahrain. I ordered coffee and asked if I could share his table.

Unfortunately he replied in immaculate English, and when I did ask him if I could practise my Arabic, he replied with a strange and, to me, unidentifiable accent.

He was, he explained, on his way back from a teacher conference in Bahrain where he had been invited to explain his own religion to a specialist gathering of Imams. He was an Iraqi Kurd from a region of desert foothills west of the great Iraqi city of Mosul. He was, he also told me, of the Yazidi faith, and when I showed no particular reaction to this statement, he waxed eloquent in describing his beliefs.

Many Muslims, he told me, hated Yazidis and would love to eradicate them, believing them to be devil-worshippers. This, he assured me, was rubbish. In fact, he went on, they believed that God had given the Devil certain powers at the time that he was thrown out of Heaven, and Yazidis merely acknowledged him to keep him from doing them harm.

Originally Muslims, they had added touches of Christianity, Buddhism and animism to their core beliefs. Their clothes included long white shirts, smart coats and caps over braided plaits. Once a year they offered the sacrifice of a bull to the Sun, and on religious feast days they danced and sang to express their joy at being alive. Their eccentricities include never mentioning the name of the Devil (*Shaitan*) nor even the sound 'sh' at the beginning of any word. They shun the colour blue, and never wear clothing which has an opening down the front. Nor will they eat a lettuce. Hardly a religion posing a threat to anyone.

I didn't meet another Yazidi for some fifty years, nor did I even hear mention of their strange faith until in 2014 when the ISIS (IS) Caliphate group attempted to wipe them out en masse. But my Bahrain coffee companion remains in my memory as a happy, simple man, and it was he who first defined the three main sects of Islam that he told me, on learning of my total ignorance of all things Islamic, I would meet in Oman.

Why, I remember him asking me, did I, a Christian, wish to fight for a Muslim army? I explained that I had joined up unaware that any real fighting was involved and that to me there was no basic difference of any import between Jews, Muslims and Christians, since we all believed in the same God.

I would soon discover, he assured me, and held his arm up high, as I imagine he did to his students for emphasis, that there was among many Muslims a great hatred of Christians, Jews *and* of Islamic faiths which differed in any way from their own.

'You have come,' he told me, 'from a land of cold people to a hot land of hot people. We Yazidi do not wish to kill a man because his belief is different from ours. Some laugh and say that we always live in mountains where the cool winds blow away anger.'

I recorded his advice in my diary and have no reason, even now, to doubt its wisdom. He said that I had chosen well to work with Omanis, because they were mostly of the Ibadhi faith and so less likely to murder those of other faiths, unlike mainline Sunni and Shia adherents.

The history of Oman's specific brand of Islam, Ibadhism, is not a happy one. The records are long and detailed, but to keep things simple I will only mention key events.

With the rise of Islam in the second quarter of the seventh century AD, Oman was one of the first countries to convert, but also, within a couple of decades, one of the first to split from the central Sunni belief that the Prophet Mohammed's successors, known as Caliphs, should always be hereditary and not elected by the people.

In AD 656, when the fourth Caliph was murdered, the Kharijite group broke away from the main body of Islam and demanded that all future Caliphs be elected. The next Caliph, two years later, led an army against the dissenters and massacred twelve thousand. However, two survivors, who fled to Oman, successfully evangelized their creed which altered the name of its followers to Ibadhis.

By AD 694 the Caliphate's court was in Baghdad and from there sent a great army to bring the Omanis back from their schism. The two brothers who ruled Oman at the time resisted the Baghdadi attack and also extended Omani rule to certain coastal tracts of East Africa where, legend has it, they also began to hunt for the indigenous people for slavery on a grand scale.

Another two armies from Baghdad followed in quick succession and finally vanquished the Omani forces with terrible slaughter. Nonetheless Oman managed to continue electing its own Imam and ignoring the Caliphate. The next Caliph of Baghdad, the self-styled Bloodshedder, is remembered for his cruelty: on one occasion, when brought the decapitated head of an enemy, he cut out the tongue and threw it to his favourite cat. He was also famous for sleeping with all four thousand of his concubines.

Of the next nineteen Caliphs after the Bloodshedder, nine died of poisoning, being starved to death or other forms of assassination.

By the year 900 the then Caliph Mutadhil Billoh ordered troops from Bahrain to subjugate the Omanis with an army of 25,000 men, including 3,500 cavalry, many clad in the new chain mail of that era.

The Imam's head was cut off, and the hands, ears and eyes of the nobles of Nizwa were removed. The Bahraini general also mutilated the inhabitants, burnt their Ibadhi books and destroyed their vital *falaj* irrigation system, of which more later.

Soon afterwards, having overrun Syria, pillaged Iraq and sacked the holy city of Mecca, where he left 30,000 corpses rotting in the streets, the anti-Muslim general Abu Tahir of the Carmathians from Iraq attacked Oman and terrified the Imamate there. However, the voting system was clearly still flourishing in Oman since, in 996 alone, sixteen Imams were voted in and then thrown out. By the year 1000 the Baghdadi Caliphate had lost all influence and the Imams were left thereafter to their own Ibhadi ways.

In all my time spent with Omani soldiers, with whom I had many discussions about religions, I never heard a bad word said about another faith. Like me, they directed their hostility against Marxists who were 'Anti-God', rather than venting their ire on different versions of their own creed.

I have no record of when the BOAC workers gave up their strike, but after a week in Bahrain, the flight we were told to check in for turned out to be by way of an ancient Fokker aircraft on charter to the Sultan which had a cooling system that worked only after take-off. When we stopped off at Sharjah, we baked in our Fokker as in an oven.

The stewardess wore a skimpy miniskirt and a most un-Islamic orange vest which accentuated her very fine figure. She gave each passenger a water bottle and was herself a welcome distraction from the suffocating heat.

We flew high above the blue-grey haze of the Mussundam Peninsula mountains, vibrating and bumping in violent thermals until, suddenly, the blue-green waters of the Gulf of Oman lay below. I studied my Oman fact sheet and found that out of a total Arabian coastline of 4,000 miles, almost one quarter belongs to Oman. Covering one hundred thousand square miles, most of it uninhabited, Oman is shaped like a boomerang with Muscat at its crook.

The Fokker lost height and I watched fascinated as the outlines of great fish were clearly delineated: sharks in pools, long-tailed rays and schools of fat dolphins.

Without warning, we roared into a narrow cliff-bound gulley, so narrow that both wingtips seemed to scrape along a rock face. Then with a heart-wrenching thud we landed. We had reached the country that we eight latterday men of the Raj had come to save from Marxist domination – or, to use a much-used leftist quip about the military, 'to travel the world, see colourful people and kill them'.

We were at Bayt al Falaj which, translated literally, means Home of the Drain. It was Oman's main airport and close to a fort with crenellated mud walls that housed the headquarters of my new employers, the Sultan's Armed Forces.

The black tarmac runnels between each massive block of runway concrete literally hissed and sizzled in the midday heat, and the white glare made it impossible to open both eyes.

My shirt was stuck to my back and shoulders as I climbed down the steps from the Fokker. The wonderful orange outline of our stewardess waved us off with the words, 'Allah protect you.'

In the shade of the nearby Customs shed we were greeted by a corpulent major with a moustache, thick rimmed spectacles and weighing at least seventeen stone. God knows how he stood the heat. He was, we soon learnt, nicknamed The Drum.

'Sling your gear in my Land Rover,' he told us. 'I'll debrief you in the Mess in an hour,' he added, waving in the general direction of a low-lying hut.

The Mess was air-conditioned, which was a huge relief. I was already seriously concerned that if I felt dizzy and disoriented after a few hours in this climate, how would I ever stand up to soldiering in it?

I had read a great deal about Muscat. Back in 1442 the leader of a Persian invasion from across the Gulf recorded that the jewels embedded in the ornate handle of his war-dagger came unstuck as the resin glue melted in the heat. The jewels also fell out of the invaders' helmets and the feathers from their arrows.

Four centuries later it was the British Navy whose ships were anchored in Muscat harbour, and one James Fraser described a visit there by HMS *Liverpool* in his book *A Narrative of a Journey into Khorasan*: 'In a single day, three Lieutenants died of sunstroke when the ship lay at anchor.'

And again in Muscat Harbour, the log of the Royal Navy anti-pirate ship *Eden* records a short stay of three days 'during which two of the crew died and several others were put on the sick list'.

In the Mess I met a newly arrived British officer, David Bayley, whose home town was Hove, where I had stayed as a post-Eton language student. He spoke good Arabic to the Mess waiter, although he had not been with the rest of us on our language course.

He was the first 'mercenary' that I met, of a goodly number, in SAF. He had, after some years in the Regular Army, become a civilian, but he had spent three years in the mid sixties fighting for Yemeni royalist guerrillas against Colonel Nasser's Soviet-supplied forces in the mountains north of Aden. He had then tried to 'settle down', but failed to defeat his lust for excitement. Additionally he knew that he was good at guerrilla fighting and the pay for 'contract officers' (polite terminology for mercenaries) was not to be sniffed at – and, as I learnt later, considerably better than the rate I received on a British Army posting.

On the other hand, should I be wounded or fall victim to any one of the various lurking diseases of Oman, I would be lovingly cared for by top surgeons and British military hospitals, whereas David and the other mercenary officers would be out on their own when wounded and dependent on their personal insurance arrangements.

Like the main Mess, the bedroom I was assigned was air-conditioned, and carrying my bags there from the car parking area was like moving between a furnace and a fridge.

I was later briefed by the brigadier in charge of SAF, a Brit who reported direct to the Sultan.

'Have you experienced action?' he asked me.

'No, sir. None.'

'Nor,' he assured me, 'have most of our officers. But I am attaching you to the Reconnaissance Patrol of the Muscat Regiment, based on the logic that most of our officers are from the Infantry, whereas you, being Cavalry, are vehicle trained, so you will get six Land Rovers and some forty men.'

I thanked him for this generous concession.

'You will spend a few months up here in Northern Oman getting to know and to train with your men before you drive down south to the war zone. The drive there is some 500 miles through and beyond the gravel desert of the Wahiba Sands.'

Taking me to a wall map, he brushed his hand across Dhofar where green areas were shown, unlike the rest of Arabia.

'These are the Qara Mountains.' He indicated the fertile chain of hills that separate the great northern deserts from a verdant coastal plain on the seaward edge of which the Sultan's palace, an RAF air station and an SAF Army base were all 'ringed by high fences'.

'The mountains are heavily forested in places and the enemy knows every pathway,' the brigadier explained. 'They are well-trained guerrillas armed, unlike our men, with fully automatic weapons. Many have been trained in the Soviet Union. We move in the mountains at considerable risk, even on foot. In vehicles great caution is needed and only one track crosses the mountains, so they mine that with anti-tank mines by night.'

One of my predecessors as Recce Patrol leader, a Scottish officer, had been blown up in his Land Rover on a track just north of the enemy-held mountains and died of his wounds. There are no helicopters to provide speedy evacuation of the wounded, the brigadier noted, and gangrene sets in quickly in the heat and with the flies.

My soldiers were to be a mixture of Omanis from either nomadic desert tribes or mountain men plus a contingent of Baluchis from Pakistan. The Sultans of Oman had for many years been titular owners of Baluchistan just across the Gulf until the current Sultan, my new boss, had sold it to Pakistan for £1 million. 'The same amount,' the brigadier mused, 'for which the Russians sold Alaska to the USA.'

He went on, 'We have three regiments in SAF and we rotate them so that each spends nine months fighting down in Dhofar, then eighteen months up here in various bases around northern Oman where things are mostly peaceful.'

I thanked the brigadier and, as the sun had at last disappeared behind the mountains that enclose Muscat, I decided to try walking outside the camp perimeter.

Smart Baluchis with rifles saluted me as I passed their guardroom. I smelt the strong perfume that many of the soldiers apply to their hair and skin. Also a filthy whiff as I passed by a line of bushes. The men, I was told, often defecated outside, but this did not cause disease as the great heat speedily desiccated the excrement.

Dusk settled quickly. Mosquitoes whined and settled on my neck. I smacked at them, momentarily worried, but then remembered that I had been taking malaria pills for a week. From the town all about the barracks came the ululating call to evening prayers in many mosques.

Back in the Mess, supper was (always) curry. I played cards with Patrick Brook, the only other Cavalry officer, or 'Tanky' as we were generally known, who I knew from German days and then the language school. He told me that he and David, the mercenary, were also to join the Muscat Regiment.

We left the Mess together and I heard the corpulent major who had met us at the airport mutter to a colleague, 'Long-haired Cavalry louts. They do us more harm than good. I can't understand why London doesn't stick to sending proper Infantry officers.'

Next morning I decided on another brief attempt at acclimatization and climbed slowly up a dusty open hillside to its rim above the camp perimeter. Sweat poured off me. My khaki cotton shirt chafed, so I took it off, but white salt-bumps began to form along my shoulders and arms so I put it back on and headed for the cool of my room.

In the evening David, Patrick and I were driven inland via a gap in the coastal mountains to the headquarters of the Muscat Regiment in the village of Bidbid. Our driver was John Cooper, our regimental second-in-command, an impressive-looking major with a lean, hard body, sun-bleached hair and the features of a Greek bandit. His personal history was also unusual.

As a Trooper in the Second World War, John had served in North Africa under David Stirling, who founded the Special Air Service. As Stirling's personal driver on many desert raids, he moved on through the years of sabotage raids in occupied France to post-war SAS campaigns in Malaya, Oman, Borneo and the Radfan in Aden. There, like David Bayley and a handful of other ex-SAS men, he had fought with the Yemeni royalist guerrillas. He operated a ham radio set in his room with a couple of impressive antennae masts outside near the parade ground. One of his fellow hams, with whom he enjoyed occasional chats, was King Hussein of Jordan.

Our route to Bidbid, which John drove at great speed, had in the 1950s been littered with mines by anti-Sultanate rebels based in the mountains. John pointed out of the vehicle window to the vertiginous ramparts of the Jebel Akhdar which was, I knew, over 10,000 feet high in places. 'We sorted them out ... up there.'

No European had ever climbed the mountain until, in 1835, two British lieutenants from the Indian Army managed it and just escaped with their lives from fierce mountain tribesmen. As late as 1950, Wilfred Thesiger, then the greatest of European travellers in Arabia, was unable to access the mountain.

In 1957, John told us, he had been about to go on leave from fighting in Malaya when his SAS squadron was flown with little warning to Oman to help the Sultan against rebels holding the heights of the Akhdar.

'We scaled those cliffs by night, sneaked behind the rebel machine gun posts and took them by surprise. Since then, the Sultan has kept an army outpost up there which is permanently manned. You'll be climbing it before long yourselves to train for Dhofar.'

My room at Bidbid was tiny, bare-floored with fly-netting

windows and, thank God (or Allah), an ancient and extremely noisy air conditioner.

That first evening I was violently sick, and for three days I never strayed far from the Mess lavatory until my stomach got used to the Bidbid water, which was piped from the shallow local *wadi* (valley).

There were no other modern lavatories in camp since the soldiers were accustomed to using stones rather than paper (as I too found necessary a year later) and no known flushing system could cope with even small pebbles.

Trying out the shower cubicle, I pulled the plastic curtain back, whereupon a spider, some seven inches across from side to side, landed on my neck. I screamed and trampled on it with my bare feet. Its legs and body were black and hairy and its mouth was a curved beak.

I slept badly.

An Arab orderly brought me tea at dawn. He carefully unstuck the spider from the floor and placed it on his tray. Looking stern he muttered, 'It is no good thing to kill such an insect for there is a chapter in the Holy Book given to its honour.'

Peter Southward-Heyton, who had been in the regiment for two years, introduced me to my Recce Platoon. I went around shaking their hands. Afterwards Peter explained, 'You *should* have five Long Wheel Base Land Rovers, each with a driver, a signaller and five soldiers, but it seems that there are actually only fifteen soldiers, five drivers and only one driveable Land Rover due to no spare parts for the others.'

A handsome Arab with a paunch introduced himself as Salim Abdullah, my platoon sergeant. He explained that Recce had for months had no officer and so nobody with clout to ensure that personnel and equipment levels were kept up to acceptable levels.

My driver, Murad, was a cocky lad who called me 'John'. He was half-Baluchi and half-Omani, so he had a full-time job trying to be acceptable to both groups. I noticed that there were tensions between the two, and also between two dark-skinned bedu-types who kept to themselves. These latter were openly arrogant and rude, even to Sergeant Abdullah.

Peter noticed my sombre manner after leaving the Recce rooms. In the Mess I felt unusually thirsty, despite having taken no exercise.

I drank three pints of cool loomee juice, limes boiled with sugar. Oman was the world's greatest exporter of limes, although in the Arab world the country is more famous for racing camels and dates.

After lunch Peter explained that, except in the war zone, the custom in summer was to avoid the noon sun at all costs. All dogs, Arabs and Englishmen, he said, are thought of as *magnoon* (mad) if they fail to observe the hour of the siesta.

So I spent an hour lying naked under a cotton sheet. The air conditioner did not work, due to a power cut.

I joined Peter for a swim. We walked down a dust track to the Sumail Valley where reeds rimmed a deep, clear pool. In the glades around us were date palms, shaded vines and fields of lucerne. The water was wonderfully cool. Peter led us back by another path which passed through a deserted village, dark with shadows of empty mud houses. This, Peter explained, had not long since been the village of Bidbid, but a smallpox epidemic had wiped out the villagers. 'Only lepers now sleep here,' Peter said. 'Never come by yourself without a gun.' His was holstered on his belt. 'The Sheikh of the Sharqiyah region hates the Sultan and has agents waiting to start trouble. And, Ranulph, take care with your own men. You can throw a stone in jest to hurry up a British soldier. Throw one at the wrong Arab and you'll be shot in the back, maybe two years later.'

I resolved to check and purge my platoon for oddballs before the time came for us to go south.

John Cooper gave me orders to take the platoon into the Sharqiyah, which was ruled by Sheikh Ahmed Mohammed Al Harthi of the powerful Hirth tribe who hated the Sultan and sought independent rule. He must be kept in his place and, by way of asserting the Sultan's rights to recruit volunteers from all Oman, I was to enter the Sharqiyah by way of the remote Wadi Tayyin and interview the Head Man of every village I came to. I was also to list the number of camels, cattle, goats, fertile date palms and adult inhabitants, and hand out recruiting pamphlets for SAF.

John gave me an official document from the Minister of the Interior, which Abdullah assured me, since I could not read Arabic, ordered the reader to allow me safe passage anywhere within the Sharqiyah and beyond into the Wahiba district.

'Do not,' John wagged a finger at me, 'go too far. There are Bani bu Ali up there. They've always been big trouble. Your predecessor patrolling this route was badly wounded in an ambush, so be careful.'

I studied my Oman fact sheet from Beaconsfield days. The Hirth tribe, the principal clan of the Sharqiyah, had long been the bane of the Muscat Sultans. Sheikh Ahmed's immediate ancestors Salih and his son Isa, who died in 1896, had been constantly hostile to Sultan Said and his father Taimur. Salih had led numerous tribal revolts and Isa became chief negotiator on behalf of 'the people of Oman' at the Treaty of Sib in 1920, which at the time settled the divisions of authority between the Sultan and the Imam. No wonder 'my' Sultan wanted an eye kept on Sheikh Ahmed.

All my attempts to turn Recce into a semblance of military order, or even to parade at a given time, were frustrated through my failure to understand the threads of constant and bitter arguments between the three ethnic groups: the two aggressive bedu, the sensitive and defensive Baluchi under their *moolah*, a big man with a mass of hair and beard, and the others (who I favoured) from Omani villages and towns, two of whom were Zanzibari-born Omanis.

I especially took to Abdullah, to Mohammed Rashid of the Beard, and to Ali Nasser who was diminutive and unintentionally funny, even liking to be laughed at.

If only the platoon were all Omanis.

Sergeant Abdullah did his level best to sort out the pandemonium while my driver Murad strove to make at least two vehicles, other than his own, serviceable. But the bedu shouted Abdullah down and went out of their way to rile the Baluchis.

The 2-inch mortar crew discovered that their mortar tube had gone missing from the platoon security store. There were mortar bombs and fuses on racks, but no firing tube. In the British Army this would have incurred a major inquiry, and probably arrests. As it was, Abdullah advised me to say nothing and to cadge one from 'A' Company, whose officer, my fellow Scots Grey, had been wounded and was likely to be absent for months, certainly for long enough to cover the period of our patrol.

'Yes. Yes,' croaked Ali Nasser in his best English, 'you do *clefty wallah*, Sahib, from 'A' Company ... Get *morsha* [mortar] and maybe machine guns, too.'

So I visited 'A' Company stores, was polite to their Pakistani quartermaster and came away with a brand new mortar tube and a .303 Bren machine gun with many metres of bullet belting.

In some semblance of order with three Land Rovers and fifteen men, we drove out of Bidbid Camp. John Cooper and Peter Southward-Heyton waved us off. God knows what they thought, for I'm sure we looked shambolic. At dusk we camped near a village called Naqsi close to the mouth of the Wadi Tayyin. In those days the rough track from Bidbid led, via the wilderness of the Ugg Valley and via Samad, to the Sharqiyah, Ja'alan and eventually to the Wahiba Sands.

I posted guards and fixed up my sleeping bag and mosquito net in a rare unstony spot. In the dark I took my shaving kit to where an inch of water trickled from a leak in the village's open canal. Two of my Baluchis did not see me as they squatted beside each other to defecate. They were holding hands. Maybe many of my men were homosexuals. I decided against asking Abdullah, or anyone else.

Mohammed Rashid of the Beard (nicknamed Abu Lahya) brought me a mug of tea in my temporary Officers' Mess. I thanked him warmly.

'Do you pray, Sahib?'

I answered him with the truth. 'I pray when I am in bed, but sometimes when I'm tired, I forget. I pray to the same God as you.' I pointed up at the stars.

He nodded and smiled. He would tell the others.

The patrol wound ever deeper into the Tayyin. There were little nimble deer, great eagles and places where big rocks from flash floods had to be pushed aside.

I began to look forward to the evening meals around brushwood fires. Murad's Land Rover held a gaggle of four goats as well as five men. Each evening he would select one goat, lovingly stroke it for a while behind the ears, then slit its throat with a razor blade.

My machine gunner, Said Salim, filled the metal plate for our group, known as HQ Section, from the main fire where the cooking was done by the two bedu.

Soft bluish segments of boiled meat and rice spiced with cloves and Indian tomato juice were eaten, while woodsmoke smarted the eyes but kept a percentage of the mosquitoes away.

The Beard, Said Salim and Ali Nasser frequently picked out the more succulent bits of meat from their side of the communal dish and plonked them down on mine. I assumed it would be polite to return them with a 'Thanks but no' smile. This was wrong, so for the next two years on patrol I accepted all mealtime goodies.

'Listen to those Baluchis,' the Beard muttered at our evening meal on the third day up the Tayyin. 'Yak, yak like jackals. Urdu is ugly.'

The bedu had initiated a screaming session. I noticed that they and the Baluchi *moolah* were thrusting their rifles at each other.

Ali Nasser explained. 'The Baluchis will not keep sentry. They say it is our turn.'

I went over to the Baluchi fire and held up a silver Maria Theresa coin – the local currency. But it turned out that nobody had heard about the 'Heads or Tails' method of settling an argument and all fifteen of my men stared at me as though I had gone mad. So I ordered the *moolah*'s section to watch the east and the two bedu the west for an hour, after which they would be succeeded by a mixed roster.

The bedu looked sullen, but the *moolah* grinned. Abdullah, who had remained quiet throughout, made out a duty list, and we slept.

On the fourth day the valley breeze ceased to blow and I woke with a sweaty body, the humidity uncomfortable even at dawn. Flies came to join the mosquitoes eagerly whining about my net. I felt dirty and lethargic. By midday my ankles, neck and arms were dotted with red spots from the sharp bites of small flies.

Masra Ain was marked on my map as a village, but turned out to be a mere clump of withered palms beside a filthy pool. The toothless hag who squatted by a bush with her skeletal husband waved a cup at us and croaked, '*Tafuddel* (Welcome), you are our guests. Eat what we have.'

At each village where we stopped I followed Abdullah into the trees, and the Omanis followed after. The Baluchis were content to guard the vehicles, for the local people eyed them with open dislike.

My tally of village property, a sort of Domesday Book, grew to

many pages as we progressed, for the village Head Men were proud
of their communal wealth.

But then we came to Zayan, the first village owing allegiance to
the hostile Sheikh Mohammed of the Sharqiyah. The Zayanis had
heard of our approach up the Tayyin and were waiting for us.

Two or three hundred men with weapons, ranging from flintlocks
to Boer War-vintage Martini-Henry rifles and a few Mark 4 Lee
Enfields like our own.

I noticed also the menacing groups of camel-borne, rifle-carrying
Zayanis silhouetted on the low cliff tops on both sides of the valley.

We halted some fifty yards short of this silent reception
committee.

Sergeant Abdullah advanced with me towards the most like-
ly-looking leader and raised his hand in friendly salutation. He
shouted a greeting, but there was no reply. We glanced at each other.
'What do you like us to do now?' he asked me.

'Whatever you normally do,' I suggested. He looked nonplussed,
so I went on, 'Tell them we are friends and just want to ask their
leader some questions on behalf of the Sultan.'

Abdullah did this and added that we were merely the advance
group of an entire Sultanate regiment. The Zayanis responded with
a furious waving of their rifles and a cacophony of unintelligible
invective.

Not wishing a confrontation, I bade Abdullah return with me to
our Land Rover and, once there, we agreed that we must turn
around rather than risk provoking an armed conflict by trying to
continue up the wadi. But first, we agreed, we would show the
Zayanis our considerable fire power.

I had managed to 'obtain' from various stores at Bidbid a total of
three Bren guns, in addition to the 2-inch mortar.

Retreating half a mile back down the wadi from the Zayanis, I
gave the entire Recce Platoon, all fifteen men, orders to conduct a
'field firing exercise' in full view of the Zayanis. The men were
delighted at the prospect. A cliff-bound area was quickly cleared of
goats and chickens and two empty 10-gallon fuel drums were placed
on rocks a hundred yards or so ahead of our vehicles.

Abdullah positioned the men in a long line and ordered the

riflemen, including the drivers and signaller, to loose off three rounds each at the drums. Two bullets out of three dozen punctured the drums. Not good.

I could hear raucous laughter from the Zayanis. But there were still the three Brens and these could not fail to damage the drums.

A wild burst of fire issued from the bedus' Bren and rock dust rose from the cliff wall some twenty feet above the drums. The bedu were ecstatic, especially when they noticed that the two other Brens had jammed.

A desperate Abdullah ordered the mortar crew to fire smoke bombs. After much fiddling with fuse settings on the bombs, two were fired in quick succession, but the elevation settings were wildly wrong and both bombs whistled high over the cliffs and out of sight.

God help us down in Dhofar, I thought.

Back at the friendly Tayyin village of Hindarut, the Wali said, 'Zayanis bad people. You did well to turn back. The sons of Al Harthi are murderous and you are few.'

Many villagers bade us share food. It was rude to refuse, but I disliked the main delicacy of sheep's eyes, which I learnt to swallow whole while smiling. The plates of sticky dates always crawled with flies and evil-looking *dibbee*, date wasps whose needles flickered in and out of their long abdomens as they moved. Flies rose in swarms from the faeces about the compounds and settled on the plates.

Ali Nasser and The Beard handed out recruiting pamphlets to young and old alike as coffee was poured out of long-necked silver jugs and handed to all of us in order of our importance. Being a Nasrani (Christian), I rated lower than the poorest Muslim, except in mainline Sunni villages whose inhabitants were less strict than Ibadis, and there I came higher on the coffee list than even the Wali.

John Cooper had bade me do my best if asked for medical help. We had no medic, but each vehicle had a first-aid bag.

One old man with puffy eyelids prodded me and, pressing his thumb against one eyelid, forced white pus to squirt onto his cheek. Villagers gathered around.

'Give him an aspirin,' Murad suggested.

I squeezed some Optrex into the loose sacs under his eyes after swabbing away more pus. I guess he was afflicted with trachoma.

Dirt-bearing flies massed at the backsides of naked babies and crawled about the lips and eyes of children who seldom bothered to brush them off. These same flies fed on the festering sores of the village pi-dogs.

Abdullah told me that tuberculosis was common, as was chronic anaemia, enlarged spleens and other symptoms of malaria. Leprosy was endemic and lepers were seldom segregated. 'Eight out of every ten babies born in Oman die before their first birthday,' I was later told by an American at the Mission Hospital in Muscat.

We left the Tayyin, gave my Domesday lists to John Cooper, who agreed that we should not have risked a fight at Zayan. Later that year two tribes in the region clashed with one another, killing a hundred or more of their number and even making the foreign news page of *The Times*.

Peter Southward-Heyton listened when I voiced my concerns that the Sultan seemed to have done nothing in Omani villages. There were but three hospitals and a dozen schools in all Oman.

'You are right,' Peter said quietly in one corner of the Mess. 'He is playing into the hands of the Marxists. Both the Soviets and the Chinese are training hundreds of dissidents from all over the Middle East, and arming them. We can expect big trouble soon. Not just in Dhofar, but here up north as well.'

The Arab world from Egypt to Jordan, from Yemen to the Sudan was in ferment. Until now Omanis had been geographically isolated from the general unrest by the Indian Ocean, the Red Sea and the great deserts to the west, but transistor radios were increasingly available, and transmitters from Cairo and the Voice of Aden beamed sedition east at a thousand megawatts – the seedlings of what, half a century later, would be known as an 'Arab Spring'.

I also discussed with Sergeant Abdullah the lack of hospitals, schools and help for the Omani people, but he merely shrugged.

'His Majesty has little money to spend. Anyway, Sahib, this has always been a poor country. Illness comes to those who sin.'

At that time the Sultan did anticipate great wealth from recent successful oil drillings in the Omani hinterland but, cautious by nature, he was determined to spend money only when he had money, and the promise of imminent funds once huge exploration costs were paid off was still just that, a promise. This conservative thinking would soon prove to be his undoing.

The great sand seas of the Empty Quarter absorbed the shock waves of Arab militancy and Marxist-supported militancy for many years, but now the Voice of Cairo reached a growing group of potential troublemakers, even in the heart of Muscat.

'Take the oil wealth that is yours,' the voice on the radio urged. 'See what we have done in Egypt ... Our new schools, food centres, roads, hospitals ... What our allies in the People's Democratic Republic of Yemen have likewise created with the help of our Chinese and Russian brothers. The route to success, Omani friends, is *revolt*! Tomorrow Said Masoul, leader of the gallant Omani freedom fighters, will speak to you at this time.'

Mounting oil revenues had reached Oman over the last three years and plans had been announced for a new deep water port, as had details for electricity and water supplies. But nothing concrete was in place, while oil revenues had already begun to alter life for the inhabitants of neighbouring lands such as the Trucial Coast and Kuwait.

Rumours spread as to a dangerous build-up of enemy forces, well trained and armed in the Soviet Union and in China, congregating at the coastal town of Hauf prior to invasion over the Yemeni-Dhofari border.

The Muscat Regiment's commanding officer made it very clear to me that when the regiment moved south to take over war operations, we would be up against a highly professional enemy with numerical and weapon superiority. I must quickly sort out the raggle-taggle Recce Platoon into an efficient fighting force or face potentially lethal consequences in Dhofar.

After a council of war with Sergeant Abdullah, we began, slowly but surely, to rehabilitate our platoon into a force to be reckoned with.

Peter warned me to keep our five Land Rovers away from dust roads if at all possible, for the *adoo*, the enemy, had a seemingly inexhaustible supply of Mark 7 anti-tank mines left behind in Aden by Harold Wilson's government.

Peter told me about Hamish Ainsley, my predecessor as a Land Rover patrol officer in Dhofar.

'He took his Land Rover deep into the scrub of the northern mountains,' he remembered. 'He had unfortunately developed a routine and the *adoo* were waiting with a 3.5-inch rocket launcher. Their first rocket hit the radiator and disabled the vehicle. They closed in to slit the throats of the crew. Hamish was already dead, but his signaller killed the *adoo* leader. Two of our men escaped.'

Abdullah and I forced a hard training regime on our little group of near-mutinous men in the furnace heat of that summer, and one result was merely the loss of a third of the soldiers who simply couldn't take the new reality of hard work.

The training was suddenly interrupted by a call for me to report to the colonel of the Muscat Regiment, Peter Thwaites, a seconded Guards officer with only one kidney.

'Make yourself comfortable, Ranulph,' he said, waving at a chair. 'You are to fly south tomorrow ... without your men ... to join the Northern Frontier Regiment for a month. They are short of officers and you could do with the experience before I let you loose with our Recce Platoon. Things are hotting up down there, so be careful.'

I packed my bags and, after a quick goodbye to Abdullah and the men, caught the flight south over 500 miles of shimmering desert to the unmarked border of Dhofar.

CHAPTER 4

The Sewage Ambush

Twenty-five years after my father was killed fighting fascism, I was on my way to my first action against communists. Far below my porthole on the highly functional little Beaver cargo plane of the Sultan's air force, the endless deserts unrolled, split here and there with centuries-old, long-dry water courses. Then, sharply delineated, a bank of sunlit cloud covered the land below.

The tannoy crackled with the Scottish-accented drawl of the pilot. 'The Dhofar mountains are below you now, gents. If you could see them beneath the monsoon cloud, you'd think we were back home. It's green as a forest down there, and full of friendly folk who want to kill you.'

A voice interrupted with landing instructions from Salalah Control. The verdant nature of the Qara, as the mountain feature beneath us was named, is a quirk of nature that runs for some thirty miles along Dhofar's southern coastline, except where the verdant Plain of Salalah separates the sea from the Qara Mountains. Quite unlike the rest of Arabia, the Qara are covered with high grasslands split by deep forested valleys. Every year between June and September, south-westerly monsoon winds speed over the Indian Ocean from East Africa and are sucked against the Qara in response to the vacuum caused by the scorching heat of the great deserts to the north of them. The Khareef (monsoon) clouds beneath our plane deposit, most years, up to fifteen inches of rain onto the Qara, forming perennial streams and waterfalls that fall in torrents for hundreds of feet over cliffs. Terrain, I reflected, made to measure for guerrilla warfare.

The Sultans of Oman have, from Muscat 500 miles to the north, nominally ruled Dhofar for over a century. Their authority extends only along the coastline, the Plain of Salalah and, for what it's worth, the arid *nej'd* or desert hinterland of the interior, but not onto the Qara heartland where the fierce *jebali* (mountain) tribes hold sway, forever feuding with one another when no external threat brings them together.

The western extremity of the fertile zone ends at the border with South Yemen. To the east, overlooking Mirbat, the last coastal village of any size, the jagged heights of Jebel Samhan are seldom blessed by the monsoon and so mark that extremity of rainfall. Where the monsoon clouds end so too does the exotic jungle growth in the valleys and grassy downs on the high plateau which turn quickly to thorn and acacia. Here, too, the many bright birds of the Qara cease to sing and wolves mark their last patrol lines.

All of Dhofar, including its offshore island of Masirah, is but the size of Wales, and over a hundred years ago at the time when my grandfather was doing his bit to prop up the Empire, the grandfather of my boss, Sultan Said bin Taimur, signed a Treaty of Friendship with the British, and this still exists today. As a result the Omanis receive military aid when needed and, in return, allow the RAF full airport facilities at Salalah and on Masirah Island, where there was also for many years a powerful radio transmitter which provided a key geographical link to the BBC Far East service.

John Cooper told me that the Salalah base had not, in fact, been needed by the RAF since the Second World War and was now considered to be an unnecessary expense to the Westminster paymasters of the overall RAF budget.

Sultan Said made clear that ongoing usage of Masirah, which the RAF did want, was available to them only for as long as they also retained their basic garrison at Salalah. This assured him that, in the event of an attack on his home, his beachfront palace in Salalah, the British would rush to defend him, if only to ensure the well-being of their garrison, which was happily positioned between his palace and

the hostile foothills of the Qara. His own air force at the time consisted of the Beaver I was sitting in and two small Jet Provost single
propeller fighters, which were safely based within the fenced perim-
eters of RAF Salalah. Emerging from beneath the cloud cover, the
Beaver flew low over the sea and touched down minutes later on the
RAF runway.

I reached for my dark glasses, for the glare on the tarmac was
intense.

'Good luck.' The Beaver pilot shook my hand and pointed to a
camouflaged open Land Rover and two equally camouflaged soldiers
inside it. A film of dust covered the vehicle, both men and even their
goggles. They wore green Arab *shemaghs* (headscarves). Their fore-
arms were deeply tanned, but both turned out to be British
mercenaries. After cursory greetings they placed my bags on the
sandbag-covered rear seat.

'Mines,' the driver explained. 'They lay them at night in between
the RAF and our camp a couple of miles down the track.' This also
explained why, instead of driving on the track, he drove haphazardly
on the bumpy ground on either side of it.

'Sorry about this,' he shouted, 'but better than being blown to
bits.'

I nodded urgently in agreement, but found myself spluttering as
dust-laden, hell-hot air entered my mouth, nose, eyes and ears. I
made a mental note never to drive anywhere in Dhofar without *shemagh* and goggles.

The SAF camp, Umm al Ghawarif (Mother of the Mosquitoes),
loomed out of our dust cloud. This was the HQ and only permanent
army camp in all Dhofar. A high fence topped with coils of barbed
wire surrounded groups of low huts and at intervals sentry towers
on stilts which boasted rotatable searchlights. This was a luxury
absent from the camp back in Bidbid, and I definitely felt
comforted.

Although midday was at least four hours gone, it was breathlessly
hot in the camp. But not as humid as in Bidbid.

I was introduced to those officers of the Northern Frontier
Regiment (NFR) currently on rest-time from their tented opera-
tional bases elsewhere in Dhofar. They were, like their counterparts

in the Muscat Regiment, a mixed bag of officers on two-year postings from the British Army or they were ex-army men turned civilian
and therefore on mercenary contracts. A spattering of Pakistani,
Indian and other nationalities added to the easy atmosphere,
although an event the previous week had reduced the level of bon-
homie in the Mess. A British seconded officer had been cleaning his
revolver at a mountain camp when, according to my informant, 'he
somehow banged the gun off by mistake and blew the Mess boy's
head to bits, poor chap.'

Unlike my own gentle colonel, the NFR commanding officer, Mike
Harvey, was a hard nut and an expert at counter-guerrilla warfare.
His hobby was karate, and he was known to his officers as Oddjob,
though not to his face. He had, during the Korean War, won the
Military Cross for leading his company of the Gloucester Regiment
out of the Imjin River trap by a frontal assault on the Chinese.

A Baluchi sergeant issued me with camouflage clothing made in
Portugal, three grey blankets and an old, bolt-action Mark Five .303
rifle with two shoulder-slung bandoliers, and a faded green
shemagh.

'Now you Lorenz, Sahib.' He grinned and thrust his hands high.

'Lorenz?' I was puzzled.

'*Heywa!* Yez. Lorenz of Arabia.'

I was shown to a bare room for Visiting Officers. I tried on my
new kit in front of the mirror and pretended to look like Peter
O'Toole as Lawrence of Arabia.

I was given a map of the Qara by Bill Prince, the officer in charge
of 'B' Company to which I would be attached for a month. There
were very few place names on this map, and those that there were
had, in brackets beside them, 'Position Approximate' or merely a
question mark. Many names, such as Habdoomer and Gurthnod,
reminded me of the Bible or Tolkien.

Bill put me in charge of a platoon with a Baluchi sergeant named
Seramad.

Dropped off near the western end of the plain by a Bedford lorry,
we patrolled silently in single file through thick mist and constant
drizzle. Monsoon midges in their swarms bit any exposed skin, raising red spots that itched maddeningly. The rain turned the soil to

slimy mud so that the simple rubber-soled gym shoes of the soldiers (and the Clarks desert shoes, aka 'brothel creepers', of the officers) gained very little traction on the slightest of slopes.

During night ambushes the monsoon midges disappeared and their place was taken by the incessant and orchestral attendance of countless mosquitoes. I prayed that my Daraprim anti-malarial tablets would cope as well with Dhofari malaria as they had to date with the northern version.

The *jebel* was, at least in some of the deep and forested wadis, an Alice in Wonderland of sudden nooks of great beauty. Spending our ambush days motionless, hidden and often enough overlooking a water source, we were privileged to see rare birds and animals and to listen to the screams of wild cats and the hypnotic calls of larks against a background choir of frogs and crickets. We looked down on sparkling pools with banks of flowering convolvulus where fish broke the surface to catch water spiders and great dragonflies of many colours darted by.

Trees with weird names and strangely shaped leaves, like the *ash'r*, the *sam'r* and the *nath'b*, scattered the sunlight into magical shafts as the long hours passed and tiny hummingbirds hovered by purple flowers.

Chameleons, some as small as my index finger, others as long as iguanas, were everywhere in these verdant wadis where flying insects and spiders provided great hunting zones for their deadly tongues.

In 1893 the first Europeans, the Ingrams and the Bents, two separate British couples interested in botany and unusual fauna, visited the Qara, and their subsequent reports included data on chameleons. They change colour, as do many lizards, not for camouflage purposes but by way of reacting to being too hot, or too cold, sick or frightened. Their great hunting tools, their tongues, are longer than their bodies and shoot out from special launching pads on their lower jaw, and they can, in a fraction of a second, trap their targets on the sticky end-pads.

Silence was key to any chance of success during nocturnal marches to lay ambushes on known camel trails, and occasional bursts of racking coughs would sound like gunshots in the dark. If a soldier on a long approach march nodded off, unnoticed by the man behind, he would be left. If you strayed from the narrow camel path, the needle-sharp camel thorn bushes grabbed at your shirt and *shemagh*.

Oddjob's policy was to suspect all able-bodied adult tribesmen on the plain of giving support to the *adoo*. So we searched every hovel, tent and cave for fugitives and weapons. Old men kept their families from starvation during the monsoon by loading their family camels with brushwood from the foothills to sell in Salalah. While they were away the women cared for their goats and children, and gave special attention to their younger camels who were vulnerable at this season, for their eyes were eaten out by flies. Many hobbled camels had ragged cloth hoods over their heads.

On a Friday, the SAF day of rest instead of Sunday, and after an especially tiring week of tick-bitten ambushes, I went on a local tour with a Dhofari bedu who hated the *adoo*, or the Popular Front for the Liberation of the Occupied Arabian Gulf as they now called themselves, and often acted as a guide for SAF patrols north of the Qara *jebel*.

Sultan bin Nashran was the adopted son of the paramount sheikh of the Bait Shaasha bedu and, being a patient man, he put up with my still stilted Arabic.

We drove first over the mist-shrouded Jarbaib, the flat coastal plain of Salalah, to the mouth of a mountain wadi which Sultan knew well. At any point, with only our personal weapons, the *adoo* might have found us an obvious target. Or a mine could have blown up our Land Rover. But I trusted Sultan's fox-like instincts of survival.

In the foothills we hid the vehicle by a rocky cleft, removed the distributor cap and walked to a chain of flowing pools. I saw snakes and a fat heron and, in one clear pool, a shoal of tiny fish.

Nashran knelt to say his prayers. There was silence all about us. The very first Europeans to visit the Qara were the British botanist explorers Theodore and Mabel Bent in the 1890s, followed forty years later by the explorer Bertram Thomas, then later still by a few men from the RAF outpost, and in the 1960s by ourselves.

During the monsoon months there was no vehicular access to the Salalah Plain, nor could any ship land anywhere along the Dhofar coast. Even back in the first century AD the author of *Periplus of the Erythraean Sea* had written Dhofar off as 'a mountainous country, hard to cross, and wrapped in thick clouds and fog'.

Thanks to the monsoon, Salalah Plain, some thirty miles long and up to five miles wide, is all very fertile with luxuriant groves of coconut palms and miles of pristine white beaches. Many types of fruit grow along this fertile coastline.

On the outskirts of Salalah town we sipped coffee at the market stall of a merchant friend of Nashran's. Cows and camels, the latter heavily laden with firewood from the *jebel*, grunted as they passed by. An ugly dog tried to lift a leg against my low seat. I asked Nashran why somebody had neatly sliced off both its ears. 'To make it hear better,' he replied.

Many of the market folk, I noticed, both adults and children, had glazed or puffy eyes. Less so with the women, perhaps due to their face veils. In the open fish market I had to keep swatting my face for flies, large and small, which settled non-stop on my eyelids and lips. Great heaps of fish, mostly sardine-sized, littered tarpaulins spread on the dirt in the market square beneath the shade of swaying palm trees.

The stench of fish was heavy on the morning air and mingled with Nashran's personal perfume, which on patrol he thankfully refrained from applying as the *adoo* have a keen sense of smell. All Salalah cattle and camels were fed on a diet of little fish, sometimes called *manchus*, but their milk was tasty nonetheless. Calves, Nashran told me, often die by choking on *manchu* bones that become stuck in their tongues and throats.

Wandering down to the beach to the east of the Sultan's palace, we passed a mix of Qara *jebali* men with indigo-stained faces, many with short camel sticks and small shields. Others, squatting beside fat black women selling fruit from small mats, haggled noisily with strange falsetto voices.

I took a few photographs, but only when unobserved as John Cooper had previously advised.

During the first week of August I took my platoon to search the Wadi Sahilnawt, well to the east of Salalah. At dawn we came to a long double-decker cave, the lower floor of which sheltered upwards of a hundred skeletal-looking cows. Flies ate at their many open sores, despite the acrid smoke from smouldering fires.

The upper ledge of the cave formed the living quarters of some forty bedu, mostly women and children. Babies screamed and mothers crooned the words *Ish kish* and *Ooskoot* (Hush now and Shut up) as an endless refrain.

There was a *seeasee* (local guide) with us who said that these folk were starving because their cows and goats had very little milk this year.

When Seramad asked why the cattle were not let out to graze on the plentiful new monsoon grass so that their milk yield would improve, the *seeasee*, Hamed al Khalas, replied that they had already lost five cows when their bellies swelled and burst due to the fresh grass.

As we left the stench of the cave dwelling, I felt helpless and ashamed. Surely we should be doing something to alleviate the obvious suffering of these people?

Instead we were supporting a repressive regime. To the Sultan, even though his only son and heir, Qaboos, was born to a Dhofari woman, all Dhofaris were disloyal and no better than animals. Two years earlier a group of Dhofaris had tried to assassinate him, since when he had distrusted them all.

Listening to talk in the Salalah Officers' Mess, it was clear that a Dhofari's lot was not a happy one due to the Sultan's edicts and restrictions. They could not legally leave for work abroad and if they were caught having done so, they were banished from their homeland forever. They were also forbidden to own vehicles, play music, wear sunglasses or use electric water pumps. There were no schools or hospitals nor, indeed, any state welfare at all.

I found it difficult to sleep in my Umm al Ghawarif room on non-ambush nights, for my conscience accused me of double standards. I resolved that I would resign from the Sultan's Armed Forces without delay. I had joined up unaware of the situation, but now that it was clear that I was part of a repressive regime, I felt that I had no course open to me other than resignation.

In the Mess I then heard talk of other officers who had suddenly terminated their service in Dhofar, and they were referred to with ridicule as cowards. Such gossip quickly spread back to their parent regiments in Germany. I could picture the faces of my fellow Scots Greys officers were I to slink back to their Mess after my first taste of active service. I would dishonour my father's memory.

So I decided to wait until my brief detachment to the Northern Frontier Regiment was over, and then I would resign from the peaceful environment of the north, which would smell less of desertion.

So the ambush patrol work carried on. One morning as we closed in on a village of clay huts in thorn country amid clusters of man-high anthill pyramids, bursts of automatic fire announced the presence of *adoo*. I felt the crack of bullets over my head and wished that I, too, had an automatic weapon. In such close bush country, even more than in open terrain, we were at a considerable disadvantage in comparison to the *adoo*, who were armed with the latest fully automatic Russian rifles that could fire twenty bullets in a few seconds. We had to cock our guns after each shot, a deadly disadvantage in any sudden contact. This was bad for our soldiers' morale.

I watched Seramad and Bill Prince closely during patrols to learn from their tactics and from their errors how they controlled seventy men in thick bush country at night, and I picked up many small, but important, tricks of the trade.

Seramad, over coffee in the camp, told me, 'If you are ambushed by big force in bush at night, tell your men to retreat when you shout "*attack*". Or shout "*retreat*" just before you attack. Is good surprise tactic of Mister Mao in China.'

Bill summarized the history of the Dhofari *adoo* which, although the current rebellion had begun only four years before, had its origins way back in the late nineteenth century when the Sultan's grandfather had been asked to visit Salalah from his Muscat palace in order to arbitrate between two sides in a bitter tribal dispute.

His decision having then been accepted by both sides, the Sultan, whose judgement visit had coincided with lovely post-monsoon weather on the verdant plain, observed how very much more pleasant Salalah's climate was when compared with that of Muscat. So he built a palace on the seafront and stayed on. His post-arbitration popularity soon vanished when the locals realized that he intended to have a permanent residence in their heartland, for they hated all foreigners, and especially arrogant Arabs from the north.

The mountain tribes of Dhofar are not mainline blood Arabs, for they originate from the Yemen and Ethiopia. They speak various strange languages and their interactive communication has been described by rare visitors to Dhofar as 'twittering like birds'.

Over the next seventy years various inept attempts to persuade the reigning Sultan or his deputies against residing in Dhofar had all failed, including the 1964 attempt by members of the local Dhofar Defence Force to shoot His Majesty as he inspected their guard of honour. He narrowly escaped with his life due to the bravery of his escort, but serious trouble started later that year when one of his drivers, Musallim bin Nuffl, was sacked for inefficiency. Nursing a huge grudge, bin Nuffl set out to gain independence for Dhofar.

Gathering three dozen like-minded Dhofari nationalists to form the Dhofar Liberation Front (DLF), bin Nuffl went to Saudi Arabia to enlist support from King Faisal who disliked the Sultan due to past land disputes.

After military training and weapons support, bin Nuffl's men managed to cross the sands of the Empty Quarter in seven Dodge power trucks and establish a hidden base in the Dhofar Mountains from which to cause mayhem to the vehicles and staff of the oil company to whom the Sultan had given Dhofar exploration rights.

Bill Prince told me that the DLF had for a while done extremely well, successfully ambushing oil company heavy vehicles and killing their crews along the so-called Midway Road, the only track crossing the Qara Mountains from the north to reach Salalah. The Sultan had this road hacked out in 1953 for the use of the oil prospecting gangs to carry their heavy equipment between the Salalah Plain and the *nej'd* wastes north of the Qara. The resulting one-lane track zig-zagged over the mountains and from time to time plunged down precipitous ramps, all ideal terrain for the *adoo* to ambush. When an early SAF group responded to these first DLF attacks, they too were cleverly ambushed.

SAF began then to send an entire regiment to Dhofar, leaving only two regiments to garrison all northern Oman. But fighting Dhofari guerrillas in mountains without knowledge of the terrain and without accurate maps was asking for trouble.

Just as the Taliban in Afghanistan would always survive as long as they could slip back and forth over the Pakistani border, so too would be the case for the Dhofari *adoo* if the British were to leave Aden and the Yemen.

And that, thanks to the Harold Wilson government in the mid 1960s, is exactly what happened. In their rush to divest themselves of the remaining British overseas responsibilities, aka colonies, they handed the Aden Protectorate over to the communist-backed Aden Nationalists.

The Soviet Union, adept at pursuing the well-tried domino theory, aimed to control the Straits of Hormuz, the key geographical feature of the narrows of the Persian Gulf through which the West's vital oil supplies had to pass.

So in Moscow the master plan was simple. Marxist-trained guerrillas would throw out bin Nuffl's nationalist DLF, take over Dhofar and Oman from the weak forces of the Sultan, and thence the feudal Gulf States, and so to the oil-rich prize of Kuwait. The only potential barrier to this plan was the Sultan's Army.

The leader of the Marxist-trained Dhofaris, Ahmad al Ghassani, based himself in Hauf in 1966 as soon as the British left Aden. He allied himself to leaders of tribes traditionally hostile to bin Nuffl's tribe, and when bin Nuffl was badly wounded in 1966 and languished in a Saudi hospital, the al Ghassani faction, later to become the People's Front for the Occupation of the Arabian Gulf (PFLOAG), set out to annihilate the anti-communist Nationalists of the DLF.

By the time of his recovery in 1968, the Marxist takeover of the DLF was complete and bin Nuffl could not return to Dhofar for fear of assassination.

Hauf became infamous for its 'Cage', a great wired-off cave wherein all suspected Nationalists, radical Muslims, or anyone at all whose motives were not at one with those of the Marxist struggle, were imprisoned.

Sophisticated weapons arrived by ship from the Soviet Union.

These included long-barrelled artillery pieces which were capable of splitting into four camel loads.

Al Ghassani's force of 400 Soviet-trained and politicized Dhofaris set out from Hauf the week I arrived in Salalah. Al Ghassani divided his force into two, half to attack RAF Salalah and half to carry on towards the east to raze the Sultan's fort at Mirbat.

The NFR Intelligence Officer, a South African major, was fascinated by the unique flora of Dhofar where no botanist had been for a century. He had a strange plant officially named after him in Latin, but his ability to learn anything at all of use about the *adoo* was nil.

However, when a wave of rumours reached Salalah market, from the wood collectors arriving off the *jebel*, that a great force from the west was about to attack Taqah, our botanist intelligence officer suggested that it would be a good idea to send a strong army presence to that coastal village.

Both Taqah and Mirbat were fishing-based villages about thirty and forty miles respectively along the coast to the east of Salalah, and each was guarded by a mud and brick fort manned by Sultanate *askars* (civilian soldiers) with a bolt-action rifle each, no uniform and no military training. Mirbat possessed an ancient radio transmitter for emergencies, but this had never yet been used.

Sending four soldiers pushing mine detectors like vacuum cleaners out ahead of our lorries, we progressed slowly along the coastal track to Taqah and conducted a fruitless search of the village. Then, three days later, we returned to Umm al Ghawarif. No sooner were we back in the Mess for breakfast, when an SOS call came from Mirbat that the fort and the town were under attack. Then the radio went dead.

Colonel Oddjob sent the entire air force, two old Provost fighters, to circle over Mirbat and to strafe any suspicious movement in the surrounding hills. The Beaver joined them, saw that the Sultan's red flag still flew from the walls of the fort and so dropped ammunition boxes out of the door onto the beach behind the fort.

Weary from our recent Taqah sortie, we set out once again along the eastern track and, halfway to Mirbat, an ammunition lorry overturned in a narrow rocky defile. It was then decided to advance for the last four miles in the dark without vehicles, and Bill Prince bade

me go ahead along the beach with two machine gunners. We trudged
for eight hours by night over the wind blown sand of the dunes. The
crash of the monsoon surf drowned all sound, and we lost contact
with the rest of the company, but dawn found us at the edge of
Mirbat beach.

I scanned the village with my father's old telescope and saw movement around the foot of the fort. We were not to know it, but as we
watched and waited for the others to catch up, the last of the *adoo*
attackers, having narrowly failed to take the fort, were even then
dragging away their wounded back to the foothills of the Samhan
jebel.

As soon as the company arrived, we spread out and advanced
across the clearing on the inland side of the fort.

A dozen turbaned heads appeared along the battlements, cheering
and waving their rifles. Then the double gates opened and the
defenders rushed out to fling their arms around us with open
emotion.

An *askar* in his early teens, his dirty *dishdash* torn, led me by the
hand to a uniformed *adoo* corpse. On the first night of their attack,
the lad said, the *adoo* had used ladders to scale the walls of the fort,
but the *askars* had just managed to shoot enough of them to stave
off this initial assault. But had it not been for the speedy response
and accurate fire of the two fighter aircraft, the fort would soon have
been overwhelmed. And without the ammunition drop, they would
have run out of bullets in minutes.

The boy kicked at the *adoo* corpse and, looking at me for approval
as a fly swarm rose from the body's leg wounds, told me that
although he had only a handful of bullets, he had killed this man
after his own friend and cousin, Nasir, had been wounded through
the stomach.

'I killed two more last night, but they have taken them away back
to the hills,' he said, grinning with pride, quite unaffected by the
repulsive sight of the *adoo*'s face puffed up and split by the heat.

The *adoo* had clearly used heavier weapons than ever before,
including 3.5mm rockets and 3-inch mortars. Great chunks of
masonry had fallen away from the fort's thick outer walls.

The *askars* had done very well. The next time a strong *adoo* force was to attack the fort, it would take an elite group of the British SAS Regiment to keep them at bay.

We searched three hundred or more houses in the town for signs of collusion. The mudbrick dwellings were honeycombed with dark cellars. We used the owners' lamps and our mine detectors. For days afterwards I stank of the house-search odour which clung to my skin and hair. And the heat seemed to increase the maddening itch of bites from fleas and tics.

The overall smell was a pungent blend of frankincense, tobacco and, mainly, the *oomah* (dried sardine camel food) which hung on racks in most of the cellars. On the Mirbat beach great piles of sardines dried in their millions, along with boxes of the fishbone fodder for camels and goats which was used once the monsoon grass dried up.

We searched the equally smelly roofs, from where the waste pipes of crude urinals and squatters led over the edge of the buildings.

We found three modern rifles, AK47 ammunition supplies, and photos of Arabs in uniform, plus many bundles of official-looking letters. All of these we took to hand over to our botanist intelligence officer.

Before we left, I waded into the edge of the sea with care, for the monsoon waves lashed the beach with violence. My clothes were soon soaked, but the hundreds of insect bites stung rather than itched, which was an improvement.

We moved back towards Salalah with great caution knowing that mines had probably been laid to await our return journey. On the second night we heard explosions from the direction of Salalah, and then a message came through that RAF Salalah was under heavy, but so far inaccurate, mortar fire.

Throwing caution to the winds our convoy speeded up and, through luck, avoided any mines that may have lurked in the hope of blowing our legs off. On arrival at Umm al Ghawarif in a lather and expecting an *adoo* full-frontal assault to follow up their mortar attack, we were relieved when this anticipated attack turned out to be merely an ambush of a sewage lorry emptying RAF sewage into a cleft close to the foothills. The driver had his legs smashed to pieces, and by the time our company arrived at the burning lorry, there was no trace of the *adoo*. Bill Prince set up his 81-millimetre mortars and told me to take the platoons forward to check the foothills for signs of the enemy's recent presence.

Between the lorry and the line of scrub which fringed the foothills, we advanced in a thin line without a shred of cover. Strangely no birds sang nor rose in alarm as we approached. The acacia bushes ahead shimmered in the rapidly rising morning heat.

We were some 300 yards from the treeline when all hell was let loose. The weight of automatic fire was intense. It should have been a massacre. We later calculated that over forty *adoo* were waiting for us to do exactly what we did. So their clever trap was successful in all but its final result.

As it was, that first salvo of high-velocity bullets went just over our heads, whereupon we dropped instantly to the ground. The signaller beside me fired his rifle blindly, took an inch of skin off my finger and blinded me with dust. I cursed him in English.

My one thought was to find cover, if only a single football-sized rock or some dead ground, but there was nothing but pebbles and weeds.

Adoo bullets soon crept lower as the *adoo* adjusted their sights. If only I had a smoke grenade. I swore that if I survived this event, I would never again patrol in Dhofar without two 38 Phosphorous grenades on my belt to provide instant cover in any ambush.

The staff sergeant to my right was up and running as he screamed 'Advance'. Well behind him a couple of his men followed suit.

Looking left, I shouted at Seramad's men, 'Rapid covering fire. 300 yards.'

Then the staff sergeant dropped with a bullet through his thigh. I took the headsets from my signaller and spoke to Bill Prince just as the first of his mortar bombs exploded in the bushes immediately ahead.

'How many of them?' Bill asked.

'Too many and all well hidden,' I replied as a bullet dug up earth between me and the radio set.

'I've got the fighters coming. Put out your red T.'

Squirming around, I pulled the ten-foot-long strip of bright red cloth and laid it out beside me pointing directly at the centre of the line of rifle flashes.

In minutes I heard the Scots accent of the duty pilot and the high whine of his Provost fighter overhead. 'Three hundred dead ahead of my T. Front edge of bushline,' I shouted at the headset.

With impressive accuracy a 250lb fragmentation bomb exploded among the clay anthills just behind the *adoo*'s position, and metal chunks whistled by.

The enemy were now shooting up at the Provost as it climbed away for a second run. As we learnt that evening, one bullet jammed the joystick control with the ailerons fully elevated. The plane climbed steeply and, about to stall, the pilot used all his strength to force the joystick forward. Somehow he coaxed the Provost back to a very exciting landing at the RAF strip three miles away.

As Bill's mortars found the *adoo*'s range, they withdrew. I advanced the men in short runs, section by section, and in the bushes we found well-sited sangars for some sixty men (or women?). There were scattered piles of empty brass cases, machine gun clips and bloodstained rags. But no bodies.

Bill shook his head. 'We are lucky. Their Soviet weapons are probably new to most of them in their first action. Their shooting can only improve. And their timing. If they had waited a few minutes you'd have all been dead meat.'

In his palace on the beach, the Sultan clearly heard the din of the battle for the first time. It was enough to make him dig into his oil funds. He ordered 3,000 fully automatic Belgian 7.62 FN rifles and a million rounds.

That week a transport plane from Bahrain brought thirty men of the RAF Regiment to guard RAF Salalah.

On 10 August Radio Baghdad announced that the Dhofar War was hotting up. 'The glorious freedom fighters of the People's Front have suffered six dead and ten wounded, but they have destroyed a Hawker Hunter and killed forty-nine of the British imperialist troops.'

The BBC World Service said nothing, for they respected Whitehall's embargo on the conflict.

On the last Friday of August 1968, Sultan bin Nashran and I drove to Salalah from Umm al Ghawarif, carefully avoiding the main dirt tracks where a 3-ton Bedford lorry had been blown up by a mine the previous day.

After buying bananas in the *sooq*, we bumped along the beach east of the Sultan's palace to the ruins of Al Bilad, which I had previously seen only when looking down from the Beaver when about to land at the nearby RAF outpost.

We parked beside a collapsed stone pillar and wandered around gap-toothed ruins, at least the size of a football field, with the roar of the monsoon surf in our ears. Crabs scuttled away, great gulls swooped, and to our south the next landfall was Antarctica.

I had seen other such ruins along the coast, including a tomb dated AD 1160 close by Mirbat and, closer to Salalah, the semi-excavated ruins of Kohr Rori, once named Abyssapolis by Ptolemy, which included defence towers and storage vats for incense, once the source of great riches for Dhofar's then rulers. In 1962 Dr Wendell Phillips, an American oilman and archaeologist who had become friends with the Sultan, had spent three seasons digging here before he fell out with the Sultan and ceased further work. He had by then uncovered evidence establishing this cliff-top citadel as a one-time centre of ancient worship of the Moon god Sin, a place of human sacrifice and incense storage.

Originally known as Sumhuran, the creek at Kohr Rori had once provided a safe harbour for ships from Mesopotamia and the Far East during the days of the Roman Empire when their gods were worshipped with frankincense, then more valuable than gold and grown only in the natural orchards of Dhofar. To colonize the land of these fabulous trees, the Roman Emperor sent a famous legion into the Saudi deserts twenty-four years before Christ's birth. But they never reached Dhofar and perished to a man in the waterless wastes north of the Yemen.

Inscriptions revealed by Phillips tell the story of the creek in 100 BC. At that time King Eleazus of the Yemen invaded Dhofar, took over its incense trade and built the city of Sumhuran. Graffiti in the ruins confirm that the Plain of Salalah was in those days known as the Land of the Sachalites, that they worshipped the Moon god Sin and that their aim as colonizers of Dhofar was to control the incense trade, then the most expensive commodity in the world.

I was no archaeologist, but I had long been an avid reader of Rudyard Kipling and secretly fancied myself as the discoverer of fabulous lost cities and remote gold mines where no man had been for centuries.

Al Bilad was not as impressive as I had found Kohr Rori, but that was partly because I had first seen the latter during our retreat by night from Mirbat when it was outlined by moon shadows racing across a starlit sky.

My studies of Dhofar history, threadbare though they were, had identified Al Bilad as Salalah's one-time harbour inlet. Sultan pushed his way past fallen pillars half-buried in sand and overgrown with snake-infested scrub – we saw four serpents of different sizes within a few minutes – until below us stretched a silted up lagoon which I knew had once hosted trading ships from China and the Indies. Marco Polo had called in here in the thirteenth century and described Al Bilad as 'a great, noble and fine city' from which many horses were traded to India and frankincense was sent to markets all over the world.

'Far greater even than Al Bilad,' Sultan told me, 'was the incense centre of Ubar, built like Paradise with pillars of gold, as described in the Koran. God destroyed Ubar for the people were evil. He turned them into monkeys with three toes on each foot.'

'Where is this Ubar now?' I asked. He waved a banana north towards the mountains and then west towards the Yemen.

'Will you take me there, Sultan?'

'*Insha'Allah*,' he said, smiling. 'One day.'

Back in my room at Umm al Ghawarif, I wrote to Ginny that we could together find the golden pillars of a great lost city somewhere in the hottest deserts on Earth.

My month on loan to the Northern Frontier Regiment over, I said goodbye to Seramad, Bill Prince and the men of the company, and flew back to Muscat.

Unrest stirred even in the heart of Oman. Arms caches were discovered, and there were strikes by previously contented workers. The heat that summer was formidable.

On the plus side, in a situation where good Intelligence can prevent trouble before it happens, a brilliant young Canadian, serving as a captain in the British Army until he joined the Muscat Regiment as one of my Recce Platoon predecessors, had recently signed on as one of a handful of 'Int-men' for the Sultan. He proved a brilliant linguist, even speaking the weird *jebali* lingo of the Dhofar mountain men. He was about to take over Dhofar Intelligence from the botanist, which, in retrospect, can be seen to have happened at the most critical period of the Marxist threat to the Sultanate. His name was Tim Landon. At Sandhurst he had become a close friend of the Sultan's son and heir, Qaboos, who, after being educated in England and the Royal Military Academy, was commissioned into the Cameronians where, in Germany, he had risen to the rank of captain before returning to Dhofar, the home of his mother, to live in the palace at Salalah with his father.

On arriving in Bidbid, I asked to see the colonel as I intended to put in my resignation, if such were to prove possible within the terms of my short-service commission.

Sergeant Abdullah heard that I was back and came to my room. We clasped shoulders. 'The men have prepared a *hafla* [party] for you,' he announced. 'Come now.'

The men were all there, even the two sour-faced bedu. I shook all their hands and tried to comprehend the welcome-back speech made by little Corporal Ali Nasser, which was oft interrupted by Mohammed of the Beard. I did understand the gist of it and realized that my brief stint in the war zone had taught me more than had the entire language course at Beaconsfield. At one point Ali Nasser provoked much mirth, even with the *moolah* and his Baluchis, when he gave a wild version, clearly from second-hand gossip, of the 'Battle of the Sewage Truck'.

The Beard ended the peroration by saying that the platoon was glad that I was back and now they would become the best Recce Platoon in Oman.

The warmth of their greeting seemed so genuine that I was embarrassed by my decision to resign and maybe let down 'my men' by doing so. I walked down to the nearby Wadi Fanjah with Abdullah and told him of my intention and my rationale.

He listened until he was sure that I had finished. Then he clasped both my shoulders and looked me in the eye as a father would an errant son.

I will not go in depth into the detail of his argument, but the gist was that Oman now had to make a choice. On one side was the old boss they knew well who had, years ago, put a stop to the civil strife and feuds which had for centuries bedevilled Oman so that, with peace, life had improved for a great many Omanis. The Sultan had done this with the help of his British friends who had never interfered with the Omanis' way of life nor their religion.

The alternative, if you believed in the wonderful dream-life talked of by the *shooyooeen* (communists), came at the cost of a Marxist revolution.

He lowered his voice conspiratorially. 'It is said that Prince Qaboos will rule in a while and, with the oil that will soon bring money, he will, thanks be to God, give us all that the communists now promise but without changing our religion.'

He propped his hands together as in the position of prayer. 'If you British leave before that can happen, then the communists will take over without a doubt. They will force us to leave Islam or they will kill us.'

I met and talked to Tim Landon when he stayed in Bidbid for a while and I came away convinced that Abdullah was right. It was a straightforward question of some 2,000 Dhofari fighters, subjectively indoctrinated in foreign lands, attempting to bring atheistic communism to over half a million people, much against their will and against their basic character. Stories increasingly emanating from Dhofar told of horrendous torture, intimidation and rape among the *jebal* tribes, perpetrated by PFLOAG bands demanding instant conversion to Marxism. Tales of old folk with hungry families being burnt and boiled for refusing to hand over their precious meat, milk and honey to the Marxist *adoo*. Those *jebalis* refusing to switch from their Islamic ways were being executed in large numbers.

I knew that I must serve my full time in SAF and make a good job of it.

CHAPTER 5

Up North

'At night we saw Muscat whose vast and horrid
mountains no shade but Heaven doth hide, though
they cover the city with a horrid one, reflecting thence
the heat, scorching us at sun setting aboard the ship.'
—*A New Account of East-India and Persia*,
J. FRYER (1698)

During my first week back at Bidbid Camp, I spent many hours
in the Recce Platoon barrack block drinking sweet black coffee
with Sergeant Abdullah, Driver Murad and the dozen or so other
serving Recce Platoon members.

John Cooper sent us on various patrols with specific missions to
different areas of northern Oman, which served to give me an idea
of the countryside, the people and my own Recce men. We travelled
in three of our Land Rovers with five of us to each vehicle. We
camped by the side of tracks or called in at the nearest SAF camp
with spare beds. I borrowed books from Peter Southward-Heyton
about the history of Arabia and its few noted explorers.

Our first patrol involved driving through the Wadi Jizzi to the
Buraimi Oasis and thence to Dubai. My job was to petition a specific
officer of the Trucial Oman Scouts, then the armed force of what is
now the United Arab Emirates (UAE), to stop sending his TOS

soldiers on leave to their Dhofar homes with their rifles, because they were suspected of using them to kill our soldiers down there.

The Emirates consists of seven Arab tribal states on the southern coastline of what Omanis called the Arabian Gulf (but which was more widely known as the Persian Gulf). Running from west to east, these states are Abu Dhabi, by far the richest, Dubai, Sharjah, Ajman, Umm al Qawayn, Ras al Khaimah and Al Fujairah. Most of their landmass is barren, low-lying desert which, known previously as the Trucial States, formed protective Treaties with Britain early in the nineteenth century.

Further west along the Gulf coastline lie the independent states of Qatar and Bahrain, where Gulf oil was first found in 1926. By 1965, three years before I visited the area, Bahrain's annual income was £6 million, whereas Kuwait, always a tempting target for Iraq, garnered £200 million annually.

Today, the current rulers of the Gulf States are just as at home in the London Savoy wearing Savile Row suits and discussing oil matters with the chairman of BP or Shell as they are in their palaces back home wearing traditional Arab dress. But a few generations back the forefathers of these same Sheikhs were often pirate chiefs and slaving moguls, with the piracy capital of the Gulf situated at Ras al Khaimah.

Two hundred years ago the night skies of the Trucial Coast would have been lit very often by fires in the villages raided by pirates rather than by the flames from burnt-off gas at oilfields.

The chief bedu tribes of the area when oil was first found were Awamir, Manasir, Afar and Bani Yas, who numbered at most some 15,000 individuals, and ruled, or at least roamed, a barren region of several thousand square miles. Today some 10,000 of these home-grown Arabs hold sway in the city of Abu Dhabi alongside more than a quarter of a million foreigners and an untallied number of mostly Asian labourers building ever more grotesque skyscrapers around an eight-lane traffic-jammed Corniche highway.

These urbanized bedu whose grandfathers were fiercely proud of their hard desert lives will often, in today's busy Gulf cities, shout, 'You stupid bedu' as abuse at careless drivers.

That greatest of all European desert travellers, Wilfred Thesiger, once wrote of the bedu of Arabia that, 'in the 7th century, avaricious, predatory and for the first time working together, they swept out of Arabia as an unstoppable Islamic wave craving for plunder and united by a burning faith.' Arabic, their tongue, is now spoken by over 250 million people, and one-fifth of the world's population professes Islam.

The President of the UAE at the time of my first visit was Sheikh Zayed of Abu Dhabi. His grandfather, Zayed the Great, ruled Abu Dhabi until 1909 when his son, Sultan, took over for four years until his assassination. Sultan's brother lasted as ruler for two years until he was murdered, and then Zayed's elder brother Shakhbut became Sheikh.

At that point family assassinations went out of fashion and Shakhbut appointed Zayed as his main representative.

Oil was found in the Emirates in the 1950s, and the Oasis of Buraimi, a fertile zone on the UAE-Omani border which consisted of eight separate tribal villages with varying allegiances to Abu Dhabi, to Oman and to Saudi Arabia, became the geographical nerve centre of the political tussles which followed.

In such a volatile atmosphere the discovery of oil was bound to cause trouble, and the main protagonists were the American oil company ARAMCO, backed by the Saudis, and the British IPC, predecessor of BP, backed by Abu Dhabi and Oman.

At one point an armed confrontation between a Saudi-American group and a British-officered Omani force was narrowly avoided.

As Abu Dhabi's ruler when the oil money first poured into his coffers, Shakhbut behaved very much as did my Omani boss in 1968 – with financial parsimony and economic caution, which translated into no new hospitals, schools or infrastructure. This did not please the people of Abu Dhabi back then nor the Omanis in my time with them.

The British reacted by staging a peaceful coup. Shakhbut was gracefully retired to Buraimi, and his more adventurous brother Zayed was appointed Sheikh in his place.

Zayed quickly doled out free housing, hospital treatment, schooling, livestock subsidies and salaries for thousands of immigrants to provide menial labour.

A few months before my mission to Dubai, the British government suddenly announced its intention to abrogate all its historical Treaties with the Trucial States and to 'withdraw' from the region. This spurred Zayed, as leading personality in the Gulf States, to found a federation of self-protection and mutual benefit to fill the vacuum caused by the precipitous British withdrawal.

Our visit coincided with complex negotiations between Zayed, Sheikh Rashid of Dubai and the rulers of the other Emirates. Three years later Zayed was to be voted President of the newly formed UAE, a position he retained until his death in 2004 when he was succeeded by his son, Khalifa. At the time of his death he was estimated to have a personal fortune of US$20 billion.

Today the Emirates own one-tenth of the world's known oil reserves and represent the non-fundamentalist face of Islam, despite or because of being the birthplace of that religion. As I write, their air force is part of the coalition to bomb and destroy the forces of Islamic State.

Nonetheless, back in the 1950s the oil access arguments rumbling on about Buraimi had led to bitter relations between Washington and Whitehall, which worsened when the Suez Crisis resulted in an open Anglo-American rift. At the 1956 meeting of the United Nations, the Australian ambassador stated, 'I was greatly distressed by the atmosphere at the UN ... the almost physical cleavage between the UK and US was one of the most distressing things I have ever experienced.'

The Buraimi Oasis oil dispute that originated such a dangerous political divide was eventually settled between the Saudis and the Omani/UAE rulers by a border agreement in 1991. It is worth remembering that the Buraimi confrontation of the 1950s between the Saudis and the US oil interests on one side and the Omani/Abu Dhabi/UK coalition on the other fortunately saved Buraimi from Saudi clutches. If Buraimi had fallen to the Saudis, many of the oil fields in Abu Dhabi and Oman (and most, if not all, their territory) would probably belong to Saudi Arabia today.

Back in 1968 our three Land Rovers left the Wadi Jizzi and the Omani Mountains before we came to the gravel deserts of the Trucial Oman, and we entered the two Omani villages of the Buraimi

Oasis to much friendly waving from the villagers. Some ten miles away beyond the fertile, prosperous Trucial villages of the oasis, I could see the dark outline of Jebel Hafeet, 5,000 feet high and reminding me of Table Mountain and my childhood. For centuries the people of the Oasis have buried their kin in the foothills of Hafeet, and local mystics, seeking cool air to help achieve inspiration, have climbed to the high ramparts. This struck me as paradoxical, since the higher you climb, the closer you are to the sun.

But warmth in the air, I distantly recalled from geography lessons, is caused by solar rays energizing atomic gases which then clash, and each little collision gives off heat. Therefore, since there are fewer atoms in thinner air, there are less collisions and less resulting heat. So the mystics were right after all.

Leaving the men at a tea-house in the south-western Trucial village of Al Ain, I drove to the Hafeet foothills intending to summit the feature and get cool. But time ran out and I only made it halfway.

I sat on a rock, swigged water and ate dates. I did not feel cool, just less hot. Below me the gravel deserts were in places coloured with strips of red dune. I oriented my map and could clearly see why this oasis had long proved key to control of south-east Arabia. Through it passed all the main trade routes, including the Jizzi road to Nizwa and thence Muscat. Water was in abundance after great distances of waterless desert and, in the heyday of the slave trade, Buraimi sat astride the 'long road of suffering' for the hundreds of thousands of black slaves snatched from their African homes and bound for servitude to Saudi masters.

We spent one night in the Buraimi village of Al Ain, having crossed over the invisible Omani border and meeting no Trucial guard or checkpoint, but the dust tracks that we had so far followed switched suddenly to Trucial tarmac with street lights and roadside shops. Our host was the commandant of a miniature fortress, whitewashed and crenellated as though transported from some Foreign Legion Saharan outpost. He was a major from a British regiment and most of his soldiers turned out to be Dhofari mountain-men. This was disturbing and I asked him if I should keep my men away from them.

He waved his hand. 'Don't bother. My sergeant will sort them out. We are on neutral ground. But,' he smiled, 'I'm glad I won't be fighting in Dhofar since, in my opinion, each of our Dhofaris is worth ten of your Omani soldiers.'

When I told him of my mission to stop TOS-employed Dhofaris taking their weapons home on leave, he simply said, 'Good luck,' and shrugged.

The journey from Buraimi to Dubai was flat and boring, and the British officer, who I will refrain even now from naming, was clearly determined to the point of rudeness to ignore my colonel's request. Since I had no other authority to approach, we left Dubai and headed back through the desert, which seemed even hotter than before. It is worth noting that no building in Dubai was, at the time, more than three storeys high.

Abdullah told me that he always found the traditional *dishdash* (one piece cotton dress from neck to ankles) less effective against heat than a simple undervest and loose pantaloons. In great heat the choice between discarding my *shemagh* headcloth which trapped the heat and sweat, or wearing it as protection from direct solar bombardment was never an easy one.

We halted in the middle of a deserted plain some miles west of Buraimi to change a half-shaft and, squatting a few hundred yards away from the Land Rovers to relieve myself, I ran some sand through my hands. It was hot and as dry as a bone. How, I wondered, did oases ever establish themselves in such lifeless ground where, if any water exists, it is many metres down.

I studied a desert animal book written by David Attenborough which explained how the air everywhere is full of invisible particles which, if only they can land somewhere suitable, will plant the germs of life. The vast majority of such particles will rot or be eaten by insects, but one or two out of many millions will survive to germinate on some invisible fungus, and a green shoot will appear with the slightest provision of moisture after years of drought.

Wind-blown organisms such as these have travelled to and from the world's greatest deserts, founding oases when rare conditions are just right. The aerial journey carrying them from place to place may have lasted for many months and spanned hundreds of miles.

Some mushroom fungi when ripe can release 100 million fertile spores within an hour, and they can produce in their lifetime up to

16,000 million which shoot into the air in puffs of vapour. Just one of these may, months later, find an acceptably damp landing ground, however apparently inhospitable, on which to procreate. However, if only a brief shower has produced such seemingly suitable conditions and is followed by a long period of drought, the fate of this 'lucky' spore's seeds will be quickly sealed. So some very clever plants have even planned ahead for such an eventuality by coating their seeds with a cunning chemical inhibitor which prevents speedy germination. Only if sufficient rain continues to saturate their landing zone will the inhibitor be washed off, thus enabling the seed to germinate.

Once back in the Wadi Jizzi, we left all traces of desert behind us, passing into the central mountains of Oman by way of the great cleft which divides them and allows traffic between Buraimi and Muscat through the Samail Gap.

Back in Bidbid we left one vehicle for much-needed repairs and four of the men for 'compassionate leave' (including Ali Nasser whose grandmother had contracted some form of pox).

With two vehicles and nine men we then drove from Muscat north-west along the coast road to Sohar, the traditional home of Sinbad the Sailor. Although the town looked nothing special to me, the famous Arab geographer, Istakhri, described it in the tenth century as 'the most populous and wealthy town in Oman', nor was there 'in all the land of Islam a city more rich in fine buildings.'

Legend has it that Sinbad, a hero of *The Thousand and One Nights*, was the son of a rich Sohar merchant who squandered his inheritance and set out on his great voyage of heroic exploits to become known the world over to generations of thrilled children.

Further north the track deteriorated and the gap between the ocean to our right and the mountains to our left became ever narrower. We had entered Oman's most northerly province, known as the Mussundam (the Anvil). Even for Oman these mountains were impressively rugged. The tribesmen who lived in this apparently uninhabitable land were the Shihu, some 10,000 of them, who spoke their own unique Zaara and Kumzari languages and carried short-helved iron axes and tiny wooden shields the size of frisbees.

Abdullah, ever a fount of local knowledge, assured me that the Shihu lived in caves, ate mainly raw fish, buried their dead under the floors of their home cave, and worshipped the twin spirits of Rock and Sea. At length the mountain sides dropped straight into the sea. The inlets which cut into these cliffs formed deep fjords in which lived inbred families of Shihu fishermen.

The narrow straits between the Mussundam and the coast of Pakistan form the Gulf of Oman, tapering north into the Straits of Hormuz, a stretch of ocean noted, even in the annals of early Greek mariners, as lethal due to sudden vicious squalls.

A cruel form of fraud was, at the time of our patrol, still being practised by people-pirates from the Baluchi coast south of the Persian border. An officer I had met in Dhofar was later posted to the coastal Mussundam town of Khasab and he told me of a starving group of 230 unemployed Indians from Kerala, south of Delhi, who had each paid their life savings to the captain of a Baluchi dhow with the promise that they would be landed in the Gulf where work was plentiful and their future wealth would be assured.

Instead, after a short but rough trip across the Gulf, they were dropped off on an uninhabited stretch of the Mussundam coast to meet their 'escort', who never turned up. They somehow found a rare friendly Shihu who guided them to a waterhole and thence to a track which eventually took them to Khasab. They were a great deal luckier than countless other boatloads of pilgrims or unemployed Asians who were thus tricked every year, landed on some desolate sandbank by their captain who, pointing over to the nearest mountain, said, 'Two miles yonder lies the great city of Muscat. God go with you.' But beyond the mountain there was neither human habitation nor water to drink. Crazy with thirst they drank sea water, and then went mad before they died while wandering through the blasted heat of the gravel valleys.

Long before we reached the northern border between Oman and the Trucial State of Al Fujairah, we had mechanical trouble and turned around. The colonel had only told me to 'show the flag' as far north as proved practical, so the state of the tracks, the failure of our radio to contact Bidbid and the lack of any Automobile Association service clearly made turning back the sensible option.

Back in medieval times, the city of Hormuz on the Persian coast enjoyed undisputed command of the wealthy Gulf commerce until the conquest of Persia by Islam.

In 1271 Marco Polo recorded with admiration the busy trade in spices, pearls, racing horses, elephant 'teeth' and cloths of gold on Hormuz. But he also complained of the intense heat and the scorching wind, even though he was not there in midsummer.

The Portuguese in 1497 sent four ships from Lisbon on a voyage of discovery which was to have a dire effect on all the lands about Hormuz, including Oman. The commander of this small flotilla was an unknown sea captain called Vasco da Gama who was sent by the King to follow up the voyage ten years before of Bartholomew Dias, the first to round the then-named Cape of Tempests at the southern tip of Africa. Da Gama carried on north up the east coast past Mozambique and, obtaining a local pilot in Malindi who knew the way across the Indian Ocean to Calicut, took all four ships there in only twenty-three days.

Da Gama had noted on his way up the East African coast that the Omanis occupied many settlements along the coastline, each self-governing and dealing in slaves. The Portuguese did not endear themselves to the Arabs, nor to the Africans.

An entry in a contemporary record describes an encounter between da Gama and two Arabs captured in Mozambique:

The captain-major [da Gama] questioned two Moors [from Mozambique] whom we had on board, by dropping boiling oil upon their skin, so that they might confess any treachery intended against us. They said that orders had been given to capture us as soon as we entered the port, and thus avenge what we had done at Mozambique. And when the torture was being applied a second time, one of the Moors, although his hands were tied, threw himself into the sea, while the other did so during the morning watch ... After the malice and treachery planned by these dogs had been discovered, we remained on Wednesday and Thursday [11 and 12 April] ... That same day [14 April] at sunset, we cast anchor off a place called Milinde, which is thirty leagues from Mombasa.

After the success of this first reconnaissance voyage, da Gama, now feted in Portugal, was sent back to India in 1502 with twenty-five ships. On reaching the Indian coast he boarded an unarmed ship taking two hundred pilgrims to Mecca. Da Gama hated all Muslims. He immediately had fifty of the women and children baptized. The rest were locked into the hold of their ship, which da Gama then set on fire. He then ordered his men to capture and plunder sixteen other boats of various sizes, which they did. A record of da Gama's Second Voyage states:

> Then the captain-major [da Gama] commanded them to cut off the hands and ears and noses of all the crews, and put all of them into one of the small vessels, into which he ordered them to put the friar, also without ears, or nose, or hands, which he ordered to be strung around his neck [after this man had been given safe conduct], with a palm-leaf for the King, on which he told him to have a curry made to eat of what his friar brought him. When all the Indians had been thus executed, he ordered their feet to be tied together, as they had no hands with which to untie them: and in order that they should not untie them with their teeth, he ordered them to strike upon their teeth with staves, and they knocked them down their throats; and they were thus put on board heaped up upon the top of each other, mixed up with the blood which streamed from them; and he [da Gama] ordered mats and dry leaves to be spread over them, and the sails to be set for the shore, and the vessel set on fire: and there were more than eight hundred Moors; and the small vessel with the friar, with all the hands and ears, was also sent on shore under sail, without being fired. In the midst of all this butchery, there came toward the Portuguese vessels of Moors of Coromandel, natives of the country, who saw the executions which were being carried out – for they [the Portuguese] hung up some men by the feet in the vessels which were sent ashore, and when thus hung up the captain-major ordered the cross-bow men to shoot arrows into them, that the people on shore might see it.

On another occasion da Gama ordered that both lips of a Brahmin, an envoy from the city of Calicut, be cut off so that all his teeth showed, and he ordered the ears of a dog that was on board the ship to be cut off and he had them fastened and sewn on with many stitches on the Brahmin instead of his own.

It is easy to confuse Calicut (originally Kozhikode) with Calcutta (now Kolkata) which is the capital city of West Bengal and the main commercial centre of East India. (Only Mumbai and Delhi have a higher GDP.) Although my paternal grandfather Eustace spent his active life largely in South Africa and the Caribbean, my maternal grandfather Percy spent his as a financial maestro in Calcutta.

Calicut, when da Gama first terrorized its inhabitants, was already known as the City of Spices. Situated on the Malabar Coast of Kerala State, Calicut became the key colonial trading post for generations of European merchants. The Portuguese set up shop there in 1498, the British in 1615, the French in 1698 and the Dutch in 1752. Apart from its global fame as the City of Spices, Calicut once wove cotton and originated the cloth known as calico.

The Egyptian Mamluks, whose navy was the only reasonably capable sea power in the Indian Ocean, tried to save their commercial trade from these new terrible arrivals, but their fleet was destroyed by da Gama's successor, Francisco d'Almeida, Governor of Goa.

Within a decade of their depredations in India, the Portuguese turned their focus on the expatriate-Omani-ruled East African port of Mombasa. Almeida attacked with eleven ships and the results were summarized in a letter written by the defeated King of Mombasa to his friend and coastal neighbour, the King of Malindi:

> May God's blessing be upon you, Sayyid Ali! This is to inform
> you that a great lord has passed through the town, burning it
> and laying it waste. He came to the town in such strength and
> was of such cruelty, that he spared neither man nor woman, nor
> old nor young, nay, not even the smallest child. Not even those
> who fled escaped from his fury. He not only killed and burnt men
> but even the birds of the heavens were shot down. The stench of
> the corpses is so great in the town that I dare not go there; nor
> can I ascertain nor estimate what wealth they have taken from
> the town. I give you these sad news for your own safety.

Two years later, d'Almeida, by then Viceroy of India, blasted his prisoners from cannons and by a reign of such repeated acts of terror had taken over most of the East African Omani settlements and their commerce from the Arabs. And in 1507 the Portuguese Admiral Albuquerque bombarded and partially destroyed Muscat city as a first step in taking it over from the Imams.

At the end of the fifteenth century when Portugal ruled the waves in the Indian Ocean, they attacked and bombarded Muscat and, on taking it, had the noses and ears of all survivors chopped off before destroying the city.

When our two vehicles emerged from Mussundam, the Hajar Mountains about 150 miles north of Muscat receded from the coastline, leaving a fertile coastal plain known as the Batinah all the way south to Muscat. Fresh water is available from a water table about twenty feet below the surface which runs parallel with the coast and allows a rich annual harvest of dates, limes and lucerne. The Batinah was home to some 150,000 Omanis who lived mostly by fishing or farming. Their homes in the date groves, known as *barustis*, were built of local mud and roofed with palm fronds.

Bananas were also a favourite crop, and the family of Mohammed the Beard produced eighteen varieties of banana, as well as dates, which they exported to Dubai.

As we passed to the east of the major town of Nakhl, Mohammed shouted, '*Nurq'l Nakhl fee Nakhl*' (my phonetic translation of his utterance), and when Abdullah gave me the English version – 'We eat dates in Nakhl' – much raucous laughter followed.

On many long flat areas of the Batinah Plain heaps of soil, like six-foot-high molehills, at precise 50-metre intervals and often in dead straight lines, were regular features.

These, I learnt, were branches of *falaj* (plural *aflaj*), the highly functional irrigation system brought to Oman by the Persians two thousand years ago. The Jebel Akhdar, the heart of Oman, is surrounded on three sides by great centres of population. On the coastal side the districts of Rostaq and Awabi, to the east the Samail Gap and Muscat, and to the south the inland towns of Nizwa and Izki. Many of these regions, their towns and their farms thrive only due to the constant and reliable water supply from the *falaj* system. I have walked for hundreds of metres down *falaj* tunnels and have written articles about them, but their principles are basically ultra simple. An underground spring in the flank of a fertile mountain is located and an area many miles away which needs water is targeted. The two are then linked in as straight a line as possible by an underground tunnel dug some 20 to 30 metres deep, with the spoil being removed via a line of shafts. If a wadi or canyon gets in the way, the tunnel crosses the obstacle by way of a simple inverted siphon. However bad a drought might be, the safe source and the immunity from evaporation avoids disaster to end-users.

Once a village or agricultural area needing water is reached, a divergent branch off the main channel brings water to the surface and, by way of many open drains, delivers it to each garden or orchard. Side pools provide cool baths in this hottest of all lands.

Many men and young boys were killed when digging out the *falaj* systems, either by rockfalls or escaping gases. Despite this, many of the main tunnels were dug deep and wide, like London sewers, and an Arab of average height could walk for fifty miles without once being forced to stoop, irrespective of variations in the surface contour of the tunnel overhead. While writing an article on the Bidbid *falaj* system (for the *Geographical* magazine), I found the skull of a young boy near an old rockfall in a deep *falaj* tunnel.

At that time, chatting to a sheikh in Bidbid, I learnt that the present dynasty of Sultans had, not long before, devised a simple but effective way of ensuring the upkeep of the *falaj* (and open canal) systems by the appointment of regional *falaj* masters each with a team of specialists who are paid by the local citizens to repair and guard their water systems. A similar scheme was put in place in the 1950s by 'my' Sultan to cover the oil pipeline against flood damage and sabotage.

The other problem is, of course, the rare but vicious storm floods in the Omani mountains (as much as 300mm of rain can fall in twenty-four hours). In Rostaq the inhabitants can usually hear the roar of a coming flood some five minutes before it powers through the town. Then massive boulders and tree trunks churn within the orange waves in their onrush through the town and all dirt roads have to be remade after each such flood. This precious water then rushes on to be lost in the Gulf of Oman.

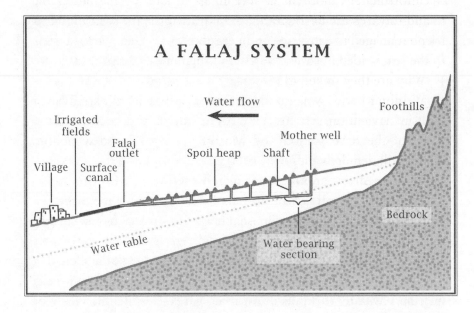

After our Mussundam patrol, I was flown to the island of Masirah and billeted in the RAF Mess with two other officers, a Brit regular like me and a mercenary type. For a week we practised ground-to-air liaison with Hawker Hunter fighter pilots from 208 Squadron in Bahrain, at the end of which activity I felt slightly more confident that the next time I found myself under *adoo* fire and without cover, I would be able to direct the Sultan's two pilots to drop bombs where I wanted and not on my own position.

In the evenings, since none of the instruction took place after dark, I twice went down to the long sandy beaches with one of the mercenaries, a Welshman with ecological interests. 'I like to kill Marxists,' he explained, 'but to save the lives of endangered species.'

One such species, he told me, was to be found right here on this island shore in the Indian Ocean, for it was the favourite nesting site of the world's largest population of loggerhead turtles.

On our second visit, an hour after dusk, we came across a moonlit beach where little turtles, mere hatchlings, were scurrying from their birth sites, their eggs having been buried just above the tideline, and they needed to reach the safety of the sea quickly after hatching or they would be eaten by gulls.

Unfortunately, most of the hatchlings headed up the beach and inland towards the RAF station and not towards the sea. My Welsh friend managed to catch two and I grabbed at another. We took them to the sea, waded in several yards and then released them.

'Why are they so stupid? Suicidal?' I asked.

'We don't know,' was the reply, 'but most people think that their built-in navigation systems are affected by light sources, such as those of the RAF station and Masirah village. Those who head inland will definitely die.'

He pointed out another endangered species down on the firing range, a huge Egyptian vulture. The RAF, he assured me, were not guilty for *their* impending demise. He was unsure who or what was to blame.

Back in Bidbid, Abdullah suggested that we take all the men on a 'Big patrol ... a big climb like in Dhofar. We maybe find out weak men and *Wallahee!* (his favourite expletive) ... we show them the door.'

This seemed like a fine idea and I put it to John Cooper, who immediately agreed. 'Go up to Sayq on the Akhdar,' and he pointed at his office ceiling. 'That'll sort them out.'

Murad and three of his drivers drove fifteen of us, including a new recruit, a medical orderly, to the village of Izki on the main road to Nizwa, where we switched to a dusty track and headed straight for the 6,000-foot cliffs of the Green Mountain. After five miles we came to a tiny village (Birkat al Mawz or 'Pool of the Plantains') where a pool and a waterfall formed the source of a *falaj* which disappeared underground after spilling across our track.

'See you here in four days.' Murad waved cheerily. I noticed that he made his drivers copy him in soaking their head cloths in the water so that, wrapped back on, they dripped down their necks and backs, for we were all subdued by the great heat at the base of the mountain.

Following Abdullah, we struggled in single file up a narrow chasm of great beauty that climbed into the heart of the mountain in a series of steps, with clear pools, shining water chutes and, all across the so-called path, huge boulders, presumably thrown around like marbles by historic floods. This was the Wadi Maydan (or Miyadin), the most beautiful place I had ever seen outside South Africa, and spoilt only by the intense heat.

My rifle and backpack seemed to get heavier by the hour as the Maydan corkscrewed its tortuous climb ever upwards. I drank great drafts from my *zamzamia* (a water bag made of tightly woven sacking which could sweat and so keep its contents cool, at the cost of slowly dripping leakage).

At length as the sun disappeared, Allah be praised, behind cliffs high above, the wadi's ascent route eased and we arrived at a spring where tribesmen of the local Beni Riyam watered their camels and goats.

An old man appeared from nowhere and watched as we all filled our water bags. Only then did he approach me and Abdullah.

After greetings and the initial traditional assurance that he had no news, he stated simply that his daughter was dying in his nearby village. She had been bitten the day before by a snake and the village 'doctor', despite applying hot irons to her unbitten leg, had not helped her. Could we give him 'Aspreen'? Reluctantly, for the heat had reduced me to a dried-out husk, despite copious drinks, I followed the old man with our medic and four men (including Ali Nasser, whose tribe was related to the Beni Riyam) back down the track for half an hour and up a side canyon to the old man's hovel. Chickens and children watched our arrival in silence and an old hag bowed her head at us beside the door of the main hut.

Inside, a girl of about ten years lay groaning and writhing on a filthy carpet. Her mouth dribbled spittle. Her eyes were wide open with a look of fear.

'Where is it bad, little one?' our medic asked. She merely moaned. Her stomach arched up from the floor.

The medic, Salim from Muscat, incised the snake bite below her knee on her badly swollen leg. She screamed briefly. He rubbed purple crystals into the wound. Then he applied Brulidine cream to the pustulous blisters of several burnt circles on her other leg where some village shaman had applied a *wussum* iron.

The *wussum* was still used all over Oman as a cure-all treatment which, as far as I could see, did more harm than good. It certainly eclipsed pain from an original sore by replacing it with a worse one, which itself was likely to cause gangrene.

Salim wrapped the bite and the burns with clean dressings and gave the girl 10 centilitres of morphine through the shoulder muscle. She must not move, he told her father. We would send another doctor down from the army camp on the plateau in a day.

By the time we rejoined Abdullah and the men at Salut, the main heat of the day had been replaced with a sticky humidity and the swarms of flies by the high-frequency song of mosquitoes. After dark and a further climb of 1,000 feet to the high plateau, we came to the army camp of Sayq, perched high above a perpendicular cliff and above a steep, fertile valley housing the main village of the same name.

The camp's officer and most of his men were away, but I found the garrison medic and he promised to tend to the girl in the morning.

When we returned from our ensuing plateau patrol three days later, the medic confirmed that the girl had died, despite his best efforts to save her.

Up on the plateau at 8,000 feet above sea level, the nights were blissfully cool. Abdullah said that there had been *thaleej* (snow) up there in February two years before.

Over the next three days we practised moving as though in enemy territory, both advancing and retreating. We used our walkie-talkies and gave each other's sections marks for silence and invisibility. We passed by isolated villages, with lonely mosques for tiny congregations, and gullies with deep cave systems.

Apart from Sayq, we visited one other Akhdar village of substance which was called Shiraija, named by its original Persian inhabitants after their own great city of Shiraz. Apart from the verdant terraces of these two villages, most of the upper mountain slopes and plateaux are dry and stony.

The local inhabitants, used to army patrols from Sayq, smiled and waved as we moved through the dust-dry streets between the cliffside mud houses. The village people lived dizzily on the side of a very steep valley, and below their houses the valley side fell away in tiers of well-irrigated terraces rich in fruit and flowering shrubs.

Every terrace was fed with water rushing along feeder channels to a terminal pool from which it overflowed in a miniature waterfall to the terrace below, and so on, terrace after luxuriant terrace for 2,000 feet of fertile orchards.

Trees and shrubs of all sizes hung heavy with fruit, including figs, pomegranates, nectarines, peaches, grapes, limes and citrons. Vegetables and ground nuts flourished, as did sweet-smelling roses and melons, and two crops of wheat are gathered each year. In short, a near vertical Garden of Eden (including snakes, scorpions, spiders and tics).

The huge amount of labour involved in building up and irrigating the terraces is generally believed to be the work of early Persian settlers, including irrigation specialists, trained artisans who were also responsible for ensuring that the great reservoir of the Akhdar in the very heart of Oman served to feed the dry lands below. The mountain's very height acts as a barrier to rain clouds so that it enjoys a far greater rainfall than the rest of Oman, indeed the rest of Arabia, even Dhofar in the monsoon.

From the Akhdar, these Persian water-wizards dug subterranean channels, in places as deep as a hundred feet and over fifty miles long, underneath the world's hottest deserts to reach distant towns and gardens. Certain tribes of these diggers were called *muqanaat* or 'men of the killers', for many of them died from rockfalls and escaping gases. They also used young boys, blinded soon after birth, who developed an uncanny accuracy when digging through solid rock in their world of darkness with simple tools, so that their tunnels ran straight between the vertical shafts and dipped but imperceptibly to maintain gravity.

From Shiraija we returned to Salut. From there we split up. John Cooper had told me that there was an enjoyable scree run from Salut directly down to the Wadi Maydan far below. I persuaded four of the men to try the 'quick way down'. The rest used the standard paths and took an hour longer than the scree route, even with rifles and backpacks.

Abdullah told me that there are but twenty-two paths to reach the plateau, some only known to a few of the Beni Riyam and still kept a closely guarded secret.

Legend recalls the original Persian attack on the Akhdar when they fought their way up one of these ascent routes, perhaps via Salut, against ten thousand Omani defenders hurling spears and boulders down on the invading army.

Back in Bidbid Peter Southward-Heyton told me the more recent history of the Akhdar and its current relevance to the worsening situation in Dhofar.

The fourth successor (or Caliph) to the Prophet Mohammed saw a period of schisms within the Islamic faith, one of which was that of the Ibadhis from Oman. They maintained the belief that the position of their religious leader, or Imam, should never be hereditary but always subject to election. But in the mid eighteenth century the Al bu Said dynasty of Oman's Sultans (who still rule) established hereditary succession despite the Ibadhi elective tradition. This caused ongoing revolts from the Imamate interior of Oman against the coastal-based Sultans of Muscat.

By the time of the First World War the tribes of the interior had elected their own Imam with his base in Nizwa, and the Muscat Sultan had lost all control and was under threat, even in Muscat. He was saved by British protection, but had to sign a Treaty with the tribal sheikhs which, although acknowledging him as the paramount leader with control of all foreign affairs, also gave the local sheikhs the right to direct internal affairs and to elect Imams.

This Treaty worked well until 1952, when the prospect of oil exploration and dreams of great wealth sparked off new troubles.

As previously mentioned, this was a case of the Saudi king with American backing against Omani and Trucial States' rulers with British backing. ARAMCO of America, having found oil in Saudi Arabia and established a bond with King Saud, was sure that there was oil to be had in the Buraimi Oasis on the Saudi border with Oman and the Trucial States. Each country had legal claims to a part of Buraimi. The Saudis' claim was based on the fact that they had occupied much of Buraimi between 1800 and 1869 before they were evicted by the Omanis. They also believed that their rightful destiny was to rule the entire Arabian Peninsula.

The British officer in charge of the Trucial Oman Levies (TOL) responded to a siege of part of the oasis by a Saudi force and was killed. In 1954 the British oversaw the removal of the Saudis and the installation of Omani and Trucial authorities in the oasis. From then on the Saudis plotted to undermine the Sultan through provision of arms and money to the Imam and the tribes of the interior. The Imam at the time, believed to have been installed with considerable Saudi help, was one Ghalib bin Ali al Hinai, who was in turn supported against the Sultan by his brother Talib, the Wali of the important Batinah town of Rostaq, and by Suleiman bin Himyar, the Lord of the Jebel Akhdar.

The Sultan's Army attacked and routed the forces of Imam Ghalib. Both Ghalib and Suleiman yielded and retired to their villages, but Talib escaped to Saudi Arabia.

The Sultan left his Salalah palace with a small convoy and drove 900 kilometres to Nizwa to accept the rebels' surrender and to abolish the ever troublesome office of the Imamate. Satisfied, he then headed back to Salalah.

In Saudi Arabia, Talib trained an army of Omani expatriates and in 1957 he re-entered Oman, reinstated his brother Ghalib as Imam and was joined by Suleiman, which meant rebellion by all the tribes of the Green Mountain.

The Sultan's Army, consisting of only six hundred men in total and led by its British officers and by Tariq, the Sultan's half-brother, set out to deal with the problem. They were ambushed and only made it back to Muscat with heavy casualties.

The Sultan used the long-standing Anglo-Omani Treaty to appeal for military assistance, and he received instant help in the form of Shackleton bombers from Aden to strike rebel targets on the plateau of the Green Mountain plus units of the Trucial Oman Scouts (formerly the TOL) and 300 infantry soldiers from the British Army.

This was a risky action, being highly provocative to the Soviet Union's regional interests and those of the powerful coalition of Egypt, Syria and the Yemen. These dangers were offset by Britain's need to retain Sultanate friendship, RAF Masirah facilities and oil prospecting favours.

Venom fighters from Sharjah took over from the ancient Shackletons and strafed the Imam's great fortress in Nizwa, but even their rockets did little damage to the solid rock walls.

Another problem for the pilots was that the Imam's flag, which flew on many rebel buildings and hideouts, was all white, and this often delayed or even prevented attacks since white flags were internationally accepted as indicating surrender.

The combined units of the Trucial Scouts, the British and Tariq's Muscat force eventually retook Nizwa and the Akhdar foothills, but the rebels held the seemingly impregnable heights of the mountain itself. Attempts to ascend by any of the known routes were easily thwarted by Imamate machine gun nests. Saudi Arabia dropped arms and supplies to the rebels, as well as landmines to lay all over Oman. Over 150 Sultanate vehicles were blown up between March and November 1958 by mines provided to the Saudis by their American allies who ignored British requests to cease the supply. The US authorities' reply was that the mines were part of an agreed assistance programme, and how they were used was of no concern to the USA.

Things did not look good, and when the Sultan appealed for more British support, the Foreign Office objected due to ructions at the United Nations.

A compromise was suggested in the shape of an SAS squadron of eighty men who would be flown secretly from Malaysia to Masirah and thence to Muscat. A carefully coordinated attack in January 1959 involved a daring nine-and-a-half-hour rope ascent of a near vertical series of cliff faces by SAS soldiers, including John Cooper, at Kamah to the west of the Wadi Maydan. Only three SAS men were killed and the war was over. The SAS melted away and Sultanate troops thereafter garrisoned the high plateau.

Securing the Akhdar ensured that, when the Dhofar rebellion began in the 1960s, supported by China and the Soviet Union, the Sultan could focus on that front without fear of serious trouble up north.

On return to camp from the relative 'cool' of the high Akhdar plateau, a number of my platoon, including Abdullah and Murad, went on home leave, and John Cooper, after receiving my verbal report of our *jebel* patrol, suggested that I too take some time off. So I went to the coast with an officer back from Dhofar who had a girlfriend at the oil prospectors' camp a few miles south of Muscat town.

'There are plenty of spare beds there,' he told me, 'and the swimming is great. PDO have their own beach.'

PDO stood for Petroleum Development Oman, a dedicated exploration arm of Shell. I packed a bag and joined my host in his Toyota pick-up.

The PDO 'village' was another world. Every building was air-conditioned, the food was four star, and there was immediate access to a keyhole cove with soft sand and a beach club-hut.

PDO secretaries in the briefest of bikinis stretched their long legs on lilos, and I recognized a tanned Briton chatting to a blonde beauty as one of the fighter pilots from Salalah.

The swimming alone was worth the visit – although the water was on the warm side of cool and alive with tiny algae and spawn, it was nonetheless the best feeling I had experienced since arrival in Oman.

That evening, with a brandy and ginger on a cool leather sofa, I read a story by a Royal Navy officer, Captain Loch, about life in the 1820s on a pirate-hunting ship along the Omani Coast.

'There are sharks, stinging rays, saw fish and poisonous jellyfish,' the captain wrote. 'Also sea snakes which appear, when swimming, to be from 12 to 16 feet long, and are venomous.' According to Loch, 'The wind was as if it had passed through an oven, causing inordinate thirst and, as the crew were on an allowance of water, it created a most uncomfortable situation.'

In mid July, Loch noted, 'The weather at Muscat was at its worst, the temperature at sunrise being 101°. The south-east wind, known as the "Ghoos", was blowing which caused a distressingly suffocated feeling.' Loch expressed great delight when his vessel, the *Eden*, finally left Muscat, 'to the inexpressible joy of all on board, for the weather had been more oppressively sultry than can be conceived, never at the coolest time of day under 96° in the shade'.

'At Muscat,' he wrote, 'unlike other Gulf ports, there is no cool season. The climate combined with the mental depression caused by the huge, forbidding black mountains which encircle the town, has taken toll of many British lives.' And again: 'Judge of our surprise when, on immersing ourselves in the sea, we found the water much hotter than the atmosphere. In hot weather the sea in the Gulf near the shore often reaches a temperature of 90° Fahrenheit.'

Bored with the total lack of action at the oil camp, I put on my coolest civilian shirt and slacks and ambled very slowly along the coastal road to Muscat soon after breakfast. The whole town was walled off with three main gates as entry points, all closed three hours after sunset. After that time nobody could walk about the town without a lighted lamp, apparently due to a street murder back in 1948.

The town squats in as claustrophobic a setting as can be imagined, in a tiny cliff-locked bay with no visible landward gap and where the black mountains fall straight down into the sea. In fact, the name 'Muscat' means 'the place of falling'. To emphasize the prison-like character of the bay, the entire harbour is dominated by two dark wizards' castles which overlook every last nook and cranny in the town. These castles were built in 1588 by the most brutal of all Muscat's many evil oppressors down the centuries, its Portuguese rulers.

The larger of these two forts, named Mirani, perched on a steep crag, was clearly built to command the town as well as to protect it, and the lesser fort, Jelali, was still being used as the town's prison. Iron and brass cannon, still in ceremonial use, nosed from the castles' parapets dating from Portuguese days.

From a smelly dockside littered with baskets full of sardines, I looked across the brilliant glare of Muscat Bay, past the drooping flags of the beachfront British consulate and US embassy, to a sloping grey rock face emerging from the far side of Muscat Harbour like some huge beached whale on which were painted the names of ships, some new and legible, others mere faded scribbles. I was told that it was customary for the crews of ships moored in the bay to produce these graffiti paintings, and one of the nineteenth-century artists was a young midshipman named Horatio Nelson.

In a nearby market I searched for a colourful seashell for Ginny who had a collection, being herself a keen scuba diver, and I was entertained by the Baluchi shopkeeper who waved his arms around his remarkable shell collection and in the direction of the bay.

All Oman, he told me, once lay under the Indian Ocean and the black rocks of the mountains all about us resulted from great submarine volcanic eruptions which in time, running north and west from Ras al Hadd at the very toe of south-east Arabia, had burst out of the sea to form Oman. Burning sun and violent storms had sculpted the final touches, the crown of Oman being the 10,000-foot-high Jebel Shams (Mountain of the Sun) up in the Akhdar.

'I often think of this when I polish my shells,' said the shopkeeper as I paid him. 'God is indeed great.'

On leaving his shop, clutching my shells, I noticed an electric fan on a table in the middle of the room, although clearly the shop had no electricity. It seemed just a case of wishful thinking.

Back then, and ever more so as Western advertising has crept over the globe, families in hot countries dreamed of an air conditioner or at least a fan, rating these items high on their must-have list. A potent form of status was, and still is, whether or not you can afford to keep cool.

I remembered the words of an old military friend, Colonel Colin 'Mad Mitch' Mitchell, from the Argyll and Sutherland Highlanders who told me that there was one place even more hell-like than Muscat in terms of its climate, and that was the town of Aden where he had been stationed shortly before the British withdrew from the Yemen.

With their town built inside and spilling over from the crater of an extinct volcano on the south-western tip of Arabia, the mostly Arab and Somali inhabitants of Aden were experts at exerting minimal effort at all times to survive the extreme energy loss due to the intense and exhausting heat, the scorching crater sand and infinite supply of lung-burning volcanic dust that sapped their desire for any action at all.

I needed to buy an automatic rifle and a Browning pistol in London before heading out for the war zone, and in order to find out about a permit, I went into a cool reception room at the British consulate. I was told to wait an hour and, with coffee, I buried my head in my travel companion book by Captain Loch, who had spent time in this same building 148 years previously on returning from a successful pirate-hunt in 1820 with his Royal Navy armed frigate.

His potted history of the Gulf stressed that Oman lay at the crossroads of the Arab maritime world. Ships had to pass by Muscat en route to anywhere of significance, whether to India, Africa or into the Gulf. Omani navies had once ruled the waves from Persia to halfway down East Africa.

They had interacted commercially with their Persian neighbours and the Turks of the Ottoman Empire for centuries before the Europeans arrived for trade.

In 1500 the first Portuguese arrived and ruled the Gulf from Hormuz and from Muscat for 150 years. Both the Dutch and the British helped rid the Gulf of the Portuguese, but their defeat came finally at the hands of the rulers of Muscat who, in 1660, were a dynasty of the Yariba tribe from the Yemen.

By the 1720s, due to weak Persian leaders at the time, the Imams of Oman became the maritime power in the Gulf, with trading ports and a thriving slave trade based in Zanzibar. For seven years from 1743 Persians ruled in Muscat, but they were thrown out by Ahmed bin Said, the Governor of Sohar, who then became Sultan of all Oman and founded the Al bu Said dynasty that holds power to this day.

Joasmi pirates from the Wahiba coast infested the Gulf for many years, but in the last years of the eighteenth century, at a time of great colonial and trade competition between the Dutch, the French and the British, the Al bu Said Sultan made the first of many Treaties with Britain and its Calcutta-based East India Company. Many other Gulf rulers were to follow. For a while Britain sent political advisers to live in Muscat on the Sultan's doorstep so as to ensure that the French were kept at bay, but their mortality rate was such (three died within a month due to the climate and disease) that they were soon withdrawn.

In 1809 the Sultan, fed up with constant pirate raids on Omani coastal villages and valuable slave-filled vessels from Zanzibar, requested that the Royal Navy put an end to their depredations.

Commander Loch describes one pirate hunt in 1818 when the *Eden* chased seven pirate ships, each towing a captured goods dhow. The pursuit, often baffled by contrary winds, took all day but, by moonlight, three dhows were taken and one pirate ship sunk.

Mariners from the *Eden* captured a dozen pirates. Loch wrote: 'They crept, knelt and prostrated themselves and showed all the extravagant misery of people who expected a most cruel and protracted death. Their own love of cruelty was such that they considered it totally out of the question that they would meet with any other treatment than that which they themselves had inflicted on the crews of the vessels they had captured – who had been most cruelly mangled and murdered as all who fell into their hands.'

Two years later, from their pirate-hunting base in Ras al Khaimah, Loch's ships visited the pirate nest of Kharak Island, home to the Pirate Chief Mir Mehenna, who was described as 'distinguished through the land for his vices and cruelty'. His catalogue of evil deeds included making his servants murder his own father in his presence because the old man preferred his other son. He killed his mother because she reproached him for his crimes, and he caused a brother and sixteen relations to be assassinated in order to gain the throne. He had two of his sisters drowned because neighbouring sheikhs had asked for their hands in marriage, which he considered an insult.

The *Eden* stayed for three days in Muscat Bay, during which time two of the crew died and several others went sick. Loch describes Muscat as the most unhealthy place in the Persian Gulf, 'and no wonder, for the surrounding hills, absorbing the rays of the tropical sun by day, emit at night the absorbed heat, raising the temperature even higher than it is at midday'.

According to a passenger on HMS *Liverpool* in 1825, three lieutenants of the ship died in a single day 'of sunstroke in Muscat harbour.

I walked very slowly back to the PDO camp, passing en route by the site of the old slave market, where at the time of Loch's first visit some four thousand slaves of all ages were sold each year. They were paraded in groups to suit the tastes and the wealth of prospective buyers. Girls from Dongola in the Sudan and copper-coloured beauties from Ethiopia sold for about 150 dollars and black women from Central Africa for just 80 dollars. It was not until 1822 that the Omani Sultan signed an agreement with the British to ban the slave trade in Muscat. And it was many British sailors' lives later that the Royal Navy eventually put a stop to most piracy and slavery in the Gulf.

Leaving the consulate and my mercenary friend with his PDO blonde, I hitched a lift back to Bidbid. I would like to recall that I was suitably refreshed by my visit to seaside Muscat, but, in reality, I was still hot and sweating.

As we left the coast and entered the rocky gap of the Wadi Samail I counted the years since Loch and his sailors had helped Oman and the Gulf rid itself of pirates and slaves. The Truce that followed between the British and the pirate chiefs was the origin of the term Trucial States, which became the title of the territories of the pirate tribes of the region. That was 146 years ago, and yet we post-colonial Brits were still, in 1968, meddling in Omani affairs. This time the target was Marxism, not pirates.

Back in Bidbid I studied the daily reports from Salalah. The monsoon clouds had dispersed in September and the bloodshed had then begun in earnest. Infiltration routes from the Yemen crawled with camel-borne supplies of heavy weapons and new bands of well-trained guerrillas from Russia and China, who infiltrated all the tribal zones of the Qara.

After various fatal clashes, SAF headquarters decreed that no unit of less than sixty men should operate in the mountains. None of SAF's three Recce Platoons mustered over thirty fighting men, and mine at the time was a mere dozen.

The colonel called me to his office and fingered his wall map of the Qara where a rocky gulley allowed a motorable track just north of the mountains and beyond the normal *adoo*-infested zone.

'Yesterday,' he said, 'NFR's Recce Platoon was ambushed somewhere here between three cleverly sited machine gun groups. Their leading two Land Rovers were shredded, as were their crews, and God knows how any of the platoon survived. However, the result is that NFR has no desert patrol ability along the northern rim of the mountains, and *adoo* camel groups are known to bring in supplies that way. So ... our Recce, *your* Recce must get down there soonest. When can you get your guys shipshape?'

I told him the truth. 'Only two of the vehicles are on the road. The equipment state is abysmal, and I need to recruit more and better men.'

'Can you do so in eight weeks?' The colonel explained why we must head south before December when the Muslim month of abstinence would begin.

I assured him that I would do my level best, and left the relative cool of his office to be hit by the roasting heat of the parade ground.

Back in my room with a warm Coca-Cola, I made detailed plans as to how to turn the platoon into a viable fighting force for the Dhofar conditions that I had witnessed and faced with Bill Prince's men.

I wrote down key rules as taught me by the SAS, and where these did not translate well with the men and weaponry at my disposal, I modified them as seemed best.

I summoned the men in our block's main dormitory and told them that the next eight weeks of training, all day and every day, would be hell and that, from now on, Recce soldiers would use their feet and not their vehicles wherever an *adoo* presence might lurk.

One of the bedu interrupted me. 'This is *magnoon* [mad],' he cried. 'We all joined Recce because we are vehicle-trained. We are no longer foot coolies like the other *geysh* [army] people. *Wallahi!* [To hell with this!]' The two bedu both spat on the floor.

Many of the Baluchis and even a few of the Omanis were nodding at the bedu's words. I had definitely put the cat among the pigeons.

The fallout did not take long. Both the bedu asked for discharge from the army, and I was pleased to see them go. Two Baluchis and three Omanis applied for transfer to the companies, all of which I encouraged.

Murad drove Abdullah and me to the other company bases spread about northern Oman, but we were careful to arrive in each case when the British major was away on leave or in hospital.

By the end of the week two dozen volunteers joined us in the Bidbid barracks, all hardened men with previous Dhofar experience. The Baluchi–Omani mix was even, with a smattering of Zanzibaris. One of the new men was a medical orderly, one a signaller with reasonable English, and two were Land Rover mechanics, which greatly pleased Murad.

I divided the thirty men into five sections of six, allotting to each a Land Rover driver and section leader. The Baluchis were evenly spread through the sections.

'*Nichna alhein al Akhl Recce, willa Baluchi, Ingleezi, Omani willa Zingibari,*' Abdullah told the assembled unit. 'We are now Recce Family whether we are Baluchi, British, Omani or Zanzibari.'

I appointed as section leaders, Abdullah, Mohammed of the Beard, the *moolah*, Ali Nasser, and Salim Khaleefa, a popular corporal and a recent acquisition. This Khaleefa knew a great number of key clerks and storemen, mostly Pakistanis, in all four companies, to whom he introduced me. As a result Recce managed to 'borrow' a magnificent supply of military stores while the company officers were still absent. Abdullah surprised me one day by his comment, in perfect English, that 'when the pussee-cat's away is the time for play.'

Within ten days Murad and his four driver-mechanics had all five Land Rovers running with an impressive back-up of spare parts, including a dozen half-shafts. The floorings of each vehicle were carefully covered with full sandbags against blast from land mines.

Each section commander carried a walkie-talkie with a two-mile range, and we never spoke, only whispered, when using them. Three sections carried BCC30 backpack radios with a Morse code range of some 200 miles.

We trained by day and by night, although I stressed that in Dhofar's war zone we would move only by night.

In the blazing oven of the Omani summer, at 10,000 feet above sea level and in the foliage of the Jebel Akhdar we trained for ten hours a day, often creeping in single file through thorn bush scrub along the floors of sheer-sided ravines wherein no breath of wind disturbed the blistering heat.

For once the moans of the Baluchis were at one with those of the Omanis, and a noticeable measure of inter-ethnic harmony crept in, for the common denominator was now shared discomfort.

We trained with live ammunition and with no stultifying safety regulations. Abdullah and the five drivers acted as *adoo*, setting up trip flares as ambushes. Movement orders were always by hand signal from man to man in bush country, and only when each man knew by heart over a dozen such signals by day did we start to move by night.

The difficult art of moving in silence in the dark requires great patience, especially when carrying weapons, supplies and heavy *zam-zamia chaguls* (water bags) for a six-day operation in the world's hottest climate. And, heavily outnumbered by the *adoo* in the Dhofar Mountains, silence would be vital to avoid detection and destruction.

Clattering pebbles, loud whispering, a stifled cough or the chink of a weapon against a rock – just one such sound could lead to disaster.

Each section boss carried on his belt a couple of phosphorous grenades to fling in the direction of a sudden ambush in order to provide instant cover for withdrawal. An added advantage of phosphorous over explosive hand grenades was that an *adoo* hiding behind a rock might escape shrapnel, but could not escape from phosphorous which, settling in a scorching shower, caused an agonizing burn to any exposed skin which would then continue to eat deep into flesh.

Constant sweat soon rotted our clothes, and sharp rocks and camel thorns punctured footwear and clothing. However, by the end of November 1968 we were as ready for combat as we would ever be, and our five vehicles left the gates of Bidbid with thirty-six of us waving rifles at the sentries and each man singing his favourite song.

Sergeant Abdullah left the army to work in his family's orchards, or so he said. I felt there were other reasons but I was unable to change his mind. We parted the best of friends a week before the platoon headed south and Corporal Salim Khaleefa took over as temporary sergeant.

CHAPTER 6

Midway

'This cruel land can cast a spell which no temperate
climate can match.'

— T.E. LAWRENCE

Our convoy headed south from Izki. Our destination, a deserted
army camp known as Thumrait or Midway, once a temporary
base for oil prospectors, was 500 miles to the south.

We passed the turn-off to the Wadi Tayyin, the valley of the
aggressive Zayanis, then zigzagged through the southern limits of the
Hajar Mountains and on through the wilderness of the Ja'alan and
the Sharqiyah to the coastal town of Sur. Once famous for its boat-
builders and slave trade, Sur was now a dilapidated place of low,
treeless mud flats which John Cooper said we should call at by way
of showing the Sultan's presence.

Murad regaled us with a fable as we passed by some very fine
buildings along the beach which seemed entirely deserted and, in
places, badly vandalized.

'They were too proud,' he said, shaking his finger at the mansions,
'so Allah told the waves to punish the rich merchants who lived
here.' He then described an infamous storm which his Baluchi grandfather had witnessed at the neighbouring town of Qalhat.

The monsoon wind had, as it did every year, blown the entire

Omani trading fleet back north from Zanzibar. The ships were fully laden and close by their home port of Sur when the great storm struck. The captains tried to anchor offshore, but the cables snapped and every ship was lost with all hands, including the best and most experienced captains and crews of Oman. The business community of Sur never recovered. Over a hundred of their ships, the entire merchant fleet of Sur, was destroyed that day, as were their jobs.

Where once famous shipwrights had built 400-ton cargo boats, there were now a handful of small fishing dhows being patched up. Abandoned wrecks like scarecrows of the sea pocked the shoreline.

I later told John Cooper that we had indeed shown the flag, but I hadn't seen a soul who was interested. Truly a place of past glories.

Ten years later when working for a magazine, I came back to Sur to record a little-known battle which had caused great dismay in the Bombay headquarters of the East India Company, and even back in Whitehall, for it involved the defeat of a British force by Bedouins.

In 1820, two years before the Sultan abolished the slave trade in Muscat, it was reported to the British and the Sultan that the rebellious Albu Ali tribe, who lived a little inland of Sur, were pirates. The Sultan asked Captain Thompson, the British officer in charge of anti-piracy in the Gulf, to help. Thompson sent his official messenger to the troublesome tribe's Sheikh to complain, but the messenger was murdered (quite possibly by bandits).

Thompson, known by the East India Company and by the navy as a zealous anti-piracy and anti-slavery man and a friend of the famous abolitionist William Wilberforce, decided, despite no hard evidence at all of any piratical acts by any Albu Ali, to mount a punitive expedition against them after landing at Sur which was a few hours' march from their village.

The Sultan himself, with two thousand Muscat levies, led the attack which was supported by Thompson with 350 East India Company troops. According to the battlefield guide, himself a wizened Albu Ali who later gave me a tour of the village where it all happened, the result was spectacular.

Armed with long swords and shields, the entire tribe attacked the Sultan's force in the date groves with such speed and aggression that they achieved a resounding victory. They wielded their razor-sharp swords with both hands, lopping off heads and limbs and allowing the soldiers no time to reload their single-shot rifles. The British commander was killed along with seven officers and 240 soldiers.

The Sultan was himself badly wounded while trying to save the life of a British soldier. Carrying hundreds of wounded men on litters with them overland, they reached Muscat five days later.

Thompson, whose impulsive attack had clearly exceeded his orders from Bombay, was hauled back there under arrest for 'disgraceful conduct' and was sentenced to receive a public reprimand.

Nonetheless, in January the following year a retaliatory force of some three thousand troops from Bombay with artillery attacked the Albu Ali's fortress and, after fierce fighting outside and inside the fortress, a white flag was eventually raised on the battlements. Five hundred tribesmen and two hundred soldiers lay dead, the Sheikh and one hundred and fifty prisoners were taken to Jelali prison and the village was destroyed.

My Albu Ali guide greatly enjoyed recounting this moment of history, and I certainly came away duly impressed by the bravery of his clan. Back in London I checked out the historical records, which tallied precisely with the old man's account.

From Sur we drove through the dune country at the northern end of the Wahiba Sands, passing by, to our east, the one-time pirate villages of the Joasmi, Junuba and the tribes of the Wahiba. Oryx and gazelle frequented these dunes.

Our route followed the south-eastern limits of the Rubh al Khali (the Empty Quarter sometimes known as the Great Sand Sea) which continues virtually waterless for 1,200 miles into Saudi Arabia and the Gulf Emirates up north.

For many hours the scenery consisted entirely of gravel and sand with low rock outcrops and, here and there, a scattering of acacia brush and dwarf palms.

Again, on the instructions of John Cooper, we took a further diversion from the main southerly track to Dhofar, this time heading west through Wahiba country towards the area inhabited by the notoriously hostile Duru, in between which and in the low dunes south of Nizwa, lay Fahud where Omani oil had been found in a rich seam. Fahud's oil was to save the Sultanate by providing wealth and progress in the nick of time. A decade earlier, when the British-owned oil company first began to establish their infrastructure at Fahud, the Duru threatened trouble, so the oilmen helped the Sultan to finance a private army, then called the Muscat and Oman Field Force, to protect them. This unit grew into the Sultan's Armed Forces.

Only a decade before our visit to Fahud, the very question as to who owned the Fahud oil was yet to be settled, for the Imam in Nizwa, backed by Saudi and American oil, made a powerful and traditional claim to the entire interior of Oman. In 1955 the Sultan, backed by the British, successfully led his army from Fahud against the Imamate forces and claimed the Fahud oil.

Fahud's oil camps were still flourishing when I flew there in 2015 to lecture to their staff. But I remember a horribly hot day during our 1968 visit when we broke down somewhere east of Jebel Fahud after our visit to the oilmen.

'Not a good place to stop,' Murad murmured from under the bonnet of our Land Rover as I held out spanners like a surgeon's assistant. He pointed at the twenty-foot-high wall of the wadi, where a shattered date palm trunk was horizontally lodged between two rock shelves and at least twelve feet above the wadi floor.

'*Sail* [flash flood],' Murad explained.

After our vehicle was back in good health and the men had said their evening prayers, Murad told me of a wadi near Rostaq where many had drowned over the years.

'All is well.' Murad's facial glances and his gestures always ensured listeners' rapt attention. 'All is dry. The sun is out. The wadi is full of goats happy grazing. A family you know from children passes by with greetings. Then – ' Murad stiffens in mock alarm – 'you hear up in the high mountains where the eagles fly the fearful rumble of thunder, wave after wave of invisible sound. Not good. Not at all good. Allah is angry. But for a while all seems calm. Then the noise is there again, but this time it is right behind you, the shaking roar of moving rock which speeds without mercy down upon you in a great brown wave in which already are the bodies of camels, men and children.'

Every evening at prayer time I tried to find shade to write in my diary, as was my habit on expeditions. I cannot regurgitate with certainty the exact turns of phrase that Murad used, in Arabic in his case, but they are as close an interpretation as possible.

Had we travelled on to the west of Fahud, we would have found our way into the heart of the greatest of all Arabian deserts, the Rubh al Khali or Empty Quarter, known to the bedu as the Sands. But along its eastern approach there lies the 100-mile drainage sink of floods from the Hajar Mountains. On evaporating over centuries of great heat, layers of salty crust have covered stinking black mud several feet deep, a quagmire which has drowned many a camel, bedu and wild animal and over which no sensible driver would take a vehicle. This is the notorious Umm as Samim (the Mother of Poison).

The drive south of the Wahiba sands was notable for its lack of scenery or landmarks of any sort. Often the soldiers dozed off on their precarious perches on bed bundles, machine guns and kitbags. These gravel deserts, known as the Jiddat al Harasis, stretch between the coast to the east and the Empty Quarter to the west, and we drove at whatever speed the widely varying surface allowed.

Travelling through this all but waterless wasteland in 1931, the diplomat and explorer Bertram Thomas revealed to the outside world the existence of a ragged tribe of nomads, the Harasis, with their own language and Stone Age survival methods. Their origins were non-Arab and more akin to the Yemeni origins of the Qara *jebali* tribes.

On his own journey to Dhofar via this route, Patrick Brook, my fellow recruit to SAF, had fallen asleep at night and then fallen out of his doorless Land Rover, unobserved by the equally sleepy driver beside him. By the time his absence was noticed and the alarm raised, poor Patrick had watched the rear lights of the convoy disappear south in clouds of dust.

Both he and I had been trained in strictly disciplined advances over North German countryside, moving very often in single file, 60-ton tank after 60-ton tank, progressing at a strictly controlled speed. But now every Sultanate vehicle moved at maximum velocity, desperate not to become bogged down in powdery sand. And ideally never moving in some previous track, whether recent or several years old. This meant a wild cavalcade advancing criss-cross without discipline over a frontage up to a mile or so wide for a desert journey by day and night of over 550 miles as the buzzard flies.

Often enough a vehicle would break through the thin gravel surface crust and crash into low gear, leading to overheating and delay.

Additionally, so as not to drive in the worst ruts and in order to avoid the choking dust set up by a previous vehicle, each Land Rover or lorry drives to the side of, rather than behind, the others. Thus the task of searching for lost detritus, such as Patrick, in the dark had to be done with care so that he wasn't missed altogether by the questing headlights of the returning convoy.

He was, on being picked up, as extremely relieved as he was embarrassed.

We spent two days and a part of each of two nights crossing the Harasis. John Cooper had allocated to Recce Platoon two extra drivers with their respective vehicles, a camouflage-painted water tanker and a standard Bedford 3-ton lorry carrying a dozen live goats and 10-gallon drums of diesel, lashed down so as not to crush the goats.

One goat a day had its throat slit before being cooked over an open fire of *hatab* (brushwood collected from wadi beds that we passed).

Sometimes an Arab (never a Baluchi) would break out in song in the back of our Land Rover. Murad would always join in. I only diarized the words, or rather my translation of them, from one song which was oft repeated during my years with Recce.

> Heywah the sun is silver
> where the date palms shade the land
> and the women carry water from the wells
> Heywah the men are riding
> on their camels to the war
> and they'll die or kill with honour, *Insha'Allah*

They beat out the rhythm of their songs with their gun butts or their open palms on the hot metal sides of the Land Rover.

One night, in the wilderness of the *nej'd*, I heard the high pure song of a lark, but by day we saw only hawks and massive vultures, the funeral directors of the desert.

Somewhere off to the east we passed by Masirah Island and its fast diminishing population of turtles and, much later to the west, the isolated Sultan's camp of Mugshin on the very edge of the Empty Quarter dune-land. When in the 1950s Wilfred Thesiger reached Mugshin, he recorded, 'Skeletons of trees, brittle powdery branches fallen and half-buried in the sand and deposits of silt left by ancient floods.' He noted that no rain had fallen there for twenty-five years, although once a great water course had flowed through the Umm al Hait (the Mother of Life). Here, a few years before, a detachment of home guard *askars* had been dropped off for a six-month stint at this dead-end spot, ideal for a dedicated Trappist monk in search of a spell of uninterrupted navel contemplation and disgusting-tasting water.

Somehow, due to record-keeping, army clerks being sacked, or because of sheer incompetence, this unfortunate detachment's existence at Mugshin was forgotten at Muscat HQ. Their radio set failed to work, they had no vehicles and no bedu visited them. There were a few date palms around the mud fort and local fauna, including lizards and foxes, for sustenance, which was lucky because nine months passed by before some relative of a missing *askar* started to ask questions, and the forgotten few were retrieved. In Britain this would have been a tabloid front-page scandal and there would have been a government inquiry. In Oman there was only cynicism, shoulder shrugging and much raucous laughter each time the tale was retold.

The Empty Quarter stretched away north to Saudi Arabia for a thousand miles from our track. In all that desert there was nothing permanent, and the wandering bedu, who dared patrol its wastes, traditionally lived for inter-tribal warfare, feuds, gossip and camels.

Had oil been discovered here or down south in the mountains of Dhofar, nomadic life would quickly have changed, as it already had for the northern bedu of the Gulf States. But, despite spending $40 million on exploration between 1953 and the mid 1960s, the Iraq Petroleum Company found no economically viable well. Only Fahud, way up north, hit the jackpot.

Corporal Salim, who had shown himself to be a popular replacement for Abdullah, had been in the Muscat Regiment for many years, including previous patrols in the Dhofar Mountains. His vehicle, beyond Mugshin, took the lead from mine and he guided us past old isolated oil camps, some no more than a single skeletal derrick and surrounding steel bric-a-brac. We passed pools of oil, steaming in the heat, where the oilmen had struck a surface anticline of no potential. But otherwise in this half-desert world of gravel plains, caked pans of gypsum, low acacia bushes and dwarf palms, the miles passed by in oppressive heat and a harsh white glare.

Despite the absence of any noticeable wind, sand devils, some hundreds of feet in height, would suddenly spiral from nowhere, rush around in a dervish dance, then disappear in a flash.

Mirages of lakes would occasionally stretch ahead across the sunward horizon, quite lifelike for a while before vanishing in haze. They were, according to John Cooper, naturally occurring optical phenomena caused by light rays being bent and thereby producing displaced images of distant objects or, usually, of the sky. They can occur anywhere where the ground is very hot and flat.

I found myself as happy as I ever remember during the long hours that we drove through the great vistas of empty desert. But I was actively angry on seeing oil drums and other detritus left by the 1950s search for oil; jealous perhaps that the oilmen had been here before me. I recall feeling thankful that they had found oil only at Fahud, now hundreds of miles behind us.

I had arrived here in these wonderful empty spaces too late for priority. Some twelve years into the future, in 1980, I would be lucky enough to lead the very first exploration and crossing of a vast area of the high Antarctic plateau and to map it for the first time. But here, in this hottest of all deserts, I was 149 years too late for priority of exploration by a non-native.

The first European to cross Arabia (but not the Empty Quarter) was, in 1819, the British Army Captain George Forster Sadlier, who was sent to persuade the Sultan of Muscat to help the East India Company destroy the Joasmi and Wahabi pirates. His ship ran aground off the Omani coast and in order to reach Saudi Arabia (where he was to request similar support against the pirates), he travelled by horse and camel all the way. He received little recognition then or since for his remarkable journey, and nobody repeated the crossing by any route until, 112 years later, the arrival in Muscat of Bertram Thomas (1892–1950).

Thomas, a native of Somerset and the son of a sailor, left school at sixteen to work for the Post Office. After service in Mesopotamia during the Great War, followed by a spell at Trinity College, Cambridge, he returned to the Middle East as an administrator with a natural flair for charming Arabs. Somehow he worked his way up to being appointed Prime Minister to Sultan Taimur of Muscat, and so was the first Briton to be Prime Minister of any Arab state.

While in Muscat Thomas became obsessed with the idea of travelling from Dhofar's south coast all the way north and through the Empty Quarter to the shores of the Persian Gulf. Suffering every type of hardship that hot deserts can serve up, he and his Omani bedu guides reached the Gulf shore at Doha fifty-eight days later, thereby achieving the first south–north traverse of the near waterless Sands.

The next man to cross the Empty Quarter was another alumnus of Trinity and like Thomas served in Mesopotamia, but they had little else in common beyond their love of Arabia.

Harry (or Jack) St John Philby, the great Arabist, famous desert explorer, MI6 Secret Service agent, Royal Geographical Society Medal winner, and much trusted diplomat, was also a traitor to British interests, a Nazi sympathizer and father to a notorious Soviet double agent within British Intelligence. He did his utmost from a position of high influence to hinder the establishment of Israel and he used his personal friendship with Ibn Saud of Saudi Arabia to ensure that SoCal and ARAMCO of America gained the enormous prize of Saudi oil concessions rather than the British oil interests as represented by the Iraq Petroleum Company.

In 1915 he helped organize the Arab Revolt led by T. E. Lawrence (Lawrence of Arabia) against the Turks, and in 1921 he took over from Lawrence as Chief Liaison Officer in Transjordan, despite the fact that he favoured his friend Ibn Saud of Saudi Arabia over Hussein of Jordan as the overall Arab leader.

In 1930, aged forty-five, he converted to Islam and took the Arab name of Sheikh Abdullah. Two years later he became the first European to cross the Empty Quarter from east to west and he is

today, as a result, generally remembered as a British hero of exploration, alongside the likes of Bertram Thomas and Samuel Baker of the
Nile.

Briefly back in England he stood for Parliament as a member of
an anti-war Mosley-type party, lost his deposit and went to Bombay
where he was arrested and deported back for brief imprisonment in
Britain.

On the plus side he made important contributions, resulting from
his extensive Saudi travels, in the fields of cartography, including
personally mapping on camel-back what was to become the official
Saudi-Yemeni border. While searching for the lost incense city of
Ubar, he came across the fabled craters of Wabar, the first European
to do so. Additionally he added greatly to our knowledge of the
archaeology, linguistics and ornithology of Arabia. Many of his
records are today held by the Royal Geographical Society.

Aged sixty, Philby went back to Saudi but disliked the new ruler,
King Saud, and criticized him in public for corruption. He was exiled
and retired to the Lebanon where, for a while he lived with his son
Kim who, like him, was a highly successful traitor to Britain. He died
there in 1960.

Next to brave the extreme rigours of an Empty Quarter crossing
(*twice*) was Wilfred Thesiger (1910–2003) fourteen years after
Philby's traverse.

I first met Thesiger in the 1970s to interview him for a travel article. I asked him to lunch in London in the salubrious setting of the
Officers' Mess in the SAS headquarters building near Sloane Square,
and I remember his lovely wrinkled smile and chuckle when the
waitress, Brenda, approached with her notepad and asked, 'Cheese
or pud, gents?'

We discovered not just a joint love of Dhofar's mountains and
tribes but other similarities. We had both been brought up since
childhood by our beloved mothers, both of whom had died in their
nineties. We had both spent our early years in Africa until, aged ten,
we had been sent to English prep schools and Eton. Both of us had
excelled at boxing, but not much else. After that he had studied at
Oxford and then begun a life of travel and exploration in the world's
hottest places.

Brought up in South Africa, I roamed the Tokai woods with the local gang. In the season of the berg-winds, I watched the fires at night on the flanks of nearby Table Mountain.

My grandfather, Eustace Fiennes, with his friend and neighbour, Winston Churchill, in the local Territorial Regiment. Grandad, like Winston, fought in the Sudan and in South Africa.

Grandad (1864–1943), at left, front row, in the British South Africa Company's Police (1890–2), when he acted against the Portuguese on the Mozambique border.

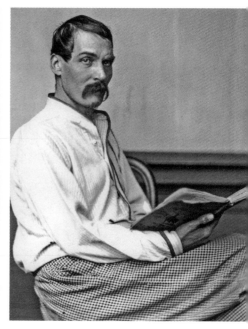

John Hanning Speke (1827–1864). Colleague and later rival Nile explorer to Richard Burton, Speke discovered Lake Victoria Nyanza.

Sir Richard Francis Burton (1821–1890). Burton was an acclaimed explorer, traveller and writer.

James Augustus Grant (1827–1892). Like Speke, Captain Grant was an Indian Army Officer and tiger hunter. He was an integral part of the great Source of the Nile controversy of that time.

Sir Samuel White Baker (1821–1893) and his ex-slave wife, Lady Florence 'Flooey' Baker (1841–1916). Baker was a multi-faceted Victorian hero, as was his wife, who accompanied him on his expeditions.

© Corbis

Doctor David Livingstone (1813–1873). Livingstone started his working life on a cotton mill, then trained as a missionary doctor. His dream was to travel throughout Africa to spread Christianity and to fight slavery.

© Getty Images

Henry Morton Stanley (1841–1904). As a journalist, he was sent to Africa to find the then 'missing' Livingstone. Stanley made his name reporting on Livingstone and thereafter made epic journeys of his own.

Charles Gordon (1833–1885). Gordon had a distinguished military career, after which he was made Governor of Equatoria in the Sudan where he mapped the Upper Nile and fought slavery.

© Getty Images

Horatio Herbert Kitchener (1850–1916). After military service in Palestine and Cyprus, he became Governor of Sudan.

Tippo Tib (1837–1905). Real name Hamad bin Muhammad al-Murghabi, his mother was an Omani with royal family connections and his father was a coastal Swahili with slaving traditions. He built his own trading empire based on ivory, slaves and political cunning. He claimed the Eastern Congo for the Sultan of Zanzibar and, with associations with the likes of Stanley and the King of Belgium, became involved in the Congo–Arab War. He died of malaria in Zanzibar.

Most adult slaves of both sexes were roped together in gangs and often with six-foot-long individual heavy beams of wood pinned around their necks, to prevent escape as they journeyed along well-used routes from their location of capture to the coast.

An awkward moment unloading one of our hovercraft from a Wadi Halfa cattle barge on the Nile.

The two hovercraft, *Baker* and *Burton*, on the banks of the Nile with the author and Charles Westmoreland.

The Atlantis of the Nubian Desert. The Commissioner of Wadi Halfa shows the author his murals, which depict the town and oasis as it was before being totally submerged as a result of the construction of the Aswan Dam.

A breakdown in the Nubian Desert – Peter Loyd at the right.

The hovercraft doing well en route to Akasha.

Bilharzia is an ever-present menace in the shallows by the banks. Peter Loyd servicing one of *Baker*'s drive motors. Nick Holder contracted bilharzia at about this time.

Baker, after the collapse of a bridge in the warzone of the Bor Forest, subsequently the scene of many massacres.

We came across an apparently endless file of black ants, some half an inch long. They packed a shocking bite, as Ollie discovered when a couple became lodged between his shirt tail and pants.

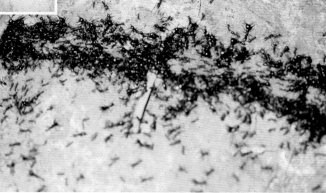

The townsfolk of Malakal watch the arrival of their first visit by a hovercraft.

I met him several times during his visits to London from his home in Northern Kenya and, finally, when I took him out to lunch near his retirement home in Surrey in the late 1990s. He was by then in his late eighties, but refused to go in my car. So we walked slowly to his favourite local pub. His balance and his eyesight were deteriorating, but he hated cars with a surprising vehemence.

He was born in Addis Ababa in Abyssinia, now Ethiopia, where his father was the chief British Minister and where his love of the remote and the wild became second nature.

Aged twenty-three, back in Abyssinia, he led an expedition through the hottest place on Earth, the Danakil Desert, to discover the source of the Awash River. Narrowly escaping murder by the locals, he knew, on returning to Addis, that he would never again be happy without the excitement of living on the edge with only the very basics of materialistic needs, with an uncertainty of what tomorrow might bring, with some plan always hatching for the next expedition and, above all, without the interference of so-called civilization and its trappings, such as cars and electricity.

In 1935 his beloved Abyssinia was brutally invaded by the Italians, but he achieved his personal revenge a few years later when, in the British Army, he played a prominent role in throwing the Italians out of 'his' country. Promoted to major he then joined the SAS to fight in the deserts of North Africa behind German and Italian lines.

At that time my father commanded the Royal Scots Greys tank regiment and played a key part in the battle of El Alamein which began the defeat of Rommel and his German-Italian Desert Korps.

At the end of the war Thesiger joined the United Nations Food and Agriculture Organization with the specific task of travelling the Empty Quarter to locate the breeding grounds of the ubiquitous locust, then the cause of many famines and much misery worldwide. During his five years as a Locust Officer he achieved two notable crossings of the Sands and travelled ten thousand miles by camel. His first crossing led him and his dozen bedu companions from Salalah via Shisr and north through the furnace of the Sands to a point due west of Nizwa, then back to Salalah on a route close to the coast, more or less similar to our own current Land Rover journey. That was in the winter of 1946/47. One day in the heart of the Sands he recorded, 'The temperature often reaches 115 and sometimes 120 degrees *in the shade* – and there is no shade.' He became close family to many of his long-term bedu companions, who knew him as Mubarreq or Miriam.

His second crossing, in the following year, started within the Aden Protectorate near Shibam, led him far to the west of his previous route but also headed north through the Rubh al Khali for 1,500 miles, including one stretch of sixteen days with no water source and the considerable danger of travel through areas of Saudi Arabia without a permit.

After many other remarkable travels in Arabia, he was turned back in his 1950 quest to climb the Jebel Akhdar. This decided him to, regretfully, leave Arabia. He wrote:

> For differing reasons, the Sultan of Muscat, the Imam of Oman, Ibn Saud, even the British officials in Aden and Bahrain had, for their own reasons, closed in on me, resolved to prevent further journeys. I had gone to Arabia just in time to know the spirit of the land and the greatness of the Arabs. Shortly afterwards the life that I had shared with the bedu had irrevocably disappeared. There are no riding camels in Arabia today, only cars, lorries, aeroplanes and helicopters.

Understanding the paradox that his travels had actually aided these very intrusions.

> I realize that the maps I made helped others with more material aims to visit and corrupt a people whose spirit once lit the desert like a flame ... I went there to find peace in the hardship of desert travel and the company of desert peoples ... I resented modern inventions; they made the road too easy. I felt instinctively that it was better to fail on Everest without oxygen than to attain the summit with its use ... Yet to refuse mechanical aids as unsporting reduced exploration to the level of a sport, like big-game shooting in Kenya when the hunter is allowed to drive up to within sight of the animal but must get out of the car to shoot it. I would not myself have wished to cross the Empty Quarter in a car. Luckily

this was impossible when I did my journeys, for to have done the journey on a camel when I could have done it in a car would have turned the venture into a stunt ... I could remember how bitterly at school I had resented reading the news that someone had flown across the Atlantic or travelled through the Sahara in a car. I had realized even then that the speed and ease of mechanical transport must rob the world of all diversity.

From Arabia in 1950 Thesiger moved to the humid swamps of the Iraqi Marshes, where he lived and travelled for eight years with the people of the marshes until he was thrown out due to a forcible change of the Iraqi government. He continued to make remarkable journeys, usually on foot in remote mountain and desert regions, and the year before I came to Oman he fought for the Yemeni royalists, as had John Cooper and David Bayley before they joined the Sultan's Army.

This little civil war, which John described as 'a skirmish', had remote Islamic origins, as did most Yemeni and Omani clashes. As in Oman, Yemenis often revolted against Caliph control from abroad and installed their own Imams. The Shia doctrine of the Imam Zaidi had survived in royalist north Yemen for a thousand years and was still the religion there. But to the south of the capital Sanaa and in coastal towns like Aden, the orthodox Sunni doctrine prevailed.

In 1962 Imam Badr of the royalist north was overthrown by republicans supported by the Egyptian Army of President Nasser. Fifty thousand Egyptian troops with tanks, artillery and bombers attacked the royalist tribesmen, but by 1966 when Thesiger, John Cooper and other itinerant Brits arrived to help the royalists, the Egyptians had, by clever guerrilla tactics, been evicted from most of north and east Yemen.

Although the USA and most of Europe recognized only the republican government of the south, the British still supported the royalists.

Many years later when interviewing Thesiger, I was spellbound by his memories of narrow escapes, cave bombings and, in the mountain fortress town of Shahra, once a major centre of the incense trade, how he had had to drink water from the public cisterns which was rife with guinea-worms and many citizens spent hours and days winding the long worms out of their legs and around sticks.

Thesiger left the Yemen in 1967, and between 1968 and 1994 settled with a Samburu family in northern Kenya from where he continued his often solo travels, always in hot, arid lands, until in his eighties his failing health forced him to a retirement home in England. He never married and once commented that 'marriage would be a crippling handicap'. He died nearly blind and suffering from Parkinson's disease in 2003.

I attended his memorial service, representing HRH The Prince of Wales who was abroad. The service was held with a packed congregation in Eton College Chapel, a building I had as a student scaled by night. I once told this story to Thesiger, much to his amusement and approval.

From Mugshin, once believed to be a main breeding ground of the worldwide locust scourge, and hence the start point of Thesiger's first crossing of the Sands, our convoy continued its journey south.

On the night of our third day's travel we reached our goal of Thumrait Camp, known to the oilmen who established it in the 1950s as Midway. When they abandoned it, they left everything behind: generators, radio aerials, living huts, cookhouse and tall derricks, all surrounded by many thousands of old lorry tyres and empty fuel drums, known to the bedu as *burmails* – a corruption of Burmah Oil. These empty drums were used by the oilmen's guides as lonely markers all over the areas they prospected. They were left in place to be covered eventually by blown sand, except in the gravel deserts where they remained as eyesores. All the oil prospectors' tracks outside the dunes also remained intact for years, since there was virtually no rain to the north of the Dhofar Mountains.

As Corporal Salim designated different huts to our five sections, a lone wizened Baluchi in khaki appeared from the cookhouse and gave me an undated scribbled note from an officer in the Northern Frontier Regiment.

'Hope your journey was good. Go at once to Habarut to secure the airstrip. Then radio Salalah for the Beaver to land and pick up an injured *askar* from our fort there.'

I tried to radio Salalah or Habarut's *askar* garrison, but failed to get through.

Weary, but realizing that a man's life might depend on our speed, we made ready to get going again after a quick meal and refuelling the vehicles. We left our two lorries at Thumrait.

We had already driven through nearly 600 miles of desert. My back ached from the bouncing.

'From now, Sahib,' Corporal Salim said, 'there may be *adoo* mines.' Thus comforted, I watched him drive off down one of many sandy tracks, heading roughly west in the direction of the Yemeni border and Habarut.

I hit one ear hard with the palm of my hand every so often to try and keep awake and so avoid the fate of Patrick Brook (and ridicule from the men of Recce). We were all very tired and very hot. Salim said it would take eight hours' driving to reach the Yemeni border *if* we stayed on the main rutted track and ignored the possibility of landmines.

'Your choice,' I told him, since he was to lead and would therefore be more likely to set off any lurking mine.

My lips were cracked, despite the protection much of the time when on the move from my Arab *shemagh* face cloth. And my eyes stung from the dust, as I found that goggles very quickly misted up.

Murad, who seemed indefatigable, shouted above the crunch of wheels on gravel, 'Tomorrow, *Insha'Allah*, the new moon will show herself in the east. Then will be Ramadan. No food or water by day all month. This is hard. *Insha'Allah* we will rest much in Ramadan, Sahib.'

Unsure whether this was a statement or a question, I replied, '*Insha'Allah.*' Many times thereafter I found this to be an extremely useful response, since it is non-committal but denotes the pointlessness of pursuing the matter any further, since God, not the officer, will decide.

At dawn we came to the oasis of Habarut, where a wide wadi crossed in front of us denoting the unmarked border.

On the low cliffs of the Yemeni side, a whitewashed, *Beau Geste*-like Hollywood dream of a fortress with little towers and crenellated battlements stood guard over the Yemeni-owned springs, while on our Omani side and also on the top of the wadi's bank our own similar fortress was situated directly opposite. Sentries could be seen pacing both sets of parapets.

The Yemeni outpost, according to our intelligence officer, Tim Landon, had originally been built as an outpost for the Hadhramaut Bedouin Legion by the British, but a year ago the British had left Aden and all of Yemen to the new Marxist-oriented government whose troops now manned the border. The tricolour of the People's Democratic Republic of Yemen had replaced that of the Legion.

Our own fort had been built only two years before, but when I returned to Habarut in 1972 it had been demolished to a heap of rubble by the Yemenis.

After greeting our own *askars*, securing the pebble-floored airstrip three miles up the wadi and, by way of a Morse code message, ordering the Beaver to come quickly, I observed the opposition's fort through my telescope. A short, moustached officer stood on the ramparts watching me through binoculars. Behind him, skylined, was the outline of a twin-barrelled machine gun pointing tactfully skywards.

Our own fort's *askars*, I noted, had no weapon more effective than their bolt-action rifles.

The Beaver touched down at noon and took away the injured *askar*. Murad, always mischievous, suggested that the man's injury was, in fact, a dose of the pox from a Habarut houri.

The temperature was 115° Fahrenheit without a breeze, but the little plane lurched upwards from the loose stones of the runway with a mere fifty yards to spare and disappeared low over our fort.

I sent a message to Salalah. Should we now go back to set up our base at Thumrait?

No! The response was immediate. We were to patrol to the south-east from Habarut and along the border to locate a suspected camel trail thought to be much used by *adoo* resupply groups. If located, we were to ambush it.

Even Corporal Salim had never been into the unknown country south of the fort. Nor had any of the *askars*, and no villager of the oasis was prepared to help the army since they grazed their goats and camels on both sides of the border, and their tribe, the Mahra, acknowledged no barrier to their free movement in any direction so long as they remained neutral.

So I would have to navigate by magnetic compass and a crumpled East Aden Protectorate chart lent me by John Cooper which gave very few place names in the relevant area, mainly because there were no places, only dry valleys between dry mountains. The border was marked as a straight line through no particular geographical feature but running directly from Habarut to Cape Darbat Ali on the coast.

From Habarut, after thanking the *askars* for the baskets of dates they gave us, we drove back east to the site of a batch of hovels named Shafia, then south into a labyrinth of wadis zigzagging between rugged cliffs up to 1,000 feet high.

We entered the widest of these valleys, one of the few with a name, the Sheetah, which ran deep into the southern *gatn*, that region of steep canyons between the dry desert and the semi-foliated western Qara Mountains.

At the entrance to the Sheetah, by a prominent pillar, we cached all but strictly relevant baggage in order to lighten the vehicles. We filled all our jerrycans with fuel and left the lorry hidden up a side nook, having taken six goats and left the rest with the lorry driver to feed and water.

My mind was full of plans to ambush the *adoo*, but the men were thinking with varying degrees of enthusiasm or apprehension of the imminent commencement of Ramadan. As a general rule Islam formed the basis of their lives, not just as their faith but socially and mentally as well. Ramadan means 'to be hot'. It arrives fourteen days later in their calendar each year because the moment of its advent depends on the first appearance of the new moon at that season.

Ali Nasser once told me with great pride that a few years back he had been the first person in his Jebel Akhdar village to shout '*Ashoof a qum'r*' (I see the moon). From then on, during daylight hours, total abstinence from drink or food is strictly maintained for a month, ending when the new moon is seen again.

That day, where the Wadi Habarut split into three wadis, Mohammed of the Beard shot an ibex, and after a feast we all climbed the wadi's bank to line its cliff and to watch the orient in starlit silence, but for the low incantation of the Quran by the *moolah*.

Corporal Salim whispered in my ear, 'Three men of religion in your village must sight the new moon before Ramadan can begin. In Pakistan they fly three *moolahs* up in an aeroplane to be sure of spotting the new moon in good time.'

This struck me as cheating, but I did not say so.

Hyenas howled from the south, the echoes repeating from the walls of many ravines.

Someone at length gave a scream of joy. 'I see her. I see her.' The men jumped about. Some hugged one another. My section, smiling like Cheshire cats, shook my hand. This gave me great pleasure for, after all, I was no Muslim.

'There will be much festive shooting at home,' someone said, 'but maybe we'd better not.'

At this meeting of three wadis, as at many random spots I had passed in this *gatn* country, piles of rocks clearly placed by humans along the valley base of cliffs indicated ancient bedu grave sites. Those wandering folk from centuries past must have watched the sickle moons of the seasons but known nothing of Mohammed or Christ.

For two days we pushed further south deep into Mahra territory, but we met no one. My map announced, 'RELIEF DATA INCOMPLETE', 'NUMEROUS HILLS WITH DEEPLY INCISED VALLEYS', and 'MANY SHARPLY DEFINED RIDGES'. An especially unhelpful comment was, 'SCATTERED SCRUB' in a valley where not even a weed showed itself.

Towards dusk on the second day at a side wadi named Etheereel, we suddenly came upon definite marks of a used camel trail heading from the direction of the Yemen and into Dhofar.

The men were by then exhausted, having drunk nothing all day, despite the frequently repeated effort of pushing our vehicles over veins of soft sand and changing tyres in the blistering heat. I too had refrained from drinking or eating during the daylight hours, a regime I had determined to follow in order to give orders from a state of 'deprivation' equal to that of my men.

So we turned back and camped a mile away, having posted a section with two machine guns and spare water bags to guard the camel trail overnight.

Next morning, with two sections, I followed the trail into an ever narrowing valley which some six hours later became a cul-de-sac with a low zone of caves and signs of past camping, including old rags and date stones. So we returned to the vehicles weary and baked. The men looked sullen, especially when I mentioned that we must be careful with our water reserves.

We continued south and, at about Latitude 17°, the Sheetah became impassable to the vehicles without a great deal of heaving and removal of small boulders.

At one point a confusion of old camel trails did cross our wadi near to where the Sheetah and the Aydim watersheds converged, but Corporal Salim, our most trail-wise expert, announced that they had not been used for many years.

Since we had no way of knowing whether or not the major infiltration route reported by Tim Landon's spies crossed our wadi at some point just ahead of us, we had no excuse for not pushing on while we still had sufficient water.

So, leaving Murad and his drivers in a boulder-strewn ravine, I took two sections who had not suffered the previous foot-slog, with two full water bottles per man and four machine guns on a south-south-east bearing, having estimated a distance of some twenty miles as the buzzard flies to the coastline. We zigzagged continually in order to avoid deeply incised canyons as we tramped along the table-tops, climbing slowly as we mounted the foothills of the coastal mountains.

At noon, through my telescope, I could clearly see the ridge line of the Qara Mountains stretching across the southern horizon, the last obstacle before the coastline of the Indian Ocean. Certain then that no west–east camel trail existed between Habarut and the Qara, we turned back.

A helicopter might have done our job far quicker and more thoroughly, although spotting camel *athar* (trails) on pebble ground in deep wadis is no easy task from the air. But there were no helicopters.

Back-tracking, we surprised two old bedu emerging from a side canyon with their skinny goat herd. We gave them dates and some of our scarce water. Where, they asked us, were we from? Hauf? At which point we realized that they assumed that we were a unit of an

Aden-based force. When Corporal Salim said that we had come from Muscat, the older man flung up his hands.

'But you will be killed,' he shouted. 'You are in the Wadi Deefan in the Yemen.' This was followed by a stream of excited gibberish. Even Corporal Salim failed to comprehend it, but one thing was clear. We were not in the Wadi Sheetah after all. We were well over the Yemeni border and in enemy territory. My map stated clearly in capital letters, 'DUE TO INSUFFICIENT INFORMATION, THE BOUNDARY BETWEEN THE PROTECTORATE OF SOUTH ARABIA AND MUSCAT AND OMAN HAS BEEN OMITTED WITHIN THE AREA OF THIS GRAPHIC.'

We returned to the vehicles, too dehydrated even to sweat. While we were away, Murad had, against my orders, taken his own local patrol (of three drivers) into a side wadi to hunt rock rabbits (the *hyrax* of the Bible). He tried to justify his behaviour by saying that he had found a recent camel trail. But he could show no signs of one.

We drove back to Habarut almost out of water.

I reflected that, had we run into an *adoo* unit in the Deefan and been reported as an invasion force of the Sultan's Army, an international incident could have been sparked.

My commanding officer in Salalah at the time, Peter Thwaites, when next we met asked what it was like in the Yemen. I asked him how he knew of my embarrassing error, and he laughed. 'Muscat Regiment is one big family. Your soldiers talk. All the soldiers talk.'

For years afterwards I had to put up with jokes about my navigating skills.

Back at Midway, or Thumrait to give it its Arabic name, the orders from Salalah were to build basic makeshift defences there, make friends with the local bedu and then find an alternate 'secret' base further to the west from which we could operate without observation by wandering camel and goat herders who, when back in the Qara *jebel*, would doubtless be quizzed by the *adoo* as to army activities in Thumrait.

The easiest of these tasks, once we had fashioned a defensive chain of oil drums filled with sand around key parts of the Thumrait base, was to befriend the locals.

In the Wadi Dawkah, an hour's drive north of Thumrait, we were introduced by Sultan bin Nashran to a family of the Bait Shaasha tribe who had camels grazing a wide area. They made us welcome in their camp which consisted of blankets thrown over a short thorn tree. The head of the family milked a hobbled camel into a tin and passed this around. As was often the case, I came last, being clearly not Muslim. I found the milk, which was warm and frothy, too salty to be pleasant.

We were then, according to Sultan later on, greatly honoured when the bedu boss produced a filthy grey bag made from the nineteen-inch skin of a *dhub* lizard. Unwrapping it, he revealed some withered strips of pinkish meat like chopped-off thumbs: slated shark guts. The smell from the bag was disgusting. It was passed around the circle. Fighting back revulsion I took the smallest piece and tried to swallow it whole while holding my breath. But it was too tough and needed chewing first. The taste was not as bad as the stench suggested: fishy and a bit rotten. Mohammed of the Beard chuckled as he watched my expression.

When we left the camp I asked Sultan why the old bedu, even when milking his camel, had used only his left hand while his right arm remained at all times ramrod stiff, never bent at the elbow.

Sultan chuckled. 'Yes. That one is a distant cousin of mine. People laugh at him because he must eat with the same hand with which he cleans himself after ablutions.'

'Why so?'

'He was once kicked and trodden on by a rutting bull camel,' Sultan said. 'His right arm was broken with bones sticking out. So a "doctor" of the Rashidi was called. The men of his family held him down, pulled the arm straight out and tucked the bones back in. Then they burnt a hole in a long desert melon from end to end into which they forced the arm. After six months they took the melon away. The arm was mended, although it would never bend again.'

Sultan and Hamed showed me plants, desert fruit and fragile butterflies, pink and blue fritillaries, that hopped about the *kfeeter* plants, tiny bobbles growing just above the ground with knotty roots curled protectively about their seeds.

'When a baby child is gripped by a *djinn* spirit,' Hamed told me, 'then we put these seeds in a piece of rag, tie it up, and hang it round the baby's neck. The *shaitan* [devil] hates the *kfeeter* so he flees to another baby.'

He showed me other plants, the gnarled *gha'ader* that provides stomach medicine for the bedu, and the *gai'sh* hedgehog bush with its sharp and deadly thorns. Many stretches of sand are littered with strings of tiny Sodom apples which, applied halved and hot to an abscess, will draw out poison as efficiently as a poultice. Heated in boiling water, Hamed had seen bedu use them to cauterize and draw jigger worms out of their toes.

Sultan once took me to an evergreen tamarisk with a pink flower. In the cool sand beneath this bush were tiny greenish flakes. He gave me one to eat. It was sweet and moist; quite possibly the *manna* of the children of Israel. Gazelle and the rare oryx can live for months without water, drinking only from the tamarisk and other juicy shrubs.

Over the next few months Sultan and his Bait Shaasha friends taught me and three of my section all about their camels. I found mounting much easier than I had thought, mainly because Sultan kept a close watch to see that I had a firm grip of the correct part of the hair at the base of the camel's neck before the animal stood up with a jerky motion, forwards and then backwards, lifting me eight feet into the air and onto its back behind the hump.

I had ridden horses on and off for years but they are well designed to be ridden bareback by humans with well-cushioned backsides. Camels are not, and their spines behind the hump jar their rider's coccyx painfully until they get the knack of how to be comfortable, if contorted, whether by side-saddle riding or, like the bedu, literally kneeling on the upturned soles of your feet.

For my first few rides I felt as though my privates were being tortured, so I switched to the lesser evil of bruised buttocks. I never really mastered the art of camel riding in comfort, but often enough, over the months ahead, wished that we were riding camels through evil terrain rather than pushing our vehicles through various hot hell-hole stretches of sand or *sabkha* where even removing 70 per cent of the air in our tyres did not help.

Racing camels in Dubai have been timed over short distances at 40 mph, and they can manage 25 mph for nearly an hour, but in soft sands on the flat they normally average 4 mph if unladen but for a rider. Our bedu's main baggage camel is raced, he told us, at six thousand paces an hour if kept away from the sort of hard ground which is ideal for a Land Rover but often painful to a camel.

Two of the toes of the broad pad of a camel's foot are joined so that the pad flattens out to provide excellent traction on soft sand. There are small water-storing sacs in their feet in addition to the main fat storage facility in their hump, but these pads are sensitive both to hot rock and sharp gravel. This means that camels are at their best in areas where vehicles have their worst problems.

Arabian one-hump dromedaries were extinct in the wild, apart from a few previously domesticated animals let loose. They weigh over 600 kilos and can digest the most leathery of desert leaves as well as brittle spiky thorns. They are highly functional, with nostrils that can flap shut to prevent sand inhalation and with thick rubbery pads on their legs and chests on which they squat.

Despite their gentle eyes with long lashes and their general air of patience, bull camels have been known to attack and kill their owners during the rut when their tongues swell up into raw pink bubbles and their subsequent copulation appears to involve a Kama Sutra-inspired back-to-back activity caused by their penis facing the 'wrong way'.

One of our visits to our Shaasha friends coincided with the arrival of a Mahra who owned an aged bull camel which he was offering as a sperm donor to fertilize the Shaasha's female camels in return for a modest fee.

In Muscat I had heard townsfolk gossip that Dhofari camels' mouths are infected with syphilis, but this is merely the product of an old legend probably sparked by the genuinely foul smell of all camels' breath.

Bedu often name their camels and clearly love them, and in desert droughts they have been known to survive without food or water for weeks using only milk from their camels, so long as the latter have available grazing.

A camel can remain in milk, providing she is kept away from bulls, for as much as four years. She may have up to a dozen calves in a working life of twenty years and can survive a long journey through the hottest, driest of deserts, unlike any other animal. She never sweats until her body heat exceeds 104°F, and although she does not store water, as is often thought, she can conserve it for days and, when thirsty, is capable of imbibing up to 27 gallons at one sitting. She can then use 95 per cent of the intake, whereas humans use only 12 per cent and excrete the rest.

The Shaasha recalled one long march by a cousin of theirs whose camels had run out of milk and, without water, he had resorted to ramming his camel stick down their throats and drinking their vomit.

A month after arriving in Thumrait we were ordered to patrol the gravel deserts to the north of the Qara Mountains and all the way from Thumrait to the Yemeni border.

I was, I realized, on a very loose rein, apart from the overall objective which was to block any possible enemy incursion from the Yemen to the north of the coastal mountains. This I could easily do by leaving half the platoon to block the Dehedoba trail while, with two Land Rovers and ten men, I could patrol further north towards or even into the southern rim of the Sands to search for the lost city of Ubar.

If radio instructions arrived which needed immediate recall to Salalah or elsewhere, I could respond within hours. It did strike me that such a course of action might be construed as dereliction of duty, but I dismissed such thoughts as overly moralistic. After all, I would still be geographically in the area designated to the platoon.

So, leaving the *moolah* in charge of the others and with his assurance that he would radio for my return if anything untoward occurred, I left with my section and Corporal Salim's.

From our camp near the pools of Ayun we headed west to the well at Tudho where we filled our water cans with enough for men and vehicles for fourteen days. Then we went north through gravel desert along the eastern side of the Wadi Aydim to an abandoned oil exploration site called Qafa. On the way we passed the wreck of one of the Dodge power-wagons which, four years before, had brought the original members of the Dhofar Liberation Force from Saudi Arabia to start the Dhofar rebellion. Salim found a promising camel trail heading north which provided good going for a few miles, but the Wadi Atinah then blocked our way for two days with soft sand and *sabkha*, a chalky layer of powder-sand just beneath a breakable gravel crust in which both our vehicles often became enmired.

If only Sultan bin Nashran or Hamed al Khalas had been with us, they would have known firm surface routes to follow rather than driving using mere compass directions.

We veered off to an old oilmen's trail leading to their 1950s exploration camp at Fasad, close to the edge of the Sands. We arrived after a great deal of manpower, sand channel usage, two burst tyres and a shattered half-shaft. I felt uneasy, for none of the men had been to this area before, but using the sun and the passage of time for direction we headed due west from Fasad wherever the terrain allowed and, after twenty-four miles of flat, stony plain, we came to a low wadi with many camel trails leading north-west. We stopped to examine them.

Corporal Salim joined me by my vehicle to kneel beside one such track. I reflected that Hamed or Sultan would probably have garnered a great deal of information from the track, but Salim said nothing.

'Could this lead to Ubar?' I asked him, for I had explained my interest that, while looking for PFLOAG of course, it would be nice to find an old city too. He had agreed and sworn all our group to silence. They enjoyed the 'shared secret', he assured me.

'*Yimkin ... Mumkin ... Insha'Allah*,' he replied, shrugging and grinning. Maybe ... God willing.

We looked up at our eight men and our two drivers still outside the vehicles. Their heads were all mummy-wrapped in green Arab headcloths from which only their dark eyes emerged, their eyelashes dusted with white *sabkha* powder.

I could see that they were unconcerned as to whether or not we traced the lost city, being happy simply to be free of the normal fear of landmines and ambush. My own fear of military censure at being so far from the Dehedoba trail did not touch them.

We moved on, having decided that all the camel trails were ancient with no sign of recent usage by bedu or PFLOAG.

When, in a narrow rocky defile which Murad had unwisely entered as an intended short cut, we jolted through a jumble of football-sized rocks and sheared another half-shaft, I decided that we must turn round just as soon as we escaped from the defile. But my desire to search the Wadi Mitan, often rumoured to be the site of old artefacts, was too strong. The wadi was, after all, only ten miles to our west. So on extricating ourselves from the defile and making Murad promise to drive without his usual abandon, we did reach the Mitan, and crossing it, for the surface was firm, we came upon a camp of nomadic Kolbani with a sizeable herd of piebald goats.

After greetings, we collected *hatab*, the dead driftwood to be found in most wadis, made two fires and, having paid the Kolbanis for a goat in exchange for a large bag of rice, gave it to Murad, our skilled executioner and butcher. Some hours later, joined from nowhere by two old Rashidi bedu, we sat around two fires, each group with its great tin dish of goat and rice.

An old Kolbani treated us, uninvited, to a seemingly endless dirge devoid of both tune and rhythm, which reminded me of the similar noise that often emanates from the Eskimos of North Greenland.

Despite this mournful lament, I noticed that the platoon members were more cheerful than I had seen them for weeks. They began to sing a pop tune known to Omanis and Baluchis which drowned out the dirge and even achieved harmony at one point. They kept the beat by slapping the butts of their rifles.

Normally any chit-chat between us when on patrol, or even in our Ayun camp, was muted, since anything above a low whisper was expressly forbidden under my platoon rules; as was smoking, belching and use of aftershave sprays. The *adoo jebalis* have a remarkably keen sense of smell and, to use an Omani expression, can hear a lizard sneeze in a thunderstorm.

A young Kolbani with a permanent scowl interrupted the silence during a lull in the merriment, firing a question at Corporal Salim while glancing at me.

Salim looked at me, clearly embarrassed. 'This boy is *shwaya magnoon* [slightly mad]. He says you are a Christian. Aren't you afraid of death, knowing that you will burn in hell? What shall I say?'

The Kolbani, the Rashidi and the platoon men were now all staring at me.

Luckily I had been told the story by Peter Southward-Heyton of just such an Ibadhi belief held by many bedu. So I was primed with the stock response.

'We *Nasrani* [Christians] are, like all Muslims and Jews, people of the Book which clearly states that we will *all* go to Paradise. It is correct that the followers of the Prophet will go there before those who follow Christ, or those who killed Christ, but the Book does not say that we will spend the waiting period in Hell ... *Insha'Allah.*'

There was much nodding of heads and the platoon men looked relieved. The Kolbani had looked nonplussed and unconvinced.

During another period of silence, I spoke to Salim since, although my Arabic was by then fluent when conversing with the soldiers, it could not cope with bedu dialect. Salim nodded and asked the old Rashidis, to whose tribe these deserts traditionally belonged, if they knew of an ancient lost city named Ubar or Wabar which had belonged to the ancient people of Ad and which was referred to in the Quran as *Irem al-Adaat*.

An intense and colourful babble instantly arose involving both Rashidi and all the Kolbani, including their elder womenfolk. Salim listened intently and eventually culled the information that, although like the Loch Ness monster there had been many a sighting of 'old ruins' in the Sands all over the place, nobody present could specify an actual location. However, the Rashidis did have a cousin who 'knows everything' and was currently to be found at or near the head of the Wadi Jadileh, only a couple of hours to the west by vehicle.

The next dawn, already sweating before sun-up and the ritual mug of Indian tea, I set my compass for the direct route to the Jadileh, took our leave of our Kolbani hosts and filled their modified vehicle inner tubes, which served as water carriers, from our jerry cans. The tubes, I reflected, were probably obtained from abandoned army or oilmen's trucks.

Before we set out I told the men that, whatever we learnt from the bedu at the Jadileh, we must then turn back to join the rest of the platoon at the Dehedoba. To my delighted surprise, they all looked unhappy at this news and Hamed Sultan, Salim's powerfully built machine gunner, said, 'But we have come a long way and the city is made of gold. We must find it before others do.'

At the Jadileh we found nowhere that could be described as its 'head', since it petered out into flat gravel here and there, only to assume the distinct shape of a wadi again. And many places were soft bad going. There were no signs of any bedu. We were clearly looking for needles in a vast haystack so, by the second evening after leaving the Kolbani, exhausted from the hellish heat of the Jadileh search, we headed south and east, luckily without further breakdowns, to our correct patrol zones. My first search for Ubar had failed. In future, I determined, I would never try again without a bedu guide. At the end of Ramadan we were recalled to Bidbid in northern Oman to train with newly issued, fully automatic weapons.

At the time our colonel was concentrating on hard training in the three northern Oman company camps. 'Reveille at 5.30 a.m. in order to get most of the serious training over before the weather was too hot,' he recorded. 'By midday the temperature rose to 120 degrees F in the shade, the sun warming the volcanic rock and shale so that the heat burned through the soles of our boots ... and the sun's heat addled the brain.'

He later added a description of a terminal training exercise with my men acting as *adoo* against the rest of the Muscat Regiment.

The dreaded Recce Platoon ... were told to be as daring and aggressive as the real rebels in Dhofar. They took this very seriously. They ambushed us before the exercise officially started, threw stones at us when we assaulted their position and blew up blanks and explosive charges in our faces. When night fell and we were securely in our *sangars* [stone shelters], they attacked us with fiendish stealth and ingenuity with an overwhelming weight of blank ammunition and pyrotechnics until, as I rallied my men and told them to sit tight in their position, the unmistakable crack of a live round whizzed past my ear. This could be dangerous, I realized, and blew the whistle.

Shortly afterwards Richard John, who had just returned from a long period of hospitalization in Britain following his chest and shoulder wounding in Dhofar, rejoined the Muscat Regiment as a company commander and suggested that my platoon act as enemy for a big night exercise in the Hajar Mountains. Unfortunately things got out of hand and over-realistic. Three soldiers were badly hurt and a Baluchi soldier crushed one of my fingers against a rock with his rifle butt. Our medic decided to cut off the damaged end of the digit with his blunt scissors in the dark. Luckily the bone defied his efforts, so he splinted the two half-severed bits together. Unsurprisingly, the wound later went gangrenous. At the time I was due a month of annual leave so, after a party in our barracks with the men, I shook all their hands. 'Come back safe to Recce,' Corporal Salim said as he dropped me off at Seeb Airport. 'Where will you go?'

'Up the River Nile,' I told him, and then added, '*Insha'Allah*.'

CHAPTER 7

The White Aeroplane

Two years earlier, during army leave from tank exercises in Germany, I had parachuted onto a 6,000-foot glacier in Norway and then completed the first recorded descent of the avalanche-infamous Briksdalsbre Glacier. That Norway team included Scots Greys helicopter pilot Peter Loyd and ex-Parachute Regiment Nick Holder who, after his spell with Gillette in Bahrain, had signed up again, this time as a captain with the Scots Greys.

At some point over the years, Nick had suggested an expedition involving no glaciers nor hair-raising parachute jumps, but far more ambitious nonetheless. His idea was to ascend the White Nile, which was one arm of the Nile, the longest river in the world at 4,160 miles from the sea to its source. Nick pointed out that almost a hundred years had passed since British explorers, mostly ex-army, had first risked their necks attempting to discover the great river's mysterious source which was known to be somewhere in the depths of Africa's unknown interior. We should, Nick announced, mark the centenary of those great men by travelling the river ourselves, which he said could be done during a standard six weeks of annual army leave if I could get Land Rover sponsorship.

As encouragement, he posted me a copy of *The White Nile* by Alan Moorehead.

The idea did sound attractive and, glancing at a road map of the whole of Africa, there appeared to be roads or four-wheel-drive tracks all the way up or near to the river from the sea, passing through Egypt, the Sudan, Uganda and Lake Victoria in Kenya.

Since Livingstone's days, hostile Nile tribes were no longer expected to kill, or even rob, visiting foreigners as a matter of course, and Land Rover had sponsored me on previous less interesting trips. By 1970 such a journey was to become impossible for many years due to civil strife in Sudan, but at the time I applied to join the Sultan's Army, there seemed no political or geographical obstacle to Nick's idea.

So in 1967 I asked Land Rover for a free vehicle. They said no, and that a 10 per cent discount was the best they could offer. However, they said they would help us to sell the vehicle when we reached Kenya.

I visited the relevant African embassies in London, all of whom said they would grant us the necessary visas. Peter Loyd was, Nick and I assumed, a mechanic since he was a helicopter pilot, so we invited him to join us.

By the time that I was on my Arabic language course prior to going to Oman, the supply of most of the requirements for our Nile drive had been agreed by civilian sponsors, or else we had been promised them on loan from friendly army stores. Where maps existed, I obtained them from London antiquarians, and Horlicks provided us with packs of iron rations. High frequency army radios came from Racal (founders of Vodafone). My fiancée Ginny agreed to organize things in England once I had gone to Oman, with advice from the hero of army expedition wannabes, Major John Blashford-Snell.

I had earlier been advised to purchase a revolver and rifle in London and take them with me to Oman. These should suffice for self-defence on the Nile.

During my language course in London, two of my original contacts at the four relevant embassies sent alarming messages warning me that visas would not, after all, be available to us, nor indeed to any foreigners without diplomatic status.

In Egypt there had long been a military stand-off with the Israelis. This had suddenly worsened and the Nile was obviously the main north–south line of defence in readiness for any Israeli attack. Worse still, the British Ministry of Defence was rumoured to be considering the sale of a batch of Centurion tanks to Israel. Were such a deal to materialize, the MoD would not want serving soldiers, who could become hostages for Cairo to hold against delivery of the tanks to their enemy, wandering around in Egypt.

And, after a period of relative peace in the region of South Sudan and northern Uganda, where rebels against the Sudanese government roamed forests and attacked army convoys, trouble was resurgent and ordinary tourists were no longer getting visas.

An article about prototype hovercraft being developed to spray crops more cheaply than aircraft gave me the idea that our expedition might become 'interesting' to both the Egyptians and the Sudanese with their vast areas of cotton crops to be sprayed. We could, by giving demonstrations of such revolutionary machines on our way up the river, become more of an attraction than a nuisance.

I approached Hovermarine, who had already made a suitable machine, but a fire burnt down their production line. Then I tried Hover-Air in Lincolnshire, who made the two-seater Hoverhawk which had a clever spray attachment to deal with crops in areas where wheeled and tracked vehicles would sink.

Hover-Air's owner, Lady Brassey, liked the idea of her machines proving their reliability on a Nile journey supported by Land Rovers carrying fuel and spares for them. A visit to Shell reaped an agreement to sponsor the fuel in remote places.

With the hovercraft theme in place, I approached the embassies once again and received a completely new and highly enthusiastic reaction. The Sudanese ambassador, who had been Prime Minister of the country a few years before, personally interviewed me and agreed to write to his superiors in Khartoum in order to acquire the visas, which were currently unavailable to normal tourist applicants.

To record the expedition for posterity, we recruited a freelance photographer, Mike Broome, and a movie cameraman, Anthony Brockhouse, to produce a documentary. Hover-Air agreed to provide a specialist mechanic. So, with a team of six, we clearly needed two Land Rovers and two Hoverhawks.

A good friend of mine married the daughter of the boss of the

Automobile Association, and he kindly agreed to give us an old retired (yellow-painted) AA Land Rover as well as an up-to-date report on Nile-side roads which were only usable in many places for a few months each year.

The flow of the main Nile at the peak of the flood season (August/September) is usually some sixteen times that of the lowest period around mid-April. And well over half the volume of water for the year flows in only ten weeks between July and September, during which period the tracks running south in the immediate vicinity of the river are submerged, forming a swamp bigger than England.

To obtain our visas we promised our embassy contacts a well-organized hovercraft demonstration on demand in Egypt, and in both north and south Sudan on specified dates. Should we make it all the way to the source of the Nile, Lake Victoria, a final show to the Kenyans would mark the end of our White Nile ascent. None of the four transit countries had previously ever been visited by hovercraft, so we had the attraction of novelty on our side, without which we would, like the vast majority of other tourists, never have received many of the regional permits necessary for travel anywhere near the Nile.

The downside of this new hover-front for our basic goal, which was merely to travel the length of the river, was that we would now have to take the machines and their trailers with us all the way, an administrative problem summarized by Nick as a 'monumental embuggerance factor'.

Long accustomed to Nick's habitual litany of complaints, I reminded him that you cannot have your cake and eat it.

'Well,' he stated, 'I am driving on this trip, not hovering.'

Since Hover-Air had already nominated their senior mechanic to operate one machine, Peter had claimed pilotage of the other, on the basis that, as a fully qualified helicopter pilot, he was already an expert at hovering.

In my earlier absence in Oman Ginny had kept a close watch on all things Egyptian, and we found ourselves experiencing very anti-Israeli feelings when one of their commando raids managed to blow up the main Nile bridge at Qena. This had the immediate effect of all tourists, whether travelling alone or in groups and irrespective

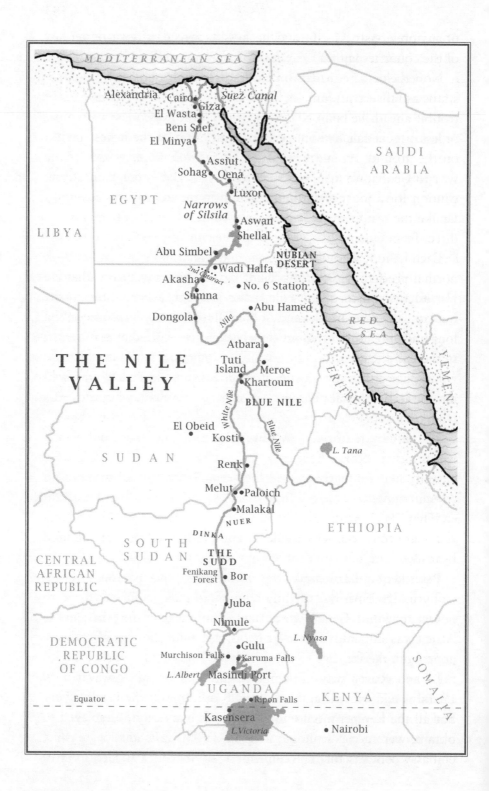

of any previously issued travel permits, being forbidden to enter any of the countries within the nine Governorates of the Nile.

Nonetheless I returned to Britain trusting in our newly acquired status as Hovercraft ambassadors and, ignoring all dire warnings of trouble ahead, we boarded a ferry from Dover in mid-February more or less on schedule and in freezing conditions with six inches of snow on the ground. Promised similar weather in France, in fact all the way to Genoa, we filled our radiators with antifreeze – strange precaution for a journey through some of the hottest lands in Africa. Unlike the rest of the team, I was well acclimatized, having arrived direct from Oman.

Each Land Rover towed a trailer tailor-made by a company whose normal product was the chassis of babies' perambulators. The two Hoverhawks, named *Baker* and *Burton* after Nile explorers, stuck out over the sides of these one-off trailers, for they were fifteen feet long and nine feet wide. So their width was 18 inches more than that of the Land Rovers.

We passed through most of France in driving sleet, and on reaching the Italian border had a great deal of bureaucratic interference from two sets of Customs officers when they saw our automatic rifle, pistol, military radios, maps and the impressive array of cameras and lenses in steel boxes.

'If it's like this with Europeans,' Nick commented, 'God save us at African borders.'

'That,' Peter said, 'is what our 3,000 sponsored Marlboro cigarettes are for – border easement. The modern version of coloured beads.'

Peter kept a diary, unlike the rest of us, so I have quoted from it from time to time over the following pages.

On arrival at Genoa we parked near the port, for our ship to Africa was still unloading its previous passengers. Although we were gone from the vehicles for less than half an hour, the locked cab of my Land Rover was broken into and my briefcase was stolen. Luckily I had with me at the time my passport and travellers cheques, but all the key permits for Africa, which had taken me so long to obtain, were gone. I phoned the Automobile Association and my embassy contacts for replacement papers to be forwarded to us at the British embassy in Cairo, and we took the ferry to Alexandria the next day.

During the ferry trip two Scandinavian hippies entered our cabin and, not spotting Mike Broome (who was about 5 foot 2 inches tall), began to fiddle with the camera gear. Hearing them, Mike sat up on his bunk, cocked my revolver, and slowly spun its chambers with his best Clint Eastwood 'Make my Day' leer on his face. The hippies went white and rapidly exited the cabin backwards.

Alexandria, where we unloaded, was once the headquarters of Alexander the Great and the greatest trading port in the world. Ships from everywhere in the then known world called there and their crews told their stories of far-flung lands and strange people. Ptolemy, soon after the time of Christ, produced the first map of the world based largely on information received from merchant princes and great navigators who called at the port.

To ensure publicity for Hover-Air in return for their sponsorship, Ginny had prearranged an Alexandria press conference. This turned out to be a non-event, but she had taken the trouble to arm me with basic knowledge concerning the history of Nile exploration and this I had swotted up during the crossing.

In 1860, the year my grandfather was born, the greatest geographical mystery in the world was considered, especially in Britain, to be the location of the sources of the Nile.

For 2,000 years different dictators, including Alexander the Great and Napoleon, had sent out expeditions to find the answer to this conundrum, but all had been failures.

The ancient Egyptians had travelled all the way through the Nubian deserts to the site of today's Khartoum where the Blue Nile from Ethiopia meets the White Nile from the 'dark hole' of the Central African jungles. Because the Pharaohs realized that Cairo and the Nile Delta existed only because of the waters of the Nile, they naturally wanted some assurance that the source or sources of 'their' life-giving river would not suddenly dry up through natural causes or with human intervention. If the Thames dried up, London would still carry on thriving. Not so Egypt. Why, successive Egyptian rulers wondered, did the Nile water not evaporate or seep away on its journey through more than a thousand miles of dry desert? The Greek travel writer Herodotus travelled up the Nile in 460 BC to locate the source, but he turned back, no wiser, at the Aswan cataract. The Emperor Nero sent a team who reached the Sudd swamp before they, too, accepted failure. But by 1860, despite the Industrial Revolution and the detailed mapping of most of the world, including Australia and India, the Nile's origins were still a mere topic of speculation as in the days of Herodotus.

Conjecture was based on the first map of the world produced by Ptolemy which was published some 150 years after the birth of Christ and showed the river arriving in what is now Cairo, via the Nubian Desert, from the Equator in Central Africa.

Further conjecture and, in the Royal Geographical Society which was (and is) Britain's nerve centre of geographical and scientific exploration, heated disagreements were stirred up by two new sources of information. Or, as some geographers maintained, misinformation.

One source was that of Christian missionaries operating from East African coastal towns like Zanzibar. In 1848 one of these, Johannes Rebmann, said that he had, on an inland trip, seen a great mountain, Kilimanjaro, with snow on its summit.

Learned RGS members pointed out that snow on or near the Equator was out of the question and Rebmann must have seen white rock. But a year later missionary Ludwig Krapf claimed that he had seen another high mountain (Mount Kenya) with a similar coating of snow. Legend has it that this claim was the origin of the saying 'a load of old crap'. A third missionary, J. J. Erhardt, then published a map of his inland journeys showing a great lake, in the same zone as these two reported snowy mountains, which he called the Sea of Uniamesi.

In addition to the wave, some would say plague, of evangelical missionaries bursting with Victorian moral rectitude and zeal to claim African souls for redemption, there were also the Arab slavers and ivory traders whose increasing interaction with the tribes of the interior caused news to be passed to Europeans in the newly cosmopolitan seaport of Zanzibar Island, where in 1832 the Sultan of Oman from Muscat had established his new court. From there his

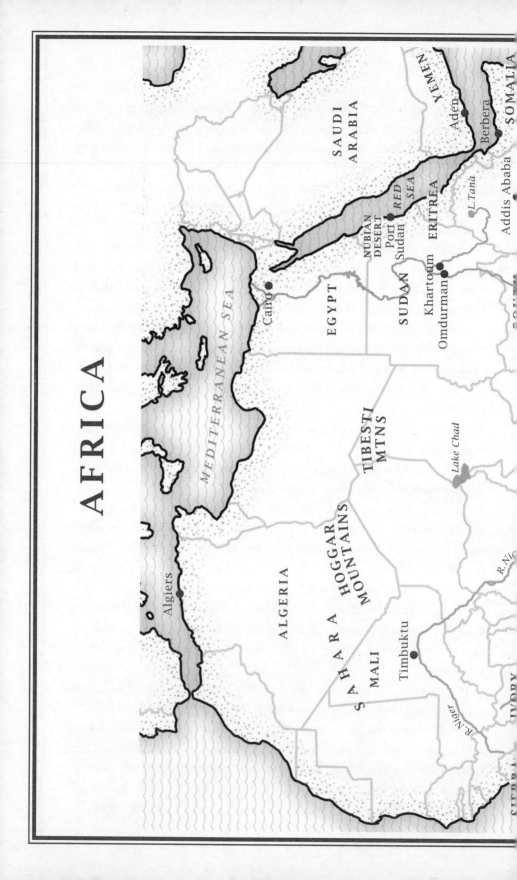

Arabs consolidated a near monopoly of trading stations on the mainland coast.

From Zanzibar these slavers reached Lake Tanganyika in the 1830s and Lake Victoria in the early 1840s. Meanwhile, the Egyptian ruler Muhammad Ali had established Khartoum as his Sudanese power base from which he sent expeditions south through the Sudd swamp regions to modern day Juba, then Gondokoro, south of which the Nile became unnavigable due to a series of cataracts. So the reported region of great lakes and snow-laden mountains was by the 1850s being slowly approached from the north and from the east. Only the hostility of local tribes prevented successive missionaries, slavers and explorers from locating the font of the great river.

By 1855 some of the great lakes in the general region where high mountains had been seen were known by name – Lakes Ujiji, Nyasa and Nyanza. Mountains and lakes are the necessary ingredients of great rivers. Streams link them all together, and although by the 1850s very little of Africa had been colonized by the European powers, all were keen to stake their claim, and none more so than Great Britain.

Due to their Industrial Revolution and with the greatest merchant navy in the world, the British were keen to protect their main trade routes both for exports and for the import of raw materials. Having successfully taken South Africa from the Dutch, they needed to ensure that the seaports of East Africa remained accessible to them and that whatever raw materials lay in unknown Central Africa would quickly become available to Britain. To this end they encouraged the Royal Geographical Society to spur on all efforts to locate the Nile's source.

In 1856 the Society selected two Indian Army officers to lead their first such mission.

The many individuals who, with support from the Society over the next four decades, eventually traced Nile waters from their very beginnings were powerfully motivated. Some, like Dr David Livingstone, had chiefly evangelical and anti-slavery ambitions, but the majority, most of whom became household names in Britain during their lifetimes, were driven by the sheer excitement of exploration into the unknown and the chance, if successful, of personal recognition. The first man to lead an RGS-supported Nile journey, Captain Richard Burton, wrote, 'The gladdest moment in human life is the departure upon a distant journey into unknown lands.'

On 16 June 1857, only 101 years before we reached Alexandria, Burton and his companion John Hanning Speke set out from Zanzibar on their very first Nile-source search.

Soviet warships crammed much of Alexandria's harbour, alongside other East European vessels involved in the ongoing building of the great Nile dam at Aswan.

If the Thames were to dry up, Britain would carry on with business as usual, but the Nile is the very heartbeat of Egypt. Since its vital water arrives by courtesy of several other countries (each of whom could, in theory, severely affect its flow by building dams or canals), it is a cause of national insecurity similar to that of the Dutch, whose nation is largely below sea level.

To the north of Cairo the Nile splits into two proud rivers, each with its own canals and dams which help irrigate the famous fertile zone known as the Delta, where the Egyptians harvest the best cotton in the world. For many years the cotton mills of Lancashire depended on the cotton fleet from Alexandria.

A Thomas Cook official approached me. His name was, of course, Mohammed and he looked entirely honest. He offered to help us 'defeat the Customs'. He was definitely a godsend, but even he with his network of friends within the Customs Hall bureaucracy found it well nigh impossible to explain that we were in no way Israeli spies despite our military equipment and total lack of any form of export licence, or indeed any paperwork at all. My explanation of Genoese thieves and replacement documents, even now awaiting us at the Cairo embassy, was sneered at. Money changed hands and Mohammed made sure that I observed each sub-table transaction, since I would in due course be reimbursing him.

God knows how he did it, but after five hours of wrangling, Mohammed beamed a beatific smile of victory and, after payment of his rightly hefty bill, he waved our convoy, complete with all suspicious items, out of the Customs zone and into Egypt by way of a mule-cluttered market square and past the crumbling fortress of Qait

Bay, which was built, Mohammed told us, on the site of the once world-famous lighthouse of *El Iskandariya* (The Alexandria). Said to be 575 feet high, this remarkable landmark included an outer spiralling ramp up which blinded mules towed cartloads of fuel for the beacon.

The jet trails of MiG fighters criss-crossed the sky above the silhouette of the fortress to remind the three of us (with recent army experience of awaiting a Soviet attack in Germany) of the ongoing Cold War. Mr Putin, the new Adolf Hitler-of-the-moment is, as I write this, threatening the world with a new conflict, but back then our worries about Soviet-inspired aggression were limited to the likely ripple effects of their ongoing troublemaking between Egypt and Israel.

At the local British consulate the car park was jammed with caravans, camper vans, Dormobiles and motorbikes, all of which it transpired had been turned back by police at the roadblocks set up at all exits heading out of town, no matter what visas the drivers held. This dampened my joy at being given an envelope sent to us care of the consulate by the Automobile Association, which contained copies of all the key travel documents stolen in Genoa.

A serious blow, also included in our forwarded mail, was a letter sent to my home address by the British embassy in Cairo. Since I had, by the time it arrived, departed to collect the hovercraft, my mother had forwarded it, as pre-agreed, to Alexandria. It instructed me to abandon the expedition altogether. This was a problem, bearing in mind that we were already in Egypt.

The letter said, 'The Ministry of Tourism has reluctantly turned down your hovercraft expedition. This must be a great disappointment to you. It is partly as a result of the recent Israeli Commando raid on Upper Egypt. Security restrictions have been increased. The authorities cannot guarantee your safety ...'

Attached to this letter was a copy of a long signal sent from the Defence Policy Department at the FCO to my regimental commanding officer which included the words, 'Any military expedition through Egypt and the Sudan would be vetoed, the more so as tensions are rising in the Middle East at present ... This is all rather depressing and, frankly, I am pessimistic about the expedition obtaining political approval at this juncture. The political ramifications, though, are legion and no amount of willingness to help can eliminate them.'

There was clearly nothing we could do at this stage other than confront our people in the Cairo embassy and hope to persuade them to let us at least try to break through whatever police or military blocks we encountered.

The Alexandria British consulate stand-in that day was a Spaniard who wished us well in Cairo, and he called the embassy there to warn them that we were on our way, as though we were likely to prove a lethal liability.

We had hoped to take the tarmac Delta Road to Cairo, but it was blocked due to a military convoy, so we had to use the more south-easterly route which was a narrow desert track flanked by salt marsh and running through endless miles of sand and gravel on the northern limits of the Libyan Desert. Sand had drifted across the track for long stretches so that, especially after dusk, there was no sign of its course.

A trailer wheel punctured, its wheel nuts jammed and, losing my temper with it in the dark, I applied too much pressure with a spanner and a nut sheared off. Peter took one look, and said, 'Dear boy – ' he sounded exasperated – 'it has a continental thread. You've been trying to tighten not loosen it.'

Since the trailer was manufactured in Cornwall, not France, I thought my assumption was perfectly natural, but Peter from then on showed alarm if I tried my hand at any mechanical activity.

Luckily Anthony had an inspired solution to the nut problem by way of a makeshift bolt, and we carried on to Cairo.

Our first stop was the airport to collect the Hover-Air 'mechanic'. This mechanic turned out to be Lady Brassey's son Charles, who was the company's sales director. He appeared at first sight to be entirely unsuited for the Nile job. He wore city clothes and, apart from a smart suitcase, carried an umbrella, a collapsible fishing rod and a pair of green wellington boots. A folded copy of the *Financial Times* was tucked under one armpit.

Our team of six was now complete and we drove to the Cairo embassy by way of the Pyramids at Giza. We came to them at midnight and parked in the sands to stand silently while Anthony filmed them. The moon had come out and was visible as a darting boo-merang between racing nimrod clouds. Pi-dogs howled from the desert behind us and I thought of the pre-Islamic days of the glorious Pharaohs whose desire for posthumous recognition had resulted in these amazing icons of early human engineering brilliance.

I had read the history of the pyramids, as described by Herodotus, which explained that 100,000 slaves had toiled with a horrendous death rate to fashion the Great Pyramids of Giza. Over twenty years later in the early 1990s archaeologists would unearth new ruins behind one of the pyramids which indicated that Herodotus had got it all wrong. Then in 2014 further digging confirmed the identity of the original labour force to be indented, paid Egyptian workers. Egypt's archaeology chief, Zahi Hawass, stated that the Herodotus myth, copied in many Hollywood movies over the years, of a multi-tude of Israelite slaves building the pyramids was rubbish. Israeli Prime Minister Menachem Begin on a visit to Cairo in 1977 stated that Jews had built the pyramids, but the chief professor at Jerusalem's Hebrew University scoffed at this on the grounds that 'Jews did not exist at the time the pyramids were built.' He also explained how the labour force, in fact, involved no more than 20,000 workers over a period of twenty years; not the 100,000 slaves of Herodotus. It was also proven by DNA sampling of skeletal remains that only ethnic Egyptians made up the work force.

The ancient Egyptians probably chose that distinctive form for their Pharaohs' tombs because of their solar religion. The Egyptian sun god Ra, considered the father of all Pharaohs, was said to have created himself from a pyramid-shaped mound of earth before cre-ating all other gods. The pyramid's shape is thought to have symbolized the sun's rays. Egyptians began using the pyramid from shortly after 2700 BC, and the great heyday of constructing them for royalty endured for about a thousand years.

The seventh-century fanatics from Arabia, when first their blitz-krieg overwhelmed the Pharaonic armies, established a fortress where Cairo now is and, at that time, the planet Mars was in the ascendant, known to Arabs as El Kahira. Hence Cairo, their new capital of Egypt. They went on to brutally sack the old Egyptian capital of Alexandria, which would never regain its former glory.

Peter's diary, 26 February: *Cairo was in a state of emergency with soldiers on every street corner and gun emplacements on bridges and public buildings. This had followed a series of Arab/Israeli incidents which had ended in the bombing of a commando camp in Syria last Monday. This does not bode well for our journey south.*

At the embassy, the military attaché, who had sent me the letter not to leave Britain, gave us a warm welcome and accepted that, ignorant of his orders, we had arrived in good faith. He arranged beds in the embassy compound for all of us.

He also explained that we could not have come at a worse time. The very morning that we had arrived in Alexandria, the Egyptian government had announced a countrywide state of emergency and instructed all citizens to watch out for Israeli saboteurs posing as tourists. Hovering on any part of the Nile inside Egypt was clearly out of the question. This was incidental to our main aim, which was to follow the course of the river by any means, but we would certainly need to use the hovercraft once we reached the Sudan, where we had agreed to give hover demonstrations, including one to the President in Khartoum.

So, since we couldn't hover, we must drive down the riverside roads to the border and, according to the military attaché, there were now over ninety roadblocks en route.

The British ambassador advised me that, although UK-Egyptian relations were currently good, they could rapidly turn bad if, as he warned me was quite likely, there was a sale by the Ministry of Defence of old Centurion tanks to the Israelis. (I wondered if any of these were the same ones in whose turrets I had spent many weeks on anti-Warsaw Pact training exercises in Germany.)

Over supper that evening the military attaché talked about past Anglo-Egyptian relations, which seemed to have see-sawed from good to bad and back to good several times over the past century or two. To summarize this in simplistic terms and ignoring pre-Islamic times, Egypt was occupied by the Arabs in AD 640 and their influence was such that Egyptians soon began to consider themselves as Arabs.

For centuries Egypt was merely part of the Ottoman Empire, but in 1869 the Khedive or puppet ruler, Ismail, became fabulously rich due to the American Civil War which increased the value of the annual Egyptian cotton crop from £5 million to £25 million. Ismail paid off the Ottoman Sultan and became, to all intents and purposes, the independent monarch of Egypt.

He splashed his wealth about with abandon and commissioned the French engineer, de Lesseps, to build the Suez Canal (more or less along the route of older canals between the Mediterranean and the Red Sea).

This new, far deeper canal was engineered by wetting the sand before excavating it, a new, more speedy technique, but cholera and other diseases caused a serious death toll in the workforce, who eventually completed the project despite the hostile climate of the eastern deserts. But it took them ten long years to do so.

'From our point of view,' the attaché told me, pointing at a large map of Egypt on the wall, 'the new canal cut the journey to India and the Far East by half compared with the existing Cape of Good Hope route. So, as the world's greatest sea-trading nation dependent on our coal-burning steamships as well as the troopships needed to defend the Empire, the canal was of huge benefit.'

The main threat to Britain at the time was the French efforts to dislodge our interests in the Near East and East Africa. Since a Frenchman had built the canal with French money, they now had a huge stake in Egyptian politics.

Khedive Ismail, immensely proud of his new canal, now declared Africa to be an island and that (despite the fact that he owned many slaves) he planned to annex the Upper Nile countries and suppress the slave trade there. He hired the British explorer Samuel Baker to command his Egyptian-Sudanese forces in order to achieve this.

After many twists and turns and battles involving the British, the Egyptians and the Sudanese, Egypt came under British rule in 1882, and the British bought all rights to the canal from the Khedive when he went bankrupt. They did, however, grant Egypt full independence under the Khedive's successors in 1922, whereupon the country was ruled by hereditary monarchs for thirty years.

In 1952 King Farouk was thrown out in a revolution

masterminded by the so-called Free Officers of the Egyptian Army, who were committed to freeing both Egypt and Sudan from British domination.

The coup leader, Gamal Abdel Nasser, became President of the new republic, with Anwar Sadat as Vice President. Nasser courted the Soviet Union as his close ally against the Western powers.

'The last real low point of our relations with Nasser's Egypt,' the attaché added, 'was, of course, the Suez crisis in 1956 when we and the French invaded, seized the canal and achieved a speedy victory over Nasser, only to be hounded out of the country with our tail between our legs following intense pressure from our supposed allies, the Americans and the UN. It's a funny old world! So you can see why we had to forbid you to come here at this volatile time of the ongoing war with our Israeli neighbours.'

Nonetheless, the ambassador and the military attaché took the extremely bold step of allowing us, despite three of our number being serving members of HM Forces, to head south, trusting to luck and in the knowledge that every other British citizen had been turned back and that we just might be imprisoned and used as a 'ransom' to persuade the UK not to sell tanks to the Israelis.

We spent our last night in Cairo at the home of a friend in the Nile-side suburb of Zamalek. I didn't sleep much due to the voices of many thousands of local Muslims with their lilting chant praising the Creator who gave them the Nile and, therefore, life. The tomcats and bullfrogs of Zamalek did their best to compete, adding to the overall din.

The road to Cairo headed due south into the midday sun. Three of us were crammed into the cabins of each hard-top Land Rover. The air conditioner of the ancient ex-AA vehicle had long since ceased to work and the heat quickly grew uncomfortable.

The natural reaction to take off our shirts was resisted due to local rules against baring any part of your trunk when driving.

Each village we came to was crowded, for we had by bad luck chosen an important feast day, Bairan al Adfah, on which to set out. The main road seemed to serve villagers as the marketplace for hawkers and vendors with their mules, carts and baskets of goods. Stray camels with supercilious expressions licked our headlights for some reason, and once the strange nature of our hovercraft was noted by children, the shriek went up, rapidly passed from mouth to mouth, of 'Tayyara Abyad' (White Aeroplane). This was weird since neither *Baker* nor *Burton* had wings (or wheels), but our convoy was soon surrounded, front and rear, by a throng of all ages, although mostly children. We could only move forward at a snail's pace in the suffocating heat, and often not at all. Nick, never patient, muttered an ongoing string of curses, including untranslatably rude Arabic ones that he must have picked up when trying to sell his razor blades in Bahrain.

Most of the crowd were good-natured but a few kicked our vehicles, especially when we tried to edge forward at faster than walking speed. Once out of the first village, Al Aiyat, we tried to go at a reasonable pace in between camels and other obstacles, but deep potholes threatened our delicate trailer suspension.

Four hours later than planned we came to El Wasta, and the first of the dreaded police roadblocks manned by an officer in a smart uniform, which must have been stiflingly hot. Behind him were a number of angry-looking goons in plain clothes.

They spread out to check our loads and to remove all the documents I could produce. We all smiled lovingly at the goons, who glowered back.

'You,' the policeman enquired, 'are the helicopter trade party from England going to the foot of Africa?' We all nodded in unison.

Peter's diary: *After a further change of escort we arrived at El Minya where the chief of police, town head and local minister of Tourism met us and wished us well. It transpired that we were the first "tourist" vehicles for ten years.*

The police chief told us, 'I have only today received orders to let you go south and to give you an escort out of my El Minya governorate and down to the Beni Suef zone. You must be careful. These are bad times. I send all other people back to Cairo.'

A couple of old vans with flashing blue lights and klaxon horns, manned by more sullen goons, appeared and we followed them with great relief down the river road. Village crowds, so impeding before, now melted away at the first sign of our escort's flashing lights.

At Beni Suef the local governor gave us coffee in a baking-hot office under a huge picture of a grinning Nasser.

At El Minya we met two gloomy Scottish archaeologists who had come to study the Nileometer of Elephant Island, an ancient stairway used centuries ago to measure annual flow rates. The police had ordered them to leave the area at once and go back to Cairo without delay.

They were a mine of information about the history of the Nile. Long before the invasion of the Arabs, the locals had established a Nile way of life which Islam hardly changed. The desert herdsmen who first settled by the river fetched water in shoulder bags, but as their vegetable plots grew in size, they needed more water and, around 2000 BC, they invented the *shaduf*, a contraption consisting of wooden poles that swivel from upright posts. Each pole has a large bucket on one end and a balancing weight on the other. The upright post of each pole is six feet further up the bank than its predecessor and it scoops water into and out of a series of pools dug into the bank at each level.

Centuries later the *sakiyeh* (water wheel) driven by oxen or camels made things even more efficient and allowed local farmers greater productivity.

In the nineteenth-century struggle between British troops and Islamic forces based far upriver, army generals such as Gordon and Kitchener powered their fuel-hungry Nile paddle steamers by breaking up *sakiyehs* for firewood in a land where wood was, and still is, as rare as gold dust.

The dejected-looking Scotsmen sadly drove north, and we followed our goons on towards El Minya, passing through intermittent roadblocks. Mike drooled at the various panoramas and exotic scenes he would have liked to stop and photograph, but we feared this would annoy our escort, the key to our progress through an otherwise forbidden land. So sly snapshots through the window were all that Mike could capture.

We came to El Minya by dusk and slept in the yard of a local school with a police detachment to whom our goons delivered us, receiving a signature from the station commander to record our safe delivery into his Governorate.

In the morning a police captain said that, if we left our vehicles with his men, we could hire a taxi to see the local sights while waiting for the escort that would take us further south. Mike and Anthony, happy as sandboys, loaded their cameras. El Minya taxis turned out to be Victorian-era hansom carriages with polished brass lanterns harnessed to noble-looking black Arab horses.

At the taxi rank on a shelving Nile beach, cabbies were lovingly washing their horses down with handfuls of sand as they stood knee-deep in the fast flowing river.

'You like English speak guide? Pay extra?' We did, and another Mohammed appeared from nowhere whose accent was that of Inspector Clouseau in the *Pink Panther*. He was well versed in Nile lore and, over coffee after a fascinating tour in three cabs, he gave us a rambling talk.

There were always, he explained, three types of boat on the Nile: the *felucca* used for haulage like European river barges and for fishing; dhows, used as taxis and for every task under the sun; and lastly, not including paddle steamers, the cumbersome *dahabiyas*. These were made from the hardest of woods, the Egyptian sunut tree, and were crewed by Nubians in smart uniforms. Nile tours were in vogue with wealthy Victorian families, habitués of the Orient Express, indulging in floating house parties and romantic honeymoons which often turned sour in the heat, thus providing excellent source material for Agatha Christie's murder tales.

Under gently flapping sails these houseboat tubs would schmooze majestically upriver until the breeze died down, whereupon the lower echelons of the crew plus local labour as necessary would harness themselves to long towlines and plod along the hot and dusty banks, their rhythmic chants blending with the on-board murmur of posh gossip.

Mohammed told us that there were no piranha in his river. 'Bad for tourists,' he explained. But there were plenty of ghost-like moonfish who, from time to time, drown sinners who dare to go swimming. They can be seen at certain times streaking through the water with their spiked backs gleaming. They can inflate themselves and produce a fart-like noise, audible from a long distance, when they deflate. Swimmers should also beware of the eel-like Nile malapterurus which can deliver a stunning shock. This creature has legs and lungs and could presumably enjoy time on land if it wished.

Crocodiles and hippos, Mohammed added, were both common all the way to the Delta and the sea until well after the time of Christ. They were worshipped as gods but hunted by Pharaohs. One King of the Hyksos once ordered that all hippos near to his palace should be killed as their nocturnal roars were ruining his sleep.

Since Russian engineers had begun the building of the Aswan Dam, the resultant lake, named Lake Nasser of course, had grown wider each year and had formed a barrier down-river into which no crocodile or hippo could venture.

'This,' said Mohammed, looking genuinely sad, 'is bad for tourism.' But he waxed ecstatic about the unbeatable taste of the local Nile perch. 'In Uganda and up there – ' he waved to the south – 'the perch are giants, but their taste ... *N'yurgh!*'

I failed to recognize the expletive, and asked him if it was Arabic.

'No, sir, it is not Arab and I am not Arab. I am Egyptian. Very few Egyptian people are Arab. They come here only maybe one thousand years ago. We are from the people *before* the Pharaohs.'

Our cabs took us then to Abu Mengal, eight miles in all of underground burial chambers, including many thousands of coffins containing mummified baboons and ibises, the revered creatures of the pharaonic god Thoth.

From Minya a new escort, even more sullen than the previous lot, led us south past Assiut, Sohag and Qena. In between towns the land was rich in orange and citrus groves with a multitude of lovingly designed clay cotes with windows and ledges for the doves that fertilized the crops.

Breeze-waving palm trees bordered fields of cotton and sugar cane. Waterwheels clattered and children splashed merrily in disease-riddled stagnant pools. Several of the little girls who came to stare at us had eyes glazed by trachoma.

At the village of Samhud our escort stopped and their commander was given a handset by his signaller. There was clearly an emergency for he told me abruptly, 'You go on.'

'On?' I was puzzled.

'Yes. Yes.' He pointed upriver. 'In Qena more police for you. We busy.'

So, for the first time we located our road maps. Nick navigated and we took a wrong turning which led us deep up a labyrinthine network of sugar cane lanes. Turning our convoy around was a major exercise, but eventually, and briefly free of any escort, we fetched up in Qena.

Qena means black country, for it was here that the Pharaohs' engineers mined the hard black stone found nowhere else. Qena's clay was also known to be superior, and all Egypt's waterwheel buckets in pre-metal days were once fashioned here. We had to cross the Nile near Qena by one of two bridges. The Nag Hammadi bridge had recently been demolished by Israeli commandos, and we were met at the other by a new escort. For some reason, this lot actually smiled at us. Peter found this sinister ... like crocodiles smiling.

The bridge was floored with wooden planks for lorries down one side and with a railway line on the other. Eight hours after our arrival and with thanks to over forty bridge guards with slung rifles, plus, reluctantly, our escort policemen, we managed to manoeuvre our trailers (which were both too wide and too low-slung for the available width and height of the rails) on to and over the bridge.

The Qena police dropped us off at night at the apparently unmanned police station of Luxor. Uncertain whether or not we would again need to map-read, we unrolled our main Nile map on the dirt floor of the police compound. It was an impressive sight, for the roll-up map showing the Nile from its Mediterranean estuary to its Lake Victoria source was 18 feet long.

We discussed our progress to date against the red marks I had previously made on the map, noting vital dates at key points if we were to keep ahead of the sandstorm season in the Nubian Desert and the first rains in South Sudan which would quickly block all further vehicular progress for eight months. We agreed that we were a week behind schedule, but, once out of Egypt, we should be able to catch up.

A dark shadow fell across the map. Four armed police gazed down at us and their boss reached down for the map. He rolled it up and pointed into the police station, the lights of which he switched on. Other police ransacked our gear.

Our interrogation was slow and confusing, since it depended entirely on my Omani Arabic and hand-waving by all present.

In short we were told that we would be arrested, that our radios were like those of the Israelis, and that the hovercraft mission was a clever disguise for our spying activities. Why did our map, which showed all the Nile countries, only have extensive pencil marks and numbers alongside the Egyptian Nile?

Because, I explained, we made the marks only when we reached the relevant places, since they were our records of progress to date.

The interrogation was a relaxed affair compared with that which I had undergone three years previously during SAS training in Wales, and it ended with our dismissal, complete with all our papers and equipment, except for our main map which the police annoyingly retained.

We were told to leave our vehicles in the compound until our new escort arrived the next evening. Meanwhile, we were welcome to tour Luxor. Hiring a guide, we spent the day imbibing quaint stories about Pharaohs, their tombs, their mummies, their murals and their animal gods.

At sunset our escort duly arrived and led us past the Narrows of Silsileh, where the river was but 85 yards wide at low flood and where Pharaohs once prayed (begged) for a high flood level the following year.

Such prayers (by Cairo's modern Pharaohs) are no longer necessary, thanks to the Aswan Dam which, since its completion in 1970, ensures a predictable water level in the Delta and an extra million acres of arable land in Egypt as a whole.

The dam was impressively huge and was soon to become the largest in the world. Arriving at the police headquarters, our equipment was again checked item by item, as were our papers. From unseen police cells we heard intermittent screams, but we were more worried by the news that we could, under no circumstances, drive the 200 miles of desert from Aswan to the Sudan border at Wadi Halfa because all usable tracks had over the previous few months been submerged under the rising river waters. We must travel on board a

barge towed by a tramp-steamer which we must meet at the temporary loading ramp at Shellal, twelve miles south of the dam.

Peter's diary, 2 March: *To the surprise of the many East European
technicians and to our great relief we passed through the Aswan
rocket base and into Aswan town where we were to load our vehicles onto the ferry. Here we were met with great ceremony due to
an extraordinary incident at the Sudanese shipping office in Cairo.
Ran had been accused of presenting a forged passport to the super-
visor who exclaimed that he knew the real Sir Ranulph
Twisleton-Wykeham-Fiennes because he was his soldier servant in
1942.*

At Shellal, the good news was that a boat would leave for Wadi
Halfa in twenty-four hours, and the bad news was that its barges
took passengers and camels but not cars of any size.

A sizeable wad of piastres and several cartons of Marlboro cigarettes persuaded the ferry's skipper, whose entire face appeared to
consist of a nose embedded in a beard, to load all our machines onto
one of his barges 'if Allah permits'.

Allah took the form of an ingenious loading procedure devised by
Peter, plus the sweating efforts for several hours of a great many
Nubians in white robes, five German students and two Californian
hippies who thought that hovercraft were 'dead cool'.

Baker was the last unit to be force-fed onto the barge and ended
up with its hull protruding well over one side of its parent vessel.

As with many expeditions, cliques form and our group total of six
worked well. Nick and Peter, Charles and me, Mike and Anthony, left
no 'outsider' to feel awkward.

When the tugboat tooted its departure, we all lined the deck of our
barge and prayed that *Baker* would not fall off its precarious perch.
When we reached the lakeside village of Wadi Halfa (Green Valley)
the hovering would begin. Meanwhile, we were thankful to have all
but escaped from the uncertainties of the Israeli-Egyptian conflict.
We celebrated with great quantities of tea to wash down our sponsored Horlicks rations, for dehydration was rapid following any
labour such as the manhandling of the heavy machines.

The water used by all passengers for the next three days for drinking, cooking and washing was scooped out of the lake in buckets tied to ropes. Green algae and anonymous brown slime floated in this beverage. In the lake and in all the slower moving backwaters of the Nile, there lurked the microscopic death bug, bilharzia (named after Theodor Bilharz, a contemporary of Richard Burton).

The sickness is highly unpleasant and its later stages often involve an agonizing death. There was at the time an available cure consisting of a six-month series of painful deep stomach injections, but there was no known prevention other than avoiding all skin contact with the water in an 'infected' river. In 1932 when records were first kept, 60 per cent of the population of the Egyptian Delta had a water-borne form of hookworm, and the statistics for bilharzia, although not recorded, are thought to have been similar.

Even spray from a paddle can contain the bilharzia parasites, and if a droplet settles on human skin and sunlight causes the spray to evaporate, the parasite will burrow through the skin's pores to escape the heat. They then make their way slowly to the liver of their new host where they feed and breed, and a new cycle of worms will leave the body in excreta. Once back in a river, pond or canal, the worms use water snails as their host bodies. At this stage they are most vulnerable to destruction by spray from an aircraft or, as we were keen to demonstrate, a hovercraft.

On Lake Nasser, or Lake Nubia as most Sudanese called it, we used our water filtration pump bottle to prepare water to drink. Unfortunately an altercation between Nick and Anthony some weeks later ended with one hitting the other with our only filtration bottle, which was broken beyond any hope of repair. So, thereafter, we drank unfiltered Nile water, bugs and all.

Bilharzia, otherwise known as schistosomiasis, is a waterborne disease occurring in most tropical countries and currently afflicting over 200 million people worldwide. It is caused by any of three species of flukes, called schistosomes, and is acquired by bathing or wading in infested lakes, rivers and irrigation systems. Schistosome eggs are passed from an infected population into water and are particularly prevalent in the waters of the Nile valley in Egypt. The eggs develop into tadpole-like creatures known as cercariae which enter the human body, usually under finger and toe nails. Once in the bloodstream they mature into adult worms. Complications of long-term infestation can cause liver cirrhosis, bladder tumours and kidney failure.

Since the 1980s, treatment of the disease has been revolutionized by a single dose of a drug known as praziquantel, which kills the flukes and prevents damage to internal organs. However, back in 1969 such remedies were unknown.

Nick described his treatment in a letter to me some time after the end of the expedition.

Our water purifying kit involved pouring the water into an open receptacle, waiting up to a quarter of an hour as the liquid filters through gauzes which filtered out the various contaminants, drip by drip, until you have sufficient purified water for a cup of tea. I'm afraid that patience was a virtue that I wasn't born with, and I noticed that the purified water didn't look or taste much different from the unpurified water. There is an old Arab saying that he who drinks the water of the Nile will always return. Reasoning that you have to be alive to return and no mention had been made of purifying kits, I decided it must be reasonably safe to drink the water straight from the river.

After the end of the expedition some six weeks later and on returning to the UK we were all checked out for the early signs of such diseases as Malaria, sleeping sickness, etc., and to my utter amazement I was diagnosed with Bilharzia.

I was admitted to the Royal Hospital for Tropical Diseases in St Pancras, London. The then cure for Bilharzia was the injection of 10cc of some drug directly into the stomach through the muscles of the abdomen. For someone of my age and fitness, such an exercise was difficult to perform if I was conscious as I would automatically tense and tighten up, so they decided to give me a general anaesthetic and I was admitted to a ward.

The next door bed was occupied by a poor fellow who had

just returned from Africa with a tapeworm. Tapeworms, sometimes called cestodes, are parasitic worms which live in human and animal intestines, are ribbon-shaped and can grow up to 30 feet long. They are usually contracted by eating under-cooked meat or fish. The worm has suckers or hooks on its head which attach to the wall of the intestine.

My poor friend was naturally permanently hungry, and the highlight of every day was the arrival of his breakfast, lunch and dinner. The meals were served by two nurses, and the routine was the same. The meal would arrive, and my friend would attack his with gusto, and then, having finished in record time, his hand would shoot up and he would ask for more. The two nurses would reply in unison, 'You can't have *any* more.'

As the days went by, my poor friend got thinner and thinner and the tapeworm got longer and longer, until one morning we were all surprised to see him emerge from his bedclothes and slowly shuffle out of the ward. A couple of minutes later we were amazed to see our skeletal friend arrive back in the ward, dancing with glee. 'I've got rid of it,' he cried, 'come and see.' We all trooped out of the ward and headed for the lavatories, and stared in amazement at the worm. It resembled tagliatelle and had completely filled the bowl of the lavatory, and had even spilled out onto the floor. An incredible sight which I will never forget.

We were both discharged from the hospital that same day and celebrated by having a slap-up dinner at the Ritz.

As the level of the lake rose annually, various landmark antiquities and tombs were submerged, but a few were saved by expensive relo-cation to a height that the lake would not reach. The most famous of these were the twin temples and statues of Abu Simbel. From my 'bed' on the front seats of the AA Land Rover, I spotted the lights of the archaeologists at work across the moonlit waters of the lake, the third largest man-made lake on Earth.

On the third day as we neared Wadi Halfa we were surrounded by desert wasteland for hundreds of miles in every direction. Sudan is a vast country with, at the time, only four million scattered inhabitants. We crossed the unmarked border and beached in shallows in the dark. Bullfrogs and chanting from the nearby unseen Customs hut vied with the leaden heat to keep me from sleeping. But it felt good to have left Egypt behind and to have entered Africa's largest and most mysterious land.

CHAPTER 8

To Please the President

Our fellow passengers, encumbered only with hand luggage, clambered off the barges or the tugboat into a rowing boat that took them from the anchor point and over the shallows to the beach and Wadi Halfa's Customs shed.

Leaving the ever-practical Peter with the seemingly intractable problem of unloading, I waded ashore and shook hands with the immaculately dressed Customs officer who had been warned by telegram of our arrival, and to whom Ginny had, a month back, sent a list of our equipment. His office, a prefab shack, was two miles away from the current tugboat 'terminal' at the ever-moving site of Wadi Halfa village. We drove there in his ancient Dodge by way of vague dirt tracks and, after stamping my papers and passport, he introduced me to the Commissioner, Sayyid Ibrahim. Like everything else in Wadi Halfa, his shack was only temporary, moving each year away from the ever-rising lake edge. The total rise to date since the dam's inception was 158 metres, and a further 26 metres was expected before completion. Then a permanent village would be built on the site of an existing station on Kitchener's old railway line to Khartoum.

Lovingly painted murals decorated Ibrahim's plasterboard walls, depicting the old Wadi Halfa before it was submerged. Less than a decade ago, tourists from all over the world had flocked to see the unique oasis town of verdant gardens where exotic fruits and flowers grew in the shade of palm trees, yet where, around its abrupt oasis perimeter, barren deserts stretched in all directions and long-forgotten bedu trails marked with the sun-bleached skeletons of camels led to nowhere.

The huge economic benefits of the dam have gone entirely to the Egyptians. They did make a payment to the Sudanese government in faraway Khartoum of £15 million to compensate for their lost land, but a mere pittance of this total had reached the Wadi Halfa inhabitants who lost their homes.

Sudanese Army units were sent to Wadi Halfa in 1958 to forcibly evict the population and to rehouse them in faraway Kassala Province, where they were to be trained as farmers.

A handful of determined Wadi Halfans, all Nubians, refused to leave their desert homes and, once their oasis was under water, they lived entirely by fishing, since nothing would grow in the sand. 'We are a proud people,' said Ibrahim, his chest rising as he spoke. 'We are the golden people – *Nub* means gold.'

Ibrahim and his tenacious fellow diehards called themselves the Guardians of the Border, for they mistrusted their land-hungry Egyptian neighbours and believed that the correct frontier of the Sudan should be back north at Aswan, as once it was.

'If we had all gone to Kassala,' Ibrahim commented, 'what would have stopped the Egyptians moving in here? There are no border markers in the desert.'

From his briefcase, Ibrahim produced a recent copy of the *Daily Telegraph* with the headline, 'Concern for Nile Expedition'. Nothing had been heard of our whereabouts for two weeks and the authorities had become alarmed. No telephones were working at the time, but Ibrahim assured us that as soon as he could he would send off telegrams to inform the Foreign Office and our families of our continued existence.

His other news was that the President and the entire Supreme Court of Sudan were to attend our proposed hovercraft demonstration in Khartoum on 14 March. This gave us exactly seven days to hover and/or drive the course of the Nile for a thousand miles, so I told Ibrahim that we must leave just as soon as we could unload from the barge.

Peter had devised a cunning system of winches, pulleys and ramps which, together with a good deal of Nubian muscle power, managed to unload all our machines with minimal damage either to them or to the side of the barge.

Charles, in long khaki shorts known as 'empire-builders' and green wellington boots, fixed propeller units to the steerage systems, filled fuel tanks and checked the edges of the hover-skirts for splits. Then, starting all six engines without trouble, he and Peter purred (not roared) off towards the far bank of the river, which was over a mile away.

Hover-Air had calculated that a distance of 105 nautical miles could, in theory, be covered by the two Hawks before they would need refuelling by the Land Rover group. They could only carry a load of either two adults or one adult and three jerrycans of fuel.

It was agreed that we must split up our two amateur mechanics, so Charles would skipper one Hawk while Peter drove a Land Rover.

Anthony with his cine camera would sit beside Charles in the leading Hawk, and I would follow with a load of three cans strapped in beside me. Nick and Mike would crew the AA Land Rover. All seemed happy with this and, bidding farewell to Ibrahim, our two groups set off, one into the desert and the other up the Nile.

I kept some distance behind the other Hawk because any ripple on the surface affected the hover-speed. Clusters of black rocks sped past the side windows of the cockpit. The speedometer showed a steady speed of 25 mph. Soon after dawn the great red orb of the sun rose above the desert horizon and another scorching day began. Stiflingly hot in the cabin, I tried sliding a side window open, but instantly regretted doing so due to the bilharzia-laden spray that was sucked inside the cabin and all over me.

I tried the walkie-talkie linked to Charles, but heard only crackle on all frequencies. Our HF radio which could be used to speak to Peter was packed in a waterproof container and out of reach. The hovercraft could not simply stop in mid-lake, and the river was still a mile wide. It must land because once the hover-skirt sinks down 'off the hover', it fills with water and the 200cc lift engine has too little power to clear the water out of the skirt to allow the machine to hover again.

I found myself scanning the nearest bank at all times to try and spot and record any shelving beach with a gentle slope just in case there was a breakdown and a sudden need for a landing site.

At some point we passed the village of Sumna, an isolated oasis like Wadi Halfa but not yet fully submerged, where we dodged between the tops of palm trees, minarets and crenellated rooftops. I counted some forty locals waving from the beach beyond the submerged village, but saw no shack or tent.

One of *Baker*'s drive motors gave up the ghost at midday, but with enough of a spluttering warning to enable Charles to beach before total breakdown. He told me that he could fix it and, since we did not need to reach our planned rendezvous with Peter at the village of Akasha, 150 miles away, until the next day, we decided to camp where we were, close to the point where the Second Cataract had once rushed by the Temple of Bohein, erstwhile headquarters of a Nubian Empire that ruled all of Egypt and part of Libya in 750 BC. The Great Temple of Bohein had been partially saved from being submerged and was then resurrected in a Khartoum Museum, thanks to a UNESCO grant and the foresight of the Sudan Antiquities Service's founder, the archaeologist Naj Madun. I met and interviewed him in Khartoum that summer, by which time he confirmed, with well-deserved pride, that his teams had saved over 90 per cent of all the sites of great archaeological value along the Nubian Nile.

We slept well on our mats without mosquitoes, there being no stagnant water for miles, and we did not use our sleeping bags due to the heat. I heard in the scrub all around us the rustling of rats. Ibrahim had warned us that close to the lake's edge there lived many lizards, scorpions, rattlesnakes and other vipers, even desert wolves. 'And crocodiles?' I asked him. 'Of course,' he replied, 'they are one of the gods of the Nile.'

After breakfast Charles fixed his faulty engine and fiddled with the knobs of our radio until Peter's voice came over sounding tired. After watching us depart he had collected a local guide who had made his name in the pre-dam days and in the immediate vicinity of Wadi Halfa. His name was Ali, and Peter did not beat about the bush in summarizing his ability as a guide. 'Pathetic.'

Within two or three miles of Wadi Halfa, the sandy track petered out and gave way to a plethora of disconnected tyre marks half-buried by blown sand, through which the Land Rovers roared and slithered in second gear. The low suspension and small wheels of the trailers, unladen though they were, often dragged through the sand like ploughs.

'The hovercraft,' said Mike, his voice clear in the background, 'were a mistake. They will cause nothing but trouble with their stupid trailers—'

'I heard that, Mike,' I cut in, 'and I'm sure you're right, but you need to remember that they are also the only reason that we've been allowed to get this far.'

By midday, Peter said, the heat had become unbearable as they pushed and hauled the trailers one by one through each new soft patch. Frequent stopping and starting caused strain on the clutch of the older vehicle, and this began to overheat, so they had tried driving after sundown. This had proved even more difficult since, in the trackless wilderness, the low ground tended to take them away from the Nile due to a west-east barrier of broken hills with cul-de-sacs at every turn.

By midnight they had completed seventy miles, less than half of which were in the correct direction. Ali had admitted that he had no idea where they were. The clutch on Peter's vehicle burnt out. He could not be certain that a usable track to Akasha actually existed now that the old riverside route was submerged, for even the AA had been unable to ascertain this when asked. Peter advised that, if we were to make it on time to the Presidential demonstration, we must cut our losses at once, repair his clutch and catch the next available steam train from Wadi Halfa to Khartoum. That way we might still just make it.

I saw his logic, and agreed, since we probably had just enough fuel to turn around and hover back to Wadi Halfa. If we did the Khartoum demo satisfactorily, we should get Presidential blessing and could then commence our journey up the White Nile on schedule in order to beat the rainy season.

Anthony, who had successfully filmed our hovering, was ambivalent as to our next step, but being of a naturally provocative nature he commented that our two hovercraft were in a huge lake with a storm brewing and visibility verging on nil. Two-foot-high waves were already lashing our beach and we were not entirely sure that we had enough fuel to make it back to Wadi Halfa, even if we had no further breakdowns hovering over the now choppy surface of the lake. Meanwhile, he added, our Land Rover group was broken down somewhere in the Nubian Desert without a guide and with their outward tracks likely to be covered over quickly by blowing sand. 'A right balls-up,' was his crude summary. At that point I mistakenly thought that things could only get better.

Somehow, over the next two days and nights, we did get both hovercraft back to Wadi Halfa, at one point having to abandon Anthony on a remote rocky headland where he was scared witless by three four-foot-long horny-backed lizards with teeth. He made for high ground and failed to film the monsters, to his subsequent regret.

Back in Wadi Halfa, Ibrahim said that there was one old Nubian ex-guide named Tawfiq who might be able to locate Peter's lost convoy without having to call up a military helicopter from Khartoum, should one be available with Presidential blessing.

Tawfiq proved to be as successful as Ali was useless and, despite having to conduct his search largely in the dark with blowing sand, he managed to find the convoy. The members of the team were highly relieved to see him, for they were firmly convinced that they were way off route.

Back in Wadi Halfa, they had little to say of their nightmare experience, wanting only to sleep well away from the great heat of the Sumna Bowl and the stinging, blinding sand.

Through sheer good luck, a train was due to call at Wadi Halfa the following day with some open rolling stock bound for Khartoum, and this train would get us to Khartoum just in time for our date with the President. To celebrate our brief stay in his district, Ibrahim organized for the local football team to come to our Nile-side camp that night with their Nubian drums and best dancers.

Anthony set up his tripod and Peter unearthed a bottle of Glenfiddich. Mike was busy preparing a makeshift source of light by which, after the dancing started, he could take atmospheric photos. This involved pouring petrol into a ten-gallon drum which he had half-filled with sand. As he was pouring neat petrol from a full jerrycan into this sand container, the resulting fumes ignited. The dull thud of exploding fumes was followed instantly by screams from Mike who, wearing nothing but shorts like the rest of us, was a ball of flames. He dropped the jerrycan which, by sheer good luck, he had almost emptied. Leaving whatever we were doing, three of us rushed towards him. He ran blindly from side to side, screaming and wildly clawing at his head. He appeared to be alight from knees to hair, and due to spillage the sand around him was also on fire. We rolled him over beyond these flames and, scooping up handfuls of sand, applied them to his back and his arms.

His hands, being soaked in fuel, were the worst affected part of his body, and fresh spurts of flame flared from them even when they appeared to have been dealt with.

He eventually stopped screaming and sat up moaning, probably in shock. Great flaps of blistered skin hung in shrouds from his arms, lower thighs and stomach. Raw and bleeding patches on his back showed where our sand-rubbing had been too violent.

I wrote to Peter Loyd in 2015 to check his memories of that sorry event, and received this reply:

> Maybe I have blanked that terrible episode out of my mind. I do remember Mike starting to top up the half jerrycan cooker filled with sand that had burned itself out some time previously. Its latent heat combined with the fearsome midday sun must have caused it to reignite. The thump from the mini explosion was so unexpected that he dropped the jerrycan of petrol which splashed back onto him causing an immense fireball. Never have I run so fast to catch up with him as he fled the scene and you and I reached him together, tackling him to the ground and smothered the flames with our bodies and quantities of sand.
>
> I thought then that perhaps we should have warned him in advance of the possibility of reignition, but the original fire had been out for such a long time and I'm sure that none of us would have thought twice about topping up.

I gave him a morphine jab and applied Gentian Violet cream with paraffin gauze dressings over the larger patches of raw flesh, for the sand, in the area where we were, had for at least a year been used as a latrine, there being no plumbing in the walkabout village. As a result, the danger of infection from the sand and the immediately attentive swarms of flies was high.

Ibrahim showed us a hut that his people used as a hospital, and a local man with a basic medical kit was summoned. Mike was laid under a mosquito net to keep the flies out, but the heat was pretty unbearable and salty sweat exacerbated his open wounds. The medic told us, 'Twenty-five per cent burns. He will be okay. Train tomorrow.'

The Nubian football team danced by the light of Mike's fuel container and the throbbing beat of their goatskin drums shook the moonlit night. Some sat on the hovercraft and drummed their bare feet against the fibreglass hulls. Others danced a slowed-down version of the foxtrot in the sand, with hands clapping to the rhythm of the drums.

The train turned up on time at the desert terminus a couple of miles from the village. We loaded the vehicles and hovercraft onto two flatbed units by way of our portable ramps. Then we laid Mike out on a bench in an almost empty passenger compartment and took it in turns to mop his sweat and keep the flies away.

Ibrahim, his local helpers, Tawfiq (but not Ali) and the entire football team turned up to wave us goodbye.

The engine and carriages, according to the Sudan Rail steward who sold us tickets, came from Britain long before he was born. But, and he sounded proud, they never break down.

The compartments were like ovens if you closed the windows. If you kept them open, choking clouds of dust mixed with soot set us off coughing and wiping our eyes. Better to sweat and simmer. Mike groaned much of the time whenever the morphine effects dissipated. I fed him bananas, aiming carefully at his mouth as the train jerked from side to side.

I thought back to my SAS training about burns, but remembered little so checked in my Expedition Medical Guide to see if Mike did indeed have only 25 per cent burns and of what severity grading. The booklet suggested that:

First-degree burns involve the uppermost layer of skin. They are characterized by erythema and pain, and often heal spontaneously within a week (think sunburn). Second-degree burns may be subdivided into superficial partial thickness and deep partial thickness burns. The former extends into tissues containing glands and hair follicles. This type of burn is painful, may form blisters and weep fluid. These burns do not heal well and often result in infection and severe scarring unless skin is grafted. Third-degree burns are full-thickness and appear white or tan because there is no blood flow to the surface. They may also appear dry or charred, and are frequently painless because the nerve endings are damaged (like a cooked chicken breast). Fourth-degree burns extend into muscle and bone, and as with third-degree burns, usually require skin grafting.

Burn size is judged using the Wallace Rule of Nines. In this rule-of-thumb method, the victim's palm is equal to 1 per cent of the total burn surface area (TBSA), arms are individually worth 9 per cent, each leg is worth 18 per cent, and the front and back of the torso are also given a value of 18 per cent. It is not uncommon, even in larger hospitals to transfer a patient with burns larger than 20 per cent TBSA to a dedicated burns centre. Burns involving the feet, genitals, joints and face are equally tricky and are frequently transferred to specialists as well.

The booklet gave an example of how very bad burns can be survived far beyond normal expectations. A fighter pilot in the Battle of Britain, Tom Gleave, took over 253 Squadron the day after his predecessor was killed. His fighter was hit and one wing fuel tank caught fire. The flames grew fierce, wrapping round his feet and climbing to reach his shoulders. Plywood and fabric burst rapidly into flames around him, accelerated by fuel from the breached tanks. In a few short seconds the centre of his cockpit had become the head of a blowtorch. The aluminium sheet in which the dials of his control panel were set began to melt. But he was far too high to ditch the aircraft; there was nothing left that he could do but attempt to bail out.

Gleave was tethered to his plane by the oxygen mask attached to his helmet. He reached down to rip this from its attachment, but the searing heat beat him back. With his arms outstretched he could see that the skin of his leg was in much the same state. His arms and elbows were also burnt and the skin hung in charred folds from his hands and wrists. His head and neck too had been exposed to the inferno and his eyes were little more than slits. His nose had been all but destroyed.

Somehow, after a lucky landing, he staggered across the field towards a gate on its far side, shouting for help.

You can just about bear to hang on to a mug of hot tea at 42°C. That's just five degrees higher than your normal core body temperature; pretty unimpressive really, but that is where the limits of human endurance lie. Everything from your digestive tract to your DNA start to fall apart at 45°C. And that's where the physiology of thermal injury starts. As temperatures climb, cells lose their capacity to self-repair, vessels begin to coagulate and tissues become irreversibly altered and later begin to die. This all happens around 60°C. Aircraft fuel can burn at over 1,000°C.

Thanks to the McIndoe Burns Unit, Gleave made a full recovery. Looking at Mike I reckoned that he would be fine so long as his wounds could be cleaned up as soon as possible.

Charles and Peter planned details for our hover demonstration in two days' time, while I read a relatively informative travel manual about the Sudan. It is a country of over 900,000 square miles, which is equivalent to Italy, Belgium, Spain, France, Portugal, Scandinavia and Britain lumped together, but with less roads and rail than any one of these countries. Their most obvious line of communication, the Nile, is the longest river in the world but its waters spend seven months each year rendering nearly all tracks within 100 miles of it unusable because of flooding.

Sudan seems well placed for trade with neighbours for it shares more common borders than any other country in the world. But jungles, swamps and deserts often vie with wars and ignorance to obstruct trade altogether.

A recent British Army expedition was described in the Khartoum press as having arranged a major press conference in the city to celebrate a unique vehicle crossing of the Libyan and Nubian deserts from Kufra. The article ended by saying that they had never arrived. Perhaps they were still out there (as we might have been, but for Tawfiq).

The ticket collector, on checking my travel permits, commented, 'You plan to drive on south from Khartoum? You will be the first foreigners to go down there for a *very* long time. Indeed, I am surprised that you have received such permits at all. God's blessing be with you in those bad places.'

We stopped at Atbara and, for some reason, at Station Number Six where there was nothing but a signpost in the sand announcing STATION NUMBER SIX. Then at Berber we bought crushed dates from a platform vendor, a mile from the site of a great victory parade of General Kitchener's Anglo-Egyptian troops. Our railway line was, in my grandfather's day, pioneered by Kitchener engineers, and after Berber it heads through arid desert in a straight line, cutting out the great Nile loop with its ancient capital cities of Dongola and Meroe. River and rail rejoin at Abu Hamed and then run together all the way to Khartoum. At Atbara, once a large slave market, I checked our Land Rovers and switched the Egyptian flags attached to their mirrors for Sudanese ones. We had considered doing this at Aswan, but had forgotten in the rush.

At Khartoum's main terminal we unloaded the convoy and I called the British embassy, who sent a cab to lead us through teeming market streets to their walled compound.

The military attaché, doing a sensitive job in a country riven by civil war, took personal responsibility for our expedition and made it clear that our route would take us smack through the middle of the most active war zone. If he had had his way, we would never have received permission to head south of Khartoum, especially since two of us were serving officers. He made it clear at once that the only good 'brownie point' of our existence in the Sudan would be if all went well with the hover demonstration in front of the President the following day.

He had Mike taken by ambulance to a private clinic and then telegrammed Ginny, who arranged flight tickets for Mike and treatment by a London burns specialist. Before his departure, Mike lent me his cameras and gave me a lecture on how to use them.

The attaché had put all arrangements for the demonstration in the highly capable hands of Ali Karrar, a retired military governor of the Blue Nile Province, who had, during the recent military regime, been one of three chief ministers advising the President.

He interviewed me with much finger-wagging. I responded with much head-nodding. He understood that I was a military man and knew that I would agree to 'our' demo being run with precision. He had checked out the best place for the demo, and the weather forecast was, surprisingly, good. This was because any time now the Khartoum *haboob* season would arrive when dust clouds invade the city from the surrounding deserts. It could then become impossible, Ali stressed, to see your own hand stretched out, even on an otherwise cloudless day. No door or window can keep the fine dust out of a house, and this would be no good for our demo! 'But,' he laughed, 'tomorrow I have personally forbidden the *haboob*.'

Our machines, he said, must do exactly what he was about to explain from the moment the President and the ministers arrived. A number of those who would be in the President's entourage could directly affect our movements once we left Khartoum to travel south. The rebels down there, he frowned, had of late been receiving much external aid from 'Christian' sources with a resulting flare-up of violence in the very regions that we must pass through on the only north–south track to Uganda.

And, he added, even with full Khartoum permissions in place, we still might be stopped or arrested by local authorities who tended to be laws unto themselves. Telegraphed orders from Khartoum often received long-delayed replies due to phone wires being cut by the rebels.

Charles and Peter, armed with binoculars, accompanied Ali and me in the official car to the Nile-side site he had chosen. The Blue Nile from Ethiopia meets the White Nile from Kenya between Khartoum and its northerly suburb of Omdurman. Close to this junction and just off the Blue Nile's residential bank is Tuti Island situated in mid-river. Opposite the island Ali showed us the exact spot where the Rolls-Royce cavalcade of the President would park in order to watch their first hovercraft in action. The local media would also be out in force ... so *no* breakdowns!

Standing on a headland not far away along a riverside path, we could see the confluence of the two great rivers, the Blue Nile from the east and the White Nile from the south. Beyond this junction the town of Omdurman, with its mass of mud buildings, shimmered in the heat haze. The colour of the two rivers was a dirty brown. I gazed up the corridor of the Blue Nile as far as the overall glare allowed and I thought of the Scots explorer James Bruce who, in the 1770s, managed to locate the source of that river.

Born to a family who upheld a claim to the throne of Britain, Bruce was briefly a Consul in Algiers, but he became intrigued by the ancient tales of Herodotus. He decided to find the Blue Nile's source by way of Ethiopia's Red Sea coast. After numerous hardships he located the source, Lake Tana, 900 miles upstream of Khartoum, and the spectacular Tissisat Falls, which he placed accurately on his map. After twelve years of travel in many remote and lethal regions, he returned to Britain where King George III and various geographers of the day disbelieved his account of his travels. Only after his death in 1794, caused by a tumble downstairs and being grossly over-weight, did later travellers authenticate his stories. Dr Livingstone finally set the record straight and described Bruce as 'a greater traveller than any of us'.

Turning to my left, the wider White Nile powered into the Blue, having already flowed for 2,000 miles from the heartlands of Africa and about to speed north for another 2,000 miles to the sea.

The central building on the bank, set amid gorgeous flowering gardens, was Gordon's Palace, alongside Kitchener Avenue and a number of ministry buildings. Ali showed us a recent *Daily Telegraph* article which stated that our 'expedition was doing much to improve the friendship and goodwill between Britain and the peoples of Egypt and the Sudan'. This seemed a touch premature, but Ali looked pleased with it. He took me then to meet the key minister, the boss of the Sudan Security Police, who was clearly hostile to any foreign-ers heading south, with or without hovercraft. He and Ali conducted a heated conversation which my Omani Arabic failed to compre-hend, but as we left the building, Ali showed me his crossed fingers as a sign that things could go either way.

The great day duly arrived and Charles stationed *Burton*, the more reliable craft, on a shelving beach in Omdurman, a few minutes' hover from the demonstration site on Tuti Island. Meanwhile Peter unloaded *Baker* on the bank where the President would be parked so that he could explain to His Nibs and other interested parties the finer points of the Hoverhawk, especially its unique ability to spray in places where no land machine or aircraft could reach.

Ali, in buoyant mood, assured us that the public turnout already at the demo site promised that the event would be Khartoum's largest ever commercial demonstration.

Charles sprayed Damp Start over every working part of *Burton*. At exactly the right time, and on walkie-talkie confirmation from Peter that the President was watching, Charles revved all three engines and *Burton* slid away down the beach in a sudden cloud of camel dung spray which scattered a crowd of onlookers, and then surged into the Blue Nile with a powerful wind astern and headed for Tuti Island.

The presidential convoy had arrived dead on schedule and a military band in front of Gordon's Palace struck up as the three purple Rolls-Royces drew to a regal halt, Sudan flags flying from their bonnets. Everybody saluted (whether or not they wore hats).

The President was a little man with thick spectacles. I shook his proffered hand and then those of the three chief ministers who stood immediately behind him. They were also small.

I introduced Peter to the massed crowds by way of a loudspeaker system and by liaising with the President's interpreter.

Charles arrived on time and a murmur of anticipation rippled through the crowds. At maximum speed, Charles executed a series of 60-degree skid turns directly below the President and a line of army generals with medal-spattered uniforms.

The Hoverhawk then danced about with Peter using the radio and telling Charles what to do in response to the rapturous cheers of the onlookers.

Charles suddenly turned *Burton* towards Tuti Island and headed at 30 knots straight for its beach. The President grunted in alarm and then released an audible sigh when the machine simply left the water and roared up the island's beach, went over a couple of low sand dunes and returned to the river. A murmur of wonder, as at some magician's mysterious illusion, followed this amphibious display. So Peter told Charles to repeat it.

Half an hour of island-hopping later, Charles advised Peter that *Burton*'s drive engine was beginning to overheat and he was himself sweating like a caged pig as *Burton*'s windows were jammed shut.

Peter gave the radio's microphone to the President who said hello to Charles and congratulated him. The microphone then went from general to general, allowing each to greet Charles and tell him to exercise some order or other. One wanted Charles to reverse and another asked if the machine could dive to the riverbed.

Eventually Peter took back the microphone and ordered Charles to head back to Omdurman before he or the machine overheated.

The President and his entourage, both the military and the civilian types, thanked me and again shook hands. The President said that there was definitely a great future for hovercraft in his country and he wished us well for our continued journey south. This last blessing was music to my ears.

Within the hour the crowds, after much clambering about on and inside *Baker*, disappeared for their siesta.

A few months later a military coup overthrew the President and his government and began to display a violently anti-Western policy. A number of Khartoum-based British businessmen were jailed for 'spying activities'. But this was in the future and we cared only for the immediate moment and, specifically, to make much better mileage with speed in order to beat the imminent start of the annual rains which would quickly block any chance of us clearing the vast Sudd swamp zone of the Nile.

As we basked in the success of our demo, black thunder clouds gathered south of Khartoum.

CHAPTER 9

The Sudd

For thirty miles south of Khartoum, a low land of rolling grass-lands through which the White Nile sped to meet its Blue sister gave us an easy ride on both road and river. Then at the Jebel Aulia dam we loaded both Hawks onto the trailers and drove them to the nearest point where road met river near a usable entry beach. This was close to the camel village of Ed Dueim.

We camped where great flocks of smelly goats and families of camels waded and dipped in the shallows to drown their fleas, and where they appeared to hold their heads back to gargle with mouthfuls of filthy water.

At dusk, unlike in Nubia, the day's heat did lessen a touch, but the clammy atmosphere of high humidity made us quickly tetchy, a mood considerably aggravated by the noisy swarms of flying ants that seemed to favour attacking our eyes, nose and lips. In Arabia the desert flies usually disappeared at dusk, but not in Ed Dueim where they buzzed about, fat and slow with a potent bite.

Within a week of leaving Khartoum I nursed a number of raw spots in various parts of my body where scratches and sores had suppurated and grown into swollen areas which failed to respond to my antiseptic cream.

My finger, squashed and half-severed on exercise back in Oman, was now badly infected and, as a result, throbbed much of the time. Various open sores on my feet and ankles refused to heal, which made wearing shoes uncomfortable, and barefoot walking was inadvisable due to the omnipresent camel thorns which were needle sharp.

We propped the machines up on jerry cans, in lieu of heavy jacks. This was precarious but workable and our mechanics, Charles and Peter, wriggled underneath both Hawks with pop rivet guns to strengthen the skirts wherever river flotsam had caused tears to develop.

We woke early, boiled water for coffee and set out in order to make maximum mileage, ever mindful of the imminent rains. Soon all tracks within a hundred miles would be submerged by the swollen river, making them impassable for the next seven months. Since all our planned refuelling camps were, of course, beside the river, no Land Rovers meant no fuel for hovering. We therefore wasted no time and put up with minimal sleep.

Most nights beside the river were accompanied by an orchestra, at least till midnight, consisting of the croak of a thousand giant toads, the churr of nightjars, the beat of distant drums and the querulous hooting of marsh owls.

We came to Kosti and found a muddy spit below the road bridge, and there we waited for the Hawks. They were very late due to a sudden increase in the floating rafts of water hyacinth, over which hovering was a rapidly learnt and very necessary skill. Peter explained the problem thus: 'Because any matter that gets between the skirt and its contact with the water breaks the vacuum of the cushion of air on which the Hawk floats, you need maximum speed to traverse each new stretch of hyacinth. So you have to be constantly aware of your speed and of the exact extent of each new obstacle ahead which you can't avoid. If your speed runs out before you reach clear water beyond a given "cabbage patch" – that's what I call the hyacinth isles – you will grind to a halt enmeshed in it. Then the only way forward is to lean overboard and methodically clear away the "cabbage" by hand and bit by bit.'

Whenever we were forced to wade in the shallows, we kept an eye open for snakes and crocodiles, especially the latter. The green-eyed Nile crocodile is the biggest of Africa's twenty-three crocodilian species and accounts for as many as 200 human deaths a year, typically by exploding from the shallows to pounce on anyone on the riverbank. It is smaller than its saltwater cousin, found in Australia and south-east Asia, but none the less daunting in its dimensions. The larger of its kind will measure up to 20 feet and weigh 1,650 lbs (730 kg). When it achieves this considerable size, the crocodile will take not only fish but zebras, small hippos, wildebeest and humans. These creatures, a throwback to the age of dinosaurs, which can hold their breath underwater for two hours, are the indisputable kings of the river. But they haven't had it all their own way. During the colonial era and beyond they were hunted until populations were desperately small. Particularly prized was their rough reptilian skin used for shoes and handbags.

I hoped that the crocodiles that doubtless watched our own passage up their river and through their hunting grounds would be put off grabbing us by the noise and unusual appearance of our hovercraft. The two that I saw in the swamp zone were sunbathing on a papyrus island and looked docile. Their jaws were half open which, according to the all-knowing Charles, was to keep them cool, rather like dogs panting.

'Further upriver,' Charles added, 'in Lake Tanganyika and the Burundi region of the Ruzizi River, there is much perennial civil strife and bodies are often tossed into the river which provides a ready food source for the local crocs. In that area individuals have been measured at 25 feet long and weighing a ton.'

'Snakes,' Charles continued, 'are also at home in the river, especially where the water hyacinth attracts large frog populations. When my accountant was canoeing last year on the Ugandan Nile, she was bitten at a riverside night-stop by a black mamba. The tour guide sucked at the twin holes of the bite, but she died in less than an hour.'

Unfortunately we found parts of the river where the green weed formed barriers that stretched, with very few gaps, right across the waterway. Only Peter's admirable skill prevented him from being trapped in mid-river on many occasions. Charles said that river fishermen were increasingly worried that their industry would soon be wiped out in Tanzania, Kenya and Uganda unless some means of eradicating the floating plant (*Eichornia crassipes*) could be found. 'Maybe a larger hovercraft with spray tanks would be the answer,' he mused. 'Especially since the water trapped beneath the floating bulbs is a known breeding ground for such deadly diseases as cholera, bilharzia and malaria.' In places, when hauling a hovercraft out of the river, we had to wade through several yards of floating weed and could often walk over the solid mass of vegetation. Insects love the fetid heat and the abundance of rotting debris which provides an ideal spawning ground. Mosquitoes, giant wasps and every form of fly choke the air, and dragonflies feed off butterflies, spiders and death's head moths.

Romolo Gessi, an Italian colleague of General Gordon of Khartoum, wrote of the Sudd, 'In the dead calms in these vast marshes the feeling of melancholy produced is beyond description. The White Nile is a veritable Styx.'

Word passed around of our arrival in Kosti and in no time at all several hundred locals were climbing all over the Hawks, making it next to impossible to work on them. We decided not to camp at all until we could find a human-free area.

During the brief period we spent on the Kosti mud-spit, several rafts of the mauve-coloured flowers of the hyacinth floated up against the spit and separated the Hawks from the nearest open water by the length of a football pitch. Our attempts to charge down the spit at full speed failed dismally and merely ensnared both machines in the heavy dragging weed.

We all waded out up to shoulder level with our feet ankle-deep in glutinous Nile mud. Peter tried to start a drive motor and showered Nick and me with slime. Charles commented that we were blacker than the locals.

With the aid of a tow rope we hauled *Burton* back onto the spit and then spent several hours clearing a five-foot-wide hoverway as far out as we could wade and where the wind direction did not cause our freeway to be quickly refilled with 'cabbage'.

Charles and Peter then drove at full speed down the spit and along the freeway, managing – just – to break through the remaining weed into open water. With great relief and up to our necks in slime, we watched the two Hawks disappear upriver.

We all grew to hate the hyacinth which sticks some six inches out of the water with mauve flowers sprouting from green leaves and with bulbous stalks and roots which are buoyant and blown about in islands by the prevailing wind.

Anthony switched between the Hawks and the Land Rovers. At
Kosti the main rail track crossed the road bridge, which was too
narrow for our trailers. We blocked the rails over the plank-bridge
and waited until a lorry arrived with thirty or so hitch-hikers
bouncing about precariously on top of its cargo. Together they
managed to hoist one of our trailers above their own load and high
enough to avoid the constricting side fences of the British-made
bridge.

Nick later found a fisherman with a rowing boat nearly as big as
our remaining trailer. For money and a pack of cigarettes he agreed
to ferry our trailer over the river. So after ten hours our convoy
finally set off south from Kosti.

Peter's diary, 17 March: *Hovering had seemed remarkably easy
until we reached the first of the water hyacinth near Kosti, some
200 miles south of Khartoum. This attractive flowering weed
slowed us down so much that we couldn't get 'off the hump' – a
term given to the configuration when the friction of water is too
great to allow the craft to rise on the air cushion and therefore one
moves like a leaking boat rather than a magic carpet.*

*It was at this point that we decided to lighten the load, and I
travelled alone until the next rendezvous point some 50 miles
upriver. I was happily weaving in and out of the clumps of weed
when my starboard engine cut out, and I spun violently to the right
and half submerged. Now I really was alone, or was I?*

*In the far distance and close to the bank stood an extremely tall
and naked man with a spear, gazing intently into the water. As I
paddled slowly towards him he looked up and shouted in perfect
Queen's English, 'I think you probably have the incorrect petrol/
oil mixture for today's heat. If you have any neat petrol I'll help
you sort it out.' This was a staggering statement from someone
who could never have seen a hovercraft before. It turned out that
he was the local prince down from Oxford visiting his tribe for a
spot of fishing. 'My English friends tell me that salmon fishing is
the finest sport, but this requires far more skill.'*

*As I hovered onward to meet up with Ran, I couldn't wait to
recount my Alice in Wonderland experience.*

The days and nights passed by, a time of sores and dirt and sweat, but also of meeting interesting people. At one camp five men appeared with nigh on 300 camels. Each carried a shield, some four feet long, and a heavy broadsword slung over a shoulder. They had only to whistle for the camels to come to an obedient halt – something I had never before witnessed in Arabia.

We learnt that they were men of the Manasir, a small proud tribe from the Northern Province who wandered into the lands of certain other tribes at great risk due to deadly feuds from decades past. They knew every path by the Nile for a hundred miles in all directions, and they knew weird ways of hunting, such as training venomous snakes which they tethered near known drinking holes and allowed to bite deer, which then died. Once the poison had coagulated, the venison could be roasted and eaten.

They waved as our Hawks roared away in the morning and laughed when their camels scattered in all directions.

In the district of Renk the locals, mostly Dinka, grew isolated patches of lucerne and dourra wheat out in the scrubland where the road moved away from the river. Here the road lay beneath coats of red dust which spumed behind Nick in the lead vehicle, kicked up by his trailer and which I had constantly to wipe off my goggles.

In the isolated Dinka village of Paloich we stopped at a hut with a Coca-Cola sign and bought a meal of beans and dourra flour. There was no Coca-Cola but there were Tetley tea bags. The dourra balls were tasty and our teeth crunched on numerous raisin-like bits, which turned out to be large weevils. The tea trickled like nectar down our dust-dry throats.

At the remote hamlet of Malut near Renk village we were searched by a detachment of local Dinka police, who locked up our weapons and radios in their hut. They told us to camp in their compound for safety. The wretched-looking prisoners in the compound's lock-up, who smelt even worse than we did, watched our every move with intense concentration as though we were aliens. They chatted and spat through the long night. I found it difficult to sleep in the dark throbbing heat with the whine of mosquitoes searching for some small rent in my mosquito net or a bare limb laid carelessly close to its gauze.

Peter, who had become an expert at hovering between the omnipresent hyacinth isles, told us of large otter-like animals that played on muddy platforms amid the cabbage plants, and obese herons apparently too idle to fly, even when approached closely by a Hawk, who remained dozing on their personal hyacinth lilos and fished with a languid movement of their great beaks as they drifted along with the current.

Soon after leaving Malut, a brief but violent storm passed us by with a startling exhibition of forked lightning and thunder, enough to announce the Apocalypse from a dark grey sky.

The storm clouds soon lifted and the heat from the sun redoubled after its brief absence.

The interior of the cockpits, Peter said, felt like miniature sauna baths. Each driver and Anthony carried three pints of water at the outset of each day, but Charles, heavily built, had drunk all his water by midday and lost sweat in streams. A hand used by the driver to wipe sweat from an eye at the wrong moment when dodging between obstacles could spell a blocked Hawk, which meant the other craft also had to stop as soon as a sloping beach could be found on which to land.

After hundreds of miles with no indication that we were in the twentieth century, other than a single Coca-Cola sign, Malakal was a sudden shock with its concrete airport buildings, radio tower and high wire fencing with brightly coloured Shell/BP signs on tanker lorries. From the airport, the town itself stretched away to the south, hugging the river with shady avenues of palms.

Ancient paddle steamers were moored to crumbling piers, and gangs of children shrieked with pleasure as they dived into the river from the gaping windows of these once proud Queens of the Nile.

The majority of locals here were Shilluk, who have little or no use for clothes. Adult women often wore inadequate G-strings, well-endowed men sported only shoulder-slung spears, and teenagers as naked as monkeys congregated about us in intimate groups as we tried to work on the Hawks.

Soon after our arrival the local police chief, a Dinka but trained by the Leicestershire Police Force, came down to the river.

His predecessor in Malakal, who was British, had been drowned with his wife when caught in a local storm while boating.

'No photographs of naked people,' the police chief told me. 'They can be used as propaganda by our enemies down south.' He did not expand on this, but I warned Anthony to be careful when filming.

'But,' he observed, 'I need people in the film and I can't tell them to get dressed.'

I agreed and left it at that.

The police chief wanted an official demonstration which would be seen as having been organized by him. We agreed to provide one on the only gently shelving bank not hemmed in by hyacinth platforms. This was a muddy slope between lines of anchored paddle steamers.

While the police chief sent his runners to villages in the neighbourhood and to all the local suburbs, we drove the Land Rovers to the demo site where Peter and Charles filled up with fuel. Our plan was to head south by river and road immediately after the demo and with an armed road escort promised to us by the police chief 'because,' he stressed, 'the enemy are active immediately south of town. They may do nothing for days, and then they attack our outposts, mine the tracks and lay ambushes in the forests.'

On the face of it the government forces were in control all the way to the Ugandan border, but lone enemy machine gunners could, and did, annihilate entire convoy groups while avoiding major conflicts with the Sudanese Army. The larger rebel units kept to the swamp country and to more remote forests.

On the muddy bank beside the Land Rovers, great bundles of hippopotamus hides in long thin slices were being rolled into temporary hyena-proof storage shelters by naked Shilluks, their faces, necks and shoulders scarred with tribal cicatrices. Trotting about among these workers were Arab supervisors in clean white robes, armed with notebooks and taking tally of the hides, and higher up the bank they were sifting and weighing sacks of dourra grain.

For several hours before the announced time of our demonstration, groups of locals arrived on the bank and stood about gossiping. Some climbed the great neem trees that overlooked the river, others boarded the paddle steamers, and an ever-deepening crowd lined the roped-off space for our vehicles and the Hawks which the police had thoughtfully erected to give us a place for preparatory work at the launch site.

By the time our police chief arrived to a drum beat, which quietened the din of the crowds, many hundreds of onlookers were massed around our patch.

Anthony had mounted his tripod on the roof of the AA Land Rover and was busily filming everything, including the groups of men wearing the colourfully plumed bush hats of the Sudanese Army. Five steamers had arrived that morning from the south with soldiers on leave from the war zone.

I heard the roar of the Hawks starting up and left the police chief, who was chatting to various VIPs and army men, and shouldered my way to the Hawks via many a bouncing breast and other such obstacles. Peter gave me a walkie-talkie, slammed his cockpit door shut and powered away down the bank, covering me and many onlookers in mud and slime.

Ecstatic cheering and a much repeated expletive, which sounded like an orgasmic '*Wau*', greeted each aerobatic manoeuvre of the two Hawks, waltzing between hyacinth rafts and skimming ever closer to the hulls of the paddle steamers at top speed.

Many onlookers sat on overhanging tree branches, which bent ever lower under their weight. Others waded, or were pushed by those behind them, into the shallows.

I joined Anthony up on the cab roof, from where I could see the full size of the crowd. I estimated that some two thousand onlookers were pushing forward to get a better view of the Hawks. Dinka were there in groups, as were Nuer, Shilluk and the lighter-skinned Azande.

I shouted into my walkie-talkie telling Peter to do his first fast landing up the bank into our cordoned-off area. To the crowd it would look like a disaster, since boats don't normally charge land at speed.

Everything then happened at once. Peter accelerated towards us, the police lost control of the great crowd as it surged forward, and the muddy landing zone was suddenly crawling with naked children more or less the same colour as the mud.

Peter had his windscreen wipers on as usual in order to clear the spray from his front window. Since by now the spray was muddy, he could see very little detail and failed to spot the children dead ahead on the landing beach. He carried on.

Peter's diary, 21 March: *I gave a demonstration of the hovercraft's abilities to a large crowd at Malakal before we attempted to navigate the Great Sudd. As I was coasting fast into the landing space kept clear by whip-handling police, the crowd broke through and rushed excitedly towards me. It being impossible to stop dead in a hovercraft, I found myself in amongst them, knocking them over like ninepins. I couldn't turn off my lift engine for fear of squashing someone, but the weight of people on the side pushed me down on top of some little boys flattened in the rush. This rather blackened my day as an eight year old got caught under one skid and was badly hurt.*

I caught a glimpse of Peter's horrified expression pressed close to the windscreen as he swung his steering wheel wildly in a vain attempt to avoid the bodies he now saw immediately ahead.

I heard screams and howls of pain above the clamour of the crowd. I jumped off the Land Rover and fought my way to the waterside and the Hawk. Peter had cut the drive motors but had left the lift motor going so as not to sink down into the mud. He had, by his last-minute manoeuvre, managed to avoid a closely packed group of children, but had scooped up some smaller boys and dragged them into the thick black mud beneath the machine's skirt.

Nick joined me to scrabble in the slime, as did three policemen. Others tried to keep the crowd and anxious parents from pressing forward.

One policeman felt a small arm and pulled its owner out, still alive but bleeding badly from various cuts. A second boy was found and pulled onto the bank. He was vomiting, badly shocked and missing one ear which had been torn off.

The crowd began to chant in anger and the police, using short rhino whips, tried to disperse them.

With admirable speed, an old Peugeot van with a red cross on its side and with blue light flashing and klaxon clanging arrived on the scene. Three or four children were carried into the vehicle, and as it departed two policemen openly apprehended Peter, presumably to keep angry onlookers from attacking him.

The injured children were inspected at the hospital as we waited, and a new police officer, with impressive rank stripes on his uniformed shoulders, introduced himself as Inspector Achmed. He told us that Peter was under arrest and would be taken at once to the Malakal Police Station, while he, Achmed, would decide what to do with him. We should report to the police compound at once with all our convoy in order to avoid a possible Dinka lynch mob, as most of the injured children were of that tribe.

During a long wait for Achmed's decision, we debated what we should do if Peter was sentenced to a jail term. Should we stay in Malakal to ensure that every effort was made to have him released and at least make sure that he was looked after and fed until he was released? That course would almost certainly condemn our already slim chances of following the Nile to its source because of the necessity of getting to the south of the swamp zone before the imminent rains submerged the river tracks.

I am ashamed to relate that the unofficial vote was that we would do our utmost to use our Khartoum contacts in the Sudanese government to have Peter repatriated to England, while the rest of us carried on south to complete the expedition.

Late that night Achmed appeared looking stressed. He had, it transpired, consulted long and hard with the local public prosecutor and a prominent Malakal Justice of the Peace. Together they had searched the relevant law books (still those of the previous British Administration) and had been unable to locate any law which dealt with hovercraft.

'The accident,' Achmed summarized, 'was caused neither by a boat nor by a road vehicle, and since the British neglected to establish any legislation against hovering vehicles, we have telegraphed Khartoum to make a decision.'

Achmed explained that the law has to be seen to be especially fair in the south because the majority of the barristers are from the north and are therefore suspected of being government stooges. The law, due to an alarmingly high death rate from traffic accidents on the narrow muddy tracks in and around Malakal, was habitually strict with offenders and was wont to hand out stiff sentences.

Achmed had, however, now been advised by Khartoum that he had done well to publicize the arrest of the British pilot, which should satisfy any potential objectors. To our great relief he then announced that, since no existing law had been transgressed, Peter would be quietly and immediately released from jail and, with our armed escort, we must leave Malakal at once. Under no circumstances would it be safe for us to hover between Malakal and the Ugandan border, and there was every possibility that we would have to abandon all our vehicles over the next fortnight, depending on the timing of the rains and enemy activity. If that happened, our escort commander would decide what to do with us. Vehicles bogged in the Sudd would be un-boggable for at least seven months. Within a fortnight at most, the whole area would be a vast lake bigger than England.

Our escort lorries would be the very last government convoy to head south that year. We left Malakal that night with a highly relieved Peter, who would long remember his memories of his 'time in a Sudanese prison'.

Steamers could reach Juba, the military headquarters of the Sudanese Army on the southern edge of the Sudd, in less than a week from Malakal once a navigable post-rains route through the Sudd swamp zone was established. A century before, Nile explorers had been considered extremely lucky to do the same journey in a month.

The river between Fenikang and Bor Forest is up to 21 miles wide in places, even during the dry season, and even when nobody tries to kill you en route it is one of the most inhospitable, hostile places on Earth.

Not even the very best river pilots who have traversed the length of the river many times after a long apprenticeship would be entirely confident of the best route, since the main watercourse is forever changing. A single storm can, in a few hours, alter the geography of the river by sundering great islands of rotting vegetation and forming new obstacles by submerging reeds, ambatch and cabbage under others during the passing of mini bore waves, crushing animals in the process.

Dead hippos, elephants and even crocodiles float by the steamers, their bodies bloated in the suffocating heat, and herds of deer starve to death on floating islands that were previously joined to the mainland.

Hour after hour the potholed tracks that our Land Rovers followed led through bush country where no animal, bird or human was to be seen although, in a clearing, Achmed pointed out an overgrown Dinka rain shrine.

Most of the southern tribes are pagan, he explained, despite ongoing attempts by Khartoum to Islamize them. They believe in the power of appointed rainmakers to bring the rains whenever they are needed, so they treat them almost like gods except when they fail in their job and then the Dinka and Shilluk murder them, usually during an unusually long drought when they bury them alive or strangle them very slowly with ropes of plaited reed.

The Madi tribe roast bad rainmakers over embers and collect their body fat for use as a medicine, while the Bari lash their unsuccessful rainmakers to tree roots, cut open their bellies and allow birds to peck out their entrails.

Rain arrived at first in showers and then as a steady downpour. The track followed by our convoy quickly became as slippery as though it had been coated in grease. The lorry drivers were experienced and the large wheels on most of their vehicles were designed to cope with mud. Nonetheless, our convoy leader looked highly stressed and allowed no stops or any overnight rest. The soldiers, high on the lorry loads and huddled miserably together over dripping sub-machine guns, glared at us understandably each time we were the cause of a new delay.

One of the trailer suspensions snapped, so we abandoned it and helped twenty of the soldiers heave *Baker* high up on to the top of a load of petrol cans.

Progress was often only possible in first gear and four-wheel-drive through the quagmire of orange mud.

At four a.m. one night our convoy commander halted on a rare bit of high ground. This was Mogoch, and its five occupants assured us that the track would rapidly deteriorate to the south. We were still in Dinka territory, but near Mogoch, a sub-tribe of theirs, the Than, lived in the Sudd all year round on elevated patches of reed with fish and hippo meat for food.

Nine miles short of Bor we entered a dark forest, a notorious centre of activities by the Anya Nya rebel army who demanded independence from the Khartoum government. They were well armed by many countries and by their Christian neighbours in Uganda, as well as by various worldwide Roman Catholic movements.

In a clearing just before entering the forest, the convoy stopped, everyone jumped to the ground and the commander ordered all weapons to be loaded and cocked.

Achmed prepared his Sten gun and Nick made my 7.62 rifle ready with six full magazines to hand.

We were deep inside the forest when a huge storm broke overhead. The thick jungle foliage took the brunt of the lightning, the wind and the rain, but the noise was deafening. Each deepening pool that we ploughed through sent cascades of mud onto the windscreens but, even driving semi-blind, it was necessary to keep at maximum revs in second gear to avoid bogging in.

The forest suddenly cleared and a raised track announced Bor village, where Achmed guided our two Land Rovers and remaining trailer with *Burton*, all entirely mud-coloured, to the police compound.

Going through the forest on top of his host-lorry, *Burton* had been hit by an overhanging branch of a tree and damaged beyond repair. Sadly we left him with the District Commissioner, a well-educated northerner to whom Bor was the last of a long succession of outposts. He wrote to me a year later saying that *Burton* was performing a valuable job in his two-acre vegetable garden as a hippopotamus scarer.

Sadly, as I write this, many thousands of civilians are killing one another in Bor and in the surrounding villages as a result of the civil war which followed close on the heels of South Sudan's hard-fought independence.

The history of the fighting goes back to Sudan's independence from both Egyptian and British rule. Soon afterwards black Africans in the south, who were either Christians or followers of traditional beliefs, feared domination by the Muslim northerners. For example, they objected to the government declaring that Arabic was the only official language. In 1964 civil war broke out and continued until 1972, when the south was given regional self-government, though executive power was still vested in the military government in Khartoum.

In 1983 the government established Islamic law throughout the country. This sparked off further conflict when the Sudan People's Liberation Army in the south launched attacks on government installations. Despite attempts to restore order, the fighting continued into the 1990s.

Eventually in 2011 South Sudan became a sovereign state which officially ended the conflict we had witnessed in the 1960s. Unfortunately the new country, inhabited by many distinct tribes, soon boiled over with ethnic jealousies, mainly between the Dinka and the Nuer. The troubles began in 2012 in the capital of Juba and soon spread north into the Sudd where for decades Dinka and Nuer had lived side by side in harmony.

My memories of 1969 Bor are of an oasis of well-ordered life on an island bounded by swamps to the north and west with, to the south, vast forests of game, home to the little-known Lotuko-speaking tribes. Bor means 'ditch' in Dinka, but the village is on ground high enough to avoid flooding, even at the highest water levels. Avenues of shady sycamores and squat bungalows surround a playground where townsfolk gossip, and this is overlooked by the police and the district commissioner who use the same offices and rules as their British predecessors did.

We had beaten the rains of the north Sudd and were nonplussed, or, in modern parlance, gobsmacked, to be told by the commissioner that we would, under no circumstances, be allowed to continue along the riverside tracks to Juba.

'Why not?' I asked him. 'The President in Khartoum led us to believe that all would be well *if* we reached Bor before the rains came. And, by the skin of our teeth, we have.'

'The government choose to believe what the army tell them and what is good propaganda. But I assure you, the very last road convoy for the year to or from Juba was last week, since when all the bridges have been blown or washed away by floods. This has happened by mid-March each year since 1965. But no trouble, my British friends, no worry, you are safe here and can go by river to Juba.'

'But our vehicles and our remaining Hawk?'

'Again, no problem. We will put them on board too. Meanwhile you are my guests in Bor, thanks be to God.'

'Thanks be to God,' I repeated, being well drilled from Oman. But my mind was racing. We had expected to reach the Ugandan border and fast roads within a week of making it to Bor, and thence to Nairobi by 30 March, the date when the RAF had agreed to fly Peter and Nick back to rejoin their regiments on time. Meantime, the rest of us would provide a hover demonstration on Lake Victoria in early April, as agreed with the British embassy in Nairobi.

The commissioner hoped that a suitable steamer heading south would call at Bor within a week. If it did, we could still make Nairobi and Lake Victoria on time. Resigned to unalterable circumstances, we stayed on in the commissioner's bachelor home.

He played backgammon with Peter, discussed world politics with Charles and Nick, had his broken camera repaired by Anthony, and spent long hours telling me of the hot, humid and back-of-beyond postings that he had suffered.

The worst troublemakers and killers of all had been the Galla of Ethiopia, who castrate victims of feudal or tribal murder and tie their mummified parts to their war-belts. They kill women on the slightest suspicion of sorcery by tearing out their kidneys. If a person shows early signs of a contagious disease, they are burnt to death in their home with their entire family.

He showed me round 'his village', as he called it, and in the main communal cattle kraal, where the native hump-backed cows had curving horns some two feet long, he pointed at the deep gaping scars where large chunks of flesh had been torn from their flanks.

He put this down to wolves and hyenas, but stressed that anthrax was responsible for more cattle deaths than were marauders. And many cattle herders die of anthrax, an agonizing way to go. They love their cattle to the extent that, even though a wealthy tribesman may own two thousand head of cattle, he will seldom kill a cow for meat, preferring to eat his beef only when a cow dies – often of anthrax. Yet a few hundred miles to the south, their Masai cousins casually slice tasty chunks of raw meat from living oxen, avoiding only the vital arteries of the poor beasts.

Most of the Dinka we met looked content and healthy – a tall, handsome tribe. The men, on reaching puberty, have their lower incisors knocked out and their tribal markings cut into their cheeks and foreheads. Their traditional enemy were the Moralay cattle raiders, who also kidnapped women and children, sometimes from villages over a hundred miles from their own. The Moralay are notorious for a high incidence of syphilis.

The commissioner reserved top marks for the Shilluk, the finest craftsmen in the south. Their paramount chief is traditionally 'retired' when old age renders him impotent or generally ineffective, and his wives then throttle him in his sleep. That way a younger ruler will take over, to the benefit of all.

At dawn on 27 March, with Nick and Peter getting decidedly nervous about becoming 'absent without leave' from their regiments, we woke to hear the welcome sound of a ship's siren from the direction of the river.

Struggling into shorts, for we slept naked under nets, we ran down to the Nile to find a small tugboat towing two fat barges laden with Bor's last shipment of dourra flour prior to the flood season. As soon as it was unloaded, the skipper told the commissioner that he must take us to Juba without delay.

This was our last chance to avoid a very long stint in Bor, but the skipper refused to take our two Land Rovers on his barges. He seemed to think that the Anya Nya might believe that they were bound for the government troops and would shoot up his ship.

The commissioner saved our bacon by various (to us unintelligible) arguments which eventually changed the skipper's mind. So long as we provided the labour without involving his crew, we could lash a vehicle to each barge once all the dourra was unloaded.

This went without a hitch and, with a sincere hug of gratitude for the commissioner, we left the village with Charles roaring off in *Burton* from the playground's beach to merry cheers from the good folk of Bor.

The commissioner and the police had stressed that Charles must stay within sight of the tug at all times, which annoyed him as he

Ginny masterminded the Transglobe Expedition between 1972 and its completion in 1982.

Father Charles Eugène de Foucauld (1858–1916). De Foucauld served in the French Army in North Africa, before becoming a dedicated Trappist monk and settling in the Sahara, living among the Tuaregs of the Hoggar mountain region. He was murdered in 1916 and beatified by the Pope in 2005.

Ollie (foreground) and Simon in the Sahara.

For 50 miles we drove along rocky tracks into the canyons of the Hoggar and, at 8000 feet, came to the pass of Assekrem.

Simon, in the Sahl region of Goundam, examines the cadaver of a cow. Skulls and carcasses littered the bush. Simon developed malaria soon after we entered the Ivory Coast jungle region.

Charlie (foreground) and Simon clear the brush beside the Bandama Rouge River. Here Charlie found a 9-inch black scorpion in his tent.

I split the platoon into three groups: one to find a safe route to the desert, one to ambush the Dehedoba trail and the third to patrol the Sands.

In the great gravel deserts that skirt the Empty Quarter we helped the companies' artillery along our dizzy 'road' from the desert to the enemy-held Qara.

My section of the Reconnaissance Platoon in the Dhofari *nej'd*. Far left is Ali Nasser. Far right is Said Salim.

A *jebali* family at home on the Plain of Salalah. The mother is in her early forties.

A bedu family we came across living in a cave near Habarut in the Dhofari *nej'd*.

When we camped in the frontier wadi's oasis of Habarut between the twin fortresses, one on either side of the border, the atmosphere was tense and heavy with the hostility of the Mahra inhabitants. They disliked the Sultan's army, for they felt that all Habarut should be Yemeni territory.

Our long stint in ambush hides were memorable for the unwelcome attendance of ticks, scorpions, midges, mosquitoes, biting ants of various sizes and colours and, always, the background awareness of being in territory held by a cunning and aggressive enemy.

The longest time our sections stayed motionless in a single ambush was four days and nights.

Tim Landon and his Intelligence group in Salalah. When he told me where and when to lay an ambush in the mountains, I could usually be sure of exciting results.

Ali Nasser.

Said Salim.

Mohammed of the Beard.

Salim Khaleefa.

Every month, if our work schedule allowed, we came to the Pools of Ayun to wash away the sweat and the dirt, and to fill all our water containers.

Said bin Ghia, a sheikh of the Bait Qatan jebali tribe, was one of the earliest *adoo* but he switched to our side and led me on many ambush patrols, once being shot through the wrist right beside me.

The hidden cleft called Fiend Field that the author and Fiend Force used as their base near the Dehedoba Trail, from which to mount patrols and ambushes.

could have reached Juba, by his own estimation, in a day. But we were quietly glad that he did not try it alone as we feared that he might never be seen again. Our skipper was from Dongola near Aswan, had been up and down the Nile all his working life yet even he did not know every meandering vagary of the ever-changing routes through the Sudd.

He sometimes took a wrong turn into a cul-de-sac as banks of reed and cabbage floated across and confused the main waterway. At such times his crew used sounding poles with skill to find the deep-water channels.

So Charles was reduced to hovering in circles at minimal hover speed. Each time he passed us, his scowl was more pronounced. We refuelled him by passing half-full jerry cans to him from off the side of the barge.

Hippo and crocodile appeared from time to time, as did the occasional waterbuck. Colourful birds were everywhere, but none of us was ornithologically aware or able to identify them apart from the obvious flamingos and herons.

At night the skipper manoeuvred his clumsy craft with cunning into still water zones downstream of solid-looking banks, at which point a weary and sweat-drenched Charles would tie up alongside. The mosquitoes and other biting insects had to be seen and heard to be believed. After dusk on deck we either sat or lay on our camp beds, tucked under our nets. Unfortunately I was unable to control my bowels all night long due to the many litres that I drank all day, as well as suffering with an indisposition that I shared with Charles which he termed 'dourra-weevil diarrhoea'. Clinging to the rear of our barge, my buttocks were easy targets for the biting mosquitoes, and swatting them while holding on to the rear rail of the barge was a risky business.

We were clearly not welcome on the tugboat itself, the wheelhouse of which was sandbagged against machine-gun fire with three heavily armed soldiers as escort.

Once under way at dawn the skipper's method of negotiating acute river bends was to steer at full steam for the outer bank and bounce off it to facilitate the turn, often against a strong current.

After three days of this giddy journey, Charles had lost a great deal of weight and looked haggard. So it was with great relief that we all greeted the sound of our 'foghorn' announcing our arrival at Juba, a couple of river bends before the town came into view.

Juba, situated close to the notorious old slaving centre of Gondokoro, was clearly a military town and also the Customs post between the Sudan and Uganda, even though the actual border was a hundred miles further south upriver. The site was originally, in 1922, a trading post and British Army camp.

We arrived on a Friday, the Muslim day of rest, so everything was closed, including the Customs post. By using every letter of introduction I'd been given in Khartoum, we managed to locate a Customs officer whom we annoyed enough to make him and his wife keen to get rid of us. Then, using the same tactic, we persuaded the army general in charge of Juba to load *Burton* onto one of his lorries that same afternoon and drive us through thick forest and over well-guarded canyon bridges. The whole region had experienced a scorched-earth policy and widespread massacres some ten years previously, details of which were still kept a closely guarded secret by the Sudanese government.

Nonetheless, Anya Nya guerrilla bands continued to ambush the road and, when major offensives were mounted against them, they faded, ghost-like, over the border into Uganda. We saw no living soul or animal all the way to Nimule, apart from three long green snakes, which seemed to favour the hot murram (hardened dirt) road surface as a basking area. They moved off in quick blurs of powerful motion as our lead vehicle approached.

That night we came to the Nimule border post. Unless we crossed the border and let Peter and Nick in the old AA vehicle rush to Nairobi, 400 miles away, they would miss the RAF flight home. But the border was closed.

My faith in humankind, especially Sudanese sergeants, was elevated considerably when our convoy leader, understanding our problem that Peter and Nick could be in danger of being accused of 'desertion from their army', broke international law and woke up the Ugandan border officer and his wife (whom he clearly knew) and drove his Sudanese Army lorry over the border in order to unload *Burton* safely in Uganda.

We all hugged the portly sergeant, including his shoulder-mounted rifle and bandoliers, and gave him our last bottle of Glenfiddich. He beamed his pleasure, and asked us to tell no one that he had crossed the border or 'we maybe start new war'.

Peter and Nick, deciding not to hug the rest of us, bade us goodbye, wishing us a safe passage to the source of the Nile and went on their hasty way to Nairobi airport. We received a telegram a week later confirming that they had made it back, complete with the AA Land Rover, on the RAF transport flight, and neither was in trouble for their lengthy absence. Mike Broome, they reported, was 'much better'.

Ninety miles from the border port was the banana town of Gulu, where a storekeeper rented out small Isuzu vans with flatbeds. He drove north at once and, with help from the Nimule Customs officer, his pretty wife and three border guards, we heaved *Burton* onto the flatbed. The Hawk protruded well over the rear and the sides of the platform, but the driver, paid in advance, did not object.

After a long drive through endless banana plantations and following in the murram dust of the Isuzu, we passed by the Karuma Falls in thunderous spate and on to Masindi Port. Then through deep forests, where the early Nile source searchers had suffered at the hands of treacherous native kings less than a century ago.

'If we could but tune in,' Charles said, lifting one hand off the steering wheel to touch his ear, 'we could hear the long scream of anguish, of pain and hopelessness of the million slaves who trod this road.'

We took a road signed to Entebbe Airport and came to a bend from where we could see what appeared more like an ocean than Lake Victoria, the main source of the Nile as confirmed by explorers Burton and Speke exactly one hundred years ago. Charles and I broke open two bottles of Coca-Cola and toasted our dead compatriots.

Charles pointed south. 'Of course you can say that this lake has many rivers down there that feed it and that they are all sources of the Nile,' he said. 'One such comes into the lake from Rwanda at a village called Kasansero, the home of the dreadful Nile perch which well-meaning Brits introduced to the lake.'

He described how in the 1950s, when Uganda was still a British colony, administrators had decided to create a new fishing industry. They failed to foresee the damage which the huge and aggressive Nile perch would soon do, colonizing the lake in no time and killing off most of the existing stocks. They grow up to two metres and can weigh 150kg. As mummified perch have been found in Nile-side tombs, they are believed to have been worshipped by the ancient Egyptians.

Kasansero became globally notorious on two counts later in the twentieth century. In 1985 the citizens began to die in their hundreds of an unknown sickness which many thought was a new version of malaria. It turned out to be the AIDS virus which subsequently spread around the world.

Nine years later, in 1994, Kasansero's river spewed over 10,000 bloated corpses into the lake during the Rwandan genocide. These then drifted north to empty out of the lake via the Ripon Falls at Jinja and into the White Nile.

Charles drove us to Jinja to photograph the great hydro-electric power station and dam built in the 1950s where once explorer Speke had made his name by sending a telegram to his supporters at the Royal Geographical Society to announce his discovery with the words, '*The Nile is settled*.'

The military attaché in Kampala had organized a major hovercraft demonstration at Gaba, on the shoreline of Lake Victoria. Hundreds of commercial and military guests, one of whom was a rotund sergeant named Idi Amin, watched and clapped as *Burton* roared from the grassy bank into the water and back to land without noticing the difference.

The East African press turned out in strength, and export orders flooded in. Back home the Ministry of Technology, astonished that the Hawk had survived the rigours of the journey, organized a sales tour of the USA and Canada, and small hovercraft, previously stigmatized for unreliability, began to be taken seriously.

As I watched Charles glide over the great inland sea of Lake Victoria, the attaché touched my shoulder. 'Well done, Ranulph,' he said, 'you made it, but you have had the most amazing chunk of luck. We were all expecting you and your team to end your days in the forest or in some godforsaken prison.'

Like the early explorers, we had failed to follow the exact course of the entire length of the great river, but we had savoured a taste of its perils, extremes of climate, and had met some of the brave, strong people who survive along its length. As the attaché said, we had been lucky.

Since the days of Burton and Baker, Africa had grown a great deal less dangerous. But, a few years later, Idi Amin and others would perpetrate mass tribal murder, as would the Hutu of Rwanda, the Congolese and the jihadis of Nigeria. We had squeezed, by chance, between various bloody episodes of history.

CHAPTER 10

The Explorers

'Heat, madam! It was so dreadful that I found there
was nothing for it but to take off my flesh and sit in
my bones.'

—SYDNEY SMITH (1771–1845)

The story of Nile explorer John Hanning Speke begins when, aged
twenty-seven, he left the British Indian Army and joined another
ex-Indian Army officer, Richard Burton, already famous for previous
adventures, to search for the source of the Nile with the full support
of the Royal Geographical Society. At first the two men approached
their mission from the Somali coast. At some point they were
attacked by Somali tribesmen. Speke was stabbed by spears and both
Burton's cheeks were skewered by a javelin, but they escaped and in
1856 tried again. This time they travelled inland from Zanzibar some
540 miles to the village of Ujiji on the shore of Lake Tanganyika,
which they claimed as their first great discovery.

Before they could set out to find a river flowing north out of their
lake which might prove to be the Nile, both men were crippled by
sickness and by the terrible heat. Burton lost all feeling in his feet and
hands and Speke became temporarily blind.

Eventually, partly recovered, they canoed with lake fishermen as
guides and almost reached the north end of the lake when the guides

would go no further due to a hostile tribe in that area. When questioned all the locals swore that the only river at the lake's northern end flowed into, not out of, the lake. So, defeated and dismayed, they retreated to Tabora, their previous base and an Arab trading post back towards the coast. Here Burton recuperated further, but Speke, who recovered more quickly, decided to follow up a rumour of a much bigger lake directly north of Tabora.

Burton was later to regret his decision not to go with Speke as the greatest mistake of his life. Speke and a small group of porters reached the unknown lake in three weeks of travel. It was vast and Speke had no doubt that it must be the Nile's source. He named it Victoria.

He rested on the southern shore for three days, then returned to Burton at Tabora. He had no evidence to support his claim, such as the sighting of a sizeable river flowing north *out* of the lake, but he had convinced himself, nonetheless, of his remarkable discovery.

Burton tried to persuade Speke to go easy on a triumphal announcement. He was, of course, keen that the initial Lake Tanganyika discovery, in which he was the chief personality, should constitute 'the triumph', and not Speke's Victoria.

The two men agreed to make no announcements until back in England. Burton, however, needed a period of rest from his various illnesses when in Aden, so Speke carried on alone and as soon as he reached London made an announcement with the enthusiastic backing of the RGS and resultant acclaim from the media. The RGS, aware of the need to gain proof of Speke's assertions, decided to send Speke back to Africa as soon as possible and without Burton who, on his return with his Lake Tanganyika 'success' story, was largely ignored. He was enraged and, hating Speke, began a long campaign to discredit him.

Speke chose, as his new travel companion, James Grant, another Indian Army officer but very different in character from Burton, being modest and deferential, not aggressive and conceited. They arrived in Zanzibar in the summer of 1860 and made their way to Lake Victoria with a great many delays en route.

It had taken Speke three weeks to reach the southern shore of the lake on his previous journey. But now it was over a year before he actually made it to the lake due to delays with porters and illness, including malaria and agonizing leg ulcers which Grant endured.

Their problems, during their long and arduous travels, were experienced by many of the nineteenth-century explorers and included the ease with which they succumbed to malaria and their horses and oxen to the tsetse fly. Burton wrote of the tsetse and other insects: 'The path was slippery with mud, and man and beast were rendered wild by the cruel stings of a small red ant and a huge black pismire. The former crossed the road in dense masses like the close columns of any army ... Though they cannot spring, they show great quickness in fastening themselves to the foot or ankle as it brushes over them. The pismire ... is a horse-ant, about an inch in length, whose bulldog-like head and powerful mandibles enable it to destroy rats and mice, lizards and snakes.'

The tsetse fly is slightly larger than a standard house fly, is greybrown in colour and feeds at the hottest time of day. The flesh of any tsetse-bitten animal is poisonous, so cattle herders in the tsetse belt of Central and Eastern Africa (north of the 27th latitude line) lead a precarious existence. The disease carried by the tsetse is known as African sleeping sickness (or trypanosomiasis) and it enters the body of the bitten person or animal via a tiny parasite which infects the brain and the spinal cord by way of the lymph and central nervous system. Sometimes symptoms can take months or even years to develop and can damage the kidneys, heart muscles and brain.

The name 'sleeping sickness' reflects that form of the sickness involving dementia, convulsions, loss of bladder control and increasing listlessness, leading eventually to a coma and death.

In certain areas of Eastern and Southern Africa, especially where there are large herds of cattle, up to 20 per cent of the human population can be infected. The flies like bright and dark colours, so wearing clothes of muted colours that blend with the background is a good idea.

There are twenty known species of tsetse, including the *nagana* which go for cattle and others that specialize in humans, often giving them the sleeping sickness. You know when you have been bitten as the bite delivers a sharp stinging sensation.

Add to the flies and the ants the various varieties of blood-sucking tics and killer-bees that attack as you brush past their habitats and you begin to realize some of the early explorers' constant irritations. There were also endemic sicknesses, including leprosy and the pox. Burton wrote of the latter:

> On the way we were saddened by the sight of the clean-picked skeletons, and here and there the swollen corpses, of porters who had perished in this place of starvation. A single large body [of porters], which had lost fifty of its number by small-pox, had passed us but yesterday on the road, and the sight of their deceased comrades recalled to our minds terrible spectacles; men staggering on blinded by disease, and mothers carrying on their backs infants as loathsome objects as themselves. The wretches would not leave the path, every step in their state of failing strength was precious; he who once fell would never rise again; no village would admit death into its precincts, no relation nor friend would return for them, and they would lie till their agony was ended by the raven and vulture, the hyena and the fox.

Quite apart from their travails with insects and illness, Speke and Grant could only advance towards their hoped for objectives with great diplomacy and patience through the lands of the Bantu kingdoms north and west of Lake Victoria. There were at the time three such fiefdoms, the first of which was Karagwe whose King Rumanika was friendly. He warned them that the kingdom they would next have to traverse on their way north would need warning of their approach. While they awaited this king's response to their messenger, they were shown around Rumanika's harem. Despite the fact that most of the women were teenagers, they were so fat that they could not stand up but only slide around their floor mats on their knees and elbows like seals. They fed only on milk sucked through straws and, should they fail to drink the stipulated daily amount, they were whipped. Nonetheless, King Rumanika was considerably more civilized than his northern neighbours.

King Mutesa of Buganda, who ruled from a village not far from modern Kampala, capital of Uganda, eventually sent his permission for Speke to visit him. Grant had to remain in Karagwe as his leg was still an open sore, so Speke went on alone.

When three months later Grant joined Speke, their party continued northwards but split into two missions – Grant to open the way
north into the third and last Bantu kingdom, Bunyoro, whose king
was known to be hostile to strangers, and Speke to check out a river
that Mutesa said flowed north out of Lake Victoria.

Speke was therefore by himself when he came to the Ripon Falls
at Jinja where, overjoyed, he named the outflowing river the Victoria
Nile, after his Queen.

All he now needed to do was to rejoin Grant, head north to
Gondokoro and announce his great discovery to the RGS and to the
world.

He was also to record some of the barbaric behaviour of King
Mutesa who, on accession to the throne of Buganda, had put to
death some sixty of his own brothers by burning them alive.
Whenever he presided at tribal courts he doled out such tortures as
the slicing off of ears, hands and feet, the burial alive of wives with
their dead husbands and the sudden chance execution of women
from his seraglio. A girl might cough in his presence or open a door
at the wrong time, and her head would be chopped off.

Every day, Speke reported, two or three women would be selected
for death and would be dragged away for execution without explanation. Henry VIII of England was a saint by comparison.

When Speke and Grant eventually escaped from the clutches of
the third of the Bantu kings, Kamrasi of Bunyoro, they were
exhausted and so missed the chance of visiting another great lake
(later to be named Lake Albert by explorer Samuel Baker).

In 1863, after three years of toil and illness, they made it to
Gondokoro where they were met by Baker on whose boat they travelled to Khartoum.

Back in London both men, but especially Speke, were met by a
tumultuous welcome and received many honours. Various geographers and Speke's erstwhile travel companion, Burton, published
erudite arguments questioning Speke's 'discoveries', and soon both
the media and the RGS, and also the public, divided into two camps,
those who believed Speke's theories and others who supported
Burton.

A year after his return, Speke was invited to meet Burton at a public debate in Bath about 'The Nile Question'. Halfway through the debate, Speke said, 'I can't stand this any longer,' and left the room. The next morning, with the main hall full and Burton on the stage, Speke failed to appear.

After a while it was announced that the previous afternoon Speke had joined his cousin on a shoot near Bath and, climbing over a wall, had shot himself. Whether accidentally or not was never ascertained.

Until his own death, Burton continued to criticize and question all Speke's claims that he had discovered the source of the Nile.

Burton and Speke's contemporary Samuel Baker, whose Nile-based work brought him fame as great as theirs, did his best, while exploring, to put a stop to the horrors of slavery.

The middle of the nineteenth century was the height of British imperial power. The list of its acquisitions, almost all in Samuel Baker's lifetime, is astonishing. Britain by force and treaty acquired Singapore in 1819, Malacca in 1824, Hong Kong in 1842, Natal in 1843, Lower Burma in 1852 and Lagos in 1861, and had claimed sovereignty over Australia and New Zealand by 1840. The American President James Monroe famously warned Europeans not to meddle in his country's affairs in 1823, but the British already had Canada.

Baker was still at school in 1837 when Victoria became Queen of England and its empire, the greatest in history. God was an Englishman, according to the cynics of the day, and by the 1860s when Baker's fame was in the making, a popular parody of a well-known hymn was:

Onward, Christian soldiers
On to heathen lands
Prayer books in your pockets
Rifles in your hands

Baker's chosen colony, where he set up a farming business, was Ceylon (Sri Lanka) which, once operating successfully, bored him. In 1855, the year before Burton and Speke set out to find the Nile's source, Baker was into hunting in a big way, including the shooting of rogue Ceylonese elephants. In one of his early books – he was to become a prolific author – he noted that elephants were proficient swimmers and when floating, even when dead, they remained so high in the water that six men could ride on them as though on a raft. Some years later in Africa he noted that many Zulu drums used leather cut from elephants' ears. And he wore khaki as camouflage when hunting long before it was introduced in the British Army.

Back in Europe in 1855 his wife died of typhus, leaving him with four young children whose care he entrusted to a succession of nannies. While travelling in Hungary, by then aged thirty-five, Baker attended a slave auction and bid successfully for a seventeen-year-old Hungarian girl whose parents had died and, by bad luck, had ended up being sold. On return with her to London, Baker found society, and indeed his own family, to be disapproving of his new 'wife'.

After trying various 'jobs' in Europe, Baker wrote to his sister in 1860, 'My magnetic needle directs me to Central Africa.' He applied to the Royal Geographical Society for a place on the planned Zambezi expedition of the Scottish missionary Dr Livingstone, but he was turned down. So in 1861 he and ex-slave Florrie, with whom he was by then living as man and wife, travelled, without any official endorsement by the establishment, on their own project to locate the source of the Nile, or at least to find and 'save' the then-missing Speke and Grant expedition.

From Aswan they crossed the desert with guides and sixteen camels. The great heat made Florrie ill and they rested a while in Berbera. They noted (as we did one hundred and seven years later) that the Nile water was 'undrinkable'. Baker also recorded his fascination with the way that Arab women squatted, naked under their robes, over jars of burning incense to ensure that their nether regions smelled pleasant.

Baker's various travel books seldom mention his children. By the time of his first Nile journey he had not seen his eldest daughter, who was thirteen years old, for six years. Florrie, childless, was horrified to note that many Europeans living in Khartoum married young slave girls whose vaginas had been partially sewn up to ensure chastity prior to their sale. On arrival in Khartoum the Bakers were put up at the consulate. The Consul himself, a Welshman named Petherick, had headed south to try and locate Speke and Grant.

After an unpleasant voyage through the Sudd, the Bakers reached Gondokoro (Juba) in early 1862 but of Petherick, Speke and Grant they found no trace. So they made camp in the sweltering heat and depressing humidity, both suffering from malaria, during which Baker somehow put down a mutiny by his own party. Two weeks later, Speke and Grant duly appeared – three years after their last known sighting by the outside world. This meeting was rather like that, a few years later, of Livingstone and Stanley. When Petherick (and his wife!) turned up at Gondokoro, after their own troubles with the locals, Speke was not only ungrateful for their attempts to locate him but, subsequently and vengefully, ruined Petherick's reputation.

He was, on the other hand, very friendly to the Bakers, and when Baker asked him, now that he, Speke, had apparently discovered the source of the Nile, what might be left for him and Florrie to usefully look for, he was as helpful as possible. Why not, he suggested, search for Lake N'zigi? This lake was reported by Arab traders to exist to the west of Lake Victoria, and the Nile might well run through it. Speke and Grant had not been able to check its existence.

Baker gave his boat to Speke and Grant, who left for Khartoum, as did the Pethericks. As soon as they had gone Baker had to put down a second mutiny, which he did through sheer force of character.

Arab slavers then became the only possible support for the Bakers to progress over the next dreadful year before they reached the Victorian Nile in Kamrasi's kingdom. En route they had suffered every form of hardship and constant bouts of fever. 'White ants and rats, robbers and smallpox are my companions and neighbours,' Baker commented mournfully in his diary. Florrie very nearly died on the journey from Kamrasi's lands to Buganda, but through sheer determination and against all odds, they made it to Lake N'zigi.

After such a discovery (as I was later to learn to my cost in Oman) it is sensible to stake your claim before somebody else does, and the Bakers, elated by their find, were keen to get back to Gondokoro and announce the discovery of their lake to the world.

Much later, with hindsight, they would probably regret that they did not visit the southern end of Lake N'zigi, which would have made them realize that it was a good deal smaller than they thought, and certainly it was tiny when compared with Speke's Lake Victoria.

As it was, they did not entirely give in to the urge to rush homewards because Baker, by calculating the elevation of N'zigi compared with that of Lake Victoria, knew that there must be a waterfall delivering the waters of the Victoria Nile into his lake.

Some thirty-five miles up the river flowing into the N'zigi at its north-eastern end, he came to the waterfall which he described as 'a grand stream ... pent up in a narrow gorge scarcely 50 yards in width; roaring furiously through the rock-bound pass ... [plunging] in one leap of about 120 feet perpendicular into a dark abyss below ... the greatest waterfall of the Nile ... ' He named it the Murchison Falls after the President of the Royal Geographical Society.

With the help of Kamrasi's warriors, the Bakers made it back to Gondokoro by Christmas 1864, almost two years after they had left that hellhole.

A nightmare voyage followed to Khartoum where they stayed until June 1865, avoiding the plague which killed thousands in the city.

Back at last in London, Baker officially married Florrie. In 1866 he was knighted. He wrote books, even a novel, became a proper father to his long-forsaken daughters, and it took at least three years of post-Nile recovery before boredom set in and he then took the job of Governor-General of the Equatorial Nile Basin, paid for by Khedive Ismail of Egypt whose ambition was to rule all of Sudan. He also announced his desire to abolish slavery in his entire kingdom. (This was a touch cynical since he, personally, retained many hundreds of slaves of both sexes.)

Baker saw his new job as, first and foremost, the suppression of slavery down the Sudanese Nile and then the annexation of the Nile Basin to Egypt. Since Ismail remained in faraway Cairo, Baker Pasha became the sole power in Sudan with his chief assistant, as ever, his loyal wife Florrie. He was now in charge of half a million square miles of Africa.

On arrival in Khartoum he found that the acting Governor-General there had just despatched eleven steamers up the Nile on a slave-taking mission, which was, of course, encouraging the very activity that Baker was tasked to stamp out.

Baker was to find that, because he was determined to abolish slavery down his stretch of the Nile belonging to the Sudan, he was thwarted at every turn by the Arab slavers who would, he knew, have otherwise been his best supporters in subjugating the hostile tribes to his (and thus the Khedive's) authority. As it was, he had to make do with an army of mostly ex-convict Egyptians and, considerably better material in his opinion, semi-trained Sudanese soldiers. From the ranks of the latter he recruited a crack squad of loyal men as his personal guard.

This army crept up the river in three groups, two in sailboats and steamers, including the Bakers, the third overland with oxen and camels to haul prefab steamers in sections for use above the cataracts.

The Sudd levels were high that year and the floating islands of hyacinth and papyrus were chaotic. Florrie wrote of unbearable mosquitoes and the river alive with snakes, crocodiles and hippos (which snorted all night). Men sickened daily in the grinding heat. At Sobat he released his first convoy of 150 slaves and married some off to his soldiers in a two-way voluntary manner. He was later to write about these ex-slaves' feistiness in asserting female rights long before the London suffragettes were to do so.

By early 1872, with a year of his contract as Pasha still to go, Baker's active force had shrunk through death, disease or desertion from sixteen hundred to five hundred but, as intractable as ever, he set out to extend the Khedive's authority further south than Gondokoro. He established garrisons at Fatiko, Unguro and as far south as Masindi. Wherever he and his main force happened to be, slavery disappeared and 'Egypt ruled', but once he moved elsewhere the slavers returned like quicksilver.

Kamrasi died, but his son Kabba Rega put together an army of five thousand warriors and attacked the Bakers in their Masindi outpost. Through sheer bravado and superior discipline, they survived, burnt down Kabba Rega's village and retreated to their compound.

When a further attack was narrowly survived and knowing it would take too long to call for reinforcements from Khartoum, the Bakers and their entire garrison conducted a hair-raising retreat overland to Fatiko under constant attack by Kabba Rega's spearmen. Ten of Baker's group were killed, but the others survived against remarkable odds. Over the next few months, eventually with reinforcements from Khartoum, Baker extended his garrisons and rescued many thousands of slaves. When his contract was ended, he and Florence said a sad goodbye to their many loyal African friends and, in Cairo, he received the highest awards from the Khedive. His legacy, as he saw it, was that the slave trade in all Sudanese Equatoria was ended and Egypt's authority was now extended to the Equator. He was of course wrong, but he had certainly done his best. Back in London, the media lauded the Bakers who took over the halo of Livingstone as the greatest of anti-slavery crusaders. His successor, the evangelical General Charles Gordon, was not a Nile explorer but, thanks to Baker, he had a navigable river to use on his own sallies to the south of Khartoum.

On returning to England, the Bakers 'retired' to Devon, but each year, until Samuel died at home of a heart attack in 1893, they travelled around the world, sometimes hunted and saw old friends. Baker's last words were to his wife, using her nickname, 'Flooey, how can I leave you?' She died twenty-three years later. Theirs was, to my mind, the greatest of all stories of true love.

In the pantheon of famous Nile explorers, the name of Dr David Livingstone is decidedly more famous than that of Baker, Burton, Speke or Grant.

Livingstone, born in 1913 in Scotland to a poor family, was a devout Christian throughout his life. He first worked in a local cotton mill, then studied medicine and became a doctor then a missionary. Aged twenty-seven he sailed to Cape Town as a fully fledged member of the London Missionary Society. He headed north to find a suitable place for his mission and home, and his early adventures, including being mauled by a lion, involved successfully locating both Lake Ngama (1849) and the Zambezi River. North of the Zambezi he veered west above the Kalahari and blazed a route to the Atlantic coast at Luanda.

This first remarkable journey involved a 1,500-mile struggle against the threats of great heat, jungle, disease, hunger and tribes who loved to kill strangers. Despite fever and exhaustion, Livingstone and his loyal group of porters then retraced their footsteps to the Zambezi and decided to follow its course. In doing so he located the great waterfall that he named after Queen Victoria. Reaching the coast at Quelimane in 1856, he sailed back to Britain and international fame, being the first man to have crossed the entire African continent from west to east.

He returned soon afterwards on a British government-sponsored Zambezi expedition to find a route along that river using steamboats and, his own venture, to set up a Christian mission. Both missions failed and his wife died in 1862, but Livingstone had nonetheless gained a wealth of scientific and geographical information by the time the Foreign Office recalled him in 1864.

That same year the claimed Nile-source discoveries of Speke were undermined by the general belief that, in September, he had shot himself as a tacit admission that his claims were false. That, together with the ongoing bitter controversies of Burton, Grant, Petherick and others, was causing great embarrassment to the RGS who, hoping to resolve the Nile puzzle beyond all doubt, sent the redoubtable, if ageing, Livingstone back into hell. He went willingly, for he had his own theories about the Nile's source which were based on the ancient comments of the likes of Herodotus, not on the modern claims of Burton, Speke and co. And above all, he wished to end the horrors of the slave trade and to introduce Christianity to the tribes.

Between 1866 and 1871, following his own deluded theories as to the geography of the Nile, he fought his way, with sickness and tribal hostility always against him, to the lakes Nyasa and Tanganyika. To advance at all he was often forced to accept help from Arab and Swahili slavers, the very devils he was out to defeat. In 1871 he finally decided against any further collusion with them when, to the west of Lake Tanganyika, he witnessed a massacre by slavers of hundreds of natives, mostly women and children, along the banks of the Lualaba River. He retreated to Ujiji on the west bank of Lake Tanganyika, where the famous incident of his 'rescue' by the Welsh journalist Henry Morton Stanley occurred. This was as a result of worldwide interest in and concern for Livingstone's fate. The RGS had sent relief expeditions, but Stanley, sponsored by a New York newspaper, found him first.

The two men spent the next three months together in a further search for river outlets from the lake. When Stanley departed, Livingstone went west back to the Lualaba River, but soon discovered that it flowed west into the Congo and might not be a Nile source. He died when, travelling in swamp country, he was stricken by fever in 1873. His body was taken by his loyal porters to Zanzibar and he was buried in Westminster Abbey. He never founded a mission nor converted more than a handful of souls. Some say he converted nobody! Nor did he finally solve the Nile controversy. But he did help to end slavery in Africa, and in twenty-first-century Zambia and Zimbabwe where European names of towns and features have been Africanized, the name of Livingstone has not.

In 2005, a year after Ginny died, I married Louise and in November of that year we were invited to join an expedition to recreate the last few days of Livingstone's 1855 journey down the Zambezi to the edge of Victoria Falls.

Planned by Simon Wilde, a white African with a guest lodge further down the Zambezi, the expedition aimed to celebrate, to the very day and date, the Scottish missionary's arrival at *Mosi-oa-Tunya* (Smoke-that-Thunders) which he renamed Victoria Falls.

One of the team, Russell Gammon, was a local safari guide and historian, and the paddlers of our *mokoros* (dugout log canoes) were Zambian rivermen, Lemmy Nyambe, Victor Sikushaba and Saad Mweembe.

Our first night was spent in a thunderstorm at a camping ground on the banks of the Zambezi 120 miles upriver of the Falls. Simon apologized in advance for the weather we were likely to experience. It was unfortunate, he said, that Livingstone had done his journey in mid-November 'when the hot dry season reaches its scorching crescendo and the first big storms of the rainy season arrive'.

We were given some advice by Russell, our guide: 'Do not trail any limbs in the water. Approach the water after dark with great caution. Crocs are natural predators that hunt from an ambush at the water's edge. If a croc comes for you, which is unlikely, you'll have heard stories about jamming an arm down its throat to make it let go, but if it's a big croc in deep water, you're basically buggered.'

Other riverine information included the fact that hippos are the cousins of horses and, clumsy though they look, they can charge at 30 mph, and they, of all the large animals of Africa, are also the biggest killers of humans. They kill more people than lions, buffaloes, crocodiles and elephants combined. They are also incredibly territorial and defensive of their young and they don't like people – and nowhere are they more dangerous than on land.

We set off at dawn with our boatmen standing at the back of our three *mokoros*, exactly as Livingstone had travelled. The balance was difficult. Louise sat behind me in the front canoe and we accused each other of causing every wobble. Louise was five months pregnant with our daughter Elizabeth, but we kept this a secret from the others and she paddled with the best of them.

The river was low after a long drought and on the many sandbanks past which it flowed there were a multitude of birds which Russell identified as skimmers, waders, herons, cormorants, multi-coloured kingfishers, ibis, vultures and fish eagles.

Our paddler Lemmy shouted, 'Ippo', and pointed to dark heads, like rocks except with ears. They looked at us suspiciously and then, to our relief, submerged.

Around the campfire one night when the talk turned to Livingstone's motives, Russell said, 'In thirty years he only converted one African to Christianity, and that man later reverted. Yet he never grew disheartened by this because he loved Africa and the company of Africans. More than anything, I think, he liked the sheer animal pleasure of moving through wild, unexplored country.'

Richard Grant, one of our team from faraway Colorado, wrote later that when the rainclouds went, 'the sun came out and tried to sear holes in my skin. I've spent most of my life in hot places but nowhere has my white skin ever felt so worthless, so fundamentally impractical, as under that African sun.'

At Mambova Island there were rapids where the boatmen told us to put away our paddles. We gripped the sides of our hollowed-out logs and thrilled as our skilled paddlers made it safely through.

Villagers cheered from the riverbank. A topless lady washed a blue plastic chair in the shallows.

Like Livingstone, we left our dugouts at the beginning of the much more serious Katambora rapids and went on a two-day bush walk around them. A local named Isaac Sitali, who used to be a poacher and knew the land well, was our guide. Russell said, 'It's the hottest day yet, hotter than a snake's arse in a wagon's rut.'

We followed fresh tracks bigger than dustbin lids in the soft ochre sand and came upon an enormous bull elephant tearing branches off a tree and stuffing them in his mouth. We heard a thundering, crashing sound approaching through the forest. This was a great sight that I'll never forget. Two separate herds, each of some four dozen elephants, advanced, seemingly in slow motion, although the little ones trotted, and the herds moved in parallel. This, Isaac told us, was to avoid confrontation between the males of each group.

The noise of an aircraft nearby caused sudden panic, and with much trumpeting and raised trunks, both herds thundered off at speed, fortunately not towards us. These elephants were here, Isaac explained, because it was the last piece of untouched, unpoached forest along this stretch of the river.

At our camp that night hippos grunted close by our tent and hyenas howled at the moon.

For the rest of the journey we were back in our *mokoros* paddling through an area of protected National Park land with an abundance of wildlife. Hippos and crocs by the dozen, elephant herds on both banks, warthogs, kudus and all manner of deer.

There was only one tense moment when a lone male hippo confronted us in a narrow channel, and we paddled with great zeal for the nearest bank to avoid him.

On the last night when we were camping on an island a hippo waddled between our tents while we slept, leaving fresh footprints to record its visit.

It was 48°C (119°F) as we paddled through the last rapids and around the last hippos and Livingstone Island came into view with the smoky spray of Victoria Falls behind.

The British High Commissioner, various dignitaries and the media welcomed our arrival in a furnace-like marquee with a band, tables with white cloths and silver salvers groaning with goodies.

After speeches about Livingstone we unveiled a fine bronze plaque in his honour on a rock overlooking the Falls. A kilted piper played 'Amazing Grace' nearby.

Then guides led us into the river and we waded out to Devil's Pool, a deep roiling pocket of wonderfully cool water on the very lip of the Falls. I remember the all-powerful roar of the falling water, the dancing rainbows in the spray and a comment by Russell on the sad irony that Livingstone, who devoted his life to end slavery, died of dysentery in a remote African village eighteen years after seeing and naming these great falls and never learning that the slave markets had finally been closed down.

Following his 'rescue' of Livingstone, Stanley's subsequent expeditions were planned and executed with ruthless ambition. Using an easily portable 40-foot wooden boat, he circumnavigated Lake Victoria, checking off each riverine inlet and outlet. Then, trekking overland, he did likewise along the west and south banks of Lake Tanganyika. His subsequent voyage of 7,000 miles each way along the Congo (Lualaba) River proved that it flowed into the Pacific Ocean and not the Nile.

As for his attempts to stop slavery, Livingstone's death sparked renewed pressure by British voters on their government who reactivated Royal Navy anti-slavery manoeuvres off the East African coast, concentrating on Zanzibar.

The slave trade in Zanzibar was dominated by Arabs, mostly of Omani descent, but Arab slaving had been active in Africa since long before the advent of Islam and along the east coast long before the Omanis established their coastal empire there.

Although the British abolitionists are remembered as mainly missionaries like Livingstone, the effective operations on the ground were those of the armed forces.

In 1814, a year before the Battle of Waterloo when the foreign ministers of Europe met to carve up Napoleon's empire, the British representative, the Duke of Wellington, was asked what Britain wanted. To the surprise of their other allies, he replied, 'An end to the slave trade.'

From 1807, before Livingstone was born, until the middle of the century the Royal Navy liberated some 150,000 slaves at sea, sometimes landing at slaving ports to destroy slavers' camps.

As early as 1822, the Omani Arabs signed a treaty which proscribed the sale of slaves to Christian countries. To monitor this, the British and Americans sent Consuls to Zanzibar as observers. Nonetheless the treaty was largely circumvented and the trade continued.

Obstacles to slave-trade control included the fact that the Americans and French refused the 'Rights of Search' to the Royal Navy, and there was a massive demand in the mid to late nineteenth century for ivory products, including from Britain. Slaves were needed in great numbers to carry this heavy commodity to coastal ports.

In 1856 the makers of cutlery in Sheffield alone ordered 170 tons of ivory. Other popular goodies for the middle classes included billiard balls, dildos, chess sets, umbrella and door handles, crucifixes, napkin rings and combs. By the late nineteenth century over 200 tons of ivory was arriving annually in Zanzibar along with 25,000 slaves.

The slave trade sustained Zanzibar's ivory trade. The Arab traders and their African armed gangs, including many ex-slaves, took beads, cloth and guns to tribal chiefs in the interior in exchange for ivory and slaves which they brought back to Zanzibar by a number of routes.

A common belief of missionaries, other than the few who reached the interior and actually witnessed the slave trade in action, was that the issue was a simple opposition of Good (the natives) and Evil (the traders). But slavery was an infinitely more complex issue and had been for centuries. The majority of individuals involved were the Africans themselves. They actually staffed the caravan-raiding parties, fought tribal resistance when necessary and provided the Arabs with their women as needed.

Tribal leaders allied themselves with slavers in their attacks on neighbours and, in return, gave their victims to the Arabs. Poor people sold their children as slaves. New chiefs bought slaves to bury alongside their predecessors to ensure that the late departed warriors were well served in the afterlife.

The most famous slave trader of all, the ruthless Tippo Tib, was himself the grandson of a slave. His gangs operated over a region of more than a thousand miles inland from the East Coast.

By the time of Livingstone's death in 1873 there were various well-used routes for the slaves to be marched to the coast from the location of their capture. En route, in order to prevent escape, most adult slaves of both sexes were roped together in gangs and often with six-foot-long individual heavy beams of wood pinned around their necks.

After much suffering on the journey, sometimes for many weeks, they would reach the nearest coastal slaving port where they were jammed on board dhows, seldom more than 30 to 35 metres long, for the journey to the island of Zanzibar. Each dhow carried between two hundred and six hundred slaves, all crammed below decks on specially constructed bamboo shelves with about one metre of headroom. There was not enough room to sit, kneel or squat, just a crippling combination of the three. Sometimes slaves were closely packed in open boats, their bodies exposed day and night to the sea and the rain. They were thirsty, hungry and seasick and many died of exhaustion. Meals consisted of a daily handful of rice and a cup of stagnant water. Sanitation was non-existent and disease spread rapidly. When any illness was discovered, infected slaves were simply thrown overboard.

Shortly before the dhows reached Zanzibar, the slaves were inspected. Most could not straighten their legs for several hours, all were weak and dehydrated, and the many dead bodies found collapsed on the benches were disposed of overboard.

By the time the (lucky?) survivors were dragged up the filthy mud shoreline to the slave lines by the so-called Customs House for collection by their 'importer', they were dazed, even traumatized. Many were then branded with a red-hot iron. They had been wrenched from their homes and often their families, abused and beaten, led off in gangs to an unknown future, witnessed death, starvation and violence on the march, forced to watch torture, mutilation and rape, and all this before their grim seaborne voyage to the hellhole of Zanzibar.

Almost as hot and health-sapping as Muscat, Zanzibar was, for a European, a posting to be avoided at all costs, but if the Foreign

Office in London sent you there, you could hardly say no. At the time of Livingstone's stay there in order to prepare for and launch his expeditions to the interior, the resident British Consul was John Kirk, a Scotsman who, unlike his predecessors, had actually travelled inland, witnessed the savagery of the slave trade and was as determined as Livingstone, with whom he had worked and travelled for long periods, to stamp it out.

The Zanzibar of his day was a violent town. Further north of the Customs House was the Sultan's palace, and along the beachfront nearby were many fine-looking houses where the rich traders lived. But behind these lay the dark shanty town of Malindi with its warren of alleyways. The island was bounded on one side by a creek and elsewhere by the sea. Along the creekside hundreds of dhows were beached. At night, fighting between rival slaver gangs often broke out and as the evening breezes died down foul smells of decay, faeces and rotting flesh pervaded the town. The beaches were strewn with refuse, offal and the corpses of slaves which were torn at by stray dogs, since nobody would bury them. The narrow streets were filthy and disease-ridden, horned cattle roamed there, as did aggressive gangs kicking at diseased and dying slaves who crawled groaning along the gutters. Malaria, syphilis, smallpox, cholera and dysentery were endemic and killed off the majority of Europeans posted to the town, including a number of John Kirk's predecessors. There were no competent doctors.

Few Europeans brought their wives with them. They kept mistresses, drank heavily and soon died. Somehow Kirk's wife, Nelly, managed to share his life and his work there.

Islamic law was largely observed, adulterers were beaten through the streets with clubs and more serious crimes were dealt with by mutilation or public execution.

Sultan Barghash was not the ultimate power in Zanzibar, for he would soon have been ousted or murdered had he upset the cabal of Arab slaving clans that formed an unofficial parliament. He was also badly affected by elephantiasis, another disease endemic in the town which caused victims' legs and genitals to swell, and this was difficult to hide under normal clothing.

Burton recorded, 'The scrotum will often reach the knees; I heard of one case measuring in circumference 41 inches, more than the patient's body, while its length (33 inches) touched the ground. There is no cure ... '

John Kirk, under orders from the Foreign Office and especially the influential Bartle Frere, was determined to get Barghash to sign a lasting agreement to ban *all* the slave trade in his Sultanate. He understood the limitations to Barghash's powers, so he acted with cautious but patient determination during the years of his miserable posting. Only the presence of his wonderful wife Nelly kept him sane.

Kirk was well aware of the awkward history of Britain vis-à-vis slavery. For over three hundred years Europeans had used slave labour from Africa to develop their colonies in North and South America and the Caribbean. Britain during that time had become the greatest beneficiary and the most extensive practitioner of the traffic. But it was also the British who first developed an intense moral repugnance against what they most of all had encouraged and practised. They felt a particular guilt about this 'of all evils, the monster evil', and in 1873, urged on by the death of Livingstone and consequent political pressures, Parliament sent warships to blockade the Zanzibar slaving fleets. This was Kirk's moment. The key was to persuade all the slaving clan chiefs to agree to a new and final ban on the trade, not just the Sultan. With subtlety and great diplomacy, Kirk succeeded, and once his document was agreed by all, signed by the Sultan and sent back to Frere and the Foreign Office, Kirk applied the agreement with a relentless determination. On 8 June 1873 a proclamation was posted on the wall of the Customs House: 'To all our subjects ... know that we have prohibited the transport of raw slaves by sea in all our harbours and have closed the markets which are for the sale of slaves through all our dominions. Whosoever therefore shall ship a raw slave after this date will render himself liable to punishment and this he will bring upon himself. Be this known.'

The trading of all slaves was now forbidden and the slave market, the oldest institution in Zanzibar, was closed by Sultanate soldiers and the auctioneers were forever forbidden to return.

So Kirk, Frere, Livingstone, William Wilberforce and many others were finally successful in helping to shut down the Zanzibar-based trade. On the African mainland slave trading carried on until the time when the Germans were defeated in the First World War and Britain took over as the East African colonial power and crushed the trade altogether.

I was lucky to get the chance to travel up the length of the Nile a century after the age of its explorers and of those who put a stop to the river's evil trade in people. One of our hovercraft, *Baker,* is still somewhere on the banks of the river at Bor, and *Burton* now resides in the Portsmouth Hovercraft Museum. And the five of us will always have our memories of the mightiest, hottest river on Earth.

CHAPTER 11

Fiend Force

Back in England, my poisoned finger received long overdue therapeutic treatment, but a friend in Dhofar sent me a letter warning me in confidence that things were not going well for the army there and, as a warning to me personally, that there were bad internal troubles with my Recce Platoon.

So, with my finger still swollen and twisted, but in view of the worsening situation in Dhofar and scared of being thought a coward, I left Ginny and my mother and went back to SAF without delay. After all, a broken leg might be a reason for prolonged leave, but a bent finger would merely be considered an excuse.

I flew straight to Salalah. Then, in the Beaver, out to the *nej'd* desert and Thumrait, where the men of Recce were awaiting my return.

As the plane bumped to a halt, some thirty half-dressed soldiers came running out of the huts. They grabbed my bags and my rifle, jostling to shake my hand and all talking at once. I felt a real flood of emotion and affection for these men. The warmth of their welcome was unexpected, and I treasure it now in my memory over forty years on.

After much coffee and gossip and talk of their ambush successes and near escapes, the sun went down and I walked outside the camp with Salim Khaleefa to hear the not-so-good news.

In my absence a new sergeant had taken the place of Abdullah.

Nobody liked him, even though he was of the Hawasana tribe, as were most of the platoon. The Baluchis hated him for he openly despised them. 'They no longer sleep and eat among us Arabs as they did.' Salim shook his head sadly.

However, fate was kind to us for very soon after my return the sergeant left the platoon of his own accord and Salim Khaleefa took over again, as he had from Abdullah. He spoke with the Baluchi *moolah*, and inter-ethnic relations soon returned to their old amicable state.

The platoon medic, used to dealing with stubborn wounds in conditions of extreme heat, applied a foul-smelling ointment and daily dressings to my finger and soon killed the bacteria. I no longer needed antibiotics, but the finger remains crooked to this day.

Soon after my return, the colonel in Salalah decided to mount a major attack on a system of caves near the Yemeni border, which Tim Landon's spies had confirmed as the *adoo* headquarters in Western Dhofar. No army unit had been there before, but one of our companies was already holding a high, barren ridge called Deefa which overlooked the Dhofar coast some thirty miles to the south. The area between Deefa and the sea was mixed thorn scrub and forest cleft by steep valleys.

The colonel aimed to strengthen the Deefa garrison of 'B' Company under Patrick Brook by moving my Recce Platoon and also 'C' Company, who were at the time camped halfway along the Midway Road between the Salalah Plain and Thumrait.

Murad made our six Land Rovers ready for the long journey into the mountains and Salim doled out all our Thumrait supply of mortars, grenades and bullets to Ali Nasser, Mohammed of the Beard, the *moolah* and another Baluchi corporal. Said Salim collected my section's supply.

A hundred men from 'C' Company in their lorries came to join us at Thumrait. They were singing and looked confident. We followed their dust cloud towards the Yemen, at first on flat gravel plains then climbing via the only drivable track up a dangerous, easily ambushed ramp which led to Deefa. This ramp had been picketed and cleared over the last week with mine sweepers.

Late on the second day we reached the bare rock of Deefa ridge, with a line of dense scrub immediately to our south. At dusk we came to Deefa Camp, a bald hilltop ringed with shallow trenches and a scattering of khaki tents on its crown.

Our intention must have been obvious to *adoo* watchers. There were now over 400 Sultanate soldiers scurrying about, by far the greatest number to have gathered in one spot in Dhofar, probably ever.

As we later learnt, a warning went out to all the *adoo* groups in Western Dhofar and to their base at Hauf, just over the Yemeni border. They closed in from all directions onto the region between Deefa and their cave headquarters. Then they waited.

The colonel sent both 'B' and 'C' Companies down into the scrub after dusk. Fearing an *adoo* attempt to take the Deefa Camp in their absence, my forty men, including the drivers, were to defend the hilltop trenches and be ready to respond to any cry for support from the companies.

We watched and waited through the day in the searing heat. At dusk we laid trip flares, for tongues of mist crept up from the treeline, dulling our vision despite the moonlight.

From the forests that fell away to the coastline, explosions and long bursts of machine-gun fire echoed up the ravines to our ridge, and soon after dark Patrick Brook called me on the radio. Both companies, he reported, had met fierce *adoo* opposition long before reaching any signs of an enemy headquarters.

Patrick's 'B' Company commander had recently been hospitalized due to drinking bad water, and he had been replaced with a newly arrived Royal Marine major, soon nicknamed Taweel (tall) by the men. This man was dogged by bad luck, and his men believed that he was troubled by a *djinn* (spirit) because the *adoo* seemed to outwit his every move, which, of course, resulted in dead and wounded soldiers.

When 'B' Company returned on our second day at Deefa, they looked thoroughly downhearted and bereft of the normal Omani good humour.

Patrick's upper arm was bandaged where a bullet had passed through between the bones. I made him a coffee in one of the tents and he told me that his men had successfully ambushed a dozen *adoo*, but on the way back to Deefa through thick scrub they had themselves suffered a close contact ambush. Patrick was leading with his magnetic compass when it happened. 'The noise was terrifying. Not only the guns in the close confinement of the bush, but the incredible sound of branches splintering all about you and the whine of ricochets from the rocks underfoot.'

One bullet sliced through Patrick's left arm and another smashed the radio he carried in his right hip pocket. He then crawled back to the machine gunner behind him. A bullet had passed through that man's skull and exited behind his ear. Taking the gun, Patrick wriggled back to the next soldier, his sergeant, who was writhing on the ground with one of his eyes removed by a bullet. Passing by a third casualty, Patrick gave the gun to a Baluchi who began to fire back into the bush ahead.

The enemy faded away unseen, but it took Patrick's men twelve hours to manhandle their wounded on stretchers back to Deefa. The blinded sergeant died en route.

On our third night at Deefa, the colonel called us south into the scrub to cover 'C' Company's return. Unlike 'B' Company, they looked confident enough though clearly exhausted, for this thorn scrub country was hellishly hot day and night.

As they passed close by in the semi-dark, we heard the scrabble of rocks and the creak of stretchers. I noticed many shirts and trousers ripped by thorn.

One man grinned up at me from a stretcher. I met him back in camp awaiting evacuation. A bullet had passed through his upper thigh and his genitals.

At one point in the midst of a labyrinth of thorn bush ravines, 'C' Company had run out of water and the Beaver had flown low, at considerable risk from *adoo* bullets, in order to drop two hundred sackcloth water bags over their exact location. All but three of the bags had split open on impact, so tins full of ice were later dropped. These took a while to thaw, but slaked the soldiers' great thirst.

The Sultan's two jet fighters had been of no help, due to the thick thorn bush cover and the frequent mists.

The whole operation, planned to last five days and to reach the enemy's Caves Complex, had to be withdrawn after only three days in order to avoid a major disaster, due to the unexpected strength and efficiency of the *adoo* and their weaponry.

Soon after the operation, Deefa Camp was shot up from the nearby treeline and, without enough troops in all of Dhofar, the colonel was forced for a while to withdraw all units from Western Dhofar. Among his post-Deefa operation comments to me while playing poker in a company tent one night were, 'I noted, Ran, that *your* Recce men cough a lot less on patrol than the company men.' I explained that I always left coughers behind in camp as to me they were potential killers for the rest of us. The colonel raised his eyebrows, 'In that case I'm surprised that you ever have enough active men.' He believed that generations of malnutrition in Oman had induced a high rate of tuberculosis in our soldiers.

He did later write that he was 'amazed how fit the soldiers were' and that, 'In spite of the fierce heat of the sun reflecting off the rocks, the soldiers seemed to have no difficulty in saving the water in their bottles. I found thirst the most painful part of the exercise.'

He had lost the use of one kidney years before and I was full of admiration for him because he was always keen to join operations himself.

The British had withdrawn from Aden in June 1967, less than two years before our Deefa operation, and already Chinese, Russian and Iraqi-trained, Marxist-indoctrinated, guerrilla troops had overrun all Western and much of Central Dhofar. Soon they would encircle the vulnerable Plain of Salalah and the Sultan's Palace.

New manoeuvres by ever-stronger *adoo* units forced our colonel to reposition his meagre manpower, and I was ordered to drive over the Midway Road from Thumrait to Salalah and to concentrate throughout the imminent monsoon season on laying ambushes along the foothills of the Qara Mountains. The so-called Midway Road was, in fact, a single-lane dirt track which in 1953, when the oilmen first came to Dhofar, the Sultan had sanctioned to be prepared from Thumrait (or Midway, as the oilmen called it) and hacked all the way over the Qara *jebel* and down to the Salalah Plain. Hundreds of labourers, mostly from Aden, completed the work between two monsoon seasons and without any trouble from the local *jebalis*.

On the track between our regimental HQ at Umm al Ghawarif and the RAF station a mile away, the *adoo* laid mines by night, one of which blew up the Land Rover of my Australian friend Spike Powell (who went by the nickname of Muldoon). He was a professional mercenary who knew all that there was to know about Marxist insurgents and their weaponry. From information gleaned by Tim Landon's spies, Spike had identified many of the new high-calibre weapons now in Western Dhofar which were poised to be brought into Central Dhofar as soon as the camel caravans needed to haul such unwieldy loads could safely do so without risk of being spotted and obliterated by the Sultan's two-plane air force. This heavy weapon move would be possible just as soon as the monsoon mists clamped down on the *jebel*. Katushka rockets and 12.72 Shpagin machine guns were included.

The downside of the monsoon for the *adoo* was that no camel, even lightly laden, could manage the steeper mountain trails once their surface was coated with glutinous mud. They could only move along the gentler foothill tracks on the northern rim of the Plain of Salalah, and this, the colonel stressed, Recce Platoon must prevent. 'Ambush the villages where the *adoo* go to get food and the wells where they drink,' he said. 'And always vary your routine or *they* will get *you*.'

So, night after night, we drove towards the mountains without lights and halted out of earshot of the foothills. Then we headed on foot for whichever of the valley mouths we intended to ambush over the next three days and nights.

Sometimes one of Tim Landon's guides led us to the mouths of specific wadis. Said bin Ghia was a sheikh of the Bait Qatan tribe and a founder member of the purely nationalist Dhofar Liberation Front (DLF).

Before one ambush briefing he told me his story. In 1964 the DLF leader, Musallim bin Nuffl, had coerced Said into his fledgling group of anti-Sultan Dhofaris. Until then Said had lived his adult life up in Bahrain as head gardener at an American Forces golf course. After training at an Iraqi Army camp in Basrah, ninety DLF warriors, including Said, boldly set out to cross the western sector of the great Empty Quarter desert from Saudi Arabia, whose army rulers gave them their six Dodge power wagons and a healthy supply of weaponry because King Faisal disliked Sultan Said of Oman.

Said bin Ghia told me about that little-known but remarkable journey through a land where previously only camels had travelled. They had driven through great barriers of sand dunes, their food always gritty with blown sand, often lost and always thirsty.

Two Dodges had to be towed and a third was repaired by Said battering a metal coffee pot to replace a piston ring. They drank water from the radiators or the stomach juices from gazelles that they shot. They fixed leaking radiators with flour and sand.

On finally reaching the Saudi-Yemeni border and the Sands of Dakaka, they were betrayed by their own leader's uncle. One of the Sultan's aeroplanes then spotted them in the open desert and destroyed all the vehicles. When, soon afterwards, their weapons dump was discovered and seized, Said gave himself up in Salalah and began his work for the Sultan's Intelligence group who, he admitted, had proved pretty ineffective prior to Tim Landon's arrival.

Said was soon trusted by the many army patrols that he led into *adoo*-held territory. He knew that he was a VIP target for the PFLOAG *adoo*. He still had family and other contacts in the Qara, and Tim gave him cash to keep him in favour with potential sources of *jebali* intelligence. Since defecting from PFLOAG, he had grown fat and idle for he was an enthusiastic gourmand from his UAE golf club days, but he was still useful as a guide and interpreter of the *jebali* tongue. Many of the Qara *jebalis* hated him as a traitor and they knew that he could tell when they lied to the '*geysh*' (the army). But they also respected him as a rich man, despite his humble *jebel* origins, seeing his heavy gold Rolex, his embroidered silk *shemagh* and the glinting gold *khanja* at his waist.

Said visited me in mid-June soon after the monsoon had clamped down over the mountains, the foothills and the plain all the way to the sea. 'Your men are now in danger,' he said. 'Certain *adoo* groups are currently working out how to trap you. They will ambush one of your ambushes.'

He explained that two of the Qatan tribe who had been accepting cash and rice from us in return for good information on where best to lay our ambushes had been arrested by an *adoo Idaara* (execution squad) and taken to a PFLOAG torture and execution site in Hauf, known as The Cage. They had identified our Recce Platoon with our six Land Rovers and noted our ability to move quickly and quietly all over the plain. From the two men, PFLOAG were also aware that our usual ambush strength was a mere two to three dozen soldiers. Luckily one of their number had gossiped to his brother who was paid by Said for news. He had been disgusted by the cruelty of the PFLOAG interrogators at Hauf, whose favourite methods of persuasion all involved heat, especially heated rods applied to eyes, nose and ears.

This was, of course, nothing new since for centuries burning or boiling people alive has been used as a legitimate punishment. It featured in biblical accounts and during Roman times. Heretics and witches were purged by the power of flames in the Middle Ages in England, while Jews and lepers were burned by the thousand after being blamed for the Black Death in France. The Spanish Inquisition killed countless thousands this way, while Spanish Conquistadors used to subjugate native Indians in South America by 'cooking' them on metal pans. The use of fire was a strikingly visual way to demonstrate society's perceived outrage at a crime while at the same time putting the rest of the population into a state of fear.

When Mary I came to the English throne in 1553 she tried to impose Catholicism on a country that had been religiously reformed by her father, King Henry VIII. Nearly three hundred Protestants were burned at her behest, including Bishops Nicholas Ridley and Hugh Latimer in Oxford. With admirable courage, Latimer turned to Ridley as the pyre was being lit and said, 'Be of good courage and play the man; for we shall this day light such a candle by God's grace in England as I trust shall never be put out.'

But there can be little doubt that being burned alive is agony and this quote was probably attributed to Latimer to reinvigorate the faith of surviving Protestants.

Accounts that survive from the Middle Ages talk about white bones showing up through the flames and flesh falling away like a 'red raw' curtain. According to one witness, it took about forty-five minutes for someone to die after the pyres were lit. Only the lucky few would suffocate in the smoke before the blaze reached them.

Boiling alive was less commonly used as a punishment, but it was nonetheless legalized in 1532 by Henry VIII to punish one criminal in particular. Richard Roose was a cook found guilty of poisoning the porridge of his boss, the Bishop of Rochester. He was judged to have committed treason and was boiled alive, roaring 'mighty loud', according to one chronicle. Women who watched the protracted death fainted, while men admitted that they would prefer to see the headsman in action. That English law was repealed in 1547.

In 1675 Sikh martyr Bhai Dayal Ji was boiled to death in India after refusing to convert to Islam. He is said to have died peacefully quoting from Sikh scriptures. Once again the account of his composure may be religiously motivated to give solace to the faithful. Modern accounts from people who have suffered significant scalds by water talk of intense pain before falling into a coma.

It was a punishment used across Europe, and as late as 1687 a man was boiled in oil in Bremen for assisting coin forgers. These barbaric practices largely ended with the age of Enlightenment. Although it didn't signal the end of capital punishment, rational thinkers did set about limiting the suffering of the condemned.

At the time of writing, Islamic State terrorists have used the Internet to publicize their horrific video of burning alive a Jordanian fighter pilot inside a metal cage. *Plus ça change.*

In order to make ready their major plan to overwhelm the Sultan's Army in Dhofar by the end of the year, PFLOAG needed to consolidate their big weapons along the northern edge of the Plain and in the deep forested wadis debouching onto the Plain. This they could do without fear from any of the three companies that made up the entire army presence in Dhofar because all three were bottled up in their separate camps with their every move under *adoo* observation. Only our Recce Platoon, which moved silently and only by night with an unpredictable ambush pattern, could therefore upset the overall *adoo* plan of the great PFLOAG leader, Ahmad al Ghassani, in Hauf.

'The only current task of certain *adoo* commandos is to eliminate your unit.' Said was echoing what Tim Landon, following information from other sources, had already warned me about.

That week we had no guide and only sixteen active men (those without monsoon coughs, the sound of which during an ambush could give away our presence). Our target was the village of Darbat.

In less troubled times the Sultan had married a local Darbat woman of the Bait Maashani tribe. Their son, the Sultan's only heir, was Qaboos, educated in England, militarily trained and commissioned as a British regular officer in the Cameronians until his early twenties, when he returned to Salalah where the Sultan kept him under close supervision (for their family had a history of internal strife and coups). The village of Darbat, situated in the fertile mouth of the Darbat Valley, sprawled around a lake immediately above a vertical 800-foot cliff-face known as the Abyss of Dahaq, a place rich in local legends of human sacrifice and oracles. Also, during the rainy season, it was the site of the greatest waterfall in Arabia. The Dahaq cliffs stretched west–east for a mile between two peaks, Jebel Darbat and Jebel Nasheeb.

Said Salim was the only member of Recce who had, two years before on his first posting to Dhofar, been to Darbat at a time when it was known to be free of any *adoo* influence. Sergeant Mohammed had, therefore, appointed him as our guide. I don't know of anybody I have ever met who was more suitable to earn the description of 'ninja' than was Said. He could move with cat-like stealth, was acutely observant and was given to wearing a sheathed stiletto-like knife, which was against army regulations, but I could foresee circumstances where he could, with a silent knife, be uniquely useful. So, unless soldiers from outside Recce were present, Said could wear his ninja knife openly. He was at all times beside me on patrols, as was Hamed Sultan, a powerful Zanzibari machine gunner.

By this time and over a campfire in a desert area, Said, Ali Nasser and the Beard had decided to dispense with the traditional 'Sahib' (Sir) when addressing me away from non-Recce folk. They determined, after much laughter and debate, to call me Bakheit bin Shemtot bin Samra, which translates roughly as John of-the-ragged-clothes, son of the Thorn Tree (due to my unkempt appearance, they explained). So from then on I was simply Bakheit to the men of Recce.

Meanwhile, back at Salalah headquarters and always keen on code names, Patrick Brook and the Colonel had chosen my nickname as 'Fiend', so Recce became Fiend Force and individual Recce soldiers 'Fiendeen'.

On our slow and silent climb through shrubs and acacia and up the slippery slope on the eastern side of the Dahaq cliff, we of Fiend Force were surprised by the descent of a herd of cattle with unseen herders. We crouched low in the darkness, but when a herder yodelled and a woman from far above us trilled a reply, Said touched me and whispered, 'They know we are here. We will need to be very, very careful.'

Once the cattle had all passed by, sliding between bushes, Said scooped up a smattering of liquid green cow dung and wiped it over his trousers. I whispered to Mohammed and the other section leaders to have their men do likewise, especially on the hair of the Baluchis who, against my orders, still used smelly hair creams. Dhofari *jebalis* have the ability to detect any smell which is not normal to their existence.

'They never move cattle on wet slopes by night,' Said whispered. 'They must have heard the Land Rovers way out where we left them and then sent the cows to locate us. They are cunning as rats. We must be very, very quiet.'

The escarpment was steep. We were all fit and, without gear, would have made it to the plateau at the top of the waterfall cliff in an hour. But the sound of a single rifle clashing against a rock would betray the direction of our movement to hidden ears.

Most of the Darbat villagers were indigenous *jebali* Qara, but mixed-blood Zanzibari slaves had over the past two centuries settled there, and most of them were now prime *adoo* material.

In Salalah *sooq* (market), Hamed Sultan, my machine gunner, often spoke to Zanzibari Dhofaris. He was a first-generation Omani Zanzibari.

After two hours we emerged on a level with the upper rim of the cliffs, and moonlight turned the monsoon mist a hazy yellow above the Darbat lake so that the vague outlines of village huts in the lakeside cultivated fields were visible. Above us the wooded escarpment continued to rise.

At this point Salim Khaleefa with seven men went past us in two groups heading for a vantage point on the slope above the village.

My section split likewise. Said, Hamed and my signaller stayed with me. I watched through my telescope as the others faded into the gloom.

A wild cat screamed above us in the woods. Hamed leaned close. 'That is no *senoor* cat, Sahib. That is *adoo*. Zingibaris of Darbat. Their night signals are those of their forefathers from the rainforests of Usumbara and Ukambani.' Said nodded. 'They know we are here, Bakheit. They will cut us off. We must move while we can.'

I had seen and heard nothing to suggest that our presence was rumbled. No dogs barked, for there were no dogs in Darbat. Only wolves, foxes and hyenas.

But I trusted Said and used my National walkie-talkie to whisper Salim's section back down. I told them that we must move back to the plain before dawn as we were probably compromised.

I knew other British officers who would think my actions weak, and even cowardly, but I had never shirked an ambush before nor did I subsequently unless advised to do so by the normally imperturbable Said and the aggressively anti-Marxist Hamed, whose parents had been killed by Marxists in Zanzibar.

'They will by now have blocked the slopes below us,' Said warned me. 'We need another route back to the plain.'

We agreed to head off on rocky ground where we would leave no footprints in the mud nor pass close by the village. The only feasible route was to creep along the very edge of the abyss on the cliff top to the far side of the Darbat plateau, then, once clear of the rock face, to find a way back down to the foothills.

Said led the way with his rifle slung over one shoulder and a white phosphorous grenade in his left hand ready to provide immediate cover in the event of a sudden ambush.

As we moved through the maize fields beside the lake, treading only on hard ground, we passed unavoidably close to animal stockades with thorn fences, and by the time we reached the rocky edge of the abyss, we had left no footprints.

The wind blew from the north with a whiff of burnt dung, so our own sweaty body odour would be less detectable, even to the locals. We were lying prone on the ground when two men came out of a hut to our front and smoked together for half an hour. Soon dawn would break and our predicament would become dire. We were halfway across the width of the cliff face when the monsoon sky lightened and our silhouettes would soon be clearly visible to any watcher in the nearby huts.

Hamed pointed to a wooded hillock which sprouted from the plateau. 'We could hide there for now,' he mused, 'and then, tonight, carry on across the village fields to the far side of the cliffs.'

It made good sense. Crouching low, we reached the little hill and, splitting again into four groups, found shelter behind boulders. My group wriggled with our guns into a shallow cave where we disturbed an army of black ants. I killed as many as possible, but was bitten again and again throughout the following day – one of the longest, nastiest and hottest of my life.

There were scares each time a goat herd or lone villager approached our position, but it seemed that by dusk we were still undetected.

All day long we had observed our intended escape route – the clear, flat ground that stretched between our hide and the point where the cliffs of the escarpment became merely a steep forested, but negotiable, descent. As far as we could tell, only cattle had been there, and we had seen a single large herd driven through at midday.

Said said that this was a good sign because the *jebalis* never took cattle into an area where they could see that the *adoo* planned an ambush.

But when the herd was still there after dusk, Said grew uneasy since, due to wolves, big cats and cattle thieves, herdsmen normally took their cows back to their byres by nightfall. So he suggested that we wait for a while.

Between slowly wafting waves of moonlit mist, we watched a sudden commotion among the cattle, and through Said's binoculars, better than my telescope at night, we saw a dozen figures drive the herd towards the escarpment's edge and along our intended escape route. We conferred quietly. They must know, we agreed, where we were and had deduced where we were heading. Assuming that they were waiting in the scrub some few hundred yards away, we determined to trick them. Said and Hamed waited in the cave with the machine gun. I took the other section from the hillock and headed off at sixty degrees from our escape route, making the occasional noise and leaving our boot prints clear in muddy places. On reaching forest, we waited in the undergrowth until Said called on the walkie-talkie. He sounded elated.

'When you left,' he said, 'we saw and heard nothing for two hours. Then the cows came back and many men. They moved below us and on to the village. They must believe you are headed further up the wadi and will plan to cut you off once you are well into the *jebel*.'

We agreed to meet at the far side of the cliffs as originally planned, and did so with scrupulous care to be wraith-like. We reached the edge of the plain by dark, and three green flares fetched Murad. We had narrowly avoided entrapment in our ongoing and deadly game of nocturnal chess.

In 1895 the first Europeans to visit any part of the Qara Mountains were a couple of avid botanists who, having heard of the unusual climatic conditions in Dhofar, determined to discover new plants there. Through a mixture of cunning, charm and good luck they obtained the Sultan's permission and went with guides and guards into a few of the Qara wadis, causing a sensation with the *jebalis* in their impractical Victorian garb. Their botanic efforts were highly successful.

Some sixty years later, Thesiger crossed the *jebel* on his way north from Salalah and, using his maps, the oilmen arrived in the gravel wastes just north of the *jebel*. In 1964, when the first army patrols probed some of the intermontane valleys and high pasture plateaux, they were the first Europeans to do so and, ever-menaced by possible ambush, they were inclined to stay on the Salalah Plain and keep *jebel* patrols to a minimum. So when Fiend Force arrived to penetrate some of the thirty valleys leading into the *jebel* from the south and lay ambushes wherever the constantly varying terrain favoured us, there were still many ravines wrapped in *Alice in Wonderland* vegetation, peppered with caves and deep in *adoo* country where white men were talked of by wandering bedu to marvelling audiences of Qara *jebalis*.

These Qara mountain folk's history can be guessed at but with no great accuracy for their ancestors left nothing but scattered graveyards. There are no ruins in the mountains and no potsherds of antiquity. Even the oldest *jebalis* know few tales of their forebears.

Archaeologists from digs in the Yemen say that the Qara were not the firstcomers to Dhofar. First came the Hamitic Cushites from Egypt who, in Dhofar, were known as Shahra and built the city of Robat whose ruins lie beside Umm al Ghawarif camp. Much later, they were overrun and enslaved by the Semitic Qara from the Nile lands and Ethiopia. These men came by way of the Yemen as part of the Joktanite invasion. Joktan was a descendant of Shem the son of Noah, and the book of Genesis states that Joktan's descendants advanced as far as the Yemen and those under Ophir as far as the mountains of Sephar, now Dhofar.

In the back of Murad's Land Rover we carried steel ammunition boxes containing bullets, grenades and mortar bombs on top of a layer of sandbags to protect us (some hope!) from death following the detonation of a mine. On top of the boxes the five soldiers of my section laid their bedding bundles on which they perched. In one of the bullet boxes I kept my supply of books, all on topics related to my search for Ubar. Ginny had collected them or borrowed them (sometimes against regulations) from the library of the Royal Geographical Society and given them to me when I was on leave. Said Salim called it the 'Ubar Box'.

A well-thumbed bargain book by a Cambridge archaeologist, Paul Bahn, had introduced me as to how to teach myself to find a lost city. It soon became clear that the discovery of ruins had a lot to do with luck, not just skill and knowledge. Bahn wrote:

Archaeology is like a vast and fiendish jigsaw puzzle invented by the devil as an instrument of torment since: (a) it will never be finished, (b) you don't know how many pieces are missing, (c) most of them are lost forever, and (d) you cannot cheat by looking at the picture. Much of the time archaeological evidence is so patchy that anyone's guess is as valid as anyone else's. You cannot prove anything. Where the remote past is concerned, nobody knows what took place. The best that can be offered is an informed guess ... Some eminent archaeologists have built their entire careers upon convincing bluff.

Nonetheless I decided to collect all available clues from all available sources and to become the Number One Ubar Expert while I was still in the ideal employment set-up for locating a lost city in the most inhospitable place imaginable.

To list some of the background facts, many of them very disjointed, will give an idea of the type of haystack in which I would be searching for the Ubar needle.

The first obvious clue was that the location of the ruins would need to be somewhere between the product that the original inhabitants wished to sell, in this case incense, and the intended market, especially places to the north of Saudi Arabia.

Second, there would need to have been an ample supply of water, which may or may not by now be covered by dunes.

Third, historical clues would need to agree, at least approximately, on the best region to start searching. I was sure that the existence of Ubar could not merely be a myth or desert mirage because references to its existence have kept occurring in literature over a period of more than fifteen hundred years. Prior to that, the Arab traders of incense would have kept all references to their trade routes and incense orchard locations a close secret from the competition of Greek and Roman traders. That period with no records, a dark hole known as the *Jehalia*, the Age of Innocence, is even darker than the corresponding period in Western Europe owing to the lack of new conquerors of Arabia who might have kept records.

At the height of the Roman Empire the Dhofar merchants were exporting over seven thousand tons of frankincense by secret land routes and by sea every year while managing to hide the actual location of the orchards from the Greeks and Romans whose pagan gods demanded that prayers and all ceremonial events, including burials, weddings and births, were accompanied by the burning of incense.

In terms of geographical history the whole of the Arabian Peninsula was too hot and arid for human habitation around 6000 BC, so no trading centre would predate 5000 BC. This was not a very helpful clue!

I studied both the Old Testament and the Quran (Koran) with care and both were helpful in fairly nebulous, often contradictory, ways. For instance, different translations of the Quran gave differing histories of the lost city of Irem, but they all talked of 'the people of the Al Akaf', and this was significant to me because the region of the Wadi Mitan and the nearby rim of the Sands were still called Al Akaf by the local bedu.

According to Quranic history, the Adites or Ubariti were a tribe descended from Ad, the son of Uz, the son of Irem, the son of Shem, the son of Noah. Ad's own son Shedad settled in Al Akaf and built Irem. Unfortunately the inhabitants of Irem/Ubar/Wabar became idolatrous and evil, so God destroyed them, in the same manner as he wiped out the biblical Sodom.

At this point the Quran gives some worthy clues to Ubar-searchers. I quote: 'And into Ad was sent a desolating wind that turned all to ashes ... And we destroyed their cities ... Against some we sent a sandstorm, some were seized by a great noise. For some we cleaved open the earth and some were drowned.' I concluded that Ubar had been demolished by a natural disaster which could have been a tsunami, an earthquake, a volcanic eruption or, most likely in the Wadi Mitan area, a sandstorm.

The *Encyclopaedia of Islam* postulates that Wabar is 'north of Mahra country and within the Rub' al Khali (Empty Quarter)'.

Noah's Ark, Atlantis and the Lost City of the Incas had no greater supply of historic reference behind them, yet explorers from many countries have made great efforts trying to find them. Ubar, the Atlantis of the Sands, was another such riddle yet, up until 1969, only two expeditions had been officially allowed into Dhofar to search for it: that of Bertram Thomas and of the American Wendel Phillips. The latter had subsequently been told by the Sultan never to return to Oman.

One of the reasons that Dhofar's early history is so hard to establish is the scarcity of their ancestral remains or written records, other than graffiti in caves in a script as yet undeciphered, as the four different tongues of the Dhofari tribes – Mahra, Shahra, Harsusi and Botahari – are all different from Arabic.

The Bible is not helpful in terms of clarifying the well-known legend that the Queen of Sheba was involved with Ubar and that she colonized the Dhofar incense orchards. Legends do suggest that she left her Yemeni capital of Marib in 930 BC to visit King Solomon, the third King of Israel, in Jerusalem in order to establish an incense trade agreement, but biblical references to her incense territories are muddled, either being the lands referred to in the Book of Ezekiel or the more northerly Sheba referred to in Genesis.

Confused by the welter of conflicting Ubar clues, I decided to concentrate on known facts.

Frankincense trees grow only in the specific climatic conditions to be found in Dhofar, certain islands off the Yemeni coast and Cape Guardafui in Somalia, and the Dhofar trees produce by far the best and most prolific harvests. Ignoring maritime trade, the routes from the *nej'd* incense zone to reach the key markets in the north of Arabia must all pass through vast waterless tracts of the Empty Quarter, and all the Rashidi bedu whom Sultan bin Nashran had quizzed for me agreed that the traditional camel caravans carrying sacks of dried incense involved one herdsman for fifteen camels with well over a hundred camels per trip. This meant that they would take on a considerable amount of water as far north as possible before entering the Sands. This in turn meant that Ubar's site must be at the northern end of a significant wadi taking water from the Qara *jebel* out towards, and historically into, the Sands.

Both the Sultan's best desert guides, Hamed al Khalas and Sultan bin Nashran, agreed to guide us to likely wadis in the *nej'd* whenever Fiend Force was next sent north over the mountains for patrol duties back in the *nej'd* and the Sands.

Said bin Ghia led us one night from the Umm al Ghawarif camp into the Wadi Naheez where its seasonal floods exit onto the plain and have washed out a cliff-flanked channel for some distance towards Salalah and the coast.

Said knew a *jebali* family who were at the time camped with their cattle in shallow caves within this channel.

Laying an ambush on the *jebel* side of these caves we stayed there for two days. Non-stop monsoon drizzle kept us all under cover and my own section camped within the main *jebali* cave among the *jebalis* and hug-a-mug with their cattle. Smoke from their dung fires hung low like fog and drove away the voracious monsoon flies. Without the smoke, men and animals would have been driven crazy.

Salim Khaleefa paid the head of the cave *jebalis* for one of their goats which they killed and boned and then heated the meat in the ashes of a wood fire. We ate with them including, post-goat, a pudding consisting of glutinous flour balls dipped into an open jar of wild honey. This was still in the comb and the bedu ate the wings and abdomens of dead bees caught in the honey without seeming to notice. Finally we shared their drink, pink and soupy, which Said assured me was nothing sinister, merely cow's milk mixed with the boiled pulp of tamarind fruit.

After the meal all the remnants were placed by the women into a bloody goatskin and hung from the cave ceiling. Then, prior to patrolling our outer ambush ring, I sat back to digest and listen to the musical sound of the *jebali* chatter and the bleating of goats, all the while watched intently by ten very grubby little children. I rubbed tears away, for the dung fumes were acrid.

On another patrol to the foothills of the Naheez and on an unusually dark night, Said seized my shoulder from behind. '*Waqaf*, Bakheit,' he whispered. 'Stop!' I was about to walk over the edge of a sinkhole some 70 feet deep and 30 feet wide known as Ghaur Fazl. We rested that night further up the Naheez in a deep cave. En route, as usual, I never followed the obvious footpaths notable by the shine on the pebbles and rocks because on the softer sandy sections the smaller enemy mines, nicknamed 'scrotum-thieves', were often laid in such places. So I was wont to thread my way along less navigable routes which in verdant wadis like the Naheez involved the risk of disturbing snakes. There were many species, including the spotted rock snake which can glide up almost vertical surfaces, the tiny threadsnake and the *ekis* carpet viper which can kill in six seconds.

Said warned me to avoid sleeping in caves if there was a reasonable alternative. The main danger was from the tics which could bite into your skin without you feeling anything and then, in sucking your blood, they infect you. Some cause raging irritation and fever, others deep ulcers and lesions. They are hosted by the foxes, goats and leopards that frequent the caves. Other denizens include hyenas, civet-cats and lynxes. Wolves, Said told me, usually keep to the more open places but are the worst predators of cattle.

Blood-sucking flies, an unfortunate by-product of the Qara

monsoon, forced the *adoo* down to the foothills where our patrols became correspondingly more dangerous. Tim Landon once sent us to the western edge of the plain to ambush the spring of Mugshayl close to the sea. The date was 20 July 1969, and on the surface of the moon that night at the Sea of Tranquillity, Neil Armstrong planted a flag in the lunar dust.

Monsoon waves crashed against the cliffs below me as, unaware of this historic event, I watched the moon's reflection dancing on the waves. In that part of the Indian Ocean dorsal-finned Indian rorqual whales, over a hundred feet long and the largest of all living creatures, cry into the night like humans. Great mammoths, and even vicious hammer-headed sharks, provide food for fifteen-foot-long sawfish with six-foot saws. These lesser monsters attack with speed and rip their giant victims' bellies out. Then they feed at leisure on the entrails of the threshing leviathans.

One day our platoon was ordered to the Salalah Palace, where the Sultan greeted me in front of all the men lined up by our vehicles.

'These are your men?' he asked. His English was without an accent. He shook my hand, his turban at the level of my shoulders. His face was gentle like his voice. He was little in stature and, in his billowing pantaloons, a touch dumpy – an Arab version of Queen Victoria. Above his fine white beard there twinkled the warm, brown eyes of Father Christmas. Since my job was to fight and possibly die for him, I was pleased that I found myself instinctively liking him.

'Yes, Your Highness.' I bowed as I would to the Queen. 'The Reconnaissance Unit.' After an English education in India, he had ruled Oman wisely for thirty-five years in the days of no oil revenue. Now the money was beginning to pour in, but cautious by nature, he had no desire to rush into crash programmes of modernization with undue speed. I felt respect and loyalty for him, knowing that I would continue to fight his enemies and, if necessary, die in his service despite disliking his shortcomings. I had often blackened his name when we were refused extra food to give to half-starved *jebalis* and when issued only aspirins for the sick and dying.

His son Qaboos was somewhere in the palace kept well away from any potential plotters. But, unknown to the Sultan, his own chief intelligence officer, Tim Landon, whom he permitted to visit

Qaboos weekly for tea as they had been friends back at Sandhurst, was the chief co-ordinator of secret British plans to replace the Sultan with his son as soon as was humanly possible.

Back in the 1950s the Middle East section of the Foreign Office had contrived the successful removal of Sheikh Zayed of Abu Dhabi when his lack of reform and progress had helped the arguments of UAE revolutionaries, and Whitehall had engineered a coup to replace him with his more progressive younger brother. So they had form!

Now that the British handover of Aden to a leftist Yemeni regime had enabled Russia and China to reach the point of imminent take-over in Dhofar, Whitehall had woken up rather late in the day to the Soviet-inspired threat to the Omani side of the oil-vital Straits of Hormuz. So a repeat of the Zayed coup was put in place, involving Tim Landon, senior representatives of PDO (Shell) in Muscat, Qaboos himself, the Wali (Mayor) of Salalah, and senior British officers in the Sultan's Armed Forces.

The coup was planned for the summer of 1970 and, once completed, massive military support would be sought to defeat the *adoo*. This would include the SAS, a helicopter squadron, jets from the Jordanian Air Force, and thousands of crack ground troops from the Shah of Persia (Iran).

The problem was that, for various reasons, none of this could be put in place until after the monsoon season. Yet the Marxist forces were all but ready for their superior ground forces in Dhofar to crush the Sultan's Army before the New Year dawned.

Whitehall's main action man on the ground in Dhofar was Tim Landon, and he had the ability to thwart the subjugation by PFLOAG of the *jebali* tribes in Eastern Dhofar, including the Eastern Mahra and the Bait Howairat to the east of the Midway Road.

The PFLOAG leader entrusted to suppress any rebellion against the *adoo* in the East was their political commissar, Salim Amr, once a worker in RAF Salalah, who had risen through cunning and cruelty to the notice of PFLOAG recruiters and had been sent to Odessa in the Soviet Union for training. Now he was appointed overall PFLOAG commissar in the Eastern Dhofar region.

Amr ruled the east through his *Idaara* execution squads, all trained in the Yemen by the East German HVA in the art of persuasive torture. His local liaison officer was Musallim Ali. I knew these names well because of a subsequent close and lethal encounter with both men.

Tim Landon decided to trap Salim Amr by a series of ambushes which were set up in caves overlooking a long-standing Fiend Force ambush target in Amr's tribal region, the spring of Arzat.

David Bayley, one-time Yemeni War mercenary and current commander of 'A' Company, was the first to take a stint in the Arzat cave system. I met him the day after his return to base. His face was a mass of red spots, many bleeding. His arms, ankles and neck were similarly marked and he scratched furiously at the livid blotches as I watched.

'The little bastards eat you alive from dawn to dusk,' he muttered. 'The caves are a living hell.'

And they were. Despite the mosquito nets wrapped around us, the flying ticks were small enough to wriggle through the mesh in their hundreds. At dusk, leaving us all itching in the stifling heat, they disappeared and a whining hum announced the arrival of the cave mosquitoes.

One night, returning from an Arzat ambush, one of Murad's drivers overturned his vehicle in an unseen ditch and Hamed Sultan was crushed to death. We all sorely missed him.

Prodded by Tim Landon, the Sultan finally allowed me a large issue of supplies to give to the half-starved inmates of the foothill villages. Over our shoulders we carried sacks of flour and rice, sugar and tea, milk powder and spices by night from the Land Rovers to village headmen. Tim also gave me cash and some *jebalis* began, for the first time, to tell me of their anger with the *adoo*. 'We do not like them, but what can we do? The government doesn't help us, until now, nor give us protection. We have so little food, but we must give what we have to the PFLOAG men or they beat us. If we pray, they torture and even kill us. They rape our daughters. They are blasphemers.'

Radio Aden announced that the 'freedom fighters' of Dhofar had located a Sultan's propaganda group who were trying to bribe the simple folk of the mountains to turn against PFLOAG. These brave freedom fighters would, however, soon eliminate these imperialist lackeys.

We made the mistake one night of telling a woman in one village that we would bring her starving children and sick husband more food and medicine at the same time the next night.

The result was a narrow escape from a well-positioned ambush. Only Salim Khaleefa's acute observation at the very last minute saved us from a wipe-out, but our guide, Said bin Ghia, was shot through the wrist and two of our Baluchi were badly wounded before we escaped from the village. I took over the machine gun while Said Salim carried the portly Said bin Ghia over his shoulder and back to the Land Rovers. Next day I found that a bullet had split apart the butt of my rifle.

Tim, at a weekly ambush discussion, warned me to be hyper-alert at all times in the light of the *adoos*' growing strength. I assured him this was already the case, but to ensure my future avoidance of *adoo* traps, he recounted two tales about late friends of his.

The previous year the SAF officer Hamish Emslie had led a Land Rover patrol in the gravel deserts just north of the scrub-zone, an area then considered fairly safe, when an *adoo* group had fired a 3.5-inch rocket at the lead vehicle, killing all the occupants including Hamish.

'And,' Tim added, 'Alan Woodman, down in the forests of the Wadi Naheez on foot patrol was hit by a bullet in his guts. I remember hearing his voice, very faint, on our radio calling for help. But help was, as always, slow in coming and Alan died in great pain ... So, Ran, I repeat, take no unnecessary risks. Be invisible.'

Al Ghassani, the notorious leader of PFLOAG in Hauf, made sure that the fate of all *jebalis* who failed to obey his new regime was made known throughout Dhofar. Old men had their loins, backs and stomachs held down on beds of hot charcoal, others were thrown over cliffs after being flogged, and still others had their eyes gouged out with hot spoons in front of their families. Fear was an important weapon to help PFLOAG in the difficult struggle against such a deep-rooted faith as Islam.

Setting up his base in Eastern Dhofar, where no army patrol had ever ventured, at the mountain village of Qum, Salim Amr and his brown-uniformed *Idaaraat* drew up their lists of known and likely 'traitors'. When the time was ripe, he had only to point his finger at an individual to condemn him, or her, to death or worse. He had no need to rape a pretty girl who took his fancy, for a word to the head of her family was enough to ensure her favours.

The one fly in Salim Amr's ointment was, perversely enough, the local PFLOAG liaison officer Musallim Ali in the eastern sector, an earlier member of the Dhofar Liberation Front nationalists. He was clearly anti-Sultan, but not, to Salim Amr's mind, sufficiently in tune with PFLOAG's extreme policies and aims to fight, not only for the freedom of Dhofar, but for a united Marxist community from Aden to Kuwait with full ownership of its own oil rights.

Musallim Ali's belief was that they, the *jebalis*, must indeed get rid of the Sultan and his foreign friends, but without accepting the new burden of Marxist Maoism. Furthermore, Musallim was reported to have said, 'Marxists say, "What is yours is mine"and take it. But we Dhofaris have always said, "Take all that I have. You are welcome to it."'

A powerful group of Eastern Qara fighters under their influential leader, Hafidh bin Abdullah, backed Musallim Ali and suggested at public meetings that they would remain loyal to PFLOAG only for as long as their traditional Islamic beliefs were not attacked, as was clearly happening in the rest of Dhofar.

Al Ghassani was aware that his assault on Salalah could go ahead only with the full participation of the eastern tribes, and he relied on Commissar Salim Amr to root out quickly all the eastern trouble-makers and eliminate all the religious reactionaries. In mid-September the monsoon began to lift, revealing the Qara Mountains in all their post-monsoon glory. Verdant, high rolling downs above steaming jungle and menace in the valleys below.

Unpleasant things now began to happen for, despite our best attempts at blocking the trails from the west, many heavily laden camel caravans had crossed through the Central Dhofar *jebel*, along with well-trained armed units and their heavy weapons. Meanwhile on the Sultan's side, no extra men, weapons or even a helicopter was added to our strength.

Adoo land mines now peppered the plain to deadly effect, and, for the first time, anti-personnel mines were placed around the garrison camps of the three companies. Little plastic mines no bigger than torches, but sufficient to blow a man's leg into his stomach, to tear off his scrotum and to blind him. And *adoo* execution squads came by night to coastal villages with target lists, so that even inside the perimeter wire of Salalah town, many civilians lived in fear.

In the Salalah suburb of Arzat, one Sultanate guide, Naseeb, was shot at point-blank range by his own brother, an *adoo* squad leader.

Spike 'Muldoon' Powell, our only Australian officer, decided that, although we in the Sultan's Army had no anti-personnel mines of our own, he would make some. Using empty beer cans, torch batteries, detonators, electric wire and plastic explosive, he formed a production line in his office.

I was given fifteen such 'mines' to plant a few months later and very nearly trod on one when, just before leaving Dhofar, the time came to remove them.

I only know of two victims of these 'Muldoon' mines. One was an armed *adoo* and the other a company soldier who went to urinate where he had been warned not to. He was badly hurt and his officer, a friend of mine, Eddie Viturakis, entered the minefield and dragged him clear, luckily avoiding other mines. Soon afterwards Eddie was murdered by one of his own soldiers, a drug addict, who then fled to the *adoo*.

Tim Landon told me that, eight weeks before, a group of five hundred uniformed *adoo* with two hundred camels had crossed into the eastern sector of the *jebel* with heavy weapons that included *Meemtoos*, US Army Browning M2 .50 machine guns (originally captured by the Viet Cong), alongside British 81mm mortars.

Rakhyut, the only Sultanate stronghold on the coastline to the west of Salalah to hold out against *adoo* attacks, now fell to the *adoo*. Only a few Sultanate *askars* had defended the fort which was easily overrun and the Muscat Regiment was too overstretched even to attempt to retake the town. Later reports detailed the execution of the garrison including the town governor. This left PFLOAG undisputed masters of two-thirds of Dhofar, with every likelihood of imminent overall victory by way of an all-out attack on Salalah once the eastern sector was secured.

Our colonel did his best to prepare for the worst, and on 17 September, once the mountains were finally clear of mist, all available army units were mustered at either end of the Midway Road, as that dangerous trail over the mountains was called, the only link between the northern deserts and the Plain of Salalah. There was no other way that the Sultan could receive supplies other than by lorry convoys over this trail, for he had no cargo planes and no navy, other than a single armed dhow.

The *adoo* had mined the entire length of this road over the Qara and had laid well-planned ambushes in readiness for the army's post-monsoon attempts to clear the way for our convoys.

The colonel's plan was to send 'B' Company, now led by Taweel (the lanky Royal Marine captain recently posted from Britain), to open the road from its northern end, while 'C' Company with elements of 'A' Company and my Recce Platoon would advance from the Plain and the southern foothills.

Up north, Taweel was caught with most of his men on open ground some four miles into the mountains at a notorious ravine known as Ambush Corner. He had with him an old 25-pounder cannon (polite name 'artillery piece') and, as its three-man crew swung it round to blast off at an *adoo* machine gun, they were wiped out by another hidden *adoo* group.

Caught in crossfire, any position other than lying flat in the grass was suicidal for Taweel, so he was unable to crawl back to his Land Rover radio to call up the Sultan's two jets for support. He could only lie and watch his men being picked off all about him. He noted that, on striking the ground, some bullets exploded, scattering rock and shrapnel. This was a new addition to the *adoo*'s arsenal. One such bullet set Taweel's ammunition lorry on fire, and as the flames roared towards the load of artillery shells, the Baluchi driver bravely tried to douse the inferno. He soon fell with a bullet through his head.

A junior British officer, just arrived from Muscat, managed to wriggle back to the radio and the jets soon arrived. The *adoo* melted away from that particular ambush.

Meanwhile, at the other end of the road some five miles south of Ambush Corner, we reached the last of the foothills before the track began its steep climb up the mountainside. All hell broke loose at that point. I led all the men of Recce in four well-coordinated sections ahead of the company lorries. We found that great boulders had been rolled down to block the track. We managed to shift these with difficulty while under fire. Several firefights later, we reached Ambush Corner, met up with Taweel's survivors and waved on the convoy. Lorry after lorry rolled past, screaming in low gear down the infamous ravine.

The convoys would take three days to complete this vital resupply run. Each night, with our long-time guide, Hamed al Khalas, we moved out from the track to ambush likely *adoo* ambushers the following day. As we lay motionless not even swatting at flies, the heat was all but unbearable. We longed for dusk.

At one point Hamed spotted six armed *adoo* in uniform moving from hut to hut in a village below our hide. I had only to call in artillery fire, but hesitated when I heard the loud laughter of children coming from the huts, and so funked making the call. My men, even Said Salim, were extremely annoyed by my reluctance to engage such a lucky target. Once the *adoo* unit left the village and moved into the surrounding scree, I did bring artillery fire down on them, but by then it was too late to be accurate.

Soon after the road clearance, I heard that a minor mutiny had occurred in the 'B' Company camp, and the men had refused to serve under Taweel any more. They were sure he had a *djinn* (spirit), and too many men had been killed since he took over the company. He was forced to leave the camp and his men threatened to shoot him if he returned.

The colonel flew out to 'B' Company to calm things down and to appoint another officer as the new company commander. He also rearranged the companies to form a loose blocking 'line' of outposts across the entire *jebel* from sea to desert at the point where the forested zone was at its narrowest. He called this the Leopard Line.

As during the previous year, I was given the entire *nej'd* region of semi-desert, some one hundred miles stretching from the northern cliffs of the Qara to the sand dunes of the Rubh al Khali, to block with my force of six Land Rovers, thirty men including drivers, one 3-ton ammunition and supplies lorry, and a water tank bowser.

This meant crossing the Midway Road once more from Salalah. We came under heavy fire from the foothills. Corporal Salim and Ali Nasser leapfrogged their sections forward, all jinking fast like rabbits as they ran. We gave them covering fire, then with the *moolah*'s men and my own we sprinted up the hillside with bullets zipping overhead.

The mortars of David Bayley's 'A' Company opened up and helped us clear the *adoo* position. A week later Tim Landon said that six *adoo* were buried that morning. He also learnt that a heavy Russian Shpagin machine gun was hidden deep in the Arbat Valley east of Ambush Corner. He detached Recce to hide in the valley until Bayley's company, with our help, could entrap the Shpagin crew.

Things did not work out that way. At least sixty *adoo* were using the Shpagin as bait with a well-sited ring of ambushes. 'A' Company was forced to withdraw with its dead, and by midday we were alone in the bottom of the Arbat; twenty of us split into four sections.

All the men understood the perilous nature of our position. We had, after all, survived in *adoo* territory, heavily outnumbered, easily cut off with no means of rescue or evacuation given a single casualty to carry, over a period of many months. That we had survived this long was due to a singular skill we had slowly developed for nocturnal movement with silence and speed and always using the easiest terrain rather than attempting to force a noisy way through scrubland in order to follow a crude compass bearing.

But down in the Arbat we knew that the *adoo* would look for an army backstop to the defeated company attack on their Shpagin group. We could not risk retreating from our hides in daylight, but we needed to escape from the valley before the *adoo* searchers discovered our location. Salim Khaleefa agreed that the less evil option would be to stay put for the seven long hours till dusk and pray that we remained undetected.

The heat and the flies notwithstanding, nobody moved a muscle. But towards noon two young girls came into the knot of scrub where we lay. Their eyes widened in fear. Said Salim touched me, his eyebrows raised in questioning mode and his stiletto unsheathed. I shook my head but, to be shamefully honest, I regretted my decision as soon as the girls had run off.

I remembered the words of an SAS veteran who had once trained me. His group had been surrounded by tribesmen in the Radfan mountains in 1967. 'The bastards got our officer and one other, but the rest of us got away. They cut off both our men's heads and paraded them about on poles in Sanaa. It was our officer's fault. He could have had us all killed. An old shepherd had spotted us and, by the book, we'd have slit his throat. But our captain said no, and the old boy told the Radfanis our location.'

Two hours after the two girls disappeared we heard the thrash of people moving through dry grass. The sound came nearer and we moved out of our hides as silently as we knew how.

Somehow our long hours of 'ninja-training', as Ali Nasser called it, paid off, and after half an hour spent creeping through low undergrowth, there was no longer any sound of third-party movement.

My signaller whispered, '"B" Company has been ambushed on their retreat. They called in the planes, of which one has been hit.'

Night came at last and we made it safely back to the *nej'd* and our vehicles.

Later the Sultan's Armed Forces summaries recorded of Fiend Force operations against the *adoo*: 'On 30 July, after an ambush on the escarpment north of Taqa, the platoon was engaged by the enemy from five different dominating locations and sustained one slightly wounded. Captain Fiend rallied his men and conducted a skilful withdrawal (the only course open), frequently exposing himself to aimed enemy fire and firing the .50 Browning machine gun himself.' And, 'On 3 August in the Wadi Thimreen, Fiend Force was engaged by an enemy force of 20 to 30 armed with automatic weapons. The platoon assaulted and outflanked the enemy groups and forced them to withdraw.' And, 'In October, as part of Operation Green Cap, Fiend Force again demonstrated their determination to operate independently with a small force in an enemy area.' And, 'The endurance, judgement and initiative on independent operations of Fiend Force have proved the ascendancy of a small SAF force over larger enemy groups on many occasions.'

The Midway Road was used only once again that year as the *adoo* in the Central region of the Qara became too strong for the army. My Recce Platoon never used the road again, and when I returned with a TV crew in 1973 there were only three SAF officers in Dhofar who had ever motored over the Qara.

By closing the road, the *adoo* controlled all Dhofar from the Yemeni border to the lands of the Eastern Mahra tribe. Once this troublesome tribe was subjugated by PFLOAG, the Plain of Salalah would be cut off with its back to the sea. The colonel's chain of blocking outposts, the Leopard Line, was certainly a good plan, but time would tell whether or not it would prove effective in blocking further PFLOAG supplies and men getting through to the east.

We of Fiend Force were determined to let nothing and nobody through at our northern end of the Leopard Line.

Back in Salalah for a visit to the medical officer to sort out bad desert sores, I met up with Patrick Brook, who had just had a surreal experience. An *adoo* had been caught with a backpack loaded with anti-tank mines. By chance he had been taken to Patrick for questioning and they had instantly recognized each other.

'Last time I saw him,' Patrick told me, 'he was a smart British–trained sergeant in the Dhofari Squadron of the Trucial Oman Scouts in Sharjah, to which I was briefly attached before my posting out here. He had come to me for his Leave Pass. I signed it for him! Yesterday, when he was brought to me handcuffed, he gave me back his old Leave Pass and apologised for "being late back".'

CHAPTER 12

The Hottest Place on Earth

The desert guides, Sultan bin Nashran of the Bait Shaasha tribe and Hamed al Khalas of the Bait Maashani, were assigned to Recce while we worked in the *nej'd*, the vast volcanic region between the Qara Mountains and the Empty Quarter, wherein only bedu survive, including those belonging to the tribes of our two guides.

We split into three groups, having left our two lorries with their drivers hidden near the Pools of Ayun, our fortnightly replenishment point for water and the only place available for those who wanted to enjoy a body wash.

The purpose of this three-way split was to cover our huge area of responsibility. Each group had two Land Rovers, ten men, a High Frequency radio and two machine guns. We were by then past masters at avoiding tracks likely to be mined. But we could never afford to be complacent. David Bayley had left one of his mountain outposts lightly manned for two days while his company was away on patrol. The outpost was surrounded, isolated soldiers were killed and their weapons seized.

We never developed routine schedules nor returned by our outward route, except when forced to by an unavoidable bottleneck. In such cases we always approached the danger zone with caution and after sending pickets out on foot. We knew that it would only be a matter of time before we too suffered an ambush or an attack, probably when and where we least expected it.

One ravine which we had to pass through beneath the cliffs of Haloof was almost certainly under observation by *adoo* watchers. We determined to do what our predecessor SAF Recce Platoons had tried but failed to achieve: to find a safer alternate route. So one of our three groups under Ali Nasser was tasked to search high and low (literally) for an alternate route through the maze of *nej'd* canyons, wadis and mesas.

A second group under the *moolah* and Mohammed of the Beard would ambush and patrol the Dehedoba trail, the most obvious infiltration route for camels from the Yemen. This left only the endless wastes between us and the Yemeni and Saudi borders where *nej'd* and sand dunes met. Since the Sultan had no helicopters and no desert patrols in north Dhofar, other than us, we needed to penetrate deep into this poorly mapped region to ensure that no *adoo* supplies were sneaked through by any means. My section led this third patrol group, together with Corporal Salim Khaleefa and with Hamed as our guide.

Before splitting up for our first three-way operation, we checked our schedules for daily radio calls, using Morse once voice contact was lost. And I warned everyone for the umpteenth time to be erratic in their actions, setting no daily patterns of movement and never relaxing their guard.

Over the months to follow, often in scorching sands with shimmering mirages of mixed-up rock, lake and sky, I grew very close to the men of my section of Fiend Force. They became as near and dear in my thoughts as my own faraway family. It was during this period of the Leopard Line blockage that I determined to find the Ubar ruins that had so successfully eluded my predecessors, Bertram Thomas, Philby, Thesiger and the American Wendell Phillips. I persuaded myself and, I think, my men that since our military task was to search the area north of the Dehedoba trail up to the Yemeni and Saudi borders, which we were genuinely doing, there was nothing wrong in looking for ruins as well as PFLOAG camel convoys. Our previous short search in the Wadi Mitan area had made me feel guilty of improper usage of Sultanate vehicles and men for a private venture, but this time we could genuinely claim that we were searching an area designated in my instructions, whether in the *nej'd* or the

Sands, so long as we stayed on the Omani side of the Saudi and Yemeni borders.

When my group's Land Rovers called in at the pools of Ayun after a fortnight's patrol near Habarut, the colonel sent me a message which boosted my hopes of finding Ubar. The new order was to find another 'new route', this one to lead from Thumrait to Habarut but avoiding the current roundabout trail based on the old oilmen's tracks to their various drilling sites. This new route, the colonel advised, should, where feasible, pass by or near to known water holes, thereby covering the likely ports of call of *adoo* arms convoys.

Since I had deduced that water holes were as good a clue as any in the search for the location of Ubar, this new order from on high was fortuitous.

Knowing that sooner or later it was likely that Fiend Force would run into trouble and need injury evacuation from the *nej'd*, we needed to find a usable flat airstrip with no rocky bits and a length of at least 400 metres.

With Hamed al Khalas as our guide, from our base in Ayun we patrolled in great heat to the west and south-west, sometimes in the vehicles and sometimes on foot, filling our *chaguls* (water bags) from remote springs that we would never have found but for Hamed. Names of these gem-like springs were often strange, but three that I do remember are Thint where Hamed said the *adoo* had once camped for months by the water hole, Abrun and Al Ghayl, lost in a godforsaken wilderness of lava valleys. From Thint one sultry evening Hamed led us, weary and thirsty, to a high gravel plateau.

'This,' Hamed gestured all around him like Moses showing us the Promised Land, 'is the most narrow place on the Dehedoba trail.' We walked to a flat stretch where Hamed pointed to a faded set of tracks.

'The Beaver aeroplane,' he said. 'This runway was once used by oilmen for bringing supplies. Maybe for one month only.'

I looked on my old 1954 oil map and, roughly at our current position, was printed *Pasadena: Position Approximate*.

I measured the usable, reasonably flat stretch of the old runway at a maximum of 350 metres, just enough for a Beaver to take off at sea level (whereas we were over 1,000 feet) in cool temperatures (not in the current furnace heat at dusk) and without much of a load. I hoped that I would never need evacuating from here. However, Hamed took us a mile or so to the north of the strip along craggy ridges to a tiny, hidden nook surrounded on three sides by gravel hillocks. This was an ideal defensive position in which to camp and hide our vehicles, yet be close enough to observe the narrowest part of the Dehedoba infiltration trail.

This became one of our bases for many months. Patrick Brook, now the adjutant back in Salalah, named it Fiend Field.

From there and the easily reached pools of Ayun we made long journeys into the Sands, saw places seldom seen by anyone but bedu and laid ambushes to kill people about to kill other people. I remember it as home. Hamed once pointed at the near horizon, at a low ridge running west–east. 'Only there can the *adoo* and their camels come by from the Yemen,' he told us over a well-cooked dish of goat and rice. 'Or else much further north where the *nej'd* ends and the sands begin.'

The *nej'd* looked lifeless and harmless. In reality every crack in the crumbling gravel of our new home concealed something that slithered or crawled. Over the next few months Fiend Force sent foot patrols out twenty-four hours a day from this base. When on patrol elsewhere we left but a single section in radio contact and well concealed among the sweltering hillocks of Fiend Field.

Concentrating on water holes and always with an eye on Ubar as well as the *adoo*, we drove east from Ayun and Thumrait to the seldom seen oasis of Andhur. I had studied the records of Thesiger and Thomas, the first Europeans to visit the ruins there. In 1952 they were followed by Wendell Phillips who completed superficial excavations which revealed a pre-Islamic fort, clearly built to guard and control the harvesting and storage of the frankincense collected from the surrounding area, in which grew the finest incense trees in the world.

We left the vehicles in the Wadi Shiswaws after a three-hour drive among gravel canyons, and we followed a line of crumbling crags above the tiny oasis and its sudden array of date palm trees until we

came to the ruins of a single small room within a larger stone enclo-
sure. Immediately outside this unimpressive shack were the
two-metre-long troughs of cut stone, which Phillips had assumed to
be storage containers for dried frankincense gum.

Hamed disagreed about the purpose of the troughs. He clearly
found them distasteful, hardly even glancing at them. According to
legends passed on by some *jebalis* and long before Islam came to the
Qara, priests had performed human sacrifice here. To appease the
Moon God Sin, young girls were buried alive in the sand, captives
were brutally circumcised, disputes were settled using trial by ordeal,
and incestuous wedlock was encouraged.

When Murad said we would need to do a lengthy repair job on
our vehicle before moving elsewhere, Said Salim was definitely not
happy. The place was evil, he said. Later at Ayun (a happy place!)
Said explained the nature of the devil to me.

'The *Shaitan* [Devil] is powerful whereas we mortals are weak
because God created us only from congealed blood and from the
water poured out from between the loins of man and the breastbone
of woman.'

I confessed to Said that I had not known this.

Frankincense today is a booming export for the health and perfume markets of the world and comes from Somalia, India and
Ethiopia, whereas the Dhofar trade has dwindled.

Historically, the infant Jesus was brought frankincense by Arabs
on camels from the East, along with gold and myrrh, because it stood
for holiness. Pagans in Rome and elsewhere revered it in the belief
that their prayers would the better reach their gods along with the
wafting of incense smoke, whether at ceremonies or merely at personal prayer.

There are records of its use in Sumerian temples in 2500 BC.
Shortly before his death, Alexander the Great was planning to invade
Arabia in order to control the incense trade.

The anonymous Greek merchant who wrote the *Periplus* as a
guide to sailors a few decades after Christ's birth mentioned Eastern
Dhofar and, specifically, the Abyssapolis of Ptolemy (Darbat's waterfall) where he noted that frankincense 'lies in heaps'.

Marco Polo wrote of the great cost of the incense and that the

Dhofar rulers made a profit at source of 600 per cent. World demand was voracious during the Roman Empire. Great storage halls were built adjacent to the Temple of Jerusalem. Chaldean priests burnt many tons annually at their temples in Babylon. Pliny wrote, 'Let us only take into account the vast number of funerals that are celebrated throughout the whole world each year, and the heaps of odours that are piled up in honour of the bodies of the dead ... It is the luxury of man, which is displayed even in the paraphernalia of death, that has rendered Arabia thus "happy".'

By the 1930s over 1,000 tons of prime frankincense were being exported by sea annually from Dhofar, and a lesser amount from nearby Somaliland where a similar hot, dry climate allowed the growth of frankincense trees, but these produced an inferior product which could be harvested only once a year, whereas the Dhofar crops were collected in spring and again in the summer. Pliny noted that the best orchards were to be found in the great dry heat of the *nej'd* to the north of the Dhofar Mountains (for example, the Andhur region).

With Salim, Murad and Mubarreq Obeid (Hamed Sultan's replacement on our machine gun), I left the others drinking tea around the Andhur ruins and, taking an empty ammunition box and a machete, visited a nearby ridge where a dozen incense trees grew seemingly straight out of the rocky ground. Their roots must be extremely determined.

'Bad folk,' Salim informed me, 'once did this ... but no sex.' This confused me at the time, but I later found that he was right. The Dhofar rulers who controlled the orchards were wont to send prisoners from Salalah to collect the gum, but nobody who had recently slept with a woman or touched a dead body was allowed to pollute the sacred trees by touching them.

The Mahra bedu whom we met at Andhur sometime later showed me which of the weird, contorted little trees, once the chief source of Arabia's wealth, would produce the best sap, how and where to make incisions in the bark of the trunk, and how many days (three to five) to wait before returning to scrape off the dribbles of milky resin. The harvesting must take place only between March and August.

The end uses of the incense were many and diverse. For instance, women drank it as a powder mixed with water to help the birth of stubborn babies.

Long before garlic was used to ward off Transylvanian vampires, frankincense was burnt at the doors of wealthy Arab houses to ward off evil spirits (and to keep insects out).

In China and India, Arabia and Africa, the plague was thought to be kept at bay with incense burnt twenty-four hours a day, but only by the rich for it literally cost more than gold, weight for weight.

Quite apart from the huge tax at source, the costs incurred in transport overland were substantial. The camel convoys for journeys over a thousand arid miles, often through lands roamed by brigands demanding exorbitant protection money, had to be financed. Finally, on reaching Alexandria, the embarkation port for Roman and Greek destinations, heavy export taxes were exacted.

My own Andhur outing to gather incense ended in failure because when, several months later instead of the recommended five days, I next visited the specific trees we had slit, the four of us disagreed as to which trees we had incised. So I went to Salalah where I bought several packets of cured frankincense and, back in London, tried to sell it at a profit to shops catering for standard church goodies. I was politely told that 'nowadays our incense is made from fish glue.'

My entrepreneurial failure notwithstanding, the global incense trade in the twenty-first century is booming. Twelve per cent of upmarket perfumes and skin care products use it as a highly marketable ingredient.

American chemists analysing frankincense have isolated anti-inflammatory, anti-carcinogenic and antiseptic properties with numerous curative and preventative uses, including therapeutic massage, aromatherapy, control of arthritis, and even DNA repair functions.

Production of frankincense is, at the time of writing, negligible in Dhofar and is confined to satisfying the market for gift-wrapped luxury packs sold at mouth-watering prices in five-star hotels in Muscat and Dubai. This does not, of course, worry Omanis because black gold from Fahud has more than compensated for the old white gold from Dhofar.

I treasure the memory of that night at Andhur by the incense troughs. The sky was crowded with stars and edged by a crescent moon. A wolf howled from the east where the labyrinthine canyons of the Wadi Thawbah cut through the *nej'd*.

From the high crags of the nearby Valley of Maghtabara the reply came from other wolves, and I thought of Thesiger who had camped here some years before. He had written of wolves on a journey he had made from Salalah to the Yemen … A bedu had left his two young sons at a well with bags of sardine fodder for his camels. He was gone for only a day, but during that time wolves ate all the sardines and killed the children. Their father found both his sons' partly eaten bodies.

While in the *nej'd* I heard many wolves, but saw only two in all my time there. On both occasions we were moving silently in file and the wolves fled as soon as they saw us.

At about this time my signaller gave me a note of a Morse code message just received from Patrick Brook, the Muscat Regiment adjutant at Salalah headquarters. A week previously I had sent back on the Beaver a Zingibari soldier who had briefly been 'taken over by a *djinn* spirit on Dehedoba duty'. He had stayed terrified after the *djinn* had left him, so he was of no use to Fiend Force.

Patrick's message was brief. 'Ref Spooky Man, Salim Mayoof, he claims that your Said Salim has stolen his soul and he cannot return to [north] Oman until it is released. Suggest you send a signal back to me saying that "Soul has been released". All ideas welcome.'

I checked with Said Salim, who shrugged, smiled and commented, '*Mayoof magnoon*' (Mayoof mad). He agreed, however, that he would very happily release Mayoof's soul if he had inadvertently and unknowingly removed it at some point. I confirmed this to Patrick and never again saw Mayoof.

From Andhur we drove back west, took on water, supplies and six goats from our base by the pools of Ayun, then headed west with Hamed al Khalas to check waterholes.

Hamed led us first by way of the Wadi Ayun and, in places, tracks beside it to a little-known spring by the confluence of the Amkun valley and another at the Ayun's juncture with the Wadi Harazon, at which point Mubarreq Obeid killed a gazelle which made a tasty change from goat.

About two miles north of the last spring, called Abkah by Hamed, we came to an important camel trail crossing the wadi and an underground spring called Umm al-Shaadid or Maashaadid. Hamed was full of praise for the water here, as a French waiter might discuss a favourite wine. 'The sweetest water in the world,' he called it, and he reminded us of his reputation for identifying the source of any water in the Dhofar *nej'd* by smell or taste alone. He could thus assure me that this Shaadid water came from the pools of Ayun.

'Then, listen well, Bakheit, for you wish to find the place called Wabar, and this water flows on by way of Hayla and Khadim to the distant well at Shisr.'

This was indeed good news on both the military and the Ubar fronts.

Curious to see how bedu watered camels at Shaadid, since the water surface was said to be 45 feet down a narrow curving shaft, I let myself down this shaft using the bucket rope, a tattered length of hemp. The drop seemed greater than predicted, the heat was stifling and the shaft descended in separate lengths with bottlenecks between them where the original diggers had gone off at tangents to avoid boulders or had dug deeper as the water level dropped.

Hamed had warned me, '*Shekohf! Ghool!*' (Beware! Snakes!) but I was more disturbed by the bats that clearly nested in holes off the shaft. My head-torch shattered en route, and in the gloom I found the flutter of the bats' leathery wings and the stench of their dung disturbing. Relieved to escape the suffocating oven, I was greatly impressed at the bedu who must spend hours down at the water's surface filling a great many buckets for their thirsty camels.

At times we swapped duties within our other Fiend Force sections after meeting up at Ayun or Fiend Field. We lived permanently on the move when not on Dehedoba Watch.

The dead wood with which we cooked was quick to turn to red-hot embers, giving out little telltale smoke and only the faintest of glows in the dark. The trees that provided most of this *hatab* were *sam'r*, acacia, euphorbia and camel thorn.

Various large carrion birds, including buzzards and kites with their shrill keening mew would circle and indicate the position of some new and edible corpse, more often than not in wadis with scrub and *hatab*. We often camped in these places since we had limited space in the Land Rovers to carry *hatab* for the evening fire. This wadi-camping was a dubious advantage, from my point of view, since, where there was *hatab* there were also spiders, and I had had a spider phobia since childhood. Keen to avoid showing fear in front of the men, I had a problem trying to hide my instinctive panic when approached or, worse still, crawled over by even a small spider.

The incidence of camel and wolf spiders in these *hatab* wadis was, unfortunately, quite common. The camel spider can jump as much as a metre, is difficult to squash, being squat and strong, has large eyes and a beak with which it can cut into and eat the flesh of animals or humans. Hamed told me that these spiders will often wait until an intended victim falls asleep and then inject them with a local anaesthetic so that they don't feel their flesh being eaten. On waking they find an area of skin peeled off and the surface flesh beneath gone missing. This never happened to any of us and by the time I left Arabia I had lost my fear of spiders through the frequency of forced confrontation with them.

Scorpions were everywhere in the *nej'd*, especially the sand-coloured six-inch-long variety, which were difficult to spot if motionless, and it was always advisable to look before picking anything up or sitting down. I always slept with my clothes and shoes on, despite the heat, and always, on feeling something crawling over my exposed parts in the dark, made to brush it off rather than squash it.

Hamed al Khalas lectured us on which 'nasties' were best avoided. Of the scorpions, large and small, whether green, black or light brown, none were deadly although their sting could be very painful and even incapacitate a strong man for several hours.

The snakes we saw most frequently in the *nej'd*, especially in the *hatab* wadis, were the horned viper and the puff adder. 'If they bite you,' Hamed advised, 'kill an oryx and rub its blood on the bite. Then you may live.'

Of larger creatures, we spotted a few hares which, like the scorpions, were well camouflaged and often stayed motionless until we were very close. Lizards and skinks were, judging by their tiny trails in the sandy stretches, very common but seldom seen.

Few days passed by on *nej'd* patrol without spotting small herds of Thomson's gazelle, the occasional ibex and oryx. In two years I saw only three hyena, one wild cat and two wolves, although we heard the calls of many of all these species, especially at night. Hamed assured me that mountain lions and leopards still wandered the Qara and the *nej'd*, but I never spotted them even during ambushes when we remained silent and motionless for many hours.

How any creatures survive in the great heat of the *nej'd* along the edge of the Sands was a mystery to me, but one of the books that Ginny had borrowed on long loan from the Royal Geographical Society listed the heat-survival tricks of various species in various deserts.

The feathers of birds keep heat out as efficiently as they keep it in when conditions are cold, but in great heat they flutter their throats which creates currents of air across the moist insides of their mouths. In temperatures higher than 70°F (21°C), desert vultures urinate on their own legs to cool them down.

Some desert gazelles can extract enough liquid from their food, such as leaf sap, in order to survive with no water. Jackals can do likewise with the body liquids of animals they kill, and all desert creatures have extremely dry faeces (which is why camel turds, along with *hatab*, are excellent fuel for fires). With both small and large animals a 10 to 15 per cent loss in body weight due to water loss will cause functional deterioration, and a 20 per cent loss often causes death.

Even the deep sea creatures in the 'black smokers' (volcanic underwater vents) of the Indian Ocean have learnt to live with great heat. Their homes in hydrothermal vents demand their ability to survive in termperatures hot enough to boil water.

Like the bedu, all animals try to remain inactive by day in whatever shade they can find and, when feasible, travel and hunt by night. The oryx has no clever anti-thirst mechanism so it survives by sticking to a strict daily routine of commuting forever between known grazing areas and the nearest available water source.

Larger desert animals, including the oryx and ibex, have an advantage in that they heat up more slowly than small creatures, a process known as thermal inertia.

Humans are quite good at keeping cool but lousy at conserving water. Sweating is their chief cooling function but, during very hot desert days and on the move, they can lose up to 3 gallons (12 litres) of water a day.

Because they have large-size brains, the blood cooled by evaporation of sweat on the face and head penetrates the skull via tiny veins which deliver freshly cooled blood to the brain. Other primates lack this function.

The chief advantage of the human design is that we stand upright and when the sun is high in the sky, only our heads are exposed to maximum sun heat, unlike four-legged animals whose entire back soaks up direct heat. Only our lower legs are close to the heat rising from the hot desert surface and our upright stance receives maximum cooling from any breeze. Since we have virtually no fur or feathers, we lose heat more quickly through convection and sweating. Our hair, for those who still have some, shades our heat-sensitive brains.

Tim Landon sent me money in the shape of heavy silver coins, known as Maria Theresa dollars, which were acceptable all over Oman and could be used to bribe bedu for information as to *adoo* uses of old camel trails well north of the Dehedoba, because Tim's informers had suggested that this was happening. He mentioned the names Mudhaghadhak and Amilhayt (which later turned out to be a corrupted version of Umm al-Hayat).

The money arrived along with our next scheduled goat supply at our Fiend Field airstrip, and I headed north with three vehicles and twice our normal load of fuel and supplies.

On reaching the abandoned Sultan's 1950s fort and the waterhole at Shisr, we drove north-east up the Wadi Ghadun, whereas previously our patrols had headed north-west into the edge of the Sands of Fasad.

The water at Shisr was reached by a sandy slope some twenty feet down and was, as Hamed had assured us, a continuation of the Wadi Ghadun aquifer and the springs at Ayun and Maashaadid. Shisr means cleft in the Kathiri dialect and clearly refers to the sinkhole leading down to the water. We topped up our water cans here and, heavily laden, bounced or often enough pushed our way along the Ghadun valley past a stark rock ridge that Hamed called Maliss.

That afternoon Murad's engine overheated and we stopped, exhausted anyway by the hottest few hours I could remember, in a confusing maze of wadis, to the immediate north of which great sand dunes reared up.

Hamed wandered off. I realized that he never seemed to notice or be affected by the heat. He returned in half an hour and beckoned to me. I did *not* want to walk anywhere, but could not admit this so I went with him to a corridor of sand where the tracks of a great many animals were clearly visible. Hamed squatted down and gave me a lesson on the prints which was so interesting that I forgot the heat. There were tracks of gazelle, oryx, hares, snakes, lizards, birds, locusts and, quite fresh, of camels, which Hamed said were heavily laden.

By way of this track, which Hamed explained would lead us soon to Tim's suspect Amilhayt trail, the *adoo* might indeed be gaining access to the Qara without our knowledge. We would soon find out. Wilfred Thesiger had once travelled by camel from roughly where we were for six days to the spring of Mugshin, assured by his Rashidi bedu guides that they could survive for up to seven days with no food or water so long as their camels kept going.

Once Murad gave me the 'all clear' on the vehicles, we continued north until the labyrinth of diverging wadis opened up into a single wide valley completely blocked to the north by an abrupt line of high dunes, reddish in colour and stretching away to the north-east as far as the eye could see.

'This is the Wadi Umm al-Hayat,' Hamed announced. We trudged slowly to the ridge line of the nearest dune, some 200 feet high, and I noticed that on the north side the sand fell away at a far steeper angle, to the point where, presumably, the sand grains would begin to slide away in response to gravity.

This was the southern edge of the Rubh al Khali. From here the world's largest unbroken expanse of sand stretched north into Saudi Arabia, dune after dune, some 580,000 square kilometres of nothingness, the cruel and arid conditions of which had spawned and cradled Islam. Here mountains of sand are constantly formed by the wind, only to be battered and engulfed by larger masses in the great summer storms. All life here is soon smothered by sand and sucked dry by the pitiless sun. Petrified ostrich eggs have been found here but little else, for billions of tons of sand shift annually, huge ranges alter their geography over the years and if fabulous cities ever existed, they would, I shrugged at the thought, be uncovered by chance changes in wind patterns and not by the shovel of an archaeologist.

To me, the surface of the dunes and of the hard ground between many of them was merely sand or gravel, but Thesiger had identified quartz conglomerate, porphyry, rhyolite, jasper, granite and limestone.

We drove seven miles to the south-west to the western end of the line of dunes and, finding for a while a hard gravel surface, continued north to check for further camel tracks on the far side of the dunes. We camped the night beneath a towering dune which Hamed called Yadhak.

Assuming that there was no need for silence so far north of the *jebel* where a single jet could kill a hundred *adoo* at leisure, the men were openly cheerful. There was nowhere for an *adoo* to run, and if their food or arms convoys were indeed using this area, they would be accompanied by innocent-looking youths, not armed PFLOAG fighters.

So the men talked into the small hours, squatting in the sand about the glowing embers of our fire, the Baluchis at ease with the Omanis. They were so different from the British soldiers that I remembered around the tank squadron fires on exercises in Germany. Nobody spoke derisively of their colleagues, trying to score over their neighbours in conversation. They expressed themselves without the need for constant swearing and an endless supply of beer cans. I felt happy with these Muslims without the superficial officer-soldier barrier of European armies. I was just Bakheit.

One by one the soldiers slept where they lay, and there was silence. Occasionally the plunk-plunk of cooling metal from the vehicles cut across the soft background sound of moving sand, tiny particles falling with the perpetual motion of the dunes. I remembered an old saying of Sultan bin Nashran, 'When the desert wind stops blowing, it will be so quiet you can hear the turning of the Earth.'

I lay awake, all thoughts of the *adoo* for the moment eclipsed by the excitement of searching for Ubar. It could not, I felt, be far away now.

On my map I measured exactly 70 nautical miles to the point where, a decade earlier, the American archaeologist Wendell Phillips, with the Sultan's permission, had located a deeply incised series of ancient tracks leading into the Sands to the north-west of Fasad. Once we had finished checking out this Umm al-Hayat area, I determined to head west to the grid reference that Phillips had recorded for his 'significant tracks' (52°30' West and 18° North).

I had read over the past year all the books and articles that I could find about the early explorers of Arabia. Al-Ya'qubi (AD 897), Al-Mas'udi (956), Al-Qazwini (1283) and Ibn Battuta (the 1320s). Later on came Ibn Majid (1470), Ludovico di Varthema (1504) and, in the nineteenth century a plethora of Europeans starting with the Swiss Johann Burckhardt in 1811 and Richard Burton in 1853. Burton was eager to cross the entire Arabian Peninsula but never made it due to 'the fatal fiery heat'. Three other notable Arabian explorers of that century were William Palgrave, who crossed Arabia from west to east (1863), Charles Doughty (1876) and Lady Anne Blunt (1879). All four made their journeys in the northern half of the Peninsula, the Nafud Desert, well beyond the Empty Quarter which was considered to be impenetrable.

Not until the 1930s did three very different and individualist characters, all British, decide to traverse the sands of the Rubh al Khali. First came Bertram Thomas, financial adviser to the Omani Sultan, who made the first south–north crossing of the sands in 1930. He was followed a year later by the colonial administrator, Harry St John Philby who, with Saudi royal backing, completed the first north–south crossing.

Both Thomas and Philby were on the lookout for Wabar during their separate crossings, as was, three years later, the British lone traveller and author Freya Stark, all 5 foot 2 inches of her, whose extensive journeys in the Yemen included a meeting with the Yemeni Sultan. He told her, 'Wabar is a deserted city which spirits took over when Ad and Thamud were destroyed. It lies between Hadhramaut and Oman.' Freya Stark pointed out that Arab geographers had variously situated Wabar inside Yemen, between Shisr and Mahra, between Shisr and Sanaa, and in numerous other locations. With such evidence, she concluded, it seems quite possible for Mr Thomas and Mr Philby *each* to find Wabar in an opposite corner of Arabia.

In fact Thomas never found any ruins but, somewhere to the west of where we had already searched the Wadi Mitan, his Rashidi guide had pointed at what Thomas later described as 'well worn tracks ... graven in the Plain'. He shouted at Thomas, 'Look. There is the road to Ubar.'

Philby's own search for the legendary Wabar ended with the comment, 'There is little likelihood of ancient ruins being found anywhere in the Rubh al Khali. I think it has been unsuitable for human occupation except by nomads since long before the beginning of civilization ... What then of the legend? So far as the Rubh al Khali is concerned, it is a myth and no more. We must seek *elsewhere* the site that gave rise to it. The spade may yet disclose the identity and history of Ad.'

Fourteen years after the Wabar searches of Thomas and Philby, Wilfred Thesiger first visited the Sands, and in two remarkable journeys with bedu guides completed the first two west–east traverses through the heart of the Empty Quarter, once from Shibam in the Yemen to the coast of the Persian Gulf at Sharjah, and then further east in the sands a round trip from and back to Salalah. He made no great efforts to locate Ubar but was once told by his chief guide that the ruins were definitely buried to the north of Habarut, outside the Omani-Yemeni border.

In 1955 Wendell Phillips was told by a bedu of ancient shards found in the dunes five days by camel to the west of Shisr. Phillips' subsequent search some 'four miles into the dunes' apparently followed the tracks mentioned by Bertram Thomas, but his description of exactly where these were is so vague as to be of no help at all. He concluded:

The mystery of Ubar remains unsolved. In a completely inaccessible area where today there is little or no camel traffic, a well-marked highway centuries old, made by thousands of camel caravans, leads west for many miles from the famous spice lands of Dhofar and then, on a bearing of N75°W, mysteriously disappears without a trace in the great sands. A dozen Ubars could well be lost among these high dunes, unknown even to the present day bedu. I firmly believe some day some explorer will solve the mystery of Ubar, Arabia's most intriguing lost city.

Leaving our camp at the Yadhake Dune, we made our way due west over very difficult surfaces of sand, *sabkha* crust and low canyons along the latitude line where the wadis debouch into the southern edge of the Sands. North-west of the Wadi Atinah and some five miles short of the abandoned Fasad North 1950s drill site, we split a half shaft in the worst *sabkha* trough that even Murad could remember. By then we had been on patrol for two weeks in the very northern limits of Dhofari *nej'd* without a sign of any *adoo* activity or, for that matter, any sign of a lost city or allied ancient tracks.

In between patrols I had collected many snakeskins in the desert – most of the reptiles were small and all had venom sacs. In the smaller wadi-beds, cracked and white with saline nitre where pools of rain had long since evaporated, were thickets of *ghaf* acacia and threadbare *marakh* bushes. In such places there were many snakes. Sleeping on the ground it was possible to hear the dry crackle of the serpents squirming through the thorny *chicka* brush.

None of us had been chewed at by spiders, though I twice awoke to find them under my blanket. Perhaps they came in for warmth, but the touch of their great furry legs was loathsome and both times I jumped up shuddering and could not sleep again for a while.

The spiders provided food for the desert monitors and countless smaller lizards that lived in the *nej'd*.

Even in the depths of the *nej'd* and the still emptier Sands to the north there were flies, countless thousands of them. And in addition to the flies of any particular area there were also our own flies that accompanied us everywhere, travelling on our backs and headcloths or, when we drove, clinging to the metal of the vehicles. Little scratches on my hands and legs became infected by these flies, grew larger and refused to heal.

The idea that I had nurtured that Ubar must lie at the latitude where the underground aquifers became buried in or near the rim of the Sands had not proved to be the case, or at least there had been no visible signs of any artefacts either to the north-west of Shisr,

Fasad and the Wadi Mitan, nor to the east and up to the mouth of the great Umm al-Hayat which in turn led to Mugshin.

We had been more thorough in searching all likely areas than any of our predecessors, including Wendell Phillips. Nonetheless, as we fought our way down the Wadi Atinah, I felt regret as my hopes of a great discovery had been stupidly high.

We became adept at dealing with the sandstorms which occasionally swept across our path in the region just south of the Sands. They were seldom more than surface phenomena reaching, in height, some six metres above the ground and giving us warning of their approach because they were visible from several miles away as a dark approaching haze, walls of dust or sand particles moving at speeds of up to 50 miles per hour.

In the *nej'd* we would usually drive through minor dust storms. The vehicles were buffeted and fine particles of driven sand stung our skin despite the bedding blankets that we wrapped around our faces. If the visibility dropped to a dangerous level then we would stop, but this seldom happened. In the worst storms we huddled together on the leeward side of the vehicles, having closed them up one behind the other. All weapons were kept close to our bodies and under our blankets. I remember the sensation of being altogether in another world as the roar and the rush of matter passed by while I clenched my eyes tight shut, closed my mouth, holding my *shemagh* and blanket with one hand and my rifle with the other. Then the storm passed and the silence that followed was interrupted by '*Waos*' and '*Wallahis*' from the men. The sun beat down again as if nothing had happened.

We came at length to Shisr and there received a message from Salim Khaleefa asking us to return to Fiend Field as soon as possible, for his task of finding an alternate route between Ayun and Thumrait to evade *adoo* ambushes had failed.

I knew it was likely to be a long while before I might have another chance to search the rim of the Sands, and when it did come there was no reason to believe that we would have any more success than on our last two searches. The trouble was clearly that surface searches involving areas of moving sand were inadequate. I would have to obtain air support, locate the Thomas 'tracks to Ubar', which should be easily visible from above, and follow them if necessary over the unmarked Saudi border until there were outlines of the ruins. That was the way 'proper' archaeologists worked these days, and I knew two of the Sultan's pilots well enough to ask for such a small favour as soon as my next brief leave took me to Salalah.

At Fiend Field we had a cheerful reunion with the other Recce sections, although their news was as negative as ours in terms of results achieved.

Salim Khaleefa had tried his utmost to locate another route, which did not pass by easily ambushed passes overlooked by the *adoo,* that could be used both by us returning from the Dehedoba trail and by the companies from Deefa and the western front. But sheer cliffs or cul-de-sac wadis had always blocked his way. So we switched over jobs and Salim's men headed north while we took over in the land of rocky canyons instead of dunes.

This time my section struck lucky and found what we were looking for. Nosing up and down a valley close to Ayun, Murad found a convoluted, sometimes hairy, way to the Wadis Harazon, Hayla and Yistah, which took us at length to Thumrait well beyond the reach of PFLOAG observers. This route, in fact, solved only half the problem because it worked well for our travel but not for the companies, since we would need to find yet another 'link road' up another set of ravines in order for their heavy vehicles and field guns to head west.

There were no immediate plans for the companies to move, so I took the opportunity to fly to Salalah on the next Beaver flight bringing supplies to Fiend Field. Over the previous two months in the sweltering heat of the sands, the festering sores on my neck, arms and legs had grown worse, and the swarms of flies which were our constant companions, smelling the poison, seemed to find me more attractive than the others. At Ayun our medical corporal had done his best and given me penicillin pills (his answer to all problems), but I had begun to feel feverish.

At the Umm al Ghawarif headquarters the Indian doctor advised two weeks' rest and a course of (a different) penicillin.

For a week in the extreme cool of the air-conditioned Mess, I played poker and went swimming in the sea by Kor Rori.

I remember one evening in the Mess a visiting pilot from Muscat commented on the Sultan's ongoing failure to introduce a policy of hearts-and-minds or to build schools and hospitals to counter PFLOAG propaganda. 'He ought to step down and let his son Qaboos take over.'

There was a general nodding of heads and only Tim Landon, reading a paper in one corner, refrained from appearing to agree. His face remained impassive as though he had never heard the pilot.

At that point few people knew that he was a key part of an ongoing plot to oust the Sultan.

I took the opportunity to chat up our Beaver pilot to ask if he would mind 'adding a tiny diversion' to his flight plan, like a quick flight along the edge of the Sands when he took me back to Fiend Field. 'Not in the near future,' was the reply, 'because things with the companies are hotting up due to increased PFLOAG pressures on the Leopard Line. But once it quietens down we'll see what we can do for you.'

That was that then. I would need to be patient. After a week of indolence in Salalah I was bored and feeling guilty, so I pleaded total good health due to the excellent doctor's treatment and he let me fly back to Fiend Field.

I noticed an ebullient atmosphere among the men who greeted my reappearance.

'You look well, Bakheit. Welcome back to your family. You have news?'

It was soon apparent that nobody was interested in my news. Around the campfire and with plastic mugs of tea, Ali Nasser stood up, for it was his moment of glory. He had succeeded where Salim Khaleefa's section and mine had both failed.

'After five days of hard travel,' Ali said, 'and the building of many ramps to cross deep wadis, we came to a country where *no* bedu has been before and *no* man has seen.'

He stroked his luxuriant beard and glanced at his audience to ensure that all were attending.

'Allah was good to show us the way and *I* was always correct in choosing the right route. On a high ridge I went to pray and, below me, many hundreds of feet down, I saw a great white wadi running north. At once I ran down without delay – after my prayers were ended – and found a ledge of rock which led down to the wadi floor.

This ledge will be, *Insha'Allah*, big enough for our Land Rover with some work.'

'Where does this wadi lead, Ali?' I asked, after giving him over-the-top congratulations.

'In the correct direction,' was his only reply. We failed to tie up his discovery with my map, which hardly mattered since the latter's favourite printed comment was 'POSITION APPROXIMATE'.

The morning after my return, my section and Salim Khaleefa's followed Ali Nasser's along a circuitous route, not using the lie of the land and skirting dizzy ramparts where the slightest skid would spell disaster. At length we climbed a narrow ridge to its highest point and looked down to see the wide white floor of a curling wadi.

Ali's ramp, which he proudly showed me, was a precarious ledge down which only a madman would drive in a mini car. And he would never get back up. Quite where the wadi led was impossible to tell, but here at last was a possible PFLOAG-free route for the companies from the western end of the Leopard Line to the gravel desert and so to the camp at Thumrait.

For several days we worked in chains rolling boulders down to widen the natural ledge, and in a week Murad proudly skidded his Land Rover down to the wadi below. Since it might well be a cul-de-sac valley, no more vehicles were allowed to descend until, after three more days, we had perfected the ramp. Then, to much wild cheering, Murad urged his vehicle slowly back up the precarious ledge to the summit.

Next day we all descended and, after a five-hour journey, came to a fork in the unknown wadi. This we followed until the hills fell away behind us and, in open steppe land, we sped north-east until we recognized the Wadi Yistah which led to Thumrait.

We signalled Salalah of the new safe route from the mountains, and not long afterwards David Bayley's company from the west withdrew their artillery by way of our ramp, thus avoiding the dangerous Valley of Haluf.

From then on our movements went undetected by the guerrillas, a factor that would prove vital in the events to come.

CHAPTER 13

Operation Snatch

Late in 1968 Fiend Force became involved in an event which Tim Landon was later to tell me changed the course of the Dhofar war.

An apparently trivial event can set off a ripple effect leading to a catastrophe, as when the assassination of a duke by a student in Sarajevo led to the carnage of the First World War.

In his zeal to root out the Mahra dissidents of the eastern *jebel*, the PFLOAG leader, Salim Amir arrested the two sons of a Bait Howeirat Sheikh close by his PFLOAG headquarters at the village of Qum. One of these prisoners, a man named Sahayl, detested Salim's newly arrived *Idaara* squad, who had gang-raped and nearly killed his daughter. He managed to escape and made his way to Salalah. Salim Amr instigated a search but, failing to catch the slippery Mahra, assumed that he might defect and guide the army to Qum. He determined to make ready for such an attack.

At that time I was squatting with Murad and Said Salim on a pile of rocks in the centre of the Wadi Habarut, on the border with the Yemen. To our left the Sultan's fort; to the right the Yemeni fort. Across the dancing heat shimmer of the valley between the two forts and close by the palms of the oasis, I heard the thirsty roar of four or five hundred recently arrived camels and the screams of their herders.

Villagers from both sides of this frontier oasis had clashed over some domestic squabble.

The commander of the Yemeni garrison had made a formal complaint to the Chief *Askar* of our fort who, in turn, had radioed Salalah HQ, who had told me to sort things out before the two garrisons started escalating the squabble into an armed conflict. We had immediately interrupted our patrols in the northern sand dunes and reached Habarut in eight hours.

I glanced at the sun. It was midday, so the blinding glare favoured the riflemen of neither fort.

A three-man delegation from the Yemeni fort made its way slowly towards us, led by a small man with yellow skin and a baseball cap. We stood up and shook their hands. After greetings, we sat again. The leader spoke classical Arabic which, compared with my Omani Army slang, was like the Queen's English compared with Cockney. One of his villagers had been shot by an *askar* from our fort and his men were slavering for retribution or compensation.

I apologized on behalf of the Sultan and promised to chastise our miscreant forthwith. By way of compensation, I nudged Murad who produced a pack of 200 Marlboro cigarettes, gold dust in the Yemen. I nudged him harder and he passed over the second pack. I gave these to the Yemeni, who nodded his acceptance. His stern features softening, he said, 'Your apologies are accepted. You will deal with your troublemakers. We with ours.'

Some months afterwards, the Yemeni garrison bombarded the Sultan's fort and razed it to the ground.

Back at our two Land Rovers, my signaller gave me an *Operations Immediate* signal from Tim Landon. We were to meet him at Thumrait the next morning. He would fly there from Salalah. I radioed the other Recce groups to meet me soonest at the Pools of Ayun. I knew that Tim would only shift us, pawn-like, around the desert at such short notice for a very good and immediate reason.

So we raced over gravel trails to Ayun and, leaving one section to guard the main Dehedoba trail, drove along a well-known track above the Qismeem Pass, which would take us back into the *nej'd*, from whence, as far as *adoo* or even bedu would know, we could only reappear via the same bottleneck route. We would thus be accounted for by the *adoo* watchers as having no vehicular access to Thumrait or to the Midway Road. It was as though we were bottled up in the desert. For the first time this was not, in fact, the case because we used Ali Nasser's new and hidden way of reaching Thumrait and all places east thereof. Using this 'Ali route' we arrived at our Thumrait rendezvous with Tim Landon the following day. With him was a small, dark-skinned Mahra.

'Do you know the well of O'bet, sometimes called Leeat?' Tim asked me.

I knew it well from patrols the year before. 'Yes, but we never use the water there as the cliffs above are on the edge of the No-Go area – prime *adoo* territory.'

'True,' Tim nodded, 'but that's where you are about to go. Let me explain.' He laid out a crude map of the Qara.

'Sahayl here – ' he nodded at the Mahra – 'has been cruelly treated by PFLOAG. He is of the Bait Howeirat who hate the Marxist doctrine even more than they hate us. So he has come to me to avenge his family for what was done to them earlier this week. He has agreed to lead us to his village in the upper reaches of the Sahilnawt Valley, an area never previously patrolled by SAF. It is one hundred per cent *adoo* territory, but disputed at present between the main Marxist *adoo* and the Eastern Mahra tribes who still champion Islam, like Sahayl and his clan.'

Tim went on to impress on me that the mission he was giving us was absolutely critical to the timing of major plans then underway to save Dhofar for the Sultanate if the anticipated big PFLOAG attack on Salalah could somehow be delayed. The only way to do this was to defer the PFLOAG elimination of the dissenters within their eastern ranks. Sahayl, in Tim's opinion, offered him the first chance of putting a meaningful spanner in the *adoo* works.

We must go at once, guided by Sahayl, to his village some fourteen miles into *adoo* territory and south-east of the PFLOAG base at Qum.

The mountains between O'bet and our target were a maze of crooked ravines, but Sahayl knew them by day or by night like the back of his hand. There were scattered villages and *adoo* camps, but he would avoid them.

We were to set out at once and reach the village by dawn, when two key PFLOAG commissars were due to arrive there with important orders from PFLOAG in Hauf. Until his defection, Sahayl had

A member of the Ubar
team under a frankincense
tree near Kanoon.

Frankincense congeals after the gum
has dribbled from cuts made in the
flaky tree trunk at harvest time.

Dr Ron Blom of NASA inspects an old frankincense trough.

In the great dunes of the Umm al Hadid.

One of our Land Rovers close to the dunes of Fasad, one of our Ubar search areas.

As epic a force as any I've seen anywhere, a sandstorm about to engulf my old patrol base at Thumrait.

With Andy Dunsire, 600 feet down the Tawi Ateer. We search the submerged tunnel walls for cave paintings and, hopefully, Ubar clues.

Nick Clapp, the movie director, Kevin O'Brien, his cameraman, and the author during the attempt to excavate the Oracle of Diana.

The Sultan's fort in 1959 was built to guard the well of Shisr, the only permanent watering place in Dhofar's Central Steppes. My first patrol there was in 1968.

The Naib Wali and the Council of Elders of the Bait Masan of Shisr agree to allow our team to excavate around the site of their meteorite crater and watering hole.

The author handing over Ubar artefacts to the newly appointed Field Director in Dhofar, Ali Achmed Ali Mahash al Shahri.

The UK B Team in Morocco's Eco Challenge Race in 1996. After two of our four-strong team dropped out, Steve Seaton and I (both at right) completed the multi-sport event after eight days and nights in and around the Atlas Mountains.

The author with teammates Steve Seaton and Helena Diamantides at the start of the Agadir Camel Race in 1996.

The American Vernon 'Komar' Craig (behind Beatle Paul McCartney) is awarded the 1984 World Record by the Guinness Book of Records for walking barefoot on red-hot coals 1000 degrees Fahrenheit (535 degrees Celcius). Author at top right.

Ginny's polar base on fire. Immediately around the conflagration, overall temperatures were at minus 43 degrees Fahrenheit.

The long stretches of soft sand and dune climbs in the sweltering, windless sections of the Marathon des Sables were killers.

Through the organisers of the Livingstone Memorial Expedition we stayed at ALERT (African Lion Ecological and Research Trust), where cubs orphaned by poachers are looked after and brought up in safety before being released into the wild as adults. My wife, Louise, and me, with one of the grown-up cubs.

We had a number of close meetings with elephants and hippos on the Zambezi Livingstone Memorial Expedition.

been a trusted member of the local militia, and he was confident that Commissar Salim Amr and his local liaison officer would arrive there '*bukra qabl dhuhr*' (tomorrow by noon). We were to take both men alive, Tim stressed, and with whatever documents they carried intact. If we were compromised we should call for air support to cover our escape back to the safety of the open *nej'd* north of O'bet.

Salim Khaleefa spoke no English, but he understood the movement of Tim's finger on the map as he pointed out the route from O'bet to the target. In a low voice he asked me how we could trust this Mahra. It could easily be a deadly trap.

I knew, as did Salim, of past occasions when SAF patrols had walked into carefully prepared ambushes and suffered many dead, even though their guide, out front, had survived unscathed. This was why SAF policy had recently been to accept new volunteer *jebali* guides only after a probation period under the surveillance of other, more trusted, guides, like fat Said bin Ghia and Sultan bin Nashran.

When I put this to Tim, he gave me a hard stare. 'I trust Sahayl,' he said quietly, 'and you should too. I recognize hatred when I see it, and Sahayl *hates* Commissar Salim Amr. This is a huge opportunity.'

'Why Recce?' I pressed Tim.

He laughed. 'You should be pleased, Ran. It shows what I think of your team's record on and off the *jebel*. Also, due to your clever new "Ali trail" and ramp, the *adoo* will never suspect any army action coming from the *nej'd*. They know where all the other companies are from hour to hour. I *must* have these two men, Ran, and whatever the commissar's documents contain, and we *must* strike while the iron is hot. So good luck and good hunting.' He then had to fly back to Salalah.

I briefed all the men, and some showed considerable alarm. Salim quietened them down, but they glared at Sahayl with open mistrust. None of us spoke *jebali*, as Nashran had gone on leave to Salalah, so we had to communicate with Sahayl using hand signals. Only he knew the exact location of our target and the best route to get there through *adoo*-infested country and, vitally, by dawn the next day. Any movement in such an area would invite the speedy presence of *adoo* cut-off groups and, with no possible help from the three beleaguered companies, we would not last long once the single active SAF fighter from Salalah had gone to refuel.

As soon as our five Land Rovers were ready, the ammunition doled out and water bags filled, we drove south-east from Thumrait through an area of *nej'd* where the only vehicle tracks were those we had ourselves made a year before in the rocky canyons and gravel hills between the wide watersheds of the Rubkhut and Jazal valleys. We then headed south beside the cliffs of the Wadi Waghala, where I had once shamed myself by suffering from some mild form of heat-induced dizziness in mid-patrol through not wearing my *she-magh*. Mubarreq reminded me of this with obvious relish.

Murad hid the vehicles three miles north of the little-known spring of O'bet at the very head of a tributary to the Wadi Jazal. This was closer than we would normally drive to the mountains, but a strong wind blew from the south and the wadi walls would also deaden the noise of our vehicles.

Just as we were leaving, Murad approached me, shook my hand and muttered, 'Go well, Bakheit. Be safe. *Insha'Allah.*' This he had never done before and I found it both touching and slightly ominous.

The platoon was as silent as Sahayl, despite their unusually heavy loads. I had left our Browning heavy machine gun and the 2-inch mortar behind, but had taken all our light machine guns and 200 rifle rounds for each man, which was more than normal.

Sahayl kept trying to chatter to me as we slowly scrambled up the rough cliff path, but I hissed '*Uskoot*' ('Shut up') at him. All he needed to do was to lead us to the right place by the best route and get us there in darkness. Tim had estimated some eight hours from O'bet at '*imshee jebali*' (the pace of a *jebali*).

Once up the cliff, sweating profusely, I checked all the men, then beckoned Sahayl to lead on. He seemed always to go too fast or reacted childishly when asked to slow down, and then went too slowly. If only I could follow a compass bearing or Nashran as usual, and not this mercurial Mahra.

After nearly an hour Ali Nasser ran up to me and pointed back the way we had come. In a moment and, it seemed, far out over the *nej'd*, a green illuminating flare shot up. Then another, and then a third.

'That is the second time,' Ali whispered. 'Murad must be in trouble.' We had agreed on total radio silence. I cursed, for I had only one option. I told Salim Khaleefa to listen out on his radio but to stay where he was. Lightly laden with only my section, I would return to Murad's hide to see what was wrong. Then I would double back. We should still have time.

Going down the cliff was far quicker and Murad was, in fact, fine. He had neither seen nor heard the flares, but from his position within the high-cliffed wadi that was not surprising. So we trudged back south again and arrived with Salim none the wiser as to the reason for the flares and having wasted three precious hours. The men were clearly on edge. None gave me their normal patrol grins. The flares had made them even more apprehensive. We were surely walking into an *adoo* trap. Thirty of us in enemy heartland and easily cut off from the comparative safety of the *nej'd*.

My signaller, normally a smiling and imperturbable man, even under heavy fire, whispered in my ear at a brief halt, 'We are going to our death, Sahib' (not 'Bakheit', I noted). 'This evil Mahra is well fed – proof that he is of the *adoo*. We must go back now or it will be too late.'

'*Abadan. Kull shay ba stawee zehn,*' ('All will be well') I told him. But time was flying and I felt that the whole affair was going dangerously wrong.

Sahayl persevered. He knew every minor fork in each new ravine where goats had made countless narrow foraging trails through the thick scrub. I was glad in these sweaty labyrinths of camel thorn that I did not suffer from claustrophobia. The mosquitoes attacked in humming clouds and a sticky heat emanated from the dark foliage.

There were, I knew, many small villages dotted about this Bait Fiah land and there were herdsmen who spent nights alone near their flocks. Yet Sahayl kept us unerringly clear of any human – at least as far as I could tell. And his overall pace settled down. We made good ground and the men were tiring with their unaccustomed loads. With three hours to dawn we pressed on. Salim Khaleefa came to warn me that the men wished to rest.

'Too bad,' I told him. 'We're all tired but if we're not in position by dawn, we'll be dead. Tell the men that.'

Sahayl followed high grassy shoulders above the ravines, but kept low enough to avoid being unnecessarily skylined. Towards three o'clock we moved through high open grassland and smelt the acrid tang of burning dung, which was a sure sign of a village or at least of goat herders keeping mosquitoes away.

To the south-east a patch of spreading grey sky heralded dawn. Sahayl, coming to a lone and withered fig tree, gave me a gap-toothed grin of delight. He pointed immediately ahead. Peering through the semi-gloom, I made out the bowl of a rounded valley below us with the dark silhouettes of Mahra huts dotted about.

As I turned to signal with both hands on my head for the section leaders to be briefed, a pinpoint of light pulsed from some high ground close by, but only for a couple of seconds. I might have imagined it, for I was on edge.

Merely to position our four sections around the grassy rim of the bowl, on the floor of which lay the village, would be stupid, for we would be in danger from any *adoo* on the still higher ground on all sides. We must hide ourselves in that higher ground from where we could still cover all approaches to the village.

One section climbed up a hill to an outcrop of boulders, from where they could cover the west side of the village with back-up from Mohammed the Beard's section.

Ali Nasser's section settled in a clump of thorn and scattered rocks along the shoulder of our approach route, while Salim Khaleefa's men followed mine up to high ground to the east with good cover for his machine guns. Spotting even higher ground, I moved wearily as dawn broke to a thicket on the hilltop and just by a well-used village approach path which I only noticed too late to be able to move anywhere further away.

Said Salim found a passageway into the thicket, which turned out to be hollow inside with an old *jebali* cowering in one corner and, dotted around, piles of ashes from past dung fires. Said Salim held his knife against the neck of the *jebali* to prevent him from making a sound.

Mubarreq, who had been carrying our machine gun and 500 rounds on belts all night, looked tired, which was unusual. He showed me a leather pouch with the *jebali*'s flint and tinder. 'Still warm,' he muttered. 'He made that light signal that we saw. Maybe to signal to the *adoo* below. Let Said slit his throat now.'

Sahayl entered the thicket last. He clasped the *jebali* to his chest and they rubbed their cheeks together.

'They are brothers,' Said said. 'Do not trust them, Bakheit.'

Leaving Said on watch, I joined the others for a short sleep as the heat mounted and the mosquitoes bit and filled their stomachs with our blood.

The sun was well up when Said woke me. I shook my head to clear it. The realization of our situation was far from pleasant. Humming birds darted among the white flowers which sprouted on ivy-like creepers in the ceiling of our camel-thorn hide. I noticed that Sahayl's brother had one pink and glazed eye.

Through a break in the thorns I looked south at the scattered huts below, and beyond them over the rim of the Qara to the Plain of Salalah stretching in a heat haze all the way to the coast of the Indian Ocean.

Men in dark uniforms with slung rifles moved about between the huts below. In two years of ambushes none of us had ever seen such an easy and tempting target. But we all knew the penalty of firing a shot. Our only hope lay in concealment. If and when our target group arrived, we must do our best to remain unobserved and catch them unawares. Truly a tall order but, as Said Salim had often told me, 'With Allah, all things are possible.'

Women with goats and youths with camels left the village and wandered their grazing animals into the surrounding hills.

Two teenagers with flintlock rifles came along the path which passed within touching distance of our thicket. Mubarreq let them see the black snout of his machine gun as I beckoned them into our hide with a welcoming smile. They looked terrified, but came without a sound. Said had them squat beside Sahayl's brother, and when they began to natter he shut them up with one hand clasped meaningfully about his knife.

Over the next two hours as the hide grew unbearably hot, seven more passers-by approached our thicket, saw my finger at my lips as well as our weapons pointed at them, and joined our ever more crowded little hell-hole.

Mubarreq scanned the village through binoculars and spotted two smartly uniformed men arrive from the west and enter the biggest, most central hut. And beyond the village, we noted some sixty men busily digging along a salient hill-line to the south presumably in order to prepare an ambush in readiness for an expected army attack from the Plain.

My suspicious mind lingered on the thought that Sahayl *might* be the key bait in an *adoo* plot to persuade Tim to send in the army. They would have assumed that, if such a ruse worked, there were no army elements to the north, or indeed anywhere, who were capable of such an attack, except from the Plain of Salalah.

At that point a highly embarrassing personal emergency interfered with my wandering thoughts. Since waking, I had felt sick with the familiar dull pain of lurking diarrhoea in my bowels. Normally I would have relieved myself as quickly as possible, but in such circumstances I had spent the past hours of boiling heat fighting against the mounting need to release a torrent of my stomach contents.

The hide already stank of body sweat and was crowded with *jebalis*. The last two arrivals were standing stooped as there was no space available to squat. Only Mubarreq was lying prone on his stomach with his machine gun half out of the thicket and covering the path. Said, my signaller, and I sat watching our front.

The pain in my rectum stabbed at me. I groaned despite the need for silence and knew that I could not delay a moment longer.

Scooping some small rocks around my buttocks, I lowered my trousers as my insides gave way in a noisy splatter of foul muck. Flies soon covered the wet rocks. The relief was immense but, as the pain diminished, I felt dizzy and desperate to lie down. There was no paper, so I used stones.

I hoisted my trousers up not a moment too soon, for Said pointed at the path. Two tall men approached moving fast. I released the safety catch on my rifle and slowly swung it round. I knew immediately that these were Tim's much vaunted targets for the lead man's cap sported the polished red hexagonal badge of a political commissar. We must take them alive.

Some fifteen yards away they stopped, no doubt spotting

movement in our thicket. The commissar was tall, his face scarred and his rifle, cradled in his elbow, was a Kalashnikov, a single burst from which would send a rip of hollow-nosed bullets through flesh and bone and guts. A dribble of sweat stung my left eye, but I was certain that the commissar was staring straight at me.

'Drop your weapons or we will kill you.' I kept my voice low, and aimed my gun at his stomach.

He moved with snake-speed, bending low as his rifle swung to face me, and I pressed the trigger. As though hit by a sledgehammer, his whole body arched back, his limbs spread puppet-like and he disappeared into the long grass. The other man's gun was already pointed at me when I fired again, as did Mubarreq and Said Salim.

I saw his face ripped in an instant into a red mask, his nose and eyes smashed back into his brains. Bullets thudded into his body as it settled across a thorn bush on the far side of the path.

Said instantly left our thicket and retrieved from both corpses their weapons, caps and, from the commissar, a leather satchel stuffed with documents. Said pushed them through the thorns to me and took a grenade off his belt to place, with its pin removed, under one of the bodies.

My signaller called Salalah for support, giving them our approximate location. I called the other sections telling them to withdraw at once and, fatigue forgotten, we all broke from our hides to fan out in a long, straggling, undisciplined line in order to flee north. Speed was our only hope to avoid being cut off on the way to the *nej'd*, and we moved with the wings of fear.

At the next ridge line shots zipped over our heads and, briefly, we all fired back, lightening the load of our ammunition. Sahayl led, as he had before, and our sections soon maintained a tactical distance between us, as in training. Within half an hour the two little SAF fighters buzzed our rear as we fled back to the safety of the *nej'd*, and the *adoo* never quite caught up with us.

Back in Thumrait, the men slept like dead men. So did Sahayl and his half-blind brother. Three of the men developed some form of heatstroke, and had to be flown from Thumrait to the Salalah medics.

Tim flew back the next day to collect Sahayl and the captured documents. He regretted that we had failed to bring the commissars back alive, but he was clearly delighted with the papers.

The green flares, he explained, had been fired by the Beaver pilot sent out by Patrick Brook and our colonel when he learnt that our patrol was less than thirty men, and not fifty as he had presumed, for I had forgotten to signal Salalah to let them know that I had left a dozen men to guard the Dehedoba trail, and others to protect Murad and his drivers. Quite why the *adoo* had clearly been expecting us (but from the south) Tim never established, but he assumed that it was due to Sahayl's escape to Salalah.

Months later both Sahayl and his brother were killed at a water-hole, and their father, a Mahra tribal sheikh, was executed soon after our successful patrol.

But Sahayl's personal quest of revenge against Salim Amr had far-reaching effects, as Tim had hoped. Other Mahra *jebalis* in the east followed Sahayl's example, and Tim soon had a thriving spy service in the midst of the *adoo* as they attempted to de-Islamize the mountains east of the Midway Road. Tim learnt exact locations of major *adoo* groups and when PFLOAG VIPs were likely to be there so that our two fighters could target them with bombs and rockets. Other anti-Marxists, even including some trained at PFLOAG camps, came over to the Sultan's side.

The result was that the *adoo* were so busy trying to prevent revolt in and defection from their own camps that they were caught on the wrong foot a few months later when the British plan to oust the Sultan and replace him with Qaboos, his half-Dhofari son, was successfully executed.

Tim and various Salalah-based troops entered the palace with minimal challenges from the Palace Guard, and nobody was killed. The Sultan himself was wounded in one foot, but a British officer friend of his held his hand while the wound was dressed, before accompanying the venerable old ruler to a waiting RAF plane, which flew him, his wives and his key staff to England and a private suite at London's Dorchester Hotel. There he died, after making peace with his successor Qaboos, in October 1972.

On his accession, Qaboos quickly used Oman's newfound oil wealth to ruin PFLOAG's propaganda, for he gave all Omanis and

Dhofaris exactly what PFLOAG had promised them, but without the threat to their beloved Islamic religion and way of life. He announced an amnesty to all *adoo*, which triggered a trickle, and soon a flood, of PFLOAG deserters, who then formed a counter-guerrilla force split into regional groups who were retrained by men of the Special Air Service.

Tim became a special adviser to his old army friend Qaboos, and substantial support, in the form of helicopters and jet-fighters, was soon forthcoming from Jordan, along with thousands of crack troops from the Shah of Persia and valuable support from both Saudi Arabia and the United Arab Emirates.

World oil prices doubled in a few years, and by 1975 Omani annual income reached £300 million.

PFLOAG's support from the Yemen and the Soviet Union eventually withered away as prosperity blossomed for the people of Oman. Within two years of his succession, Qaboos had wells drilled in Dhofari villages without ready supplies, and a deep-water harbour was constructed west of Salalah so that Dhofar was no longer cut off in the monsoon months. Sixty hospitals were built with free medicine for all, and by 1973 the number of students (of both sexes) in Omani schools exceeded 34,000.

Now, more than forty years after his succession, Sultan Qaboos remains today the most popular absolute ruler in Arabia, some say in the world.

During the troubled times of the Arab Spring, many rulers, from Morocco to the Yemen, were removed one by one, but not Qaboos. I like to think that the wonderful men in my one-time family, Recce Platoon, played a key part at a key time in staving off an all-out *adoo* attack on Salalah when Qaboos would have been Number One on PFLOAG's Death List.

Tim Landon loved the Omanis in particular, but all things Arab fascinated him. We spent hours in my room or his at Umm al Ghawarif during my rests there between the weeks in the desert or the ambush stints.

We agreed with the generalization that, although all humans since their beginnings have fought and killed one another for often paltry reasons, those tribes living in the hot regions of the world have proved to be the most fractious and, once attached to a particular belief, the most ardent and, often enough down the ages, the most fundamentalist (with a number of obvious exceptions such as the Christians' Inquisition and the Nazis' Holocaust).

Islam, Tim argued, originated in the great heat of the Empty Quarter. Mohammed and most of his original disciples came from isolated desert villages such as Medina and Mecca, but their DNA was that of the desert nomad. To cope with life in the inferno of the Sands meant the survival of the fittest. And of the most determined. Such people were fiercely loyal to their leaders, their religion, tribe and tradition. They were at their best under extreme conditions. They had no tradition of civilization or specific architectural identity. For them black tents, not Taj Mahals or ancient abbeys. Where materialistic riches simply did not exist, God had no rival in Mammon. When Mohammed announced Islam, God's favour became attainable but only if you obeyed to the letter the Quran's instructions as understood by your specific *mullah*.

The race to convert the denizens of the hot countries, especially Africa and Arabia, to either Christianity or Islam was definitely balanced in favour of Mohammed not Christ.

After all, great heat encourages visions to meld with reality like mirages and asceticism can easily become unhealthily important, leading seamlessly to fanaticism whereby a Mohammed or a Mahdi can exhort the hordes to devastating effect, timing with cunning the date of an uprising or a genocide of unbelievers to coincide with hot and humid weather.

Additionally Mohammed's team hit on great ingredients for their new religion of Islam which, unlike the other religions, was custom-built to appeal to Arab and African warrior alike.

To write about heat is to write about Islam, just as a treatise on cold would invariably discuss Eskimos and their codes of conduct.

Islam allows four wives and divorce is simple – highly appealing to both nomadic and African tribes where polygamy had long been a practice. Women are inferior to Muslim men, according to the Quran, and Paradise, obtainable for instance through *jihad*, opens the door to an eternity of sensual delights.

Women do badly compared with their counterparts in most other religions, but then again this has always been the case in most nomadic Arab and tribal African societies, so a majority of their women have come to accept their status.

Christianity, by comparison, works badly in hot climates. The clothes of their missionaries in their tight jackets, cravats and trousers and their women in their whalebone corsets and heavy dresses made no sense compared with cool Arab gowns. African authorities accepted slavery and polygamy as did the Quran, but not so Christianity. Mosques were designed to be cool, unlike churches.

The origins of Oman's history are not precise but can be divided into two main DNA sources: those who arrived from the south, from the Yemen (the Yemeni), and those who came later out of the northern deserts of northern Arab nomadic stock (the Nizari).

Oman, one of the very first lands to adopt Islam during the lifetime of the Prophet, soon rebelled against paying the Prophet's Council (my term) an annual tax (*zakat*) and obeying their central diktats. Instead they strove to worship under a religious leader (Imam) whom they would vote in or out as they pleased rather than the hereditary descendants of the Prophet.

To this end was formed an Islamic sect favoured by all Omanis called Ibadhism, which was inaugurated at the time of Ali, the fourth hereditary Caliph of Mecca.

The current Sultan's dynasty, the Albu Saids, managed to institute hereditary rule in Muscat in 1744 and they have ruled in the city and along the Omani coast since then, but with frequent revolts in the interior led by various Imams based usually at Nizwa.

In the same year Wahabism, a new Islamic sect, was founded by Mohammed Wahab who denounced all Islamic practices that had over the centuries diverged from the dictates of the original tenets laid down in the Quran. His disciples were told to destroy all who professed Islam but not in the Wahabi way.

The denizens of the Gulf whose income was largely gained through piracy and slavery embraced Wahabism and murdered all captives who professed other beliefs. In 1801 they invaded Iraq and sacked the Holy City of the Shias.

Their pirate fleets terrorized the seas off Oman and India and were the reason that the Muscat Sultans first asked the British for help. One East India Company horse-trading ship commanded by a Captain Sawbridge was captured by pirates from Ras al Khaimah. Sawbridge complained bitterly, so the pirates used a sail needle and thick twine to sew his lips together. They then burnt his ship, along with all its cargo of horses. Only after many years did the British navy eventually eradicate the Wahabi pirates.

Out of the hottest of the world's deserts came the northern Arabs who, in the seventh century, swept out of Arabia to form their empire. No country withstood their ferocity and within a single century they ruled from the shores of the Atlantic to the borderlands of China united by the words of their Prophet.

The most unwarlike and tolerant Arabs in the world, however, are today the direct descendants of the original north desert warriors of Oman and the Gulf States.

The intolerant Muslim groups, such as al-Qaeda, Islamic State, Boko Haram and al-Shabaab, state their aim as the formation of a new Caliphate to 'correct' the great crime of the British and French colonial powers who, in 1916, instituted the imperial carve-up of the Middle East and Africa and established artificial borders that have caused so much ongoing conflict.

The Sykes-Picot Agreement decided how best (from an Anglo-French viewpoint) to carve up the Ottoman Empire after the Great War. Islamic State, Boko Haram and their stablemates wish to abolish the artificial borders of this imperial geography which often ignored physical terrain and ethnic groupings and later caused murderous chaos between Muslims and Hindus in India. The IS concept is forcefully to establish their Islamic Caliphate as a new religious-based territory with completely new boundaries governed by Sharia Law.

IS did not create the chaos in Syria (where, in 2015, eleven million people out of a population of twenty-two million have been displaced from their homes and often their livelihood), but they have used it to their advantage.

So what did spark off the Syrian crisis? I would contend that climate change in the form of great heat fermented the rot in a land already riven by inter-sectarian hatreds, a bossy government and Great Power rivalries.

Poor harvests at the time, causing brutal global price rises for staple foods, plus a cruel drought in Syria resulted in mass movements from the baked countryside into Damascus, Aleppo and other towns and rising anger against the Assad government. A variation of this same equation is present in northern Nigeria and other lands in the Sahel zone where more heat and less rain lead to social disruption, with determined and brutal groups taking advantage of the general state of misery and anger.

In Oman, one of the hottest countries on Earth, the inhabitants have over the centuries adapted to the heat, as have the Eskimos (Inuit) to extreme cold. Furthermore, their unique and hitherto reliable source of water, and hence food, and their mountain ranges, means that social panic instigated by climate change is avoided. They have Ibhadism, but not an equivalent of IS or al-Shabaab. And we helped bring about the downfall of PFLOAG.

Despite their warlike forebears, the Omanis Tim and I had met were the most peaceful and tolerant of people. I once asked Ali Nasser why nobody in the platoon had ever, to my knowledge, said a single bad word about Israelis or Jews, and he replied without thinking, 'Because nobody ever told us to think badly of them.'

CHAPTER 14

The Heat before the Cold

I left the Sultan's Army in 1970, a month before my boss, the Sultan, was deposed, because my eight-year contract with the British Army was finished and, much as I had fallen in love with Oman, and especially with Dhofar, I disliked the idea of signing on as a contract 'mercenary' officer.

I was also keen to marry Ginny, although we hadn't decided exactly when. However, I sensed that she was getting fed up with a marriage date which, like a desert mirage, kept fading into the distance. She was very attractive and I remembered the saying, 'Out of sight, out of mind'; I feared I might lose her if I stayed on in Oman.

So one day at our remote camp overlooking the Dehedoba trail I said goodbye to the men of Recce Platoon. For me and, I like to think, for some of them, it was a sad parting. I told them that I would hope to come back to Dhofar and that I would see them again. I thanked them for being like a family to me for such a long time and for being the best and the bravest of soldiers.

Later that year I married Ginny and moved up to her cottage in the far north of Scotland where she had a job with the Scottish National Trust. We agreed to run expeditions together and, since they would have to be fully sponsored as we had no money, we would need to move to London in order to visit the hundreds of potential support companies more easily.

From our new home in a very grotty basement flat in Earls Court just beside the Tube station (purchase price £7,000), I applied for a position as captain with the SAS Reserve Squadron in Hereford, but the major in charge, remembering my removal from the Regular SAS Regiment four years earlier (for blowing up civilian property with army explosives) would only take me on as a trooper. The pay was useless, so when, after a year with the Squadron, a vacancy came up for a captain with the London 21 SAS Regiment, I took it.

We lived a hand-to-mouth existence earning what we could when we could. Lecturing about the Nile in town halls in the London suburbs to audiences of lonely old folk earned us £18 a go.

Ginny evolved a plan to achieve the first ever surface journey around Earth, travelling not horizontally but vertically through both Poles. We spent the next seven years organizing this challenge. Nobody paid us so we alternated the preparation with paid media missions.

The boss of Independent Television News (ITN), Don Horobin, asked me to take one of his film teams to Oman to interview Sultan Qaboos, and I was given a crash course in TV news reportage by Peter Snow, the ITN newscaster, and others.

We then spent two months in Oman, where Ginny worked with Save the Children charity projects in various villages, including Nizwa and Sohar. Staffed by dedicated volunteer nurses, their clinics did great service in areas where previously there were no facilities.

My ITN film crew consisted of two technicians with a wealth of frontline experience in Belfast. This was fortunate because we were reporting from the army outpost of Simba overlooking the South Yemeni border. The film crew revelled in recording the action as PFLOAG mortar bombs slammed about our foxhole.

The SAS refused to let me film them training their ex-communist counter-guerrilla bands, so I recorded an old friend, still a captain in SAF, leading a ferocious-looking line of Dhofari tribesmen charging downhill with their automatics blazing.

Another media-paid outing to Oman in 1986 involved researching and describing a lethal nineteenth-century battle between the British and Omani rebels. This entailed my return to the lands of the same Beni bu Ali tribe who had menaced my own 1968 Recce patrol into the Sharqiyah and Ja'alan districts to recruit for the

Sultan's Army. They had blocked our way up the Wadi Tayyin and, later that same year, had clashed with another tribe, killing dozens in a massacre, news of which had even made it into the *Times* newspaper.

Back in 1820 the same tribe had excelled at coastal piracy, and a British envoy working with the Muscat Sultan was sent to warn them of Royal Navy retaliation. They killed the envoy so an Anglo-Indian army of a thousand men, artillery and with the Omani Sultan himself up front, was sent to subdue the tribe.

I drove into Beni bu Ali territory from Muscat with three men, three rifles and an Olympus camera, and located not just one battle-field but five of them, since various Beni bu Ali villages each claimed the site of the battle.

Each relevant 'guide' (all old men) assured me that his tribe had completely wiped out the army of the British '*Kafirs*' and that the local wadi had run with their blood. I photographed each battle site for good measure. Documents I studied at the British consulate in Muscat did record a Sultanate defeat and the comment that the Sultan had been awarded 'the sword of honour' for being wounded while saving the life of a British soldier in the heat of the fray.

Ginny, meanwhile, lived as the third (nominal) wife of an Omani Sheikh in the mountain village of Ulyah, near Rostaq. She was commissioned by *Woman's Own* magazine to describe day-to-day life in a typical harem. She dressed as did the other wives and learnt their ways of cooking, washing clothes in the local *falaj* and conforming to the normal village rituals. She grew to love her Ulyah family and learnt to speak good Arabic, which was to stand us in good stead over subsequent desert journeys in the Empty Quarter.

After completing some media work in Dhofar, I joined my old friend Patrick Brook, by then commanding officer of the Sultan's Armoured Regiment, on a four-day race over the Jebel Akhdar mountain trails at 10,000 feet. Our ten-man team won against a dozen others, and Patrick lent me a Land Rover to go wherever I wished. Driving north to a remote Kawasena village in the Akhdar foothills, I arrived unannounced at the low mud-brick home of my Recce Platoon personal hero, Said Salim. I had not met him for sixteen years and I was bearded, but he recognized me. We clasped shoulders and laughed aloud as I searched his belt for his trademark skinning knife. He shook his head with a grin: 'No PFLOAG, no knife.'

Said's cousin, Salim Khaleefa, ex-Recce corporal, soon joined us and we talked of times past, of battles fought, of near escapes and of where old friends now were. We ate dates and were young again. When the sun began to slide I left them warm at heart with many memories.

A week later, and organized by Patrick, I joined a single Dhofari officer armed only with a .22 rifle who led me for many miles along the coastline from Rakhyut to Rayzut on the western edge of the Salalah Plain, sleeping on beaches and drinking from springs. I had known this area as the *adoo* heartland, a region where I had once feared to move even by night and with thirty armed men. There were still mines on the trails, but no *adoo*.

Various media-based projects in deserts and jungles gave us a basic income over the years, but they were never predictable. So I kept up my Territorial Army attendance. In 1970 I was sent by the SAS Reserve Squadron in Hereford on a month's jungle training in Brunei. My fellow 'R' Squadron trooper, Len Sheen, had been a mercenary in the Yemen in the 1960s but, like me, was untrained in the niceties of jungle warfare.

The RAF Hercules transport plane from Britain was loaded with equipment and some forty Regular SAS soldiers who ignored the two of us Territorials, as though we did not exist. All the bucket seats and other vaguely comfortable nooks on the aircraft were taken, leaving Len and me one metal side of the toilet cubicle to share with our kitbags. The flight stopped for eight hours at an RAF base on the island of Gan in the Maldives. Short of sleep, I dozed off in swimming shorts on a beach beside the airfield. Len woke me a few hours later and I was ashamed to find that I had failed to apply suncream and was burnt lobster-pink over much of my body by the extremely powerful Maldives sun.

The follow-on flight to Brunei was even more uncomfortable and various parts of my stomach and hips were badly sun-blistered.

On arrival in Brunei the squadron sergeant major, Wally Poxon, signed each man with food and equipment for the jungle month, all in a bergen rucksack weighing 70 pounds. On parade the RSM Geordie Tindall explained that we would be working in the jungle in groups of four with a veteran SAS instructor and that helicopters would drop us off in different locations. Because my skin where the bergen straps would rub was by then raw, I realized that in jungle conditions blood poisoning would be likely, so I requested a few days' sick leave before heading for the jungle.

Both Poxon and Tindall remembered my previous removal from the Regular SAS when I was an officer. They were now entirely unsympathetic. So I took a course of penicillin tablets and plastered duck tape all over the raw skin. In time it healed over.

The instructor with the four-man squad I was attached to was a highly capable Scot, Sergeant Trevor Henry, who taught me how to fix up a mosquito net and hammock between trees under a camouflaged groundsheet and beyond the reach of whiplash scorpions, spiders, snakes and poisonous millipedes. Each day, twice a day, monsoon rain beat down, so the forest floor was always glutinous mud. The humidity made any activity, even without the great weight of the rucksack and 7.62 FN rifle, a palpable effort. We were taught about setting Claymore mine ambushes, how to spot jungle booby traps, how to spot human presence by bird alarm calls, how to avoid leaving tracks, how, in close-foliage contacts, to kill before being killed. By day and by night we took turns to navigate to set points through dense undergrowth and along zigzag ridges following game trails.

Biting ants brushed off leaves were a constant nuisance and, as we passed, our presence was announced by the screams of hornbills and the manic laughter of long-tailed monkeys.

From time to time, as Trevor taught us, the lead scout, a role we took in turns, would halt with one hand raised and listen intently.

Before halting for a night stop, we would head round in a circle which ended back where we had passed ten minutes before so that we could observe our earlier tracks and be sure that nobody was following us.

About a fortnight after we started the training, the toughest soldier in our group went down with dengue fever from drinking unsterilized local water. A helicopter evacuated him after we had used our explosives to clear a landing zone of trees. As the trees crashed down, a shower of every imaginable tree-dwelling insect parachuted down onto us as we lay behind the tree trunks. A very large black and yellow spider bit the patrol medic, Roger Cole, on the neck, and this produced a spongy, bulbous black bump. The other 'student' in the group, a recently joined SAS captain, Simon Garthwaite, slipped on a wet rock and cracked the back of his skull. Roger patched him up and we kept going.

Some while later doing my stint as lead scout, I slipped and slid down a slimy slope. Trailing liners of barbed *attap* thorn brought me to a sudden halt, suspended by one ear. I cut myself free with my knife, but half of my ear lobe was torn away and the injury was bleeding freely. Roger pumped me full of penicillin and stitched my ear lobe back on.

At the end of the course Trevor Henry celebrated back in the base at the local *Kampong* tea-house. Alcohol was forbidden by the Sultan of Brunei, but beer and whisky were served from a china teapot into pretty little teacups.

A year later Simon Garthwaite was shot dead by *adoo* in Dhofar.

Back in London I met Ginny on her return from her Ulyah harem. For a long while her finger nails remained indelibly orange from henna. On a later Omani foray she collected a number of rare scorpions from the Wahiba which now reside in the Natural History Department (Arachnida Section) of the British Museum.

The SAS kindly gave me and Ginny an empty office in their King's Road Barracks for the next eight years, and it was from there that we organized her plan to complete the first surface polar circumnavigation of Earth and recruited unpaid volunteers to join us. Ginny also learnt to become an expert in HF communications with the Territorial Royal Signals.

The Foreign Office would only support our circumpolar project if we gained some experience of polar travel, so, via Tim Landon, I approached Sultan Qaboos of Oman, and he kindly agreed to sponsor our costs to train on the Greenland Ice Cap in 1976.

More snow fell on Greenland that year than had ever been recorded before. The katabatic winds roaring down the escarpment to the sea had been measured by an anemometer at the air base at a speed of 140 mph.

Britain's best-known climate expert, Professor Hubert Lamb, stated that so much snow had fallen that year that the Greenland Ice Cap was rendered unduly heavy, in terms of the world's balance. Since the world wobbles on its orbit, this 1976 unbalancing factor might well have altered the atmospheric circulation and, likewise, the fragile global weather patterns.

The violent snow storms that we experienced on that journey as I skied ahead of the two snowcats reminded me of sandstorms in Arabia when similar all-powerful energy had blurred my ability to think, to sense direction and to do anything other than grovel on the ground in order to escape the hostile blast of the elements.

After Greenland we did further polar training north of Ellesmere Island on moving sea-ice, and in 1979 we finally set out on the Transglobe Expedition from Greenwich heading south down the zero meridian. Our first major obstacle began at the port of Algiers where our ancient ship, the *Benjamin Bowring*, with her volunteer crew dropped off our 'land group' and sailed on ahead to pick us up when we made it down to the Ivory Coast.

Our team of five in three Land Rovers consisted of Ginny and her only helper, Simon Grimes, in one vehicle, me in another with, when we could get one, a local guide, and lastly the other two members of the surface-team (selected from 800 applicants), Ollie Shepard from Wales and Charlie Burton from Sussex. Ollie had been a beer salesman and Charlie had run a meat business in South Africa.

I noticed as the ship headed out of Algiers harbour, hooting a Goodbye signal to our three quay-side Land Rovers, that she was steaming backwards all the way. We later discovered that the ship's engine had become jammed in reverse gear.

We left Algiers in 110-degree heat at noon and headed south into the Atlas Mountains. The French had tamed the Berbers in their mountainous homeland and in the 1870s their soldiers and explorers had crossed the Atlas Mountains to conquer the great deserts to the south, which in the 1850s were virtually untrodden by Europeans.

These deserts, or *ergs* as they were known, had gradually dried out over thousands of years and their lakes had disappeared, along with all cover of grasses and bush. All soil blew away and humans moved south leaving only bare rock vistas and great dunes of sand. Like the bedu of Arabia, only the Touareg could survive in such a place.

The French had defeated the Berbers of coastal Algeria to the north of the Atlas with great brutality. In the 1840s their soldiers had conducted ruthless raids (or *razzias*) which culminated in 1868 in suppressing one uprising by the locals at a cost of 300,000 lives.

Once when eight hundred villagers hid in caves to escape the military, they were all asphyxiated by fires lit at the entrances. The French used many irregular troops called *tirailleurs* and, against the Touareg, camel-borne cavalry known as *méharistes*. The Foreign Legion, known for a while as the kings-of-the-desert, was started in 1831 by King Louis Philippe (who survived seven assassination attempts) to provide gainful employment for the many armed and dangerous ex-soldiers at large in France following the Napoleonic Wars.

Their first role was to pacify Algeria, and there were other foreign forays before the force was sent to Mexico to overthrow the government and install a European prince as head of state. In terms of the Legion, the event was memorable for a stand at Camarón on 30 April 1863 by sixty-five Legionnaires, led by Captain Jean Danjou, who had lost his hand when a musket exploded a decade previously. Surrounded by two thousand Mexican troops, Danjou refused to surrender and made the isolated men swear on his wooden hand that they would fight to the last.

For twelve hours wave after wave of Mexicans were repelled by the stalwart fighters of the Legion until the last handful who remained alive emerged, defeated as much by thirst as by the opposing force.

Although Danjou was killed early on, the prosthetic was taken back to France where it is still the Legion's most valued relic and is paraded annually on the anniversary of the Battle of Camarón. The battle characterized a fundamental tenet of the Legion, that Legionnaires should follow orders implicitly, no matter how futile they seem.

There followed numerous overseas actions, including many during the First and Second World Wars. *Beau Geste*, the novel by Percival

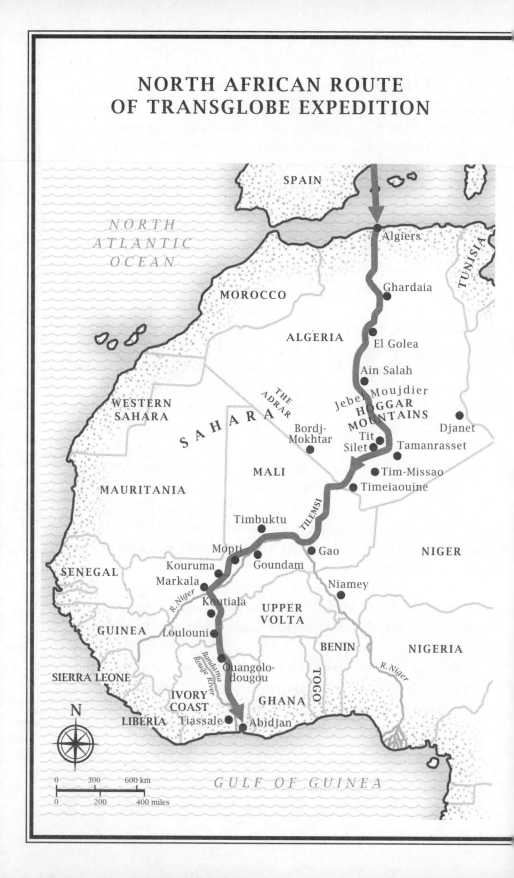

NORTH AFRICAN ROUTE
OF TRANSGLOBE EXPEDITION

*NORTH
ATLANTIC
OCEAN*

SPAIN

Algiers

TUNISIA

MOROCCO

Ghardaia

ALGERIA

El Golea

Ain Salah

WESTERN
SAHARA

THE
ADRAR

Jebel Moujdier

HOGGAR
MOUNTAINS

Djanet

S A H A R A

Bordj-
Mokhtar

Tit
Silet

Tamanrasset

MALI

Tim-Missao

Timeiaouine

MAURITANIA

TILEMSI

Timbuktu

Mopti

Gao

NIGER

Kouruma

Goundam

SENEGAL

Markala

R. Niger

Koutiala

Niamey

UPPER
VOLTA

GUINEA

Loulouni

BENIN

NIGERIA

*Bandama
Rouge River*

Ouangolo-
dougou

TOGO

R. Niger

SIERRA LEONE

IVORY
COAST

GHANA

N

LIBERIA

Tiassale

Abidjan

0   300   600 km

0   200   400 miles

GULF OF GUINEA

THE TRANSGLOBE EXPEDITION
1979–1982

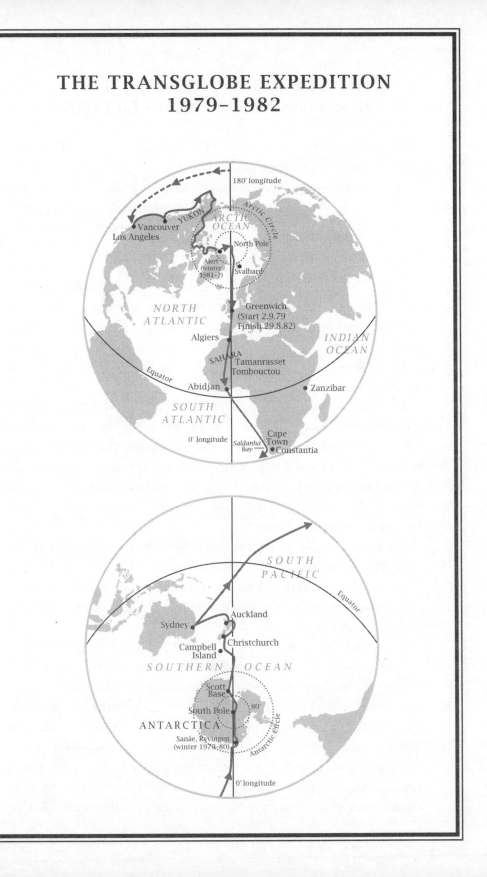

Christopher Wren, filmed in 1926 with Ronald Colman and in 1939 with Gary Cooper, has the Legion in the Sahara defending fortresses typical of those found in Morocco, which was a French protectorate until 1956. Wren claimed to be a former Legionnaire, which made the tale seem all the more authentic.

Shortly afterwards, when Algerians fought for their independence, the Legion showed its mettle by rebelling against their own government which was about to settle with the Algerians, and even plotted to assassinate the French President, Charles de Gaulle. Conscripted troops in the French Army put paid to the Legion's attempted coup. Conspirators were arrested and the problematic regiment involved was disbanded. But there is little evidence that the Legionnaires involved were in any way repentant. Today, more than seven thousand shaven-headed men in the Legion wear their distinctive white kepis, or hats, with pride. Loyal to France they may be, but it's the Legion that they inhabit rather than the country.

In 1926 Russian-born Major Zinovi Pechkoff of the Legion described the men who served with him as 'simple and modest'. 'They do not claim glory for their services. They do not even claim recognition. The most impressive thing about them is that they do not think of themselves as heroes sacrificing their lives. They do not think of themselves as martyrs; and even if they died, they die with the same enthusiasm.'

It's tough, soldiering in excessive heat. That is partly why the redoubtable ranks of the French Foreign Legion are so remarkable. These are men specially trained in the most gruelling conditions to endure everything that the jungle, the desert, and their often sadistic officers can throw at them.

For decades there was an air of romance about the French Foreign Legion, whose men were believed to be the roughest of diamonds who would willingly die for a cause that was not their own.

In the public consciousness the Legion is inextricably linked to lonely fortresses in the Sahara Desert, thanks to the story of *Beau Geste*.

That was the Legion's mid-twentieth-century history, but being a Legionnaire is still hot work today, as part of their arduous training regime takes place in the unforgiving jungle of French Guiana. This old colonial outpost in South America is where Devil's Island, once France's most notorious prison, lies rotting. Even now there is not much by way of luxury in that sparsely populated part of the world which is bordered by Brazil and Surinam. That suits the Spartan ethos that defines the Legion.

Although it's part of the French Army, the Legion has its own motto, '*Legio Patria Nostra*', meaning 'the Legion is our Fatherland', and a definitive anthem.

You certainly don't have to be French, or even to speak the language, in order to join. Those who survive their time under the muscular regime of the Legion are entitled to become French nationals, being '*Français par le sang versé*', or 'French by spilled blood'.

Entry is open to anyone older than seventeen and a half years but less than forty, who is physically fit but isn't on the Interpol 'most wanted' list. That said, a criminal past is not necessarily a barrier, although convicted murderers are no longer welcomed, and anonymity by virtue of an assumed identity is an option favoured by many.

Faith, education, marital status and nationality are disregarded by the Legion during induction, at which time rudimentary French is taught. For those among the international contingent who may not have shone at languages at school, this is frequently as hard as the physical challenges thrown down by the officers in charge of recruits. These recruits suffer beatings, with corporal punishment being a recognized method of shaping the thoughts and actions of a disparate group drawn from dozens of nations until they function as smoothly as a machine.

The French, like the Italians and British before and after them, eventually left their erstwhile hard-won colonies to self-rule followed, usually, by civil strife such as the Arab Spring.

The route that we followed from Algiers to the Sahel, and various alternates to either side of it, had been in use for thousands of years to bring slaves north to Europe, just as now, in 2015, hundreds of thousands of refugees are annually risking their lives through the same deserts on the same voyage.

Apart from the risk of drowning in the Mediterranean, the chances of dying of thirst before ever reaching the southern edge of the Saharan *ergs* are ever present through lack of water coupled with the deadly heat of the Saharan sun.

A healthy adult human body is 60 per cent water. Dehydration occurs when more water is lost – through either exercise or dehydration – than is drunk. And it only takes the water levels to drop by a few percentage points for problems to start.

At first the symptoms are bearable – extreme thirst, headache, low blood pressure, dizziness, dry skin, tiredness and irritability. Further deprivation of liquids means that the body's cells will start to shrink without the necessary replenishment, and confusion follows as the brain begins to shrivel, tugging at the blood vessels attaching it to the cranium in the process. Toxic waste products, that should be flushed out of the body with a healthy rinsing of water, remain trapped within. The volume of blood that services internal organs also declines calamitously in the absence of water. When organs are no longer properly serviced by the viscous fluid that remains in the veins and arteries of the dehydrating body, then they begin to fail.

At this point the body's temperature rises, the eyes sink and the tongue swells, making communication impossible. Within hours the victim falls into a coma, which will come as a blessed relief to those unfortunate people who are dying of thirst.

In modern times one might hope that journeys into deserts, where it is so hot that sitting still in the shade compromises fluid retention, would inspire careful preparation. Alas, dying of thirst is still one of the perils that many desperate migrants face when they seek a better life, including many people from Sub-Saharan Africa who are tempted to make an ill-prepared desert trek to find low-paid work in countries in the north of the continent or travel onwards to Europe. By the traffickers who take their money, they are barely given the same considerations as cargo. A spotlight was shone on this illicit human trade route in 2013 when ninety-two men, women and children died parched in the desert after two lorries that had been transporting them from Niger to Algeria broke down. Only twenty people survived. The UN's tally of migrants crossing the Mediterranean in 2014 was, at 219,000, nearly four times larger than the figure for the year before.

Problems begin even before the mechanical problems. One young girl died after finding the stuffy, uncomfortable ride across the Sahara too much to bear. The drivers used water from the canisters they carried aboard to soften the hard-baked ground so that they could bury her.

When one of the two trucks ground to a halt, both were unloaded and their drivers went to the nearest settlement to sort out repairs. Despite a lack of water and the beating sun, they refused to take their paying passengers to a well that was comparatively close. In desperation people finally headed there on foot rather than be marooned in the desert. When the alarm was finally raised, bodies were found in groups or singly already half-buried by sand.

There is a similar story in America where the arid southern US border with Mexico has claimed the lives of untold hundreds of immigrants who would rather risk the unforgiving heat for a new start in the US than continue their economically unrewarding lives at home.

As for the slaves who were marched, already sick, starved and exhausted, right through the Sahara from places like Lake Chad in Central Africa to the coast by Tripoli, their bones still line the old desert slave trails.

A British official in Nigeria, Hans Vischer, who returned to duty from leave in 1908 leading a caravan of two hundred ex-slaves from Tripoli, published first-hand information of these slave caravans. The losses could be as high as 80 per cent, and he calculated that during the whole period of Arab slaving more than two million miserable human beings must have been moved north along this route, the majority on foot, and only the youngest and prettiest girls and boys in covered camel-litters.

Since a profit was made on the 20 per cent of slaves who somehow survived, the equanimity with which the slavers accepted the massive death rate of their human cargo is easy to understand. The Creator, whether God or Allah, had clearly decided to ignore this world of suffering without a grain of compassion.

After crossing the Atlas Mountains, we came at length to the sand dunes of El Golea, nicknamed by Ollie as El Gonorrhoea, and we camped there between dunes as the expedition's very first scientific task was to collect sand lizards, or skinks, from the nearby Sands of Khanem for London's Natural History Museum, who had spent many hours training Ollie as a skink catcher.

Ginny, who had in the past collected Omani scorpions for the Natural History Museum, had been commissioned to collect fairy shrimps from desert ponds. These are tiny crustaceans less than a centimetre long that swim in swarms. They have hatched from eggs that may have been blowing with the desert dust for fifty years or so, travelling maybe for hundreds of miles from where they were laid by their long-dead parents. The dust has also produced microscopic spores and these now, in the water, have grown into thin filaments of algae. The tadpoles feed feverishly, and the algae alone will sustain them.

Ollie lectured us on skinks and skink-hunting.

The dune surface can become broilingly hot within a few hours of sunrise, yet coolness is only an inch or so away. Thrust your hand beneath the surface of the sand and you will feel how cold it is. Most of the dune animals are well aware of this fact and will burrow down beneath the surface to hide or to escape the worst of the heat. But the sand grains are so smooth and dry that they do not cohere. So it is impossible to tunnel. The sand simply collapses behind the tunneller. One way to move through it is with a swimming action, and several of the lizards that regularly dive beneath the surface push themselves through the sand with their legs. The best way is not to use legs at all but simply to wriggle. Several lizards belonging to the skink family do this. Their legs, very much reduced in size, are sufficient to move them over the surface but are held close to the body when they are moving within the sand. One or two that spend nearly all their time below the surface have lost their legs altogether, like the skink of the Namib Desert, which has covers over its eyes, protecting them from wear by the sand grains, and its nose is pointed, assisting it in moving. It lives by hunting beetle grubs and other insects. The tremors in the sand caused by a moving insect are detected by the skink. It swims through the sand towards the movement and then pops up to seize its unsuspecting prey.

At Khanem in great rolling dunes, Ollie set many skink traps which he baited with chunks of corned beef. The following dawn, clearly excited, he led us on a tour of his trapline. The sun rose huge, orange and early. All the traps were empty, not just of skinks but of corned beef.

Clouds of fat flies which caused constant itching and little flies that bit maddened us all day as the sweat dribbled down our necks. We wore next to nothing and Ollie recorded 122° Fahrenheit in mid-afternoon. We could not decide whether it was more unbearable inside or outside our tents.

When I suggested that we end the fruitless hunt for skinks, Simon murmured, 'We are suffering for science.'

'It is quite likely,' Ollie interjected, 'that I ... we ... might make skink history at the Museum as no skinks of a particularly rare sub-species have ever been found this far north.'

'That,' Ginny pointed out, 'is probably because they don't live here.'

After two skink-less days, Ollie decided that we should extend our trapping zone. So, armed with water bags, compass and sacks full of traps and tinned meat, we trudged deep into dune country searching for skink-tracks, which Ollie said he knew how to identify. But there were none.

'Are you sure they leave tracks?' I asked Ollie.

'Of course they do. They have legs and a tail. You must have patience. Perseverance is a necessary ingredient of all research work. Skinks don't grow on trees.'

Exhausted, we eventually returned to our camp. Everyone was touchy, even before the local mosquitoes set up their evening orchestra.

Next day, with Ollie's agreement, Simon and I set off to recruit a local skink-catcher. We had checked on how to describe what we were looking for – in Arabic, in French and even in Latin (*dhub pois-sons-de-sable* and *scincus scincus cucullatus*).

The villagers of El Golea passed us, frisbee-like, from one reputed 'skink expert' to another, until at last we were introduced to a local farmer who dabbled in skinks for no specific reason that we could ascertain. No matter, he really did know all about these elusive liz-ards which, he said, tasted good when fried.

In a small, square, mud-made hovel we met Hamou-the-Skink-Catcher. He had a colour TV, a generator and a fridge full of Cokes, which he generously bade us enjoy.

He agreed to help us out, but said we must understand that it was dangerous, and therefore expensive, work because lethal sand vipers and scorpions often inhabited the same holes into which a skink-hunter must plunge his hands in order to catch the skinks. Sand vipers were deadly, and 128 people from the local town had been treated last year alone for scorpion stings, three of whom had died. And he told us that sand vipers eat skinks. I agreed to pay Hamou according to his results.

He led us all into dunes less than a mile from the sites of Ollie's diligent hunts, and within minutes he had identified tiny skink trails. Digging both hands into slightly disturbed sand close to where each trail ended, he had produced two prime skinks in under an hour and, by dusk, a third little beauty. Back at base we all celebrated with him while Ollie 'humanely' skewered and packed the five-inch lizards into his formaldehyde bottles which he labelled with the exact grid references and descriptions of their lairs.

'Soon,' Ginny said, noting the proud smirk on Ollie's face, 'we'll have to call him Professor.'

All of us lost weight during our week's dune-trudging in the sweltering sauna of El Golea and we were pleased to head south to where we hoped the water would not taste, as Charlie put it, of skink poo.

After finally improving our driving skills and spending more time at the wheel instead of heaving bogged vehicles, we camped in the Jebel Moujdier which was fanned by hot winds from the western dunes. Ginny and I stripped naked in our tent, but we still sweltered. Mice scurried about our groundsheet. These, Ollie assured us in the morning, were in fact gerbils, which some doctors blamed for spreading the medieval Black Death that killed millions worldwide. This sparked off a big argument, since the rest of us knew full well that sewer rats were the guilty party. Nonetheless, I never again looked at gerbils or jerboas as cuddly little critters.

At one point Ginny, driving the lead vehicle, noted after we had climbed gradually to a long open plateau that the flora had altered from non-existent to scrubland with islands of scrub, acacia and even the stubby dwarf palms which are an indicator to bedu of ground water close to the surface. They can also provide sustenance in the form of a sweetish porridge that can be made from their reddish nuts.

Simon, who was in charge of keeping us in water and local food supplies, identified a 'fresh spring' at Ain Salah, which means 'salty well', and it certainly lived up to its name. Simon was blamed. One day at a lunch stop in a dry valley, I wandered off to find an object to squat behind and came across Simon inspecting a very dead cow corpse. As I approached, he mused, 'We are very short of tinned meat, you know, Ran.'

'Don't even think about it,' I muttered, not entirely sure whether he was joking.

High above us over the stark ramparts of the Moujdier range, there circled great lammergeyer falcons with their wild, buzzard-like calls.

South of Tamanrasset and in a dust storm we drove off the track at the Well of Tahadat or, in hippy-speak, the Jo-Jo Spring, where a water-guard named Spaghetti charged us three dinars for each jerry-can that he filled for us.

'You can camp for free,' he said, 'in my valley down there.' He pointed at a picturesque dry riverbed that meandered below the site of the spring.

A German hippy who was camped right beside the spring was listening, and he laughed. 'I was here last week,' he said, 'and that wadi was for several hours a raging flood fifty metres across.'

So we camped beside rather than in it.

Ollie's next task, as we headed on south to meet Anton Bowring and the crew at Abidjan, the largest city and chief port of the Ivory Coast, was to collect a very specific type of desert bat which lived in certain places on either side of the Mali border.

We were told by Spaghetti of a Touareg guide who 'knows the desert'. Ollie explained where the *chauves-souris* (bats) were, and the guide spat at his foot (his own, not Ollie's) which we had learnt meant, 'Stop there ... I know the answer.'

'Best for you will be west to Bordj-Mokhtar. But that track has not been used for five years now. Much bad sand. No piste any more.'

My Michelin map indicated a good piste to Bordj-Mokhtar, but maybe the guide did know better. After all, sand does shift.

'You do better to go to Gao by way of Timeiouine,' said the guide. 'Then I take you.'

This was good, but when I explained that we had run out of money and would pay him with tinned food, he shrugged.

'I take only money. So you go without guide. It is possible. Maybe you will not get lost in the deserts.'

Ollie asked him if he had seen bats of the sort in Ollie's photographs, which he showed him.

'The deep wells of Silet ... I have seen your bats in them.'

Ginny was a devotee of Charles de Foucauld, the French soldier monk who had founded a hermitage high up in the Hoggar Mountains. So, before the bat-hunt, we left the others and drove fifty miles along a series of rocky tracks, climbing 8,000 feet to the Pass of Assekrem, and then walked up a mountain path with a rucksack of food and a jerrycan of water from the Jo-Jo Spring to give to the elderly French friar who now manned the hermitage alone. He clearly enjoyed the spectacular views of dizzy peaks, thunder clouds and soaring eagles. His lonely chapel was festooned with an array of meteorological instruments with which he kept meticulous daily records. He greeted us with joy.

I noted from the diaries of de Foucauld that it took him an hour to walk from the hut and trudge down the rocky slopes some 500 yards in height to reach the nearest water source which, if an animal had just drunk from it, took at least an hour to fill up. 'In the nine and a half years that I have been here, it has rained twice; once, nine years ago, for 36 or 48 hours and once, five years ago, for 3 or 4 hours.'

The fact that locusts had destroyed what little grass existed did not help. At one point the priest developed scurvy symptoms. Nonetheless he treasured his lonely existence at Assekrem, of which he wrote, 'The view is more beautiful than can be imagined. The very sight of it makes one think of God.'

Ginny wrote of the Hoggar Mountains, 'Great peaks of black rock rise from the gravel valleys, the result of volcanic action. Lava flows cut through the canyons, a perfect landscape for a movie of the end of the world.'

Touareg in the Hoggar talk of their parents hunting oryx, leopards and antelope, but we saw only vultures and eagles soaring high above us. Ginny's guide book showed a photo of a stubby tree with black and white flowers which, she told me, she would love to find to keep me under control. Apparently this *Calotropis procera* was used by Touareg women down the ages as an ingredient to make *borbor*, which first breaks a man's will and then, with a bigger dose, kills him.

When travelling through the desert in the company of camel-borne *méharistes*, de Foucauld, who revelled in acts of physical endurance, would often walk behind them even in mid-summer. One French officer, Jean Dinaux, recorded:

The pace of a detachment of camel troopers is considerably faster than that of a walker. The priest continued to follow us on foot to the point of exhaustion, telling his beads and reciting litanies. He forced his pace when the terrain was difficult. From five o'clock in the morning, the sun beat down mercilessly, and the temperature in the shade varied from 40° to 50°C. Each of us downed from nine to eleven litres of water a day, and what water, bucketed from ponds in which livestock had been splashing. And the father followed along at a rapid pace.

Sandstorms, which de Foucauld often suffered, are well described by another of his travel companions, Fernand de Foureau:

We were struck by a tornado bigger than I could possibly have imagined ... vast, towering clouds of dust, of a sinister copper colour and topped by wild plumes ... covering a good quarter of the horizon. They advanced with fantastic speed and swept over us with a force that nothing could resist ... blinding everybody, blowing the baggage from the camels' backs, knocking over the mules. It was impossible to turn your back to it. Sand and gravel flew from every direction. We could not see farther than a few metres.

Most people think of a grain of desert sand as starting and ending
its life as just that – a grain. The reality of sand grains and their
behaviour in sand dunes is more complex.

The sand from which they are formed is all that remains of the
desert rocks after thousands of years of being grilled by the sun
during the day and chilled to freezing point during the night. Under
such conditions even the most durable granite begins to crack and
flake. Slowly it disintegrates into its constituent minerals. Each grain
is blown over flat rocky surfaces and is forced against other grains,
becoming rounded and coated with a red polish of iron oxide. As the
winds eddy across the desert, so they gather the grains sweeping
them into great piles. These are the dunes. Some are as much as 200
metres high and a kilometre across. Where the wind usually blows
from the same direction, the dunes are far from stationary. They
form ridges and slowly advance across the desert. The wind blows
the sand up the gentle slope of the dune to its crest. Then, with nothing to bind it, it slips down the steep front face of the dune in a
continuous series of tiny avalanches and the dune itself inches
forward.

Our route back to our camp from the hermitage was not as simple
as we had assumed and, having no detailed map of the various trails,
we stopped at a canyon junction where two trails met. Our conversation was abruptly halted when a series of explosive rumbles shook
the air, or so it seemed, and forked lightning flickered above.

We both knew that many locals are drowned every year in the
narrow wadis of the Hoggar. Even on an apparently fine day a distant storm can result in a sudden surge of brown water bearing
tumbling rocks that can sweep away men, camels and even
vehicles.

We were lucky, although when we did reach camp the tents had
been blown down, everything was soaked and the others were trying
to retrieve lost gear.

I remembered Wilfred Thesiger telling me of one great Dhofar
flood a decade before, soon after which he had seen for himself
palm tree trunks jammed by the force of water eighteen feet up
among the cliffs of the Qara's Wadi Aydam where that valley was
a thousand metres wide. He knew of Arabs who had died as a result

of a flash flood which had burst over fifty miles away from a single storm.

From Assekrem we drove west to a place called Tit where, at a confusion of dusty tracks, a battered sign pointing heavenwards announced Abalessa and, to Ollie's joy, Silet. Using our compass we selected a track which alternated between scarred black basalt and sand-filled ruts.

Eight hours later, with all our water bags empty and our bodies grey with dust, we came to an isolated well with a canvas bucket on a rope. Simon, our water maestro, hauled up a bucketful and poured it into a jerrycan via a filter.

'Little bastards,' he muttered, staring at the filter's gauze, on which wriggled a dozen hook-tailed tadpoles. 'That's just the visible ones,' he enthused. 'Hookworms, liver worms, toe worms and God knows what else. Imagine what a drop of this water would look like under a microscope.'

I gulped down a litre at once although, but for my intense thirst, I wouldn't have touched the stuff.

One of the vehicle starters went dead, and for five hours in 105-degree heat Simon struggled to fix it, blistering his fingers on the hot metal.

Four miles out of Silet village we found a series of gravel pits with shafts sunk some fifty feet down, in the gloom of which Ollie glimpsed bat-like movement. So we lowered him on a rope with his bat net at the ready. He came up batless but covered in pigeon feathers and stinking of dead animals. He photographed a long green water snake lying on the surface slime of one well, and from a lone leper to whom we gave food, came confirmation of a bat colony to the west in the wells of Tim-Missao.

For three days Simon rationed our worm-infested water as we bumped and jolted our way west and south close to the Niger and Mali borders over featureless wastes. Violent dust storms meant closing all windows and sweating like pigs. Faint tracks disappeared and, completely lost in soft sand, Ginny and I went off on foot with binoculars until we picked up the ancient piste of twin camel trails leading southwest. To our great relief that evening we came across clearly defined vehicle tracks from the north, beside which, exhausted, we camped.

All night furnace-like winds lashed our tents, and the next day we drove hour after hour through yellow gloom with our headlights on, making many halts to verify that we were still on the tracks.

Crossing riverbeds, we were often bogged down in soft, loose sand. Our eyes were bloodshot and our skin was raw in places from sand-rub. But we made it to the Mali border markers, having, for the last hundred miles, taken on as a guide a lone goat herder, with no goats, from Timeiouine.

Trailer springs fractured, tyres punctured and tow bolts snapped, but our spares supply coped and we inched south from the Adrar to the scenic vale of Tilemsi where the world about us began, slowly, to turn green. Now at our camps Ollie began to point out scorpions, spiders bigger than I thought existed, insects of every shape and colour, foxes, lizards and rabbits. By night we were serenaded by owls, nightjars, crickets and frogs. By day we passed the black tented camps of nomads surrounded by herds of grazing camels and haphazard heaps of camel skeletons.

At Gao we reached the Niger River and followed its westerly curve for 400 miles to Timbuktu. En route Ollie added three very ugly bats (of the wrong species) to his collection of bottled corpses and, always a keen ornithologist, his bird sightings included the shirka, the mouse-bird, the bee-eater, the brubru shrike, the cutthroat weaver, the white-rumped blackchat, and the hoopoe. He was especially proud of noting the blue-backed whydah cuckoo, which was 'too idle to make nests or feed babies'.

We camped in the forest of Timbuktu, which was a mistake. The sand was soft and bog-like everywhere, while the dry grass patches concealed a myriad of marble-sized burrs, sticky and itchy.

The non-stop call of vinaceous doves and hoopoes in the pango-pango trees kept us awake all night lying on our clammy lilos.

Near the village of Goundam we launched our collapsible canvas row-boat on a tributary of the Niger which led to a great reed-covered lake and some lakeside ruins where, at last, Ollie located a colony of the 'correct' bats. In one long-abandoned ruin full of big black spiders with thick webs, all five of us stretched bird-catching nets across all exits and caught six beautiful little bats with fixed smiles, which a deliriously happy Ollie immediately pickled.

By this point Simon was incubating malaria, but didn't know it.

In Timbuktu town Ginny bought a 'crusader sword', to use the terminology of the teenager who sold it to her at 'knockdown price'. It did look like the real thing, but a Westernized Arab at a Coca-Cola stall, on spotting it, said knowingly, 'Ah, you have *hadada* sword.' He shook his head knowingly. 'Made from Land Cruiser.'

This was later confirmed at Abidjan by an Ivorian antique dealer who had a number of similar swords. *Hadadas* are northern Arab craftsmen who moved from using mined iron, often garnered from meteorites found in deserts, to scrap-iron, especially leaf-springs from abandoned cars and lorries, once the latter became an easier source metal.

Floods in Niafunké blocked our route, and ferries were unwilling to cross the swollen river. So we took a 450-mile detour to Koutiala. My memories of this region between desert and jungle are sketchy, but I do remember great humidity, forests of dead and dying trees where no birds sang and where herds of emaciated cattle churned up the mire into a giant pig-pen.

We had at some point passed from desert into that semi-arid zone known as the Sahel. The common perception of this region, which is south of the Sahara and north of the rain forests, is one of creeping desertification where the desert is advancing, vegetation is dying and dire changes are taking place at various levels of ecosystem function.

Mean rainfall in the Sahel belt was adequate for local crops, but almost every year from 1970 until the present time it has been increasingly dry. Scientists now believe that this desertification is caused more by wind-blown dust than by lack of rainfall. The irradiant effects of the dust are known to influence climate change.

Food, animal feed and fuel are all in high demand in Africa's troubled Sahel region, but supply is not rising to meet demand. Researchers have analysed figures from twenty-two countries in the region, and have identified a falling availability of resources per capita along with increased famine risks. Between 2000 and 2010 the region's population grew from 367 million to 471 million, but the production of crops did not increase at the same rate. Population projections indicate that the region will be home to one billion people by 2050.

The region has already been hit by a number of famines, and

harvests are set to decrease due to higher air temperature. If future droughts occur at similar climatic magnitudes as the ones that took place in the 1970s and 1980s, the Sahel will be at risk of mega famines, the researchers conclude.

As the days passed and we moved south from the desert into the savannah scrub along its southern fringe, camels gave way to mules and oxen.

From the relatively disease-free heat of the Sahara we had now entered the humid, pestilential fringe of the tropics. River blindness, dengue fever, yellow fever and malaria lurked and would soon increase as we followed the Niger south to Mopti. There was little evidence of poverty as we drove between the roadside villages, but the Sahel has a high death rate of children and the hotter the world gets, the greater the spread of disease in such regions.

Every year seven million children die of disease and starvation and one billion have no access to clean water.

One clump of bushes where we camped produced a throng of black Arab-speaking Mauritanians who sang to us at sunset, clashing their shields with their short spears while their women bounced their multi-coloured bead necklaces against their banana-shaped breasts to a rhythmic beat.

For three days we drove south-west through foetid swampland forest and the irrigated rice lands of Kouruma until, at Markala by the Niger Barrage, we came to proper tarmac. Charlie in his shorts threw himself down and kissed this 'real road'.

Our camps were now in forest, not savannah, and under swaying baobab trees. One moonless night I heard Ginny moaning outside our camp perimeter, and when I found her she was lying on hard ground and ignoring the ants crawling over her legs. For several years she had suffered infrequent, but worsening, stomach pains. Tests had indicated a spastic colon, but this was never confirmed. I gave her aspirin, and by morning she felt well enough to drive. Twenty-five years later, suffering the same pains, she died of stomach cancer.

Simon's eyes were badly bloodshot, caused by the dust and the non-stop dribble of sweat which was made worse by his contact lenses. In Loulouni, near the Ivory Coast border, he bartered a pair of khaki shorts for guavas and yams, from which exotic mix he

produced a tasty meal. We sat round a log fire in a clearing surrounded by tall elephant grass, while lightning forked and thunder
rumbled in the rain forests all around.

We crossed the Ivorian border at Ouangolodougou and, prompted
by Ollie's last collection task for the Natural History Museum, which
was to obtain water snails from the Bandama Rouge River, we
entered the rain forest via Tiassalé.

Ginny had failed to find a single fairy shrimp in the Sahara, but
she had a second mission for the Museum which involved collecting
a certain type of termite. And, she stressed to me, there was a huge
difference between termites and ants.

I studied Ginny's detailed 'ant and termite habitat' notes:

The need to conserve moisture … dictates that a termite colony
must build a nest. Many build enormous mud fortresses. Each
labouring insect makes its own bricks by chewing earth, mixing it
with liquid cement from a special gland above its jaws, and producing a small pellet which it kneads into position on the rising
wall with a shaking action of its head. Millions co-operate to con-
struct their immense tenements. These may measure as much as 3
or 4 metres across. Some may have spires 7 metres high. Ventilator
chimneys run up within the buttresses around the sides to allow
spent air to escape. Deep shafts descend through the foundations
to moist ground where the workers go to collect water. This they
smear over the internal walls of their galleries and so prevent a
lethal drop in the humidity of their microclimate.

Ants, too, live on the grasslands, but unlike termites, have a
hard, impermeable outer skin to their bodies, so they are able to
march above ground, even in sunlight, with little risk of desicca-
tion. Harvester ants swarm through the turf, indefatigably
collecting grass seeds and carrying them back to their underground
granaries. There, workers belonging to a special caste with huge
jaws crack them open so that other less well equipped members of
the colony can eat them. Other species, the leaf-cutters, demolish
living plants, using their scissor-like jaws to shear the leaves and
stems of the grasses into easily transported sections.

Ants cannot digest cellulose any better than termites. They too

recruit the help of a fungus. It is not the same species as that cultivated by termites, and the ants eat it directly. The nests of the
leaf-cutters are not as obvious as termite hills, for they are built
below ground; but they are even bigger. The galleries may go down
to a depth of 6 metres, extend over an area of 200 square metres
and provide a home for seven million insects.

For an insect-free camp, we cleared away a patch of bamboo and
undergrowth with machetes. Charlie, nonetheless, found a nine-inch
black scorpion hiding in his sleeping bag and gave it to Ollie, who
pickled it 'in case it is of interest to the Museum'. Simon roasted a
three-day-old chicken over a fire of bamboo embers using a Land
Rover starting handle as a spit.

Ollie led all of us into the surrounding jungle and along the banks
of the Bandama with 'all eyes out for snails'. We traversed a column
of many thousands of half-inch-long black ants. Ollie swore when
one bit his backside. The tree boles all about us were massive.
Underfoot the vegetation was deep in decayed foliage and convoluted roots. Butterflies, weirdly marked moths and noisy dragonflies
criss-crossed the dappled gloom until, as dusk fell curtain-like, darting fireflies took over.

Ginny and I bathed in the dark, assured by the all-knowing Ollie
that there were no crocodiles or piranha in the Bandama.

Later in the week, once Ollie was happy with his slimy snail-haul,
we left the jungle for the coast and the Ivorian capital of Abidjan,
where Anton Bowring, Transglobe Expedition's 'marine leader', met
us and guided us through busy fish markets to our ship. Two of his
crew were sick with malaria and were being nursed by Jill, the ship's
volunteer cook (later to marry Anton). Simon, with swollen glands
and heat exhaustion, soon collapsed. He had done well to keep going
until then.

Late in November 1979 we left the Ivory Coast to steam south at our
maximum speed of nine knots over the Equator and down the
Greenwich Meridian into the Benguela Current.

Flying fish died on the sweltering decks and the ship's ancient
refrigerator system gave up the ghost, so that two tons of sponsored

mackerel, enough for the crew for the next two years, unfroze and turned into a stinking sludge that leaked into the ship's bilges so that everything and everyone soon smelt of rotten mackerel. I dread to think what would happen if there was a similar freezer breakdown on a huge modern container ship on the Asia–Europe route, the longest leg of which is from Malaysia to Port Said in Egypt. This takes ten increasingly stifling days. By the end of this, crew members say, the containers (which are refrigerated) sweat as much as they do. A power failure on this run would turn to mush a typical cargo of 33,300 kilograms of frozen fish roe loaded in China.

The weather closed in and the ship rolled forty degrees each way. Somewhere in the Benguela Current off Angola and down in Number Two hold our forklift truck broke loose and crushed a generator, which caused battery acid to run free over the cargo in the hatch below.

At times I began to fear the worst but, as we edged down towards the Skeleton Coast, the seas grew less aggressive and we reached Cape Town in time for us to prepare for the next phase of our circumnavigation, the first complete surface crossing of Antarctica by a single group.

There is no place in a book titled *Heat* for our experiences below zero while completing the first one-way-only crossing of Antarctica, but some eighteen months later Anton and his crew, still all unpaid, managed to rescue the five of us from the Pacific side of Antarctica and took us up to New Zealand and Australia, where we held an exhibition in Sydney on the quayside and right by the famous Opera House.

Ginny and I had long been fascinated by the vast heartland of Australia and had often discussed an expedition to traverse its deserts. Leaving Anton in charge of the preparations in Sydney, we stayed with an old friend from the Australian SAS regiment who regaled us with tales of early Aussie explorers.

The most successful of the Australian desert explorers was a Scotsman named John McDouall Stuart. Aged twenty-three he emigrated to Australia and worked for the South Australia Surveyor General, Captain Charles Sturt, who had by then completed several successful journeys into unknown regions of Australia.

In 1844 both men left Adelaide to explore the arid centre of the continent and locate the great inland sea of many Aboriginal rumours. They found no lake, but they did visit two great desert areas which they named the Simpson Desert and the Sturt Stony Desert. When Sturt's second in command died of scurvy, John Stuart was appointed to the job. Both he and Sturt nearly died of scurvy too but, although the latter never fully recovered and retired, Stuart, after a rest of six years, was able to mount six ambitious attempts to cross the continent from south to north. The first four did well and the Royal Geographical Society awarded Stuart a Gold Medal, their greatest honour, and one they gave soon afterwards to Dr David Livingstone on the other side of the world.

In 1860 Stuart and his steadfast colleague William Kekwick were sponsored by the Australian government to travel once again as far north as possible with various subsidiary missions. They had some months previously commissioned another expedition with more or less the same tasks. This other team was led by Robert Burke and his aide William Wills and they were already well on their way north.

In April Stuart reached the epicentre of Australia, over 1,000 miles from both the south and the north coasts. Eventually, sick, tired and with scurvy symptoms he turned back.

The same year Burke and Wills with two others, King and Gray, had struggled from their central base at Cooper's Creek all the way to the coastal marshes near to the northern coastline and they did actually reach the sea. On their desperate return journey through the central deserts, three of them by then with two camels (having set out with fifteen members and sixteen camels), they became weak through lack of food, and when Burke caught Gray stealing food he beat him. Gray died soon afterwards and the other two eventually reached Cooper's Creek only to find that their base party, after waiting for them for four months, had just left that very morning. Burke and Wills died soon afterwards and King only survived thanks to Aboriginals who fed him for months before a rescue group found him.

Soon after Stuart set out on his sixth attempt to cross the continent, a horse kicked him unconscious and trod on his hand. Nonetheless he continued on with ten men and seventy-one horses. They were attacked by Aboriginals, but in July 1862 they reached the northern coastline and the Pacific Ocean. They had achieved their goal through Stuart's dogged determination.

The Simpson Desert produced temperatures and sand dunes to rival the Sahara. Some quotes by explorers into the region include this by Ernest Giles (1874):

Being in a chronic state of burning thirst, my general plight was dreadful in the extreme. A bare and level sandy waste would have been paradise to walk over compared to this. My arms, legs, thighs, both before and behind, were so punctured with spines, it was agony only to exist; the slightest movement and in went more spines, where they broke off in the clothes and flesh, causing the whole of the body that was punctured to gather into minute pustules, which were continually growing and bursting. My clothes, especially inside my trousers, were a perfect mass of prickly points.

And about Charles Sturt (1845):

In 1844, aged forty-nine and partially blind from earlier expeditionary work, Charles Sturt left his beloved wife Charlotte and started on a third and final expedition – this time aimed straight at the heart of the continent. There, he believed he would find 'a large body of inland waters', so he equipped the expedition with a boat for sailing on this mythical sea. Instead, he discovered a sea of seemingly endless sand dunes – the Simpson Desert – and temperatures so extreme they shrivelled his supplies, prostrated his horses and burst his thermometer.

Sturt was possessed by an almost manic obsession. Scurvy was turning his men's skin black, and large pieces of spongy flesh hung from the roofs of their mouths. They were rotting where they stood, but still Sturt, now all but blind, pushed on. He wrote that he preferred death to defeat by this terrible land.

From Australia our ship took us up to the mouth of the Yukon River, from where Charlie and I (Ollie had left the team for domestic reasons) made our way by open boat and skis to the most northern island in the world. The following dark winter months we spent in two huts with Ginny. When in the spring of 1982 the sun reappeared, we left Ginny to begin our traverse of the Arctic Ocean via the North Pole.

Two weeks later, Ginny was woken by the alarm in her radio shack. She looked out of her window and saw an orange glow around the door of the neighbouring stores hut. Forgetting the temperature, which was minus 40° Fahrenheit, she rushed across to the store and, on opening the door, was faced with a fireball. The whole hut, with all our precious stores and parachutes, was a mass of flames from end to end. Ginny tried to use fire extinguishers, but she might as well have spat into hell.

She woke Simon, but they could do nothing but watch as eight 45-gallon drums of stored gasoline exploded, soon followed by our rocket flares and 7.62 ammunition.

Newspapers and TV reports all over the world screamed 'POLAR EXPEDITION IN FLAMES' and 'CONFLAGRATION AT POLAR BASE'.

Charlie and I carried on towards the Pole and arrived there on Easter Day 1982, the first humans in history to reach both Poles by surface travel. But, only a couple of hundred miles later, solar radiation had so gnawed at and broken up the sea-ice that we had to seek the safety of a floe which looked solid, in the hope that it would float us south to the ship before being crushed by collision with other million-ton floes.

After seven months out on the moving sea-ice, the remains of our floe did eventually float us to within twenty miles of the point that our ship bravely managed to reach, despite near-critical damage to her hull caused by ramming ice floes.

A month later we steamed up the Thames to Greenwich, some three years after we had left that point. Mankind had for the first time in history travelled vertically around Earth's surface, a journey never yet repeated by any route.

All the members of our team returned to their various homes across the world, including to the USA, Canada, Fiji, Scotland, South Africa, Australia and New Zealand.

Anton, Ginny and I spent eighteen months paying off the expedition debts, and then we began to plan other challenges, including how to make a living. After so long in cold deserts of ice, we yearned to get back to the hot, sandy variety.

CHAPTER 15

The Long Hunt

Ginny's hard work in the polar regions was recognized when she became the first woman ever to receive the coveted Polar Medal. This was given to her by Her Majesty the Queen. She was also the first female voted into the hallowed portals of the Antarctic Club. But given the choice of expedition work zones, she would always choose the hot ones.

In 1984 *The Guinness Book of Records* voted me 'The World's Greatest Living Explorer' in their World Hall of Fame.

In that same year Billie Jean King was their 'Greatest Sportsperson' and Paul McCartney the 'Greatest Musician'. Their choice was in each case based on the number of world records the individual had achieved in their specific field. One such record in the 'Highly Specialized' category was that of the American Vernon 'Komar' Craig who had walked barefoot over a set distance (some 40 metres) of red-hot coals at the hottest recorded temperature of over 1,000°F (535°C). When, at the awards ceremony, I asked him how he avoided badly burnt feet, he said that he wasn't certain but probable factors included the fact that water has a very high specific heat capacity whereas embers have a very low one. Therefore the temperature of the foot tends to change less than the coal. Water also has a high thermal conductivity, and on top of that the rich blood-flow in the foot will carry away the heat and spread it. When the embers cool down, their temperature sinks below the flash point, so they stop burning and no new heat is generated. Firewalkers do not spend very much time on the embers because they keep moving. Vernon assured me that he had, as yet, never been 'badly hurt' by his fire-walking and he was still seeking to beat his own heat record.

The Guinness Award did not help to get me a dependable income, although I used it in my CV with all my ongoing job applications.

By chance a good friend of my mother's answered her plea to find me a job 'somewhere exciting'. She was worried that I might end up doing something crazy and she knew that her friend had excellent Foreign Office contacts.

I met my mother's friend at our home in Sussex and he was very helpful with career suggestions, all of them naturally based on his own past experiences.

Sir Olaf Caroe had retired to write books about Asia after a highly successful professional life in the Indian Political and Civil Services between 1919 and 1947, during which time he graduated to serving as Chief Commissioner of Baluchistan and later as Governor of the North West Frontier Province.

I told Olaf that I had read all about the Soviets in Afghanistan and I wanted to do my bit against the invaders. My grandfather had fought for the Empire, my dad had fought the Nazis and I wanted to fight the Marxist threat. In Germany I had spent years with my regiment waiting for the armed might of the Soviet Union to attack, but this never materialized. So, for a chance of real action against the Soviets, not just their PFLOAG cadris I wished to join the Mujahideen guerrillas in their armed jihad against the Soviet invasion.

Olaf asked me if I liked extreme climates. I said that I did. He asked if I spoke Urdu, and I said, 'No, but I'm good at languages. I could learn quickly.' He worked hard to put me off by lending me written records, his own and those of his Anglo-Indian colleagues. Here are some excerpts from those notes which describe one of Olaf's early work areas, the United Provinces between the Ganges and Jumuna rivers and only four degrees of latitude south of the Afghan border in the same climate belt.

We used to keep wet mats made of *khas* grasses hanging over our bungalow's open doors. These helped to make the living room just about liveable for much of the year, but in the hot season every bit of furniture was burning to touch. The nights were terrible with my apartment a veritable furnace. We covered tables and chests of drawers with blankets, or the wood would split with noises like pistol shots. You took clean folded bedlinen or a shirt out of a drawer and they might as well have come out of an oven. We wore regulation Political Service clothing for many occasions ... totally unsuitable! I often felt dizzy and wanted to sit when I had to stand.

When on field journeys of inspection in the forest areas, we slept in tents ... hot as hell! By day flies were everywhere, crawling all over any food. Tree bark split and bamboo clumps crackled as though trying to scream. Mosquitoes always managed to find holes in my net and sucked my blood all night.

I asked him about the wildlife, but he clearly had no interest in the fauna.

We kept a dog and a tame mongoose to warn us of snakes. They were everywhere, especially in the rainy season. They liked our tents and the bungalow, above all to curl up in the dry toilet tubs and in our boots. They were especially frequent lodgers in the monsoon weeks when the rain filled their holes.

Apart from the snakes and other creepy crawlies, he described the monsoon as a welcome change, humidity instead of heat.

Like living in a Turkish bathhouse. Mosquitoes breed in millions. Armies of frogs hop to new pools. Every type of insect and spider heads for shelter in your bungalow. Rivers roar down dry valleys.

But the people [he assured me with a grin] are delightful for the most part. Especially the sugary bureaucrats so well portrayed by Peter Sellers. Let me give you some well known examples of their mastery of the English language ... 'An expected increment' became 'an excrement', draft texts of petitions included the phrase, 'two adults and two adulteresses', and the habit of many Indian clerks to draw out long words could cause misunderstandings. For instance, an Indian restaurant waiter asking a newly seated English customer, 'Are you com … for … table?' might well get the answer, 'No, I have come for tea.'

But [Olaf became serious] not all Indians are, of course, happy-go-lucky, nice chaps any more than we are. Think of the Black Hole. Back in the eighteenth-century in Calcutta, a city that *we* founded, the Nawab of Bengal sent 50,000 troops against the fort's garrison of a couple of hundred British Army men. They soon surrendered and at least sixty of them, including two women, were shut up in the fort's prison in a dark cellar only six by five metres in size with two small barred windows. It was mid-summer, there was standing room only and the prisoners fought to get near a window. The guards jeered at their screams. By nine o'clock at night many prisoners had slowly suffocated. There was no water. The weak were trampled by the strong. They defecated standing up. They raved, swore and fought. In the morning the guards dragged out the bodies of all but twenty-three of the prisoners and threw them into a ditch.

Olaf flicked an old newspaper cutting towards me. 'They aren't too gentle in your Afghanistan either. Look at these figures.'

Twenty-seven thousand Afghan civilians had, according to Amnesty International, been executed by the Kabul government even before the Soviet invasion, and after it hundreds of thousands of Afghan civilians had been killed in bombing raids or massacres.

I decided, after further reading about the Afghan war, and specifically about the region north of Kabul, that I would join the forces of the Sunni leader there, Ahmad Shah Massoud, known as the Lion of Panjshir. I applied in October 1984 for an Urdu language course in London and approached the boss of ITN, for whom I had previously interviewed Sultan Qaboos in Oman, with the plan that Ginny and I would produce a documentary film titled *Fighting for the Lion*. We badly needed an income.

The week before we were due to go for our key ITN interview, we were woken at 4 a.m. one morning by a call from Los Angeles and I was offered the job of Public Relations Officer at Occidental Petroleum in the UK. The caller was Dr Armand Hammer, octogenarian founder and chairman of Occidental Oil, a man of enormous wealth and power. Previously, Prince Charles had persuaded the Doctor to help the Transglobe Expedition with fuel, and I had met him on several occasions.

'I have never had a job outside the army,' I warned Dr Hammer. 'I know nothing about PR.'

This did not faze the Doctor. His attitude was that since I had persuaded sponsors to part with £29 million worth of goods for the recent Transglobe Expedition, then I must know something about public relations.

When I told Ginny the good news that our financial troubles were all over as I had my first 'real job', she turned over in bed expressing the sincere hope that my new boss was not going to make a habit of calling me at 4 a.m.

Later in the week I was flown to Los Angeles by private jet for an interview with the Doctor, who told me that I should consider myself his personal representative in Europe, not just one of Occidental's employees in London.

I explained that I already had a career in expeditions and would need, therefore, at least four months a year away from my Occidental desk. Surprisingly, this proved acceptable and I was given the job.

I worked for Dr Hammer for the next nine years with the ambiguous title of Vice-President of Public Relations at Occidental in London. The North Sea oil platform of Piper Alpha was one of my PR responsibilities, and this turned out to be a very unhappy involvement when, in 1988, Piper Alpha caught fire and 167 of those on the platform died.

Apart from North Sea activities, I was periodically sent messages from the 'good doctor' with weird, non-oil related missions. These in the early 1990s included visits to Italy to pass on handwritten messages to the exiled King of Afghanistan with the end view of reinstalling his rule in that country. This plot, according to Dr Hammer, involved the US Secretary of State, George Shultz. It failed, but many years later when I was in Kabul with the BBC News senior correspondent John Simpson, I mentioned it to the then President Karzai who found it very amusing and commented, 'There will never be another King here.'

I went with John, a group of ex-SAS security types and a BBC film crew for a fortnight's filming in various areas of Afghanistan, including a night in an isolated police post overlooking the Tora Bora caves, made famous by their erstwhile inmate Osama bin Laden. I ended up feeling grateful to Fate that I had not spent time fighting for the Lion of the Panjshir Valley ... Afghani politics and shifting allegiances were far too slippery to warrant life-threatening service there.

After the visit to Afghanistan, which turned out to be pleasantly cool and not at all like Olaf Caroe's hothouse, I was commissioned to write articles for a travel magazine on 'great snow-covered mountains', starting with Kilimanjaro.

The first Kili-Climb tour guide that I met at Arusha in Tanzania shook his head when I asked to interview him. 'Snow-covered!' he grunted, 'I have put my guide business up for sale while the going is good and Kili still has at least a sprinkling of snow to help attract customers.'

Although there was certainly more than a sprinkling, there was definitely far less snow cover on the Kili glacier than when I had last seen the mountain only a dozen years before. Like the Arctic sea-ice cover, Kili had been considerably changed by global warming in a comparatively short passage of time, which was obvious even to the naked eye.

Another part of the world where glaciers were in alarming retreat was the Andes. I went there to climb eight volcanoes near Quito. Temperatures in the Andes have of late risen faster than the global average and the glaciers that provide much of the water for towns like Bolivian El Alto are disappearing, to the alarm of the inhabitants and thanks to the greenhouse gas emission of the industrialized world.

I witnessed great lightning storms in the Andean volcanic mountains, including a stunning lightning and thunder display on Chimborazo at over 20,000 feet above sea level. My mountain guide there commented that these potentially lethal storms were on the increase. Not long before he had joined the search for a fellow guide and his Scandinavian client. He had found them both near the Chimborazo summit with a hole drilled neatly in the helmet of the guide who had been struck directly by a bolt. His ice axe was partly molten and his client, some fifty metres away, had also been killed, apparently by the electrical current having passed down the icy rope that connected the two men.

From the Andean volcanoes I flew to Texas where I visited the NASA headquarters at Houston for an interview with the lady in charge of all astronaut in-flight food. She was, at that time, experimenting with new ways of providing maximum calories for minimal weight. This was exactly what I needed at the time for an attempt to cross the Antarctic continent, manhauling all supplies for 1,500 miles and three months without replenishment.

The three NASA food experts that I met in Houston were an interesting group and, over sandwiches and coffee in their Space Center, the conversation covered all things related to how 'heat makes the world go round'. We discussed many topics which were thrown about like a game of dysfunctional ping-pong, and some of the disjointed heat-related nuggets included a discussion about the fact that my cousin Oliver Fiennes, the Dean of Lincoln, had recently left Texas taking with him the Lincoln copy of the Magna Carta with which he was touring the USA. One of my NASA hosts remembered cousin Oliver's talk about Magna Carta and how it helped form the US Bill of Rights. But he was much more impressed by Oliver's reaction when accused by the cathedral treasurer of spending too much on heating the building. He had simply erected a small glass greenhouse in the cathedral's vestry in which he lit a small kerosene heater and switched off the cathedral's central heating. The saving of costs over the next winter overrode the complaints by the freezing congregation, and the cathedral vergers could warm up their hands over the heater.

'I'm sure,' one NASA man commented, 'there are lessons there for our over-cosseted astronauts.' He added that American researchers were following up their own version of my cousin Oliver's heat-saving action. The US 'Advanced Research Projects Agency – Energy' was backing the development of a project known as Local Warming. The principle of this was that buildings are highly inefficient consumers of heat, especially in winter when a huge amount of energy is wasted heating empty homes by day and warming empty office buildings by night. Even when buildings are functional, unoccupied spaces are kept at the same temperature as those that are in use.

Little wonder then that the heating, ventilation and air-condition-ing of buildings accounts for 13 per cent of total energy consumption in America. 'Note,' he added, 'that all solar power in the country only provided 1 per cent of available energy.'

This Local Warming project was based on the premise that, apart from the modest ambient heat needed to prevent pipes from freezing, it is people rather than buildings who care about keeping warm. So why not aim heat at individuals as they move about their place of work? Local Warming's apparatus consists of a combination of pow-erful infra-red lamps, clever optics and servo motors to direct beams at people as they are tracked by a Wi-Fi based system. An alternate system being worked on uses arrays of infra-red LEDs and targeting optics that switch on and off as people move about. Local Warming estimates that, once one of its systems becomes practical and cost-effective, build-ing heating costs could be cut by as much as 90 per cent.

This led to the comment from our NASA lady host that global warming was causing 'islands of urban heat', which in turn was kill-ing off many tree species in South Carolina including the attractive red maple, and this was causing a massive increase in the populations of urban pests such as the wonderfully named gloomy sap-sucking scale insects, whose fertility rates increase greatly in the warmth.

Another problem is that the viral disease dengue fever which causes excruciating bone and joint pain and is transmitted by the *Aedes* mosquito is now present in the southern states, including Texas and Florida. And chikungunya fever, which is similar to dengue, but from a different host mosquito which is also now breed-ing in the USA.

NASA, according to a notice on the Houston canteen wall, was leading mankind's efforts to reach into space about 14 billion years after space 'began' and the Big Bang occurred. Life appeared on Earth 3 billion years ago. Humans evolved from other primates 7 million years ago. The wheel was invented 4,500 years ago. The first time great heat was used to smelt rock into iron was in 3000 BC, and good quality steel was produced by the mid eighteenth century. This helped man to land on the moon in 1969, thanks, of course, to Houston and the Kennedy Space Center in Florida.

What, I asked our hosts (their names are sadly long since forgotten), is the hottest temperature on our planet? Their answer was that, if a hole was drilled right through Earth, the temperature an explorer would experience in the epicentre would be around 7000°C.

And the hottest man-made fires? The NASA men laughed. They knew of a product produced by arsonists, known to the FBI as High Temperature Accelerant (HTA), which could speedily destroy an all-steel and concrete construction and which would reach temperatures of over 5000°F. Steel girders melt and concrete is turned to powder by this HTA. The Seattle Fire Department, analysing HTA post-arson debris, speculated that a concoction resembling rocket fuel was involved. Firefighters had to stay well clear of the infernos caused by HTA arsonists and found that water jets intended to put the fires out actually encouraged the blaze. In order to add my pennyworth of heat information, I volunteered that the biggest man-made non-nuclear detonation ever recorded was in the summer of 1917 during the trench war in northern France when a ridge line, known as Messines, was held by the Germans and seemed impregnable. British miners secretly dug nineteen tunnels under this ridge and set off a single huge explosion of over a million tons of ammonite which blew great craters along the ridge, instantly killing 10,000 Germans. The Prime Minister in London actually felt the tremor at his desk, and the sound of the detonation was heard in Dublin. My uncle was killed a week later during the follow-up attack.

Despite good advice from our NASA friends, we were never able to obtain a daily ration of 5,000 calories weighing hardly any less than those used by Captain Scott in 1910. However, NASA did subsequently agree to try to help locate Ubar by using special cameras on the Space Shuttle.

Back in the UK, I mounted a series of journeys with Dr Mike Stroud. We broke a number of polar records in the Arctic and Antarctic, but I was on a solo attempt to reach the North Pole unsupported when my 300lb sledge fell through sea-ice in the dark at minus 48°C with a wind blowing. To rescue my sledge I had to fish around in the ice-laden water to retrieve the harness ropes (which I had released to avoid being dragged into the sea myself). Using my left arm I located the rope and managed to drag the heavy sledge back onto a solid ice floe. Rapidly losing all feeling in my 'dry' hand and knowing that I already had bad frostbite damage to my wet left hand, I was extremely lucky to be able to erect at least one half of my small tent and creep into it out of the freezing cold, already shivering violently, before both my hands became useless. I then tried to light the cooker, for I knew that without heat I would die within a few hours. But with only one hand to pump the fuel I could not prime it, so I put one side of the stove in my mouth as a substitute for my useless hand and managed the pump action with the other (still just usable) hand. To my huge relief when I struck a match, a minor petrol explosion resulted, together with a high flame. I then found that the cooker was stuck to my lips due to the cold metal. Tearing it away there was blood all over the place. The cooker flame then set fire to the inflammable tent liner, but this I put out with my sleeping bag.

The feeling of warmth that soon spread through the little space in the drooping tent was the best feeling I can remember. *Heat* was at that moment the most wonderful word in the English language.

In the same vein I can remember the days of the most unbearable heat during the three expeditions with Ginny in the sand dunes of the Empty Quarter when, less acclimatized than in my army days, I felt the oppressive effects of the heat more easily.

Some time after I had left the Sultan's Armed Forces, my old friend Tim Landon (who had been crucial to the coup which ousted my boss Sultan Said bin Taimur) wrote to offer me a job in Dhofar. The work involved raising and leading an anti-PFLOAG raiding group to be based in the region of Shisr (my old Ubar-hunting camp) consisting of Mahra anti-communist tribesmen.

This suggestion fell through as the PFLOAG situation in Dhofar changed following the accession of Sultan Qaboos. When working for ITN I went to Muscat to interview Qaboos, and he asked me about my years spent working for his father and the conversation veered to my long-time search for Ubar. He showed immediate interest and quoted from the Quran, 'Irem of Ad of the many pillars.' He wished me luck when I said that I hoped to be able to continue the search and, soon afterwards, through his kindly chief adviser Dr Omar al Zawawi, sponsored one of my Arctic expeditions. His only stipulation was that we fly the Omani flag on reaching the Pole.

Ginny became as fascinated as I was by the idea of finding the lost city and she did a great deal of research into its little-known legends in the library of the Royal Geographical Society.

Dr Omar invited us to stay with him in Muscat during a visit by the Queen to Oman. By then Omani officers were slowly taking over from the British at all levels of the Sultan's Armed Forces, but Patrick Brook was still in Muscat and he sent signals to detachments of his Armoured Regiment to look after me.

In the north the country had changed beyond recognition in a thousand ways. Where fifteen years before there had been one school, one hospital and a few roads of tarmac close to the capital, there were now four-lane highways, spaghetti junctions, schools and hospitals throughout the country, free bus services, factories, museums, street lighting – indeed, everything you would expect to find in a developed country had arrived as though at the touch of a magic oil lamp.

And the overall planning had been sensible, avoiding wasteful haste and ugliness. The apparent miracle was easier to comprehend when one bore in mind that *all* ministries and *all* substantial plans were subject to the approval of one man: the Sultan. Despite his Western education, Sultan Qaboos was a strict Ibadhi Muslim and venerated the benefits of traditional values in architecture as well as in moral issues. Unlike Prince Charles in Britain, he did not have to fume in frustrated helplessness when he espied some monstrous concrete carbuncle rearing up in an Omani city; he simply ordered it to be pulled down and replaced.

In Dhofar the last of the *adoo* had surrendered to the Sultan, whose forces had in the early 1970s received military aid from the Shah of Persia, Britain's SAS, the UAE and Jordan.

Despite Patrick's help during my 1985 visit, I was unable to further my Ubar plans and the closest I came to the Wadi Mitan was a cross-country trip from Thumrait – now a square-mile complex of Sultanate forces, including a hardened runway for Phantom jets – to the Yemeni border at Makinat Shihan, well south of any likely Ubar site.

*

Back in England I met up with Nick Clapp, a freelance movie director who had edited a film of one of my polar expeditions and we had
become friends. He had subsequently made a film in Oman about the
golden oryx, had fallen in love with the desert and started to read
about the Empty Quarter explorers. When reading about Bertram
Thomas's search for Ubar, of mysterious tracks in the great desert
and a fabulous lost city, he knew that he had an ideal theme for a
movie to shoot in Oman. So, for the next two years he became a
bookworm searching for any and all Ubar clues – just as Ginny and
I had on and off for the past twenty-one years.

Nick's problem was that he knew only too well, after making his
oryx film which had been sponsored by the Omani government who
approved of that particular project, that he was highly unlikely to
obtain a permit to film in the seldom visited province of Dhofar.

Nick went ahead with his Ubar research anyway and approached
the Jet Propulsion Laboratory (JPL) in Pasadena, California, whose
Imaging Radar system on a *Challenger* mission passed over the
Empty Quarter in May 1985. Nick's contacts at the JPL, Doctors
Ron Blom and Charles Elachi, showed him radar images of ancient
stream beds and lakes, long buried under dunes, which may well
have supported habitation in centuries past.

The Ubar bug had now infected Messrs Blom and Elachi, who
kindly agreed to further radar imaging. Sadly, the following spring
Challenger exploded after lift-off killing all seven crew members, and
this affected all aspects of the planned *Challenger* programme. So
Ron Blom took to studying images from the LANDSAT and SPOT
satellite programmes instead.

By then Nick and I had agreed to work together in searching for
the lost city. I would plan, organize and lead the search on the
ground, as in the past, and he would organize and direct the mov-
ie-making. His film would be titled *The Search for Ubar* so he still
stood a good chance of finding a 'buyer' for his movie even if we did
not, in fact, find the city.

In 1986 the JPL team gave Nick an updated radar image from the
latest *Challenger* orbit which clearly showed a short stretch of the
'Thomas Road' as well as an L-shaped feature nearby.

His Majesty the Sultan of Oman came to London and paid a visit to his old friend Tim Landon, who was by then a retired brigadier living in a secluded manor in Berkshire. I went there with an updated proposal for the Ubar expedition and His Majesty reminded me that he was not keen on people descending on Oman, especially the southern part, with picks and shovels. However, he had been pleased with the Omani involvement in my polar project and would be prepared to allow me to take an expedition to the south, provided any digging was carefully controlled.

At that time I could not clearly state where I wanted to excavate, but I showed His Majesty a LANDSAT space image I had received from Nick Clapp that summer. This showed thin white lines amid the dunes which could perhaps be the ancient camel trails of the incense trade. I assured His Majesty that I would revert to him as soon as I could draw up a more detailed and specific plan to search for Ubar.

For a while another ex-Sultan's Army officer had searched for Ubar using a hot-air balloon, but he had given up the search so the coast was now clear.

In 1989, five years after JPL came up with the first *Challenger* radar image of the Ubar search area, they produced a detailed map of a number of ancient desert tracks but still no image of any potential buried site. Nick and a lawyer friend of his had also failed, despite approaching many potential millionaires in Washington DC and Los Angeles, to raise any funds to sponsor a Ubar search expedition.

Now that I knew there was no hope of a high-tech instant solution to the problem of finding Ubar, I contacted an old friend, Major Trevor Henry, who worked in an unspecified military department in Dhofar. He was the tough and enigmatic Scotsman who had been my sergeant instructor on the long jungle-warfare course in Brunei in the early 1970s. He had fought for the Sultan during the Dhofar War and had stayed there ever since. He knew more than any man alive about the country and its people and I was lucky that he agreed to do what he could to help my Ubar search. He had heard of a number of sightings of ruins or old pottery deep within the sands and, where permitted by his Omani superiors, he agreed to check them out.

Trevor warned me that delicate negotiations were in progress between the governments of Oman, Saudi Arabia and Yemen over the exact position of their mutual boundaries in the sands and it was important that no archaeological expedition unintentionally caused a border incursion before agreements were reached. He was well aware of my slightly dubious past within the SAS and I remembered the critical jungle report he had sent my 21 SAS commanding officer some fifteen years before. With Trevor as the expedition's Dhofar representative, we were off to a good start.

In the summer of 1990 I spent a hectic few days visiting twenty-two Omani company executives in Muscat and managed to raise all the necessary funds and equipment that Nick had failed to obtain in the USA. Land Rover Oman lent us three Discoveries and British Petroleum Oman gave us as much petrol as we needed.

The Sultan gave me permission to go ahead with a reconnaissance expedition that summer and agreed to aerial support from a Royal Oman Police helicopter, if needed.

Nick recruited an experienced Middle East archaeologist, Dr Juris Zarins, who was well aware that all archaeological work in Dhofar had come to an abrupt halt back in 1972 when the Oxford archaeologist Andrew Williamson had been killed near the Sumhuram ruins. His Land Rover was blown up by a landmine.

When the chance to join the Ubar search came his way, Juris saw it as a wonderful chance to visit Oman. He knew well that no new excavation work had been permitted in Dhofar for eighteen years and that prime sites existed that were almost certainly ripe for plucking. He gave little credence to the tales of Ubar and he did not like the thought that a high degree of interference with his work was likely from Nick's film team, but for the opportunity to work in Dhofar he was prepared to put up with a lot.

The reconnaissance journey was to take place in July 1990, at the time Saddam Hussein was about to invade Kuwait. Luckily nobody then knew of Saddam's intentions, so the Sultan's Office stamped all the visas.

The team consisted of Nick and his wife Kay, who was a tough but likeable probation officer who looked after our commissariat, Nick's friend George who was there, as far as I could make out, on the basis that he was helping to finance Nick's film, archaeologist Juris Zarins, Ron Blom from NASA's JPL and the film team.

We duly met up in Muscat and flew to Salalah where Trevor Henry was waiting. He had our Discovery vehicles ready, and for eight hectic days he guided us by way of many tracks that did not exist at the time of the troubles twenty-two years before.

Using the coordinates of the desert tracks JPL had obtained from the *Challenger* missions and the LANDSAT images, the Omani Police helicopter flew us deep into the sand dunes and, to the delight of Nick and Ron Blom, three distinct and dead-straight tracks led north-north-west over a low gravel plain and straight into the heart of a dune over 200 feet high. Since at this point the camel trail was covered by thousands of tons of sand, it could reasonably be assumed to be 'ancient'.

In order to refuel and save valuable flying hours, the helicopter pilot told me that he would leave us with a cold-box of Cola tins and would return in an hour or so, by which time our appraisal of the area should be complete.

An hour passed by and, the inspection completed, we sat or squatted on a mesa top, high enough to catch any breeze to alleviate the oven-like heat of midsummer. But there was no breeze, not even the slightest of zephyrs, to cool our sweat-soaked shirts. The cold-box was soon empty.

I walked around the rim of the mesa and, peering over the western side, spotted an aperture, more a slit in the rock than a cave. There was enough room for all of us and an aperture in the ceiling caused a slight through draught. After an hour and a half I noticed that a mood of nervous apprehension had descended on our little group. Even Juris was not his usual talkative self. The thought was slowly dawning that, if the wheel of fortune was to cause the helicopter to crash, we could moulder here on the mesa until the end of time. In those days there were no mobile phones in everyone's pockets!

'Ssh!' Kay whispered. 'Listen.' She thought she had heard the distant beat of the helicopter. There is nothing easier than to hear the vibration of imagined sounds when hoping for a rescue. Many a time in deserts and polar wastes I have distinctly caught the approaching beat of an aircraft engine, expected to bring vital supplies or to remove an injured colleague. But the sound was, as often as not, merely my imagination.

Two anxious hours passed by before our pilot returned. We flew to Thumrait base and then to the little-known ruins of Andhur. On the journey I reflected how, in some way, I was now back at square one. By hoping for space-age technology to identify the actual site of Ubar, I had fallen into the trap of suggesting as much to the sponsors. I had known that the glamorous mix of satellites and buried cities would excite even the most reluctant sponsor. Now, with all our space cards a busted flush, I still had to convince His Majesty and our sponsors to back the main expedition. Over the next week Trevor took us to every site of ruins in the *nej'd* and on the coast, in the Qara *jebel* and on the Salalah Plain which had ever been mentioned as being connected to the frankincense trade. Juris was in his seventh heaven and so was Nick and his camera team. They were both keen to dig and/or film at all these scenic sites – Andhur, Hanun, Kaysh, Muday and many others – some without names but none that had clues as to Ubar's faraway location.

Luckily the humidity was high and monsoon flies were about, hungry for our blood, and this discouraged too much lingering, at least at the *jebel* sites. Ron nearly trod on an *ekis* viper, but Trevor stopped him just in time.

Scorpions, four-inch millipedes and giant spiders added interest to our trek up a side valley to a wonderful cave that in the past I had only visited by night for purposes of ambush. We slithered on the orange mud and avoided the dripping lianas with their colonies of stinging ants. The cave was wide and as high as a church, with a floor deep in the animal dung of centuries. Bats chirped from the dark recesses of the rock roof as Trevor led us to the mouth of an interior passage.

'Leopards live in here,' he told us, indicating the outline of feline spoor. A portly guide from the local tribe moved ahead and knelt down at the very mouth of the lair. At that moment Trevor emitted a spine-chilling scream with a fair attempt at ventriloquism. The guide leapt higher than I would have believed possible. He saw the joke and joined in the general mirth.

With the help of a powerful torch we inspected painted figures high on the inner cave walls, blurred symbols that seemed to include laden mules or camels but interpretation as to their identity varied to reflect the individual aspirations of the viewers. Nick, for instance, was keen on camels since from an editorial point of view he could the better splice this cave sequence into a desert scene filmed a week before.

Sweat glued our shirts to our backs and our socks to our ankles, bites itched maddeningly and I marvelled yet again how local mountain folk could survive such a hell on Earth for the three monsoon months every year of their lives.

Since my last visits to Shisr and Fasad, both locations had been settled and tasteful but modern bungalows had been erected for, in the case of Shisr, a dozen families of the local tribe, the Bait Masan, and, at Fasad, a camp for a 'frontier patrol force' of young Dhofaris with desert skills whose duties included, as mine had once done, patrols along the Yemeni and Saudi borders.

I asked the head of this patrol, a Rashidi bedu, about Ubar. He spoke of Ubar's fate as though it were an integral part of his people's history.

'Maybe Irem lies in Yemen, or Saudi, or Oman. In those days there were no such borders, so no matter. Allah was good to the people of Ad who built the city, a paradise on Earth. But *they* were bad and forsook Him for other gods, so He destroyed Irem.'

The Rashidi made a pile of sand between us and then, scooping up another handful, dashed it down violently on to his makeshift city.

'Like this,' he said, 'so did Allah treat the people of Ad.'

'Is Irem of the Quran the same place as Ubar?' I asked him.

'Maybe,' he said with a shrug. 'Who knows?'

One elderly Bait Masan, Abdullah bin Salim, whose tribe's camels had long travelled the Shisr region, remembered Fiend Force from the 1960s when we had taken coffee with his family at their various desert camps. He now invited us into the new *majlis* (community hospitality room) in the recently built village close by the old water spring and the 1950s fort built by my old boss, the late Sultan.

Abdullah was now the village head and his hyperactive son, Marbruk, proudly showed us round the seven or eight bungalows. 'If you come back,' he said, 'we rent you these eight rooms if you like.'

As since the 1960s I had always considered Shisr to be the best start-point for Ubar dune-searching, this was good news.

Juris told me of a French lady archaeologist who had, years before, had a brief look at the heaps of old stone rubble all around the Shisr waterhole, but the few artefacts that she recovered were far too recent to have had any relevance to Ubar.

Nevertheless, for our main expedition, the site was geographically ideal. We took our leave of Trevor, who agreed to continue to advise and help me, and we left Oman.

Ginny had stayed at home, much to her frustration, because she had started to breed Aberdeen Angus cattle on Exmoor and could not get away. However, she was determined to come on the main expedition.

A fortnight after we left Dhofar Saddam Hussein pushed his troops into Kuwait, and Oman joined the other Gulf States in condemning this aggressive move against an Islamic country.

To put together my proposal for Sultan Qaboos I needed a convincing opinion from Juris. He was nothing if not frank. 'Didn't see any real places,' he said. 'Just some pottery at Shisr. I didn't think anything about any of the sites. Nick kept asking me and I kept saying, "I don't know." They just looked like interesting sites. I do know there is *nothing* in the Rubh al Khali. We have done the reconnaissance and have *nothing* to show for it.'

This was all very well but, were I to admit it to His Majesty or the sponsors, I feared that the main expedition would not be allowed to take place.

Some extra time was gained by the worsening situation in Kuwait. On 7 February 1991 I was forced to write to the Americans to tell them that we should postpone the main phase until November. I laid out a suggested schedule that involved archaeology on the Plain of Salalah, with Salalah as our base, then moving north to excavate at Shisr, Heilat Araka, Andhur and elsewhere, using Shisr as our base.

Nick approved of this, as did Juris, but Trevor Henry, so indispensable to our reconnaissance the previous year, warned me from Salalah that as part of the ongoing removal of all expatriates from the Omani Armed Forces he was due to leave Dhofar in the near future and we could no longer count on his assistance.

He had earlier referred me to another Scotsman, named Andy Dunsire, who had lived in Dhofar for some eighteen years and knew the country almost as well as Trevor. 'Andy works for Airwork, the aircraft engineers in Thumrait. He will give you any help that you need,' he assured me.

So in November 1991, twenty-three years after my first Ubar search, we arrived back in Salalah and set up a temporary base at the newly erected beach-side Holiday Inn – a far cry from groundsheets on the sand.

I drove to a wild and remote part of the *jebel* where, after many enquiries, I found my old friend Hamed al Khalas who was staying with a wealthy camel-herder. The two decades and more that had passed since we had worked together under Sultan Said bin Taimur had been kind to Hamed. We talked for two hours over a bowl of foaming camel's milk and I told him of our plans. He promised to guide me to any of the 'old places'. There was nowhere in Dhofar that Hamed could not find.

Sultan bin Nashran was also in good health and living in Salalah, for he had long since retired from government Intelligence. His memories of our long patrols in the *nej'd* were undimmed, but he was as adamant as ever that Ubar lay to the west of the Wadi Mitan.

Once our sponsored Land Rovers and supplies were ready in Salalah we moved to the first work site on the Plain. This was a long-abandoned well some seventy feet deep which Ptolemy had described as the Oracle of Diana. Juris wanted to excavate the shaft itself and the ruined village around the mouth of the well, so I borrowed a mobile crane from BP of Oman in Salalah.

Nick and I were lowered into the shaft inside the crane's bucket. The smell of rotting flesh was overpowering and emanated from the bloated bodies of dead foxes. I manoeuvred the corpses into polythene bags and swatted at the fat flies that settled on my arms. I tried to keep my thoughts off the glistening carpet of insect life that crawled, leapt and slithered in that foul-smelling hole.

Even inside the swinging iron bucket we were attended by a host of flying, biting insects, but the stench lessened once the foxes' bodies were gone. Subsequent lowerings took us back down with shovels and we began the task of hoisting debris into the buckets. Each time we raised a new item, be it a tattered tent canvas or a stinking mattress, hundreds of disturbed creatures of all imaginable shapes and sizes scuttled in all directions.

Unfortunately, the deep stratum of modern garbage and animal bones that formed the floor of the shaft defeated our attempts to reach detritus from earlier times, so we left the Naheez valley and headed north, via Shisr and Fasad, with eight days' supply of food, fuel and water. Andy Dunsire came as our guide, but in Fasad I asked the Imam, a gentle Rashidi named Mohammed Mabhowt, if he would take us to a specific but nameless spot out in the Sands.

Ron Blom produced one of his satellite pictures which was taken from 260 kilometres above Earth and clearly delineated each and every sand dune. Mohammed made various grunting sounds that indicated comprehension if not recognition and agreed to accompany us. One thing he could promise us: *wherever* we ended up, he would be sure to find the quickest route back out again. Just as no man could, for many centuries, travel the Sands by camel better than the Rashidi, so nowadays they were accepted as the master rally drivers of the great dunes.

This was no idle boast. Mohammed drove our lead Discovery, travelling over the softest sand and mounting the severest of slopes.

Somewhere well within the eastern furrows of the Uruq al Hadh, with high dunes on all sides, we camped and Ron extricated his Magellan GPS satellite navigation in order to locate our position to within 100 metres. We eagerly awaited the results of this high-tech magic, the box of tricks which rendered any city-dweller a capable navigator overnight. Ron appeared nonplussed. 'Odd,' he muttered. 'Very unusual. They certainly never gave any warning of this.'

Magellan had decided, for unstated reasons, to make their navigation services unavailable to ground users for twenty-four hours. So much for reliance on state-of-the-art boffinry, I mused, but said nothing, not wishing to upset Ron.

The next day we reverted to old-style position-line navigation, using the satellite pictures as though they were maps. This was a slow process involving many stops and interesting debates between the film director, the explorer, the space scientist and the Imam of Fasad, through whose familiar home terrain we were hesitantly creeping. If only we could have given him a known name as our desired goal he would quickly have taken us there by the best available route. But the faded tracks of the 'Thomas Road' had no name and their grid reference could not be speedily inferred from our own, until the latter was indisputably revealed at such a time as Ron's Magellan condescended to supply the relevant data.

There was even now no way of knowing that the elusive Ubar did not lie beneath the very sand that we trod in our wanderings that day.

When Philby had asked the famous Saudi governor, Ibn Jiluwi, where Ubar was, the reply had been: 'Somewhere in the Rubh al Khali.'

Sadly, the satellite photographs had not provided any more specific information than Ibn Jiluwi. They had shown up the 'Thomas Road', but Thomas had already established that feature and its exact location without the help of the Space Shuttle *Challenger*.

Towards noon on the following day we found the correct valley, having negotiated various sand bridges across the serried ranks of dunes, thanks to Mohammed and his impressive dune-driving techniques.

We all camped that night by the vehicles, but Andy and I, keen to savour the still beauty of the desert night, climbed to the rim of a nearby dune. The sky was wide and full of the mystery of the universe. For me this was helpful, inspiring thoughts of a future still worthy of dreams and an antidote to the narrowing outlook of middle age. I wished that Ginny was with me. She was to arrive in a week or so.

Sirius, the Dog Star, crept, brilliantly glinting, into the lacuna of pre-dawn luminosity between two crested *ergs*. Desert dew settled and tiny grains of sand whispered in their millions as they trickled down the face of their mother dunes. Allah was close by on such a night. It is written in the Quran's Chapter of the Star that: 'It is He who makes men laugh and weep, it is He who kills and makes alive ... He is the Lord of the Dog Star, He who destroyed Ad of yore, and Thamud, and left none of them, and the people of Noah before them. Their cities, he threw them down and there covered them what did cover them.'

At the break of day the clear and mellow voice of Mohammed, Imam of Fasad, sounded the morning incantation to God. The soul of Arabia, the thunder of the Saracens and the air of the desert came together in the passion of the *mullah*'s voice. No God could ignore such a sound: '*Allahu Akbar, Allahu Akbar ...* '

Later that day we established that there were two main camel tracks and, since camels were not used as load-carrying beasts before 2500 BC, the dunes that now buried them must have done so since then. This was yet another conundrum.

An expedition by the Smithsonian Institute to a Baluchistan desert monitored twenty-foot-high dunes that moved six inches a day, but only in the windy season. Juris scoffed at the idea of major sand advances in the Rubh al Khali. 'The mass of these dunes,' he told me, 'haven't moved their butts since the Ice Age.'

At this point, and thanks to Mohammed's navigation, we returned safely to our new base at Shisr, chosen for its easy central position and facilities. It was also one of a dozen sites of potential interest, both for clue-searching and for scenic film-making. Our visit there the previous year caused the following reaction from Juris: 'Sure, Shisr had a bit of pottery ... but it had nothing to do with Ubar.' Later, in 1992, he told me: 'I didn't think Shisr was Ubar, even when we started digging there.'

When first I planned which areas of Dhofar were most suitable for Juris to visit, the key person who judged the value of each site (whether a suspect JPL blip in the Sands, an old village in the steppes, or a nest of ruins on the plain) was Trevor Henry. But in the mountains our chief guide and adviser, a remarkable Dhofari of the Shahra tribe, was Ali Ahmed Ali Mahash.

Back in the 1960s Ali had, like many Dhofaris, joined the British-trained Trucial Oman Scouts. His outstanding qualities of leadership soon saw his promotion to lieutenant and he was sent to Mons Officer Cadet School in England two years after I graduated from there.

In the late 1960s we were both at the Army School of Languages in Beaconsfield, where I was a student of Arabic and he was a teacher. He was recalled to the Gulf States as a captain and, being the best young officer of his generation, was selected for a three-year posting to a British regiment. Unfortunately the Gulf Intelligence services discovered that Ali was promulgating revolutionary ideas and he was jailed in Muscat for seven years.

On his release he obtained a government job in Salalah but remained restless until, in March 1988, a fellow Shahri showed Ali some cave writings in the Wadi Naheez. Ali was fascinated. He knew that the history of his country, of his people the Shahra and the lost people of Ad, was locked within a pre-Islamic language that existed only in southern Arabia, and especially in Dhofar. He spent long hours working to try and decode the cave hieroglyphics.

Ginny arrived in Salalah, having left her beloved herd of Aberdeen Angus under the care of a trusted neighbour. Together, while the team under Juris – and always being filmed – continued their desert searches, we spent three weeks with Ali in remote and wonderful places all over the Qara Mountains.

We drove the track east from Sudh to Hadbin until it tapered out on a precipitous coastal track in the mountains west of Hasik. Then we went to the homesteads of Ali's people, the Shahra, high on the grassland downs of Kizit and deep in the Wadi Darbat where they kept large herds of camel.

Ginny, with her communications expertise from our polar years, set up radios at Shisr, Thumrait and in each of our three Land Rovers. In brief lulls, usually on Fridays, we went alone in our Discovery to areas where Fiend Force had once patrolled and fought, to the pools of Ayun and out on the Dehedoba trail to places where I had slept under the stars and dreamed of Ginny.

Ali led us to the little-known Mahra waterhole of Leeat, an hour or so east of Hanun and tucked into the base of the mountain cliffs. Years before I had twice been ambushed by communist forces at this place, and the memories flooded back of our successful Operation Snatch.

'Was it not the Mahra,' Ali loved to ask men of that tribe, 'who killed the camel of the Prophet?'

'No, no,' they would always respond. 'The Shahra, *your* people, did that thing.'

Juris's archaeological team arrived from Missouri not long before Christmas. They were all in their early twenties and none had any previous experience of Arabia. The five girls were blessed with long hair, pretty faces and well-rounded figures. I thanked God (and Juris) for an excellent selection process and felt confident that there would be no problem in Andy Dunsire finding a great number of volunteer male diggers from among his Airwork colleagues at Thumrait. If the attraction of the actual digging was not enough, this bunch of alluring American belles would surely do the trick. I nursed mental images of hundreds of randy diggers shovelling aside vast amounts of sand from our sites over the next three months.

The common picture of Western archaeological students and field diggers, as defined by archaeologist and author Paul Bahn, was in our case wide of the mark, but may well have been what our helpers from Thumrait were expecting:

Diggers, undergraduates and volunteers are the cannon fodder of any dig. They normally provide all the sweaty labour and are kept in a state of blissful ignorance about what they are doing and why. Amazingly, some even pay to be treated in this way. Their basic task is to move dirt from one place to another and occasionally sieve it into different sizes before dumping it. Useful items they take on excavations include scruffy old clothing marked 'Archaeologists do it in holes'; a pointed trowel except in France where bent screwdrivers are preferred; insect repellent; insurance against trench collapse; condoms and bottle opener...

Bahn also warns of the qualities endemic in many modern archaeologists with regard to their field reports:

A basic rule is to fill your reports with 'maybe', 'perhaps' and 'possibly'. This enables you to make an orderly and dignified retreat in case of attack. Another way to sidestep criticism is to make your prose so obscure and tortuous that nobody is quite sure what you are saying. If later proved wrong, this smokescreen will enable you to claim that you were misunderstood and that you actually said nothing of the kind.

Well into December Juris had taken his team to many sites but found nothing worth digging for. However, the film crew happily continued to film the scenic 'search'.

Two days before Christmas I was sitting with Ginny in the shade of an old wall at Shisr when I overheard two Omani students chatting on the other side of the wall. They were unaware of our presence. Both men were with us on loan from the Ministry of National Heritage and Culture and were commenting on the fact that we had been in Shisr for ten days, the teams were ready and yet all we seemed to do was to film each other. This seemed a fair summary, but it would not sound good in the wrong quarters. The two students were likely, in their next report on our activities to their boss at the ministry, to repeat these observations which would then reach the all-seeing Sultan. We would, I felt sure, then get the royal boot without delay, in the same way as had my American Ubar-seeking predecessor Wendell Phillips in the 1950s.

So Ginny and I went post-haste to Juris and told him that he must start digging at once.

'Where?' and his eyebrows rose. 'We've found no real clues yet – anywhere!'

'Dig anywhere,' Ginny said. 'It doesn't matter where.'

We explained the likely imminent threat to our ongoing existence in Oman. So Juris quickly mustered his team and they applied their tools to the nearest rubble around the Shisr well.

Months later Juris, laughing at the memory, told me, 'By 23 December we had done *no* archaeology in Shisr.' But by Christmas Day, with a workforce of four Omanis, three Asians and six Americans, he was looking decidedly perky. I asked what was up, but he was cautious.

'It's good,' he said. 'Interesting.'

'Is it four hundred years old?' I pressed him. 'Like they say? And so not the correct period for us?'

'No,' he replied, winked and returned to the room where retrieved artefacts were beginning to spread all over the improvised shelves. The team were buried in site maps, lists and hushed discussions. There was an unmistakable air of excitement.

At first Juris concentrated his small force on or close to the original rubble pile. Within a week the outline of the rock heap had taken on the clear-cut silhouette of a ruined tower connected by low battlements to a second round tower and a beautifully built horse-shoe tower to its east. Pottery and flints were hourly unearthed, including, to Juris's great pleasure, both Roman and Greek-style urns from the period that would have been Ubar's heyday.

Days later a piece of red pottery was found that was identical to the pottery style of the Jemdet Nasr period in Uruq, Mesopotamia. If carbon dating proves this to be so then it will predate previous thinking as to the commencement of trade between Mesopotamia and south Arabia from 5000 to 4000 BC. That, in turn, will affect many other evolving theories about our human history.

'I am not going out on a limb,' Juris told me, 'and saying that this is or isn't Ubar, but I will go back to the university to check out all our findings. Then I can make some statement. But I can already say that this is a very important Roman site. It probably goes back at least four thousand years.'

Of our site, Juris told me, 'So far we have walls and towers that are square and round and horseshoe-shaped. There was clearly a central tower, an inner sanctum and an outer wall which had a min-imum height of between ten and fifteen feet and a consistent thickness of eighty centimetres. Some of the original rooms, complete with hearths, have already yielded rich finds for the key periods between the second millennium BC and around AD 300, when trad-ing activities seem to have dropped off.'

He added that, 'The central site would have appeared majestic and without equal in the land to the bedu cameleers. For nine hundred kilometres of desert in any direction there was no edifice even a quarter the size of Shisr. The walls and towers would have stood out to the weary and thirsty traveller from up to twenty miles away – to them, indeed, a city of the desert.'

One notable find in the rubble was the only ancient chess set ever to be found in south Arabia. The six soapstone pieces, each two or three inches high and well polished by the fingers of the players, had lain buried for over a thousand years. Shatrinj, the forerunner of modern chess, was a Persian war game and the king was *shah*. The word for dead is *ma'at* and a victorious player, cornering his opponent's monarch, would shout '*Shah ma'at*' – not so different from 'checkmate'.

By the end of January 1992 we had found no major inscription (such as a sign saying Irem or Ubar), but nine towers were unearthed, some 60 per cent of the main outer wall, and over 6,000 individual artefacts.

Andy Dunsire had told me of a cave system in the Qara *jebel* which was six hundred feet down at the base of a giant sinkhole called Tawi Ateer, the Well of the Birds. He had promised to show me a great cavern, which I hoped might contain wall writings or at least paintings, for it was known, certainly before the advent of recent rockfalls, that *jebalis* used to descend into the hole by way of vertiginous pathways.

Andy drove me with a Range Rover full of his friends to the village of Tawi Ateer on the high plateau of the *jebel* and a mile to the north, and we trekked into the dry bush with rucksacks and ropes. Three of his friends were to camp at the edge of the 600-foot-deep crater to ensure that our descent ropes were not removed during the night.

Because I was inept with the special rope techniques that Andy used, he took an hour to make everything ready. I felt a touch giddy, for the cry of pigeons and the starling-like Tristram's grackle echoing around the vast natural chamber kept reminding me of the long drop down to the cave system.

By the time we were ready, dusk had filled the huge, perfectly rounded sinkhole and, as Andy encouraged me to let go of the safety rope by the crater lip, stars were already appearing in a sky of midnight blue. I could not see below me and my helmet torch, striking a rock, went dead. This had the advantage of making it impossible to see the 600 feet of thin rope dangling down into the void between my swinging feet.

After many minutes of painfully slow descent, the two-inch-long alloy crocodile clasp, which slid down the rope at a speed that I could control with a lever, suddenly came up sharp against a knot of rope coils. I winced as the rope elasticated. I imagined the feel of it breaking and the sudden rush of air. Panic was not far off. Sweat stung my eyes. Because all my body weight rested on the point where the metal teeth grasped the knot and since there could be no upward impetus from my dangling legs, it took me many long minutes to free the impediment without disentangling my lifeline by mistake. For a while I despaired, then a lucky tug freed the coil, and ten minutes later I arrived, shaky kneed, at the floor of the great shaft.

The foul stench of civet dung hung about in the warm air and I heard the scrabble and snarl of the striped cats in the darkness. Andy arrived after twenty minutes and I followed him, via boulders and sloping ledges, past stalactites and a descending series of passages, to the edge of a scum-laden lake. The beam of his head torch disturbed a cloud of flying creepy-crawlies.

On a previous visit Andy had secreted two Land Rover inner tubes close by, and stripping down to our pants and desert boots, we slipped into the evil-smelling waters.

Andy beckoned me away from one side wall where a swarm of wasp-like insects rose in anger or alarm from their nest.

'There are blind fish in the caves.' Andy pointed downwards and added, 'Keep close.' I nodded, needing no second warning.

For fifty minutes I swam on my black tube and soon gave up any attempt to memorize our tortuous route. Sometimes the ceiling on the tunnel approached within inches of the water and, copying Andy, I turned over and swam on my back. There was just enough room to breathe and then, when the gap improved slightly, to haul on a long cord attached to my tube to pull it under the obstacle.

I kept a nagging claustrophobic fear at bay through total trust in Andy's cavemanship, if that is the right term. But it came to me how easily he might suffer a sudden heart attack, for he was well into his fifties. How then would I find my way out of these evil waterways? Certainly not by memory.

My faith in Andy collapsed and my inner fears surged when his white beard lifted from the oily surface and he spluttered, 'Which way did we enter this chamber?'

I told him and he disagreed. We bobbed under an even lower ledge with no more than three inches of clearance and I smelled putrefied flesh close at hand. An animal skull with wet, green flesh attached in floating ribbons nodded against my shoulder – some civet or goat lured to its death by thirst.

After an hour and a half Andy shook his head, dislodging all manner of flying insects.

'I can't understand it,' he grunted. 'The main passageway must be underwater. I just can't locate it.'

So we gave up and, to my considerable relief, Andy found no difficulty in retracing his route to the entry point.

We slept on a ledge free of civet dung until dawn when, back at the base of the crater and the single length of rope, Andy attached two special grips to my foot and shoulder.

'You go first. If you get into trouble, shout, but do not look down.'

After about four hundred feet the tautly stretched rope felt as thin as string. The swish and shriek of disturbed grackles and my empty stomach combined to make the climb unenjoyable, but I managed to force from my mind the tiniest thought about the ever-increasing drop below.

When Andy joined me at the upper rim of the crater, he looked disappointed. 'Never mind,' he said, 'we'll come back when the water level drops.' My enthusiasm to find the cave graffiti had lessened, but I took care not to show it.

Some five weeks after the first key finds at Shisr, a police van with four armed officers arrived around midnight with a summons for me to go at once to the palace in Muscat. The officers drove me to Salalah and, by Royal Oman Police flight, I reached Muscat the next morning. A royal limousine took me to Seeb Palace, where various new ambassadors were being accredited. After an hour's wait in what must rank among the most splendid palaces in the world, I was shown in to His Majesty Sultan Qaboos's *majlis*. He was delighted with the success of the expedition and was keen to ensure continued excavation at Shisr until the ruins were fully revealed. He asked me to give him a list of actions I thought might best be taken to follow up the discovery.

'Is it definitely Ubar?' he asked me.

'I believe so, Your Majesty. It is difficult to know what else it could be.'

The warmth of his smile and the strength of his handshake reminded me of my meeting with his father twenty-four years before. I felt then that the long years of hoping, the setbacks and the false trails had all been worthwhile.

*

I asked in my report to Sultan Qaboos that Ali Ahmed Ali Mahash be appointed Field Director for Archaeology in Dhofar, that Juris be contracted to continue excavations and that the Shisr site be protected against damage by visitors.

To my delight, Ali Ahmed was duly appointed as director with responsibility for all future heritage work in Dhofar. I was to ensure that all artefacts were handed over to him before Juris and the team left Oman. Since I had personally given Dr Ali Shanfari, the Minister of Heritage, a document taking full responsibility for all such items, I was keen to comply.

I sat on the floor of Ali Ahmed's new office in the Ministry of Information for some three hours and handed Ali more than thirteen thousand artefacts, all fully computerized with individual reference numbers.

The day we left Salalah, Jana Owen, Juris's team leader, gave me her thoughts on the dig. 'Very exciting,' she said, 'but hot, real hot. When things started to appear it was like striking gold. It was a lucky find but it is a very significant site. Now we have at least a year's work of analysis.'

On 5 February 1992 an article by John Noble Wilford was splashed across the front page of the *New York Times*, giving the news of our discovery of Ubar. This article was picked up and given widespread coverage worldwide, for there was a shortage of hard news at the time. All leading newspapers and TV networks across the USA gave the story prime rating and suggested that the project was an entirely American-inspired success. 'Guided by ancient maps and sharp-eyed surveys from space,' wrote the respected Mr Wilford, 'archaeologists and explorers have discovered a lost city deep in the sands of Arabia.'

When in March I returned to Salalah and told Juris that the American media were implying that we were led to the discovery by satellite imagery, he said, 'That's not entirely true, but it sounds good. It sounds like technology is at work and all that kind of rubbish. The truth is, it was found by hard work and excavation. The satellite imagery allowed us to eliminate sites so that we could concentrate on the most probable areas.'

'Did all that LANDSAT/SPOT stuff about water help?' I asked him.

'No.' He was adamant. 'That's just for publicity.'

'Could there not be other Ubar sites yet to be dug up?'

'Sure there could be, but where?' he exclaimed. 'I have been all over Saudi and the Empty Quarter for twenty years and nobody has come up with another site, let alone one that is both where Ptolemy put it and has Roman pottery. Something as big as Shisr shows up on air photos. ARAMCO and PDO oil surveyors had tracked all over the Sands for thirty years, never mind the bedu and the army. Yet nobody has reported an alternative. Perhaps it is buried in sand, but sand doesn't move that fast, as you can see at Shisr.' Juris thumped his knees. 'Shisr is unique. There is nowhere like it in the desert for nine hundred kilometres.'

In April 1992 I was asked by the Oman Minister of Information to become International Adviser to the Ubar Committee, a post which I welcomed, for where else is there a people and a land of such enchantment?

CHAPTER 16

As the Sun Goes Down

Turn your face to the Sun
So the shadows will fall behind you

One summer in the early 1960s I was determined to enter the
Special Air Service but was warned that the Selection Course in
Wales was too difficult for the vast majority of candidates. So I
decided to train very hard while on leave from my regiment in
Germany. An army friend who had tried the course and failed
advised me to train by myself in the Brecon Beacons, always to carry
60lb in my rucksack and to map read by day and by night all over
terrain as featureless and confusing as possible.

One extremely hot summer weekend, somewhere in the Welsh
mountains and out of water, I overdid my efforts, suffered a dizzy
spell and a feeling of extreme nausea. I then collapsed and for a while
must have been unconscious. I emptied the ballast of rocks from my
rucksack and limped slowly back to the nearest road where I flagged
down a lift back to my car. I believe I was on the verge of hyperthermia. Maybe I had not drunk enough at the time. Either way I
subsequently took the Winter Selection Course and passed it without
difficulty. Nonetheless my memory of that hot day in the Brecons
came vividly back to me when, in 2013, I heard that three soldiers
on the SAS Selection Course that summer had all died in the same

mountains. They were on a sixteen-mile training course as part of the selection process which included an ascent of Pen y Fan, a mountain in the Brecon Beacons. The temperature hit 29°C (84°F) and, on his way down from the ascent, one soldier died of hyperthermia within two hours of becoming dizzy, and two others died days later suffering from multiple organ failure, all as a result of the high temperatures. All three men were young, tough and fit. Seven other soldiers suffered heat injuries that day.

Some thirty years after my Brecon Beacons scare I received a telephone call from Mike Stroud and he suggested that we attempt a new record for marathon running. 'It's very simple,' he explained. 'We run a standard twenty-six-mile marathon on each of the seven continents over seven consecutive days.'

'But neither of us are marathon runners,' I pointed out.

'With a bit of training,' was the reply, '*anybody* can run a marathon.'

He then went on to say that he had looked carefully at the challenge and the key to success would be to avoid heat, ideally running by night. Two continents would be hot – Africa and Asia – but research into the central computer of British Airways (our long-time sponsor) showed that existing jumbo jet flights could not give us a schedule which would allow our Asia run (which would have to be in Singapore) to be done by night.

The African location was a choice between Egypt and Libya, and we chose to avoid the latter on reading that Libya held the all-time world record for the highest temperature ever recorded in the shade (57.8°C or 136°F) in September 1922.

Singapore, which would have to fit into the pattern of BA's intercontinental flights, would need to be run during the day in great humidity (immediately after Sydney and before London). Each run would be for a different charity and for the Singapore event we chose the Singapore Heart Association because I had, some three months previously, had a massive heart attack followed by a double bypass operation and three days on a life support machine.

We tried hard to change the BA schedules but could not. Anyway, the first three marathons – in South America, the sub-Antarctic Falkland Islands and Australia – all involved reasonable temperatures.

We were unable to sleep on the flight to Singapore, and on arrival there had only three hours' rest before the pre-dawn marathon start. Mike kept a diary of that run:

It was still dark outside the hotel but it was already stiflingly hot. It was also unbelievably muggy. Although we could sweat freely, we would gain little or no benefit. It was simply too humid for sweat to evaporate and the wetting of our skin would not therefore meet its physiological needs.

Prior to starting, I asked the Sponsors whether needles and syringes could be waiting at the finish so that I could confirm my new suspicion of rhabdomyolysis and check that my kidneys were not in danger. This check is known as a creatine kinase (CK).

Within an hour of starting the run I realised that this was the marathon too far. I felt sick and my legs, although still painless, had become utterly useless as the first few miles went by. The heat was stupefying and I thought that my whole body might melt into a pot of tallow.

The remainder of the Singapore run was hard on both of us. The temperature climbed and the humidity remained total. Ran, too, was utterly exhausted, and he said later that at one point he had been sure he would fail. Nonetheless, he tottered onwards, drenched with water every few minutes by the helpers who were accompanying him.

When the CK test results came back, I was passed a slim folder by the Sponsor's chief medical officer and I quickly scanned down the printed figures. I was surprised to see that Ran's CK was raised to nearly fifty times normal. He at least was suffering from significant muscle damage. Then I looked at my own results – which took a moment or two to sink in. My CK was a shocking five hundred times normal. It surpassed anything I could have imagined and confirmed beyond doubt that I had suffered massive muscle loss. This explained the trouble with my legs.

Mike did somehow manage to complete the Singapore run and said afterwards that it was the hardest thing he had ever done. But we caught the flight that evening to London where we ran the

Europe leg, then squeezed the last two marathons (Africa and North America) into the next forty-eight hours, including flights.

The Egypt run began at the Great Pyramid of Giza with a speech from the Sponsor, Suzanne Mubarak, whose husband was President of Egypt. After the tortuous conditions of Singapore, Cairo by night was blissfully cool.

As Director of the Army Personnel Research Centre at Farnborough, Mike had access to laboratories including a heat chamber, and at one point he trained and acclimatized an army team to run one of three races rated as 'the toughest foot races in the world'. One of these was a 135-mile race in California's Death Valley, which started 282 feet (86 metres) below sea level and ended on Mount Whitney at 8,360 feet (2,548 metres). This race takes place annually in mid-July when temperatures of over 120°F (49°C) are not uncommon.

Another such ultra-marathon, over an even longer distance, is the Marathon des Sables (Marathon of the Sands) in which Mike had entered his team. His diarized account of that nightmare challenge in the Saharan deserts of Morocco made interesting reading:

The race is held annually, and each year it attracts increasing numbers of competitors. They come from all over the world, keen to pit their strength against one of the most difficult of environments, covering in one week the equivalent of five marathons – not on smooth London tarmac but over rocks, plains and shifting sand. To make matters more difficult, competitors must each carry a backpack containing all food for the entire week plus all other requirements. With this fairly heavy rucksack, rough going underfoot, and the fierce desert sun, it is not a venture for the faint-hearted and many find it difficult to understand how such a race can be run. The answer lies in our remarkable ability to cope with heat.

Running through our bare skin is a network of blood vessels that dissipate heat through the processes of convection, conduction and radiation, and if that is not enough, we also have tens of thousands of sweat glands which can automatically wet the skin to add the power of evaporation to our cooling. This ability to cope with heat stems from the millions of years of our early development in the hot cradle of Africa where our primate ancestors met a climate which would have cut down those who could not keep strong, fit and, above all, fertile through the worst of the blistering summers. Natural selection melded early humans to make them extremely heat tolerant and when, one hundred thousand years ago, they started to spread to cooler parts of the globe, they took this potential with them.

Mike found it difficult to sleep at the desert start, due to growing doubts about the challenge ahead. He had acclimatized assiduously in the Farnborough heat chamber, but now with the sand dunes of the Sahara all about him, apprehension and self-doubt crept in.

Some disconnected excerpts from his daily diary give an idea of the rigours of the event:

The heat added to my consternation. It became exceedingly warm, far worse than I had thought possible in April. By midday we were positively roasting, even lying shaded by the canopies. When the wind blew, it somehow made things worse, engulfing us in a wave of crushing heat rather than providing the relief one might have expected ...

The air began to stir and a light breeze started to flap our shelters. Within minutes the breeze rose to become a stiff wind and then a full-blown gale. It was an extraordinarily rapid change as the stars that had been gleaming with unearthly intensity disappeared behind the blowing sand. Indeed all was lost in an increasing, whirling stream of violence. Under the shelters the sand filled everything, and all but the heaviest of our belongings threatened to blow away. It led to another hurried exodus, after which there were pathetic attempts to eat without consuming too much of the wind-blown dust ...

At around 11.15 we departed, running down a trail directly into the storm. It was a bizarre experience. The sand was everywhere, and despite scarves around mouths and noses, we inhaled it, ate it, coughed it. Whatever we did with the rest of our clothing, the sand also got to our skin, and soon all moving parts became sore and

chafed. It was desperately hard to run against the constant battering, and even when we changed direction, the wind still seemed to
blow against us ...

Wherever we looked, the harsh sun shone. Its heat was reflected
from every surface, burning the face despite the dust that now
coated every one of us. Although only the second day, our lips were
already dry, cracked and swollen. I knew that my core temperature
would be running higher than was safe. Once again, I also suffered
cramps and nausea as I became increasingly dehydrated. My body
was sweating at a rate that my drinking could not match ...

With the heat and the constant pounding, my feet had swelled
up, and the shoes I wore were now tight. Several toenails were
bruised and, indeed, were later to fall off. The soles were also
blistering ...

There before me lay the desert of the movies – rank upon rank
of these huge sand hills extending to the horizon. Some were small,
some big, and some gigantic ...

The sun was high enough to eradicate all areas of shade and the
sand surfaces lapped up its radiation and then re-transmitted it.
Within the still and silent bowls, temperatures were unbelievable.
As I descended into them, I could feel the heat scorching my face
like the blast from an open oven door. The sand was so hot that it
was burning to touch, and this became a serious problem when
going uphill, for I still had to use my hands on the steeper parts of
some slopes ...

The wind had built up and was suddenly blowing in my face. Even
with sunglasses on, I found sand poured into my eyes. I knew from
my compass that I should now be heading almost with the wind. I
decided to head right. It was a struggle to walk in that direction, for
the wind must have been up to something like forty knots and the
whipping sand was painful as it scoured my legs and arms. I worked
my way sideways, head bent against the blast, looking for the route.
I began to retrace my steps – or I would have done had they still been
there. The wind had carried away all trace of my passing just
moments before. I began to grow anxious. I had only a couple of
litres of water and could not afford to mess about like this ... It
brought home to me how easy it would be to get lost completely ...

My body churned out more heat from the effort of ascent. But as I climbed, so did the sun. By the time the canyon widened and I emerged on the upper slopes of the mountains, it was beating down on me ferociously. The last thousand feet to the col were desperate. I reached the col shortly before midday and found others who had got there before me crouched beneath a small rock overhang, trying to escape the fierce radiation while they drank some water ...

As we ran across the last ten miles, even the further litre and a half of water provided at the last checkpoint could not prevent our problems. Bodies were churning out waste heat so fast that we simply could not shed it all. Simultaneously the ground, the air and the sun poured more heat into us. Hyperthermia became inevitable.

Bearing in mind that Mike, who was well known for understatement, had written this, I made a firm decision to avoid involving myself in any such hot activities. He was, after all, a uniquely strong individual, both mentally and physically. He was also at the peak of his life, in terms of the best age for endurance racing, and he had acclimatized himself and his team with long, hard training hours in a heat chamber.

So, some eighteen years later and now aged seventy-one, when my charity Marie Curie discussed the possibility of my entering this same Marathon des Sables (MdS), I went to meet Mike, who is now Senior Lecturer in Nutrition at Southampton University, to check whether he felt that I could manage it. I explained that, if I were to complete the race in 2015, I would be the oldest Briton to do so which could be used by Marie Curie to raise at least £1 million to recruit more nurses.

Mike pointed out that people over sixty-five are more prone to heat stress as their body often fails to adjust adequately to sudden changes in temperature, and they are more likely to have had a previous illness which might have altered their body's heat responses and caused them to take medicines which block or reduce their ability to sweat and regulate their body temperature. Since I had experienced two heart attacks, undergone cancer treatment, was diagnosed as pre-diabetic, and as a result was taking daily prescribed medicines, this did not bode well for entering this particular race.

However, the temptation to raise £1 million was too great to be resisted due to common sense, so I swotted up on various heat-related facts and Marie Curie obtained a last-minute entry for me.

I signed on with Rory Coleman, a top trainer of ultra-marathon runners who was based in Cardiff, and he advised me, as Mike had done, to spend as much time as possible acclimatizing in a heat chamber (or a hot country). This proved impossible, but I approached Paul Sykes, my long-time sponsor who underwrote the costs of my fundraising activities, but only when he was sure that I wouldn't be likely to die in the act.

As a result I needed to have relevant cardiac tests carried out, and these Rory organized in a heated laboratory at Kingston University's School of Life Sciences, and the outcome was good. 'To recreate the MdS environment, we set the temperature at 40 degrees and the humidity at 30 per cent,' said Dr Hannah Moir, Senior Lecturer in Health and Exercise Prescription.

> Ran was on the treadmill in there for an hour. We measured his heart rate and core temperature. He maintained his core temperature at between 37 and 38 degrees, which is really good, meaning he has a good thermal response at dissipating the temperature while he's in that thermal environment. His heart rate remained very stable at 100bpm [beats per minute], which was also what we like to see. He sweated a lot but was drinking to replenish the lost fluids. His body is very well designed for coping with extreme environments. He is the oldest person we have hosted here for MdS training, but age is not a factor in an individual's coping response with heat. He responded very well, probably much better than I would, and I'm 31.

Rory summed up some of the likely factors of the marathon.

When the body's heat regulating mechanisms are overwhelmed, this can result in death. In Morocco for the race, the temperature will be super-hot. When your body warms up the ambient air around you, you cannot dissipate that heat – you can't sweat the heat out.

You've also got the problem of humidity. Now it's about 25 per cent humidity because they have a lot of spring rain. So there is water vapour in the air, plus the temperature, meaning a British Caucasian is simply going to cook. You very quickly become hyperthermic.

Avoiding hypothermia is critical. An inability to cool the body through perspiration starts a chain of events, with other symptoms, including nausea from dehydration, vomiting and headaches. Low blood pressure can lead to fainting or dizziness, while the heart attempts to maintain adequate circulation. Confused, hostile or seemingly intoxicated behaviour can follow, while the worst case scenarios include unconsciousness, multiple organ failure and death.

Rory advised me to run in black, not white, clothing, although many top runners would disagree. Rory argued that, under their white hair, polar bears have black skin to absorb more heat. Black clothing, he maintained, absorbs both sunlight and the heat radiating from the body, but if your garments are loose-fitting and there is a wind, then that wind will convect the heat away faster than it is absorbed. White clothing reflects sunlight, but it also reflects internal heat back towards your body, so that the net effect under identical conditions is *less* cooling than if wearing black. Hence, Rory concluded, desert-dwellers like the Saharan Touareg wear loose-fitting black clothing and use black tents.

Omanis had often explained to me that they wear more than one layer of clothing in order to keep the heat out. But the reality is that the extra layer is helping to stop their sweat evaporating and thus maintaining a cool layer of air next to their skin.

At Gatwick I joined Rory and the other six runners in his team, all 'proper' ultra-runners, although one, Angus, was fifty-six years old and, I was happy to note, at least semi-geriatric.

Following my first heart attack and bypass surgery, I had been warned by the cardiac surgeon that I should never allow my heart to tick at more than 130bpm, and I had done my best to heed his advice ever since.

Unfortunately the French organizers of the Marathon des Sables had set vigorous race rules with the specific aim of forcibly removing any and all participants who, however keen to continue, were lagging behind specific cut-off times at each desert checkpoint. Also, to cull anyone lagging *between* checkpoints, there were two mean-look-ing Touareg with camels bringing up the rear. Should these camels catch up with you, their owners would tell the race organizers who would remove you either by helicopter or Land Rover.

The week before the race, Marie Curie announced my participa-tion and the national media, presumably because there was little going on at the time, gave the fact wide coverage. This had the advantage of raising more money for the charity and, from my point of view, increased my apprehension about the ignominy of failure.

I looked at the race entry data sheet, and among the facts and figures I found the following:

— There were over 1,300 competitors, and of these:
— 30 per cent were repeat competitors
— 70 per cent were international
— 30 per cent were French
— 14 per cent were women
— 30 per cent were in teams of 3 or more
— 90 per cent were alternate walking and running
— 3 km/hour is the average minimum speed
— there were 450 support staff
— 120,000 litres of water would be drunk
— there would be 300 Berber tents and 4 camels
— 120 all-terrain vehicles and 25 buses would be provided
— 2 helicopters and 1 Cessna would be available
— 57 medical staff would be available with 6.5 km of Elastoplast, 2,700 Compeed plasters and 6,000 painkillers
— the distance covered in the marathon is 250 km

A later report stated that 'there were fears that Ranulph would not be able to finish the event after the 91 km fourth stage, which saw him run for more than 30 hours with just one hour of sleep, while towards the end of the race he relied on painkillers to numb a back problem.'

And this report also stated that 'Ranulph has previously raised £6.3 million for Marie Curie. In 2007 he climbed the Eiger from its north face for the charity, and in May 2009, at the age of 65, he became the oldest Briton to climb to the summit of Mount Everest. During the Marathon, his trainer at times had to force him to rest. Ranulph said, "I was getting dizzy, I had a stabbing pain in my back and it was extremely hot. There was a period when I thought I'm not going to make it."'

When the competitors get to the checkpoints, everyone taking part in the race is given their emails by the organizers, and one towards the end from my wife said, 'Enough is enough. Elizabeth wants her daddy back, not a corpse.'

My lasting memory of the Marathon des Sables is of intense, energy-sapping heat and the twin fear of going too hard and damaging my heart or going too slow and being caught by the camels. Ninety-eight marathon runners dropped out altogether, and the other older member in our tent, in his 50's, spent time on a nasal drip completely dehydrated.

At the end I was asked for my overall impressions of the experience for an online diary:

Were there any pieces of kit you wish you'd taken?
In soft sand you get pressures on your feet and your back because your trainers are slipping. It started rubbing very badly on the part of my foot that had been frostbitten and had had the skin replaced with skin cut off my hip some years ago. So I got a knife and cut a hole in the side of the boot, but then, of course, you've got sand pouring in, so I Velcroed if off so that I had less pressure but kept the sand out. That worked very well as a modification. I'll have to patent it.

What is your best memory of it?
The finish – it was a huge relief. I turned around and gave two fingers to the camels.

And the worst?
The worst parts were trying not to have a heart attack, although recognizing the oncoming symptoms, but not being able to slow down because of the camels, the time and your watch ticking. Another bad thing was having made a mistake at night when we

were doing the 60-mile stretch, which was a very long, hard stretch
and I had a low torch battery. I thought I knew where the next foot
would land, but actually it landed three feet below where I thought
it would and I got a jolt up my back – that's when I started really
needing lots of painkillers.

When the camels reach you, you're out of the race?
Yes. On one occasion – this doesn't sound like much unless you are
there – we got to a huge sand dune area with 13 minutes to spare.
So, you can imagine when you're wanting to slow down but you
can see the checkpoint is a long way away and the camels are
behind. That's a bad situation to be in.

The French race organizer was rightly proud of the event, which
he had first launched thirty years before, and he announced that this
year, 2015, would be the toughest and longest of all to date. Most of
the 1,300 entrants listening to this announcement greeted it with
cheers, but I did not find my enthusiasm mounting.

Rory stayed with me from the beginning. On the fourth day, after
long hours of no wind and a maximum temperature of 53°C, I did
not feel good. The *Daily Telegraph* report that day stated:

*Trainer expresses fear that Sahara race could put too much strain
on explorer's heart as the team enters the fourth day of the race in
the Moroccan desert.*

Sir Ranulph Fiennes may be forced to pull out of the Marathon des
Sables as he starts the fourth day of the ultra-marathon in the
Sahara. Rory Coleman, his trainer, said, 'Today is the biggest test
for Ran. We need to be really careful. I don't know if he is going
to make it.' The explorer, who turned 71 in March, has complained
of dizziness during the 156 mile race.

Sir Ranulph, who has had two heart attacks and a double heart
bypass, said, 'I feel a rhythm under the wire in my heart where they
sewed me up. I think what brings it on is the soft sand and the
steep hills.'

Sir Ranulph is 46 miles into the fourth stage of the event after arriving at a checkpoint at 4.30 a.m. this morning, having set off at 8.30 a.m. the previous day. The explorer walked across dozens of sand dunes under the moonlight. Speaking live from the desert on BBC Breakfast this morning, Sir Ranulph said, 'Last night was pretty horrific. It's hell on Earth. You're trying to go up hills and your feet are slipping backwards in the sand. I had some really shaky moments. My head torch faded and I couldn't see the hills.'

Coleman said, 'In these temperatures, just doing one hundred paces is for anybody really hard work, let alone if you're carrying all this gear and you're 71 years of age. His heart – that's my big concern – making sure that we keep it at 75 per cent rate.' Coleman is taking part in the event for the twelfth time. Talking about the fourth stage of the race, he said, 'It was superbrutal – and the toughest Marathon des Sables stage I've ever done.'

Ranulph said, 'When I get back to the UK I'm going straight to my surgeon to see what's gone wrong with my back. Two people broke a leg. Another man thought it was all sand, but there were hidden rocks and he cut his face open falling onto a rock. Another one cut his stomach open and there were entrails around. I got away pretty lightly really – ninety-six people dropped out.'

Thanks to the support of Paul Sykes, the expertise and patience of Rory Coleman, and the dedicated fundraising activities of Marie Curie, the challenge raised over £2 million.

Back home in the UK a week after the event, there was a bitter wind and non-stop drizzle as I carted endless loads of old bricks to a dump. Shivering with the cold, I remembered my mother's old saying:

> As a rule, man's a fool
> When it's hot he wants it cool
> When it's cool he wants it hot
> Always wanting what it is not

APPENDIX I

Heat and the Human Body:
The Mechanics

The body's temperature control is the hypothalamus section of the brain. It tells how hot or cold we are, thanks to a number of sensors in our skin, within our core and in our bloodstream. If too hot (above 37°C/98°F) it signals our skin to sweat more and the blood vessels in our skin to widen which speeds up the blood flow rate and thus the rate of heat loss from the blood. It only takes 90 seconds (on average) for blood to circulate through all of our body's 100,000 km of blood vessels.

The effect of sweating lets warm water leave our body and, as it does so, it cools our skin. Our body should always maintain its core temperature of 37°C (whether we are Inuit or Touareg) unless some illness affects us.

As a general rule, the body turns most of the food we eat into heat. When working hard our muscles can briefly generate as much heat, up to 2 kilowatts, as does a small electric fire, and even when we are at rest our body only 'feels' comfortable when the air around it is slightly cooler than it is. We breathe out warm air and, in normal conditions, expect to breathe in colder air.

Anthropologists blame the sun's heat and light for our upright stance and our skin colour. Like plants, we are energized by photosynthesis and can be described as solar-powered.

Our skin pigmentation is strongly selected by climate, and our early African ancestors were probably all dark-skinned with the melanin protecting them from excessive sun damage to their skin. Those tribes that moved away from the tropics would evolve to have lighter skin, the better to synthesize the Vitamin D (from the weaker sunlight) needed for bone metabolism.

Today this rule still holds good, as evidenced by migrants to Britain from the Indian sub-continent who suffer from an above-average rate of vitamin D deficiency troubles. And, at the other end of the skin colour scale, the number of white people who settle in or sunbathe in unaccustomed hot zones and develop skin cancers.

Some six or seven million years ago in Africa there was a population of small apes that were the common ancestors of both man and of our closest cousin, the chimpanzee. The population must have then divided into two groups which started to live apart and tended not to interbreed. The cause of this division is probably that the two groups started to occupy different environmental niches. At around that time the African climate became both hotter and drier, and it seems that this led to a thinning of the forests and an increase in the areas of savannah. With a reduction in the number of trees, some of the apes started to live on the ground and then moved out on to newly open grasslands. Others remained more arboreal, living within the forests. The result was that the two groups were exposed to different environmental demands and this led to their slow evolutionary divergence. The tree-dwelling group slowly evolved towards the two species of modern chimps. The ground dwellers embarked on the path that would eventually lead to man.

One of the changes that life on the savannah appears to have prompted was a move to becoming upright, and various suggestions have been made to explain this. One is that the move to the savannah meant that the groups had less access to shade. With the sun high in the African sky, heat stress would have been a considerable problem and the adoption of an upright stance would have reduced exposure by limiting the surface area under direct rays from the sun.

Our evolutionary heritage has also granted us amazing attributes when it comes to environmental hardship. Because the ancestors of all modern humans were still living in the heat of Africa as little as 100,000 years ago and most evolutionary adaptations move very slowly, we all have an extraordinary capacity to cope with the heat if given some days in which to acclimatize and access to a reasonable water supply.

APPENDIX II

Some Key Hot Country Explorers

Cristóbal de Acuña (1597–c.1675) Jesuit priest who provided the first written testimony about the Amazon and the tribes in its vicinity.

Delia Denning Akeley (1875–1970) American plant and animal collector whose expeditions to Africa with husband Carl and later in her own right included crossing the Somalia desert and living with pygmies in the Congo. Carl's second wife, Mary, accompanied him to the Belgian Congo in 1926 to study gorillas and both raised concerns about their risk of extinction. She continued mapping and recording observations about wildlife after Carl's death.

Alexander the Great (356–323 BC) Conquered Asia, including parts of India, northern Africa and part of Europe to create a mighty empire extending from Gibraltar to the Punjab, although it did not survive his death.

Samuel White Baker (1821–1893) Sailed with second wife Florence up the White Nile hoping to discover its source. He was also a campaigner against the slave trade.

Heinrich Barth (1821–1865) Writer and mapmaker who explored North and Central Africa, he travelled in the Sahara and the Sudan for more than five years.

Henry Walter Bates (1825–1892) Travelled with Alfred Russel Wallace to the upper Amazon to study plants and insect life.

Nicolas Baudin (1754–1803) One of the earliest maritime explorers to chart Australia's coastline.

Margaret Bell (1754–1803) Veteran of expeditions in the Moab, Syrian and Arabian deserts as well as an expert on Persian culture and a British diplomat.

Gregory Blaxland (1778–1853) One of the first free men to emigrate to Australia, where he navigated a route across the Blue Mountains.

William Bligh (1754–1817) Commander of HMS *Bounty* and famously the subject of a mutiny after a voyage to Tahiti. He later charted the coast of New South Wales in Australia.

Pierre-Paul-François-Camille Savorgnan de Brazza (1852–1905) Italian-born Brazza served in the French navy and explored central Africa, eventually establishing the colony of French Equatorial Africa. He was a campaigner against exploitation of local workers by private companies.

James Bruce (1730–1794) African explorer who believed that he had located the source of the Blue Nile, but was later derided by a sceptical British public.

Johann Burckhardt (1784–1817) Explorer in Africa and the Arabian Peninsula who became a scholar on secretive Muslim communities before his death from dysentery.

Robert O'Hara Burke (1821–1861) With William Wills, led an ill-fated expedition across Australia that led to their deaths from starvation.

Richard Burton (1821–1890) Dressed as a Muslim, he visited the holy cities of Medina and Mecca, also Harar in Ethiopia. Burton discovered Lake Tanganyika and searched for the source of the Nile.

Pedro Alvares Cabral (*c.*1467–*c.*1520) Credited with discovering Brazil during a sea voyage to India, which he was undertaking as one of the earliest international traders.

Alvise da Cadamosto (1432–1480) Broke out from domestic Portuguese waters to explore Africa's west coast and daringly sailed out of sight of land to do so.

René-Auguste Caillié (1799–1838) Frenchman who wrote vibrant accounts of Timbuktu, at the mysterious heart of the desert.

Verney Lovett Cameron (1844–1894) The first European to travel equatorial Africa from coast to coast, one-time associate of Richard Burton, and the leader of an expedition to locate the lost missionary David Livingstone.

Diogo Cão (1450–1486) Explored uncharted West African coastline, discovered the mouth of the Congo River and marked his travels with limestone pillars donated by Portugal's King John II.

Charles Chaillé-Long (1842–1917) American who explored the Nile and discovered Lake Kyoga.

Hugh Clapperton (1788–1827) Born one of 21 children who later went to sea as a cabin boy, Scotsman Clapperton was both an explorer in West Africa and a campaigner against the locally run slave trade.

Christopher Columbus (*c.*1451–1506) Maritime explorer whose three major expeditions significantly enhanced geographical knowledge of the globe.

Pêro da Covilhã (*c.*1460–*c.*1526) At the behest of Portuguese rulers, he explored India, the Middle East and Ethiopia, creating new trading opportunities and pursuing the legendary Prester John, thought to be an immortal Christian king living beyond Persia.

Charles Darwin (1809–1882) 'Gentleman naturalist' who accompanied a round-the-world expedition to study rare wildlife, after which he published a long-considered theory of evolution. An anxious Darwin was left fending off criticism from the established Church, believing his theories contrary to biblical orthodoxy.

Dixon Denham (1786–1828) One of the first Europeans to reach Lake Chad, which he encountered as he tried to map the course of the River Niger.

Bartholomew Dias (*c.*1450–1500) Extensively mapped a hitherto unknown African coastline on his way to rounding Cape of Good Hope.

Charles Doughty (1843–1926) Fascination with the Arabian desert led him to live with Bedouin tribesmen, after which he produced some influential early travel writing.

Henri Duveyrier (1840–1892) In his day he was the leading authority on the Sahara's animals, plant life, archaeology and the Touareg tribespeople who lived there.

Antoine d'Entrecasteaux (1739–1793) French naval officer who explored the South Pacific, south Australia and Tasmania.

Edward Eyre (1815–1901) Sheep station manager who explored Australia's harsh interior landscape in a bid to find routes across it for livestock.

Percy Fawcett (1867–1925) Initially a military surveyor, Fawcett disappeared without trace trying to locate a lost city in the Brazilian jungle.

Matthew Flinders (1774–1814) First to navigate his way around Australia, expanding knowledge about the continent by collecting flora and fauna.

Charles-Eugène de Foucauld (1858–1916) French soldier who was beguiled by North Africa, became a missionary in the Sahara and mapped Morocco.

Vasco da Gama (*c*.1460–1524) Building on the achievements of Bartholomew Dias, da Gama forged a sea route around Africa to India and spearheaded the creation of a Portuguese empire.

Ernest Giles (1835–1897) One of the first to cross Australia travelling from east to west, traversing some of the most inhospitable desert territory in the world to do so.

Jane Goodall (1934–) Advocate and activist, Goodall was driven by a love of chimpanzees to spend years studying the way colonies lived, loved and communicated in Tanzania. Thanks to television, she brought her findings into people's homes and has received numerous awards.

James Grant (1827–1892) Part of John Hanning Speke's expedition that proved that the source of the Nile is Lake Victoria.

Freidrich Hornemann (1772–1801) The first European to travel across the Sahara from Egypt to reach what is now northern Nigeria, sending his findings home to Germany. He vanished on a subsequent expedition.

Daniel Houghton (*c*.1740–1791) An English army major who established that the upper Niger River ran towards the east before perishing at the end of another ill-fated African venture.

Hamilton Hume (1797–1873) An explorer who discovered two rivers in his native Australia.

Ibn Battuta (1304–1368) Attributed with 75,000 miles of exploration, Battuta went to most major Islamic territories to produce a substantial and historically important document about what he found.

Willem Jansz (late 1500–*c*.1629) A Dutch sea captain thought to have been among the first to conduct an inland foray in Australia.

Mary Kingsley (1862–1900) Following the death of her parents, Kingsley sailed for West Africa where she spent eight years studying culture and wildlife, labelling her expedition 'a quest for fish and fetish'. Remarkably, despite the heat, she always dressed in a high-necked blouse, a small bonnet, tight-waisted skirt and petticoats – which once saved her from injury when she fell into an elephant trap. She died of typhus working as a nurse in South Africa during the Boer War.

Alexander Laing (1793–1826) Early Western visitor to Timbuktu after a trip across the Sahara from Africa's north coast, he was murdered shortly after leaving.

Richard Lander (1804–1834) Initially a servant to Hugh Clapperton, he later emerged as an explorer in his own right, travelling to the mouth of the River Niger with his brother John before both were captured by tribesmen and ransomed to a slave trader. On a third trip he died after another attack by hostile locals.

Miguel López de Legazpi (1510–1572) Spaniard who moved to Mexico before establishing a colony in the Philippines.

Ludwig Leichhardt (1813–1848) A Prussian army deserter, Leichhardt was a plant collector in Australia who organized one expedition from Sydney which was hailed as a triumph, but he perished along with six others on a second outing, probably in the Simpson Desert.

David Livingstone (1813–1873) Missionary and doctor whose detailed observations and records – along with his long disappearances into the heart of Africa – elevated him to be one of the world's most famous explorers. A former cotton mill worker, Livingstone was driven by unshakeable faith and a desire to end the slave trade in Africa. He discovered that the Kalahari Desert did not meet the Sahara, and he named the Victoria Falls for the British Queen, but he failed in his efforts to find the source of the Nile.

Jerome Lobo (*c*.1593–*c*.1678) Jesuit priest from Portugal whose written descriptions of life in Abyssinia and Lake Tana, the source of the Blue Nile, were much later criticized by James Bruce, who also visited the area.

Ferdinand Magellan (1480–1521) Portuguese circumnavigator whose achievements rivalled those of Christopher Columbus. He died in battle in the Philippines.

Jean-Baptiste Marchand (1863–1934) French explorer who ventured into the Western Sudan and later the Ivory Coast. But he is best remembered for trying to block British colonial expansion of the Nile when there was nearly a war between the two nations before France abandoned her claims.

Francisco de Orellana (*c*.1511–1546) First European to cross South America by sailing up the Amazon, enduring heat and hunger to do so, although his first aim had been to find 'El Dorado', a lost city reputedly made of gold.

Mungo Park (1771–*c*.1806) Sent to Africa's interior by eminent scientist Sir Joseph Banks, Scottish surgeon Park suffered numerous attacks from hostile tribes as well as debilitating disease in order to explore the River Niger. After publishing a bestseller about his adventures he returned to plot the Niger's path once more and was killed when he toppled into its fast rushing waters during another attack.

Marco Polo (*c*.1254–1324) Venetian who devoted his life to travelling the unknown world, heading as far north as Russia and through the Middle East, Asia, including India, then around China. Doubt has been cast on some of his accounts, but on his deathbed he insisted, 'I did not write half of what I saw.'

Friedrich Rohlfs (1831–1896) As a soldier in the French Foreign Legion, Rohlfs became so captivated by north Africa that he was the first to travel from Tripoli on the Mediterranean coast to Lagos on the Gulf of Guinea.

Cândido Mariano da Silva Rondon (1865–1958) Before the First World War he mapped 193,000 square miles of his native Brazil, in the process becoming an expert on flora, fauna and jungle cultures.

Theodore Roosevelt (1858–1919) Apart from diplomatic and political triumphs Roosevelt was an explorer who charted the River of Doubt in Brazil alongside Rondon.

Eduard Schnitzer (1840–1892) Also known as Emin Pasha, he worked for the British and the Germans in Africa as well as conducting expeditions. A committed anti-slave trader, he was ousted as the governor of a region known as Equatoria by the rebellious Mahdi and was ultimately beheaded by Arab soldiers near the River Congo.

Georg Schweinfurth (1836–1925) Related by marriage to Rohlfs, Schweinfurth shared his fellow German's passion for North Africa and his observations were compiled into an influential book called *The Heart of Africa*, published in 1871.

May Sheldon (1847–1936) A wealthy American with a fascination for Africa, Sheldon bucked the trend, being a woman explorer with a conviction that the continent's tribes were friendly. She was largely proved right although her team flatly refused to breach the territory of the Masai warriors.

John Hanning Speke (1827–1865) Army officer who briefly saw action in the Crimea before turning explorer and discovering the source of the White Nile. Speke undertook three expeditions to the area, named Lake Victoria for the British Queen and had his claims rubbished by the irascible Burton. Although he accidentally shot himself the day before he was due to debate the touchy subject with

Burton, later findings proved that Speke's declarations about the source of the White Nile were correct.

Henry Morton Stanley (1841–1904) Best remembered for finding the 'lost' missionary David Livingstone, Welsh-American journalist Stanley colonized the Congo for Belgium and liberated a reluctant Eduard Schnitzer from an apparent Arab siege. He later returned to England and became a Member of Parliament.

Freya Stark (1893–1993) After being spellbound by stories of the *Arabian Nights*, Stark spent years travelling the Middle East, working both as a travel writer and a cartographer, this time in the Himalayas. She died a centenarian.

John McDouall Stuart (1815–1866) First man to reach the heart of Australia, the Scot finally helped to link north and south by telegraph after two failed attempts to find a suitable route. The exertions cost him his health and he died soon afterwards in near penury, despite being acclaimed for his achievement.

Charles Sturt (1795–1869) Known as 'the father' of Australian exploration, Sturt revealed hundreds of acres of valuable pasture and inspired the foundation of Adelaide following his extensive charting of the continent's waterways.

Pedro de Teixeira (unknown–1640) After helping to oust rival colonialists from Brazil, Teixeira led an all-Portuguese team along the Amazon and back to establish his nation's overriding influence.

Wilfred Thesiger (1910–2003) Although his first expeditions centred on Ethiopia, Thesiger is best known for living among Arabs in the north of the continent where he developed what he called 'a strange compulsion' to wander in deserts, including the Empty Quarter.

Joseph Thomson (1858–1895) First European to cross territory held by the hostile Masai tribe, Thomson also has a waterfall in Kenya and an African gazelle named after him. He was later a treaty negotiator between African tribes and trading companies keen to exploit the area. However, it cost him his health and he died aged just 37.

Alexine Tinne (1835–1869) As a wealthy heiress Tinne explored the Nile and its hinterlands and Central Africa in considerable style, hiring large steamers and numerous staff, including soldiers, a botanist and an ornithologist. She was killed by Touaregs as she attempted to cross the Sahara.

Alfred Russel Wallace (1823–1913) An avid naturalist, Wallace explored the insect life of the Amazon and Malaya before publishing findings simultaneously with Charles Darwin that suggested natural selection.

William Wentworth (1790–1872) Son of a woman transported to Norfolk Island, Wentworth nonetheless became a wealthy landowner and a lawyer – but he is best known for finding a route across Australia's previously impenetrable Blue Mountains.

APPENDIX III

The Paths of the Nile

To the Ancient Egyptians it was the river that brought them life. The Nile flowed through otherwise arid territory ruled by the Pharaohs, bringing a harvest of plenty. Mysteriously, the waters rose mightily every year, even when there had been no rains in Egypt. After it burst its banks, the black silt deposited by the river on farmlands encouraged the following year's crops to grow.

In fact, the Nile isn't just a single river; it is the sum total of two great rivers and many minor tributaries, some of them as yet uncharted. The waters that inundated the fields of Egypt came rushing down from far distant highlands where there were seasonal downpours, as by volume most of the waters and all the silt of Egypt's primary river come from the Blue Nile which flows from Lake Tana in Ethiopia.

However, the longer of the two rivers is the White Nile, or Bahr al Abyad, and its ultimate source is still disputed.

For years Lake Victoria in Uganda, with its northerly facing Ripon Falls, was wrongly held to be the source of the White Nile. Certainly the waters that tumbled over the Ripon Falls were known as the waters of the Victoria Nile. But at that point the lengthening effect of the rivers and tributaries flowing into Lake Victoria weren't taken into account.

In 2010 one team claimed that the starting point was in Rwanda's Nyungwe Forest, at the start of a tributary to the River Kagera which feeds Lake Victoria. However, a different tributary to the same river which begins in Burundi has been given credence too.

In any event, it is the inclusion of the River Kagera's length that gives the Nile the accolade of being the world's longest river. A further extension in length by dint of a newly discovered source will only compound that claim.

The Victoria Nile flows into Lake Kyoga where the waters that once gushed down the Ripon Falls sweep around in a half-circle and encounter the Karuma and Murchison Falls before reaching Lake Albert. Thereafter the river is called the Albert Nile.

By the time it arrives in South Sudan it is more familiar as the Bahr al Jabal or Mountain River until it encounters Lake No. Whitish clay from the riverbed here dictated that its name be changed to the White Nile.

Downstream lie the swamps of the Sudd region, a stumbling block for numerous explorers of previous generations as they were often found to be impassable. The meandering channels, lagoons and sodden fields of the Sudd cause the Nile problems too. Flow rates drop as the river thins into marshland where excessive amounts of water evaporate. A later junction with the Sobat River soon increases the river's surge.

The White Nile and the Blue Nile meet in Sudan and conjoin to head northwards towards Egypt and the Mediterranean Sea. The construction of the Aswan Dam in the 1970s brought an end to the annual floods and the destruction they occasionally wrought by controlling the waters of the Nile. In building the dam, Egypt provided itself with a reliable hydro-electric supply, although major hydro works in Ethiopia, the Sudan and other Nilotic countries could still affect the behaviour of the river.

Curiously, the Nile has existed longer than the Mediterranean Sea that it pours into. Distant millennia ago tectonic movements caused the Straits of Gibraltar to silt up, leaving the Mediterranean Sea to dry out. Water from the doomed Med evaporated, ultimately to fall as rain in the newly formed Ethiopian highlands, and from there began to carve the path of the Blue Nile. Rifts caused by earth movement following the last ice age already provided a path for branches of the Nile. While it has long been a home to crocodiles, the Nile is still a young river in geological terms.

Although it is mostly associated with Egypt, less than a quarter of the river runs within that country's borders. In its different guises the Nile touches ten other African countries during its 6,695km (4,160 miles) length: Tanzania, Burundi, Congo, Kenya, Rwanda, Ethiopia, Sudan, South Sudan, Eritrea and Uganda.

It is the enigma of the river's rise that has motivated exploration for generations. Even modern explorers are drawn to it. In 2014 former paratrooper Levison Wood walked the length of the Nile, travelling through six countries on an expedition often at risk from warring factions en route.

APPENDIX IV

The Suez Canal: A Nutshell History

Opened in 1869, the Suez Canal was immediately a key waterway linking the Mediterranean to the Red Sea.

The idea was first conceived some 4,000 years ago and on several occasions the Ancient Egyptians devoted considerable time and effort to the construction of just such a short cut.

Napoleon Bonaparte was also intrigued by its possibilities, but he abandoned the notion of a canal when he was assured that there was a large disparity in the heights of both seas. In fact, French engineers later proved that to be wrong.

By 1854 Ferdinand de Lesseps persuaded the Egyptian authorities to allow the building of the canal – which has bends but no locks as it links the coasts in Asia and Africa. De Lesseps didn't take the most direct route but connected several lakes on its 168-km (105-mile) course between continents.

Cutting into the desert landscape without the benefit of modern tools exacted a huge toll among the workforce, which was made up of thousands of Egyptian peasants. The difficulties of construction left the canal a modest 8 metres (26 feet) in depth, 22 metres (72 feet) wide at the bottom, and never more than 91 metres (300 feet) wide at the surface. Passing places were built in because it was not big enough to accommodate more than one ship at a time, so procession along the canal was ponderously slow.

Still, it represented a huge reduction in the length of time that sea journeys took, an advantage keenly felt by British ships on their way to colonies, including India.

Inevitably, having eyed the project with some suspicion from the outset, Britain seized an opportunity for greater involvement. In 1875 the hard-up Egyptians sold their national stake in the company that ran the canal to the British for £4 million, although the French remained the major shareholders. This meant that the canal now brought fewer direct economic benefits to the Egyptians than previously as Britain and France received the lion's share of the levies being paid by ships.

But, as oil assumed greater importance than ever before, the British had a swift sea route to the Persian Gulf. Indeed, Britain was given sway over many of these crucial sites at the end of the First World War after the defeat of the Ottoman Empire, which had once been the region's controlling power. Yet the pendulum was still swinging away from imperial powers.

Between the wars Britain's colonies began pressing for independence, and in 1922 Egypt was given a measure of autonomy. A later agreement permitted British troops to be stationed in the Suez Canal zone until 1956, with an option for renegotiation.

As it played out in North Africa, the Second World War brought a series of threats to the security of the canal, but in the event it remained out of German and Italian hands.

But if Britain thought that it could return to the position of unrivalled influence that it had enjoyed in Egypt for decades, it was mistaken. There had been a sharp upturn in the level of nationalism in Egypt, accompanied by a desire to see British troops removed from Egyptian soil.

In public the two countries appeared cordial enough. Behind the scenes, though, there were manoeuvrings by both sides that heightened tensions. By the mid-1960's Gamal Abdel Nasser was in charge in Egypt; for years he had been an agitator against colonialism who was happy to trade with communists as well as the capitalist West.

As for the British Foreign Secretary, Anthony Eden, he was an arch opponent of appeasement and was also opposed to any goodwill gestures towards Nasser. It was the era of the Cold War and, together with America, Britain stood firm against Soviet encroachment anywhere in the world, but particularly in strategically sensitive areas.

The withdrawal of British and American funding for the planned Aswan Dam was sufficient for Nasser to take direct action. He announced the nationalization of the Suez Canal in order to raise the money needed for the dam project.

By the time that Britain and France responded by concluding a secret agreement with Israel, Egypt's enemy, Eden was Prime Minister.

Israel, which had already been at war with its neighbours since its creation at the end of the Second World War, would attack Egypt so that Britain and France could send troops in, apparently legitimately, to safeguard the canal.

On 5 November 1956 British and French forces sprang a lightning attack, easily defeating Egyptian forces in the vicinity of the canal. But the politicians in both countries had reckoned without the loud opposition they received from America, the United Nations and at home.

A ceasefire came just a day later, at the insistence of UN Secretary Dag Hammarskjöld, preventing what was turning out to be a military clean sweep. The canal was duly closed by the Egyptians until hostilities were resolved.

Relations between America and Britain were under strain following the adventure, although it turned out to be a short-term blip. Eden compounded his domestic difficulties by insisting that there had been no talks with Israel before its invasion. His health and his career soon collapsed.

But while Britain had been taken down a peg or two in the international arena, some things hadn't changed. Soviet Russia was still keen to get a foothold in the Middle East. Britain would still provide the necessary buffer from strongholds it maintained in the region, to the satisfaction of the Americans.

APPENDIX V

Hot Deserts of the World

About one-third of the earth's surface lying above water is labelled desert. A desert is defined by its lack of rainfall, which inevitably leads to sparse vegetation and limited animal life. Perhaps surprisingly, the two biggest areas that fall into the desert category are Antarctica and the Arctic, by virtue of having little or no rainfall. For the purposes of this book, we will bypass the polar deserts – and those considered as cold like the Gobi and Patagonian deserts or cool coastal deserts like the Atacama – to focus on those with sub-tropical environments, further down the league in terms of size but higher ranked as far as temperature is concerned.

For most people, the term 'hot desert' brings a brutal sandy expanse to mind. Dune systems are immensely helpful to scientists as they can yield valuable information on past climate conditions. But that's not the only terrain found in deserts, which can have rubble-strewn floors, mud-cracked riverbeds, salt pans caused by dried-out inland seas, rocky acres, gorges, canyons and mountains. Some have cactus plants, but many do not. The largest and most significant deserts are found in Africa, Asia, Australia and America. Europe has sandy and barren stretches. The Piscinas in Sardinia, also known as the little Sahara, has the continent's tallest dunes fashioned by the region's mistral winds. But none is considered significant in global terms.

Wind is one of the key factors in desert environments. With sands being shifted by anything from stiff breezes to gales, the boundaries of sub-tropical deserts have changed over time. Without a covering of vegetation a high wind can whip up dust and sandstorms capable of engulfing buildings and dramatically altering the landscape. A possible link between an increased number of dust storms and a lessening in the amount of rain in desert regions is being looked at by scientists.

Sahara Desert: Less than three inches of rain falls annually in the Sahara, which is the world's third-largest desert at 9.4 million sq. km (3.6 million sq. miles), where sand dunes can be nearly 195 metres (600 feet) high. If that landscape was not eerie enough, the dunes of the Sahara are known to emit a whistling sound, probably as the wind plays against the hard edges of the crystalline quartz sand granules. In Arabic, the word Sahara means 'sand and gravel region'. The Sahara straddles the north of Africa between the Atlantic Ocean and the Red Sea, stopping in the north just short of the Mediterranean Sea and the Atlas Mountains. Accounting for about one-quarter of the continent's land mass, it has high points, like the 3,445-metre (11,300-foot) Mount Koussi, and low points including the Qattara Depression in Egypt which is 133 metres (436 feet) below sea level. Despite its chronic dryness, the temperature range can fall anywhere between 50°C (130°F) to a minus figure, depending on the season and the time of day.

Early this century scientists from the University of Cologne concluded that the Sahara was once a fertile savannah before a shift in weather conditions, starting about 6,000 years ago, left it arid and unyielding.

Arabian Desert: Covering an area of almost 2.33 million sq. km (900,000 sq. miles), the desert dominates Asia's Arabian Peninsula. It is the fourth-largest desert in the world, and at its central and southern reaches lies the Rubh al Khali, the world's largest sand desert, so hostile it is still partially unexplored. Also known as 'the Empty Quarter', it covers ground in Saudi Arabia, Yemen, Oman and the United Arab Emirates. There are some eighteen large volcano fields within its borders, no longer active but identifiable by the stony

ITEMS ON ISSUE
FOR Mrs Anneke Plaister
ON 19/02/16 12:51:16

4101915413
Fiennes, Ranulph
Heat
Issued 08/02/16 12:46:32
Due 11/03/16

plains left behind. There is an area known as the Great Nafud which is typified by its towering red sands.

The date palm is the most familiar of the desert vegetation in the Arabian Desert, but it also hosts juniper, myrrh and caper trees. This is despite an annual rainfall figure of no more than 35mm, when the latest annual figure for London stands at 557.4mm.

Great Victorian: The largest desert in Australia and the third-largest sub-tropical desert in the world is surrounded by more of the same. The Gibson lies in the north, the Little Sandy Desert to the north-west, while in the south there is the Nullarbor Plain, and in the east the Sturt Stony Desert. Although it receives a modestly healthy amount of rain – perhaps 200mm or more a year – the deluges are unpredictable. It makes farming impossible as only plants that have adapted to the daily heat and nightly chill will thrive. But, in addition to red sand dunes, there are grassland plains, salt lakes, eucalyptus trees and spiky clumps of spinifex grasses. The desert is renowned for its lizard population that relishes the harsh environment. Also, invasive species, including feral cats, rabbits and camels, seem to tolerate desert conditions, while some native species have become extinct.

Syrian: A mix of desert and steppe, it extends from Syria itself into Iraq, Jordan and Saudi Arabia. It is sometimes considered a natural addition to the Arabian Desert, but it is rocky rather than sandy, thanks to the lava left behind by long-extinct volcanoes. Once a barrier that posed a problem to travellers from the Mediterranean heading east, it is now bisected by roads and oil pipelines.

Kalahari: Rainfall varies across the Kalahari, with some areas receiving a respectable 500mm, although drier regions expect much less than half of that. For this reason, the Kalahari is more dry savannah than arid desert. The cool coastal Namib Desert to the west is a better example of a typical desert. However, it does not have the size of the Kalahari which, at 712,247 sq. km (275,000 sq. miles) covers territory in Botswana, South Africa and Namibia. And the Kalahari loses more moisture through evaporation than it receives from rainfall. In dry parts the desert floor is pocked with 'pans', which are shallow dips lined with cracked grey clay that gleams in the sunlight, revealing salt deposits.

Chihuahua: This is the second-largest desert in North America after the much colder Great Basin, and is the third largest in the Western Hemisphere. It includes mountain ranges which provide high, wet, cooler climates in parallel with the annual average temperature of 24°C (75°F). Covering some 362,000 sq. km (140,000 sq. miles) it straddles the borders of the American states of Arizona, New Mexico and Texas before reaching deep into Mexico. According to the World Wildlife Fund, the Chihuahua Desert is at risk from water misman-agement, over-grazing by cattle and goats, and a lack of understanding of the desert's fragile eco-system, but work is going on in the region to bring about improvements.

Thar: Also called the Great Indian Desert, this arid stretch falls into both India and Pakistan. It has mighty sand dunes, salt lake beds, sandy plains and barren hills. About 100mm (4 inches) of rain falls in the west, although the precipitation in the east can be four times that amount. The hottest months of May and June are also charac-terized by high winds.

Mojave: America's hottest desert is known for two things – Death Valley and the Joshua tree. On 10 July 1913 a world record-breaking atmospheric temperature of 134°F (56.7°C) was recorded in Death Valley, which is the lowest, driest and most scorching region of the US. (Only a temperature reported in Libya nine years later has ever exceeded this, but this has not been validated.) Nevertheless, plant life, including the spiny Joshua tree – a member of the yucca family which is found mostly, but not exclusively, in the Mojave – flourishes here. Indigenous people have endured the heat for thousands of years, but it proved tough for settlers, including Mormons, who made their way across Death Valley on the borders of California and Nevada in the nineteenth century en route to Utah. Unusually for a desert, the wider Mojave Desert has been urbanized and Las Vegas is one of a number of cities within its boundaries. That has helped to make the desert into a tourist attraction, with visitors flocking each year to see dunes, rock formations and unusual vegetation. The Mojave is now a major centre for the production of solar energy. To the south lies the Sonoran Desert, which spans Arizona, California and parts of Mexico, through which would-be immigrants risk their lives to reach the United States.

APPENDIX VI

Climate Change: Some Comments

Hot places are getting hotter, and it's generally believed that climate change is to blame. After the most recently gathered land and sea temperatures were analysed, figures revealed that 2014 was the warmest year on record. There is ample evidence to suggest that even the slightest temperature rise is statistically significant and will have far-reaching consequences.

At ground level problems appear to start in the Earth's cold regions – far more sensitive to rises in temperature than other parts of the world – but the effects of global warming are not restricted to those regions. As the polar ice caps deplete along with mountain glaciers, sea levels rise at the coast because water takes up more space when it is warmer. And inland deserts expand.

So, in hot regions it is people rather than landscapes that suffer with the inexorable march of climate change. Supplies of food and water may one day be at risk. Desperate people tend towards desperate measures – which could put world security at stake.

In simple terms, those bold assertions touch on a hugely complex matrix of variables. Although scientists talk confidently about different scenarios, there is little certainty about what lies ahead. Hundreds of books have been devoted to the thorny topic of climate change, while here am I toying with the topic in comparatively few sentences – so this is by no means a definitive view! And I am no scientist but, given my many journeys in the company of eminent scientific researchers, I do have a keen sense of awareness about this issue.

Man has, of course, burned trees since the earliest times. After the Industrial Revolution, tons of carbon dioxide were sent skyward by Western nations as they evolved sophisticated economies. Manufacturing, transport and population increases have worsened the issue. Now an estimated 110 million tonnes of greenhouse gases are dispatched into the atmosphere each day, where they trap heat and pollution and prevent the Earth's natural cooling process. Deforestation has exacerbated the problem. Trees will absorb carbon dioxide, that problematic greenhouse gas, but there are fewer of them to perform this service than ever before.

And Nature is still a massively powerful source. The eruption of Mount Tambora on one of the Indonesian islands in 1815 brought perpetual winter to many parts of the planet for three years. In the most powerful eruption of the past five hundred years, an ash cloud that spread over a million square kilometres was propelled into the sky. The blast made by the mountain's explosion was heard 2,000km away. One of the tsunamis it caused was two metres high when it hit Java, some 500km distant. Crops across the globe were left in ruins as untimely frosts and relentless rain disrupted the climate. A volcanic eruption like this is always on the cards.

So Earth has heated up and cooled down during its long history. What's notable about the 8°C rise in average temperatures over the past 150 years is the rapid rate of increase when compared with other temperature increases which have unfolded over centuries.

The argument about whether man is the root cause of the increased global temperature, or if natural phenomena are culpable, has been largely resolved.

Today, a persuasive 97 per cent of scientists think that human activity has brought about global warming problems. And each year the problem climbs higher on the political agenda.

Without touching on its causes, President Barack Obama put the threat in stark terms when he spoke in April 2015: 'Today there is no greater threat to our planet than climate change.' It could, he went on to say, no longer be denied or ignored – a commendably brave statement when many of his fellow politicians in the USA are doing just that.

He has perhaps been persuaded by US government figures which reveal that average annual temperatures in Alaska have increased by three degrees over the past six decades, and by six degrees in winter, transforming snowbound landscapes to woodland and changing permafrost to thawed soil. The effects include increased costs to infrastructure as the land changes shape, acidification of the seas, and shrinking lakes affecting migrating birds.

All over the world, climate change poses a real threat to people alive today, let alone to future generations. But some people will be hit much harder than others.

According to the Intergovernmental Panel on Climate Change, set up in 1988 by the World Meteorological Organization and the United Nations Environment Programme, the world's poorest populations are likely to suffer most from floods, torrential rain, drought, famine, disease and food shortages. In addition, numerous plant and animal species will become extinct.

WMO's latest report contains the findings of more than eight hundred scientists from eighty countries and assesses over 30,000 scientific papers. It shows that each of the last three decades has been successively warmer at the Earth's surface than any preceding decade since 1850. 'It is likely that human influence has more than doubled the probability of occurrence of heatwaves in some locations,' the report states, 'and it is likely to worsen with heatwaves happening more often and for longer.'

Critically, increased temperatures will cause crop failures and water shortages in areas that can least afford this, and among people who, ironically, have some of the lowest emissions on Earth. It is the same story for thousands of people living on the fertile plains that encircle places like Bangladesh, which are likely to be swallowed by the sea that is rising at a rate of 3mm a year. That is in addition to stronger cyclones that will wreck homes and harvests, especially in Asia. Monsoons are expected to deluge West Africa, while the east of the continent will have short-lived rains instead. Tropical countries like Sierra Leone will suffer heatwaves, droughts, floods and deadly landslides. In South Sudan, the world's newest country, desertification is already occurring after rains have become increasingly unpredictable.

In cities that have sprung up among developing nations where there has been emerging prosperity, life may become unbearably hot – a fact that will inevitably hamper continued economic growth. Climate change could usher in a new era marked by the plight of desperate refugees as people try to escape the worst of its effects. As I write this in May 2015, BBC Radio 4 has just announced that over five hundred deaths in Southern India through heatstroke and extreme dehydration occurred over the past week, and that the forecast there is for a continuing 'heatwave to severe heatwave'. In Delhi, where the temperatures were 4 degrees higher than the seasonal average, crowds have sought sanctuary in the Metro. Mortality levels are worse than in the severe heatwave of 2010, which started earlier, registered the highest temperatures for decades and lasted for months.

For countries in low latitudes, their location within the tropics leaves them vulnerable to changes wrought by the weather, with difficulties exacerbated by a loss of forests which helps to shore up against its worst effects, but richer countries have the advantage of better geographical locations and a greater potential for technology to mitigate the effects. But climate change is also a First World problem.

Australia's Climate Council has said that climate change triples the odds of summer heatwaves and doubles the chances of them being intense. It believes heatwaves there are becoming hotter, lasting longer, occurring more often and starting earlier.

With every heatwave comes an increased risk of wildfires. A new study by America's National Park Service and the University of California has revealed that fires in the forests are causing a significant amount of emissions that in turn worsen the problem. Forest fires may be started by lightning, a dropped bottle that magnifies the power of the sun, or even deliberately. Depending on weather conditions, including wind speed, and the dryness of the forest, fires can race away from attending firefighters, eating up hundreds of acres in minutes.

Despite the assertions of President Obama, climate change seems to slip off the political agenda surprisingly swiftly. Any international willingness to pull together in this great battle to ensure a stable climate is notably absent.

Any naturally occurring process to correct the balance will be tortoise slow. But there are a few positives. One bright hope is the possibility of renewable energy flourishing in these new conditions. More solar power is being generated than ever before, and there are refinements on the theme, notably in Spain with new-style power stations in which multiple mirrors focus the sun's rays to heat a boiler to 400°C. The resulting steam is passed into a turbine to generate electricity.

So technological innovation may yet save the day. There is, for example, a slow-burning solar roadways project that will have tough solar panels replacing asphalt and providing enough electricity not only to power road signs and LED lights, but also homes and factories. First mooted in 2006, it is now attracting the interest of leading players in the industry. It is just one of a host of possible game-changers bidding for a place on the top table of ideas.

Before the growing extremes of heat around the globe become simply defined as 'the new normal', I hope we can learn to pull together to save ourselves from self-inflicted oblivion. Heat is great in small doses which I have been lucky enough to experience on and off through my life. But a state of too much heat, from which there can be no escape is a fate we, the human race, must try far harder to avoid ... while there is still time.

ACKNOWLEDGEMENTS

My thanks to all those who helped my preparation of this book, including Ian Bannister, Dan Brandenstein, Patrick Brook, Kevin Fewster, Nicholas Holder, Steve Holland, Dr Oliver Johnson, Robin Knox-Johnston, Nicholas Lancaster, Peter Loyd, Quentin Morton, Jonathon Porritt, Eugene Rae, Sergiu Stanescu, Jan Turner, Simon Wilde, and Ben Wright.

Also to my wife Louise and daughter Elizabeth for their patience, to Jill Firman for the ever more difficult task of deciphering my hieroglyphics, to Ed Victor for his advice and support, to Karen Farrington for her research expertise, and to all at Simon & Schuster.

INDEX